Let Me Encourage You Again

More encouraging stories
for every day of the year

By

Mark Hopper

Mark Hopper

I THESS. 5:11

1

ISBN: 979-8-218-32215-1

Book design by Author

Printed by DiggyPOD, Inc., in the United States of America

First printing edition 2023

Mark S. Hopper
1125 Grubstake Drive
Diamond Bar, CA 91765

markh@efreedb.org
dbarhop@gmail.com

First printing – November, 2023
Second printing – December, 2023

Dedication

This book is dedicated to my wife Susan and to my four children and their spouses – Tim & Christine, Trisha & Bryan, Traci & Jonathan, and Teri & Jacob. And to my ten grandchildren – Katie, Carly, Jonah, Ellie, Caleb, Elizabeth, Emily, Janie, Landon and Emily M.

Introduction

I hope you enjoy my newest book. This is the third in the series of books designed to **Let Me Encourage You**. There is a story for every day of the year,

I recommend you _not start_ on page one but _start reading on today's date_. Some stories are seasonal so you will find Christmas stories in December and stories relating to marriage in February.

Don't be in a hurry. Just read one story a day. Each one is a _short three minute read_. I recommend you keep this book in your bathroom or on your bed stand or on your breakfast table.

And I hope you will do something in light of what you read. Make a call, mail a card, or send an email _this week_. Reconnect with an old friend or write an encouraging letter to one of your children or grandchildren.

I hope you will be encouraged and uplifted by the stories you read in this book. When you finish I hope you will pass it on to a friend or family member.

Sincerely,

Mark Hopper
markh@efreedb.org
dbarhop@gmail.com
November / 2023

Do Something

Recently my friends Eric and Susan shared with me they were reading my first book titled, *"Let Me Encourage You"* by Mark Hopper. They were reading it together - one story a day. When they read the story about one of the assignments I have used in premarital counseling they decided to do it themselves.

The story on April 29th is titled, *"How Well Do You Know Your Mate?"* It has a list of seven questions designed to help couples assess how well they really knew each other. Some of the questions included, "What are some of the happiest things that have happened in your spouse's life" and "What are some of your mate's deepest fears".

Each couple was instructed to write down their own answers individually and then share their answers with each other. The goal was to help them see how well they actually knew each other and to motivate them to improve and deepen their communication skills.

Eric and Susan had been married for over 40 years. They took time to answer one question a day and discuss their responses with each other over dinner. They said it was helpful even though they had been married for a long time.

There is a passage in the Bible when Jesus taught a large group of people on a hillside near the Sea of Galilee in northern Israel. We call this the *Sermon on the Mount* (Matthew Chapters 5-7). At the end of his sermon Jesus urged his listeners to not just hear His words but to do something in light of what He had taught them (Matthew 7:24-27).

If you read something in a book or hear something in a sermon you should do something. *The goal is not just information but perspiration.* The stories in this third volume of my *"Let Me Encourage You"* series are written with the hope you will be motivated to *do something* in light of what you read. Write a card, send an email or make a phone call.

Let me challenge you to read this book one-story-a-day. Take your time. Don't be in a hurry. Then *do something* that will encourage your family, friends, coworkers, classmates, neighbors or even a stranger. They will be glad you did and you will too.

I Love Your Book

One conversation I enjoyed after attending the first Portrait Church service was with a woman I had never met before. She waited patiently while I talked with a few friends and then introduced herself. She told me she had read my book and was excited to meet me in person. I felt like a celebrity but she didn't ask for my autograph.

She explained someone had given her a copy of my book and she had faithfully read one story a day over the past few months. She said she loved my book. She felt like she already knew me because many of the stories in the book were about my family.

This stranger also expressed her condolences over the death of my wife Jeanne. She had read about my wife's journey with cancer and offered some kind words. She felt she knew her because of the number of stories in the book about Jeanne's life and our family.

When I told this woman I had published a second book she wanted to know how she could get a copy. I asked her which book her friend had given to her. Was it the book with the white cover (*Let Me Encourage You*) or the second book with my picture on the cover (*Let Me Encourage You More*)? She said it was the book with the white cover.

I also told my new friend I was working on volume three (this book). I hoped the new book would be ready for the Christmas season.

It is very humbling when someone says the like my book and very encouraging when they give a copy to a friend of family member. The purpose of the stories in these books is to encourage people and to motivate them to do something in light of what they read. Most stories end with a challenge like "do *something today*" or "*send a card this week*" to help and encourage others.

The Apostle Paul wrote several personal letters which are included in the Bible. He wrote letters to Timothy, Titus and Philemon. His purpose was to instruct and encourage these men in the work God had given them. Let me encourage you to send a card or write an email to encourage someone *this week*. And if you are really feeling generous why not send them a copy of one of my books. They will be glad you did and I will too. Write to me at markh@efreedb.org if you need one.

No Parking at LAX

Recently a friend drove me to LAX. I was flying to Europe to visit my adult children and grandchildren in Slovenia and Portugal. He left his small car at my house and rode with me to the airport in my larger car with all my luggage. Then he would bring my car back home.

This was my first trip overseas since my wife died. I had two large suitcases plus a carry-on suitcase and my backpack. The grandkids had given me a long list of things they wanted me to bring so I knew I would be paying for extra luggage. The bigger challenge was how I would be able to get all of these bags into the terminal at LAX.

My friend suggested we park my SUV near the international terminal and he would help me get the bags to check-in. However, when we got to the airport the traffic was terrible and the parking structures near the international terminal were full. What a mess. They were doing an extensive amount of construction at LAX. Our tax dollars at work. The traffic was heavily congested and parking was almost non-existent.

In a moment of desperation I pulled my car into the entrance of a parking garage that was full. I got out of my car and unloaded all of my suitcases in the blocked driveway. I told my friend Walter I would find a way to get the bags to the ticket counter and encouraged him to drive away. He was reluctant to leave me but he followed my instructions.

Just as I was considering my options, a nice parking lot attendant saw my predicament and she brought me a sturdy airport luggage cart so I could transport *all* of my bags. I don't know who she was or how she knew I needed help but she came to my rescue. The only words she spoke were – *God Bless You.* I wonder if she was an angel wearing an LAX employee vest sent to help me in my time of need.

With the luggage cart I was able to get all my bags to the airline ticket counter by myself. I did pay $100 more for the extra luggage. I did get to my plane on time and all of the luggage did make it to my destination. The grandkids were thrilled I brought all of the things they requested. There is a verse in the Bible that says, "Bring your requests to God in prayer and He will send you help in your time of need" (Hebrews 4:16). Let me encourage you to pray and ask God for help when you face a difficult situation this week. He might just send you an angel wearing a parking lot attendant's uniform too.

Canceled

I recently heard a group of adults talking about their children and grandchildren. One of them shared they had been told by one of their adult children they had been "*Canceled*". Most of us in the conversation were unfamiliar with the term. What did it mean the adult child had *canceled* the parent"?

When I looked online I found a 14 page article on Wikipedia on the term. It referred to the popular phrase "*Cancel Culture*" which has political and social connotations. It provided this definition. "*Cancel Culture*" is a phrase contemporary to the late 2010's and early 2020's. It is used to refer to a culture in which those who are deemed to have acted or spoken in an unacceptable manner are ostracized, boycotted or shunned".

Apparently the adult child was offended or angered by something their parents had said or done. So the adult child cut off any contact or communication with their parent. They did not want to speak to their parents or have any contact with them. Maybe this has happened to you. You may have children or grandchildren who do not want to see you or talk with you. They are boycotting any contact with you. They may not allow you to see or talk with your grandchildren. They are shunning their parents.

I had never heard the phrase used in reference to relationships. When did children assume the right to treat their parents in this way? Did they learn it in college or read about it on the internet? How do children young or older think they have the authority to "*cancel*" their parents? There are several passages in the Bible which say, "Children honor your father and mother" (Exodus 20:12 / Mark 7:10 / Ephesians 6:1-2). It is unimaginable children would dishonor and disrespect their parents even when the parents may have said or done something wrong.

Parents aren't perfect. Children are not either. Disagreements will occur and arguments may not be resolved between children and parents. The Apostle Paul wrote, "Get rid of all bitterness, rage, anger, brawling, slander and malice. Be compassionate and kind to one another, forgiving each other just as God forgave you" (Ephesians 4:31-32). Let me encourage you to honor and respect your parents. Resolve your disagreements. Be willing to forgive each other. Keep communication open. You will be glad you did and they will too.

In the Living Years

There was a famous music group in the 1980's called **Genesis**. They were a British rock band who had a following around the world. Members of the band included Phil Collins and Peter Gabriel. After a successful career each of the five members formed a new band.

One of the members was Michael Rutherford. He named his band "*Mike and the Mechanics*". They had one song which is remembered by many people today - "***In the Living Years***". The background to the song is the poor relationship Mike had with his father. Mike was a bearded, casually dressed British musician. His father was a properly dressed traditional British Naval Captain. They did not see eye to eye. In the song Mike laments, "I was not there the day my father passed away. There was so much more I wanted to say". The refrain is, "*Don't wait until it is too late. Say it loud. Say it clear. Say it in the living years*".

I often share this story at a memorial service or funeral. I encourage people to reconcile their differences and express their love for their family and friends. Sadly there are many families who did not share a close relationship with their loved ones. Disagreements and divisions were not resolved. Bitterness and resentment remained. And now their family member is gone. It's too late.

So I challenge people who attend the funeral or memorial service to not allow unresolved issues to affect their relationship with their family and loved ones. I usually give a homework assignment at the end of the service and ask people to tell someone *today* how much they love them. Do it *before the day is over*. I remind them to not wait until it is too late. *Say it loud. Say it clear. Say it in the living years*.

I wonder if there is someone you are not talking to because of some unresolved issue. Have you "*canceled*" your family or loved ones? Jesus said, "If you are offering a gift at the altar and then remember your brother has something against you, leave your gift there at the altar. First go and be reconciled to your brother and then come and offer your gift" (Matthew 5:23-24).Let me encourage you to take the first step to reconcile. Ask for their forgiveness for what you have said and done that hurt them. Accept responsibility for what you did. And be willing to forgive them for what they may have done or said to hurt you. They will be glad you did and you will too.

January 6
My Space

Many years ago we built a new classroom building at our church in Tucson. The church was growing and we needed more space for the nursery and young children. In addition, we planned to launch a new preschool when the new building was completed.

We hired an architect to draw up the plans and submitted them to the Pima County Building Department. The new building was designed to meet the building and safety requirements for a licensed preschool too.

We hired a local contractor to do some of the work and we did a lot of the construction ourselves. We began to spread the word about the opening of the new preschool. My wife Jeanne and two other women were the first faculty members. Classes met Tuesday – Friday from 8:30 to noon. I think there were a dozen students in the first class.

The new building was very helpful for Sunday School classes too. Teachers were delighted to have larger classrooms for the children and a new nursery for Sunday mornings and the mid-week programs.

However we did not foresee problems would emerge between the preschool teachers and the Sunday School teachers. Both groups expressed frustrations with the other. Preschool teachers complained the Sunday morning teachers were using their materials and the Sunday morning teachers were frustrated the preschool teachers were taking up most of the cupboards and storage space.

The solution was to change their perspective. Both ministries were important. One was not more important than the other. I suggested the teachers look for ways they could help each other. Don't complain about the supplies and storage cabinets. Start asking what each of them could do to help the other ministry succeed.

The Apostle Paul wrote, "Each of you should look not only to your own interests but also to the interests of others" (Philippians 2:4). If you are experiencing conflicts with other people in your family, work or school let me encourage you to put their interests ahead of your own. Watch for an opportunity to help someone *this week*. They will be glad you did and you will too.

Mountain Climbing

Some people are professional mountain climbers. Some have their sights set on the tallest peaks in the world. My mountain climbing experiences were much smaller but still memorable.

The first mountain I climbed was *Camelback Mountain* in Phoenix, Arizona. Camelback is a landmark in the middle of the city. It really does look like a camel if you view it from the south side. If you are flying into Phoenix make sure you sit on the right side of the plane. You usually get a clear view of this famous site.

I remember climbing to the top of Camelback on the 4th of July with my brother Steve and a few of our high school buddies. We thought we could get a better view of the fireworks around the city on a summer night. But we were too high and too far away to really see the displays around the city. And we didn't bring a flash light so we stumbled down the mountain in the dark.

Another famous landmark in Arizona is *Picacho Peak* between Tucson and Phoenix. I climbed to the top of this landmark with some friends from our Tucson church. It was not a difficult climb but there were some narrow parts getting to the top. It is fun to drive down Interstate 10 and remember climbing to the top of Picacho Peak. Did you know there is an artist's sketch of both Camelback Mountain and Picacho Peak in the opening credits of the movie *The Three Amigos*? Watch and see!

The tallest mountain I have ever climbed was with my son. Mount Wrightson rises over 9,000 feet above the desert on the southern edge of Tucson. It is slightly higher than Mt Lemon on the northern side of the city. Tim and I climbed to the top of this landmark in the spring of 1988 when he was 13 years old. The trail was easy to follow as we hiked from the desert to the top in one day. I remember it was a gentle but steady climb. We actually hiked through snow near the top. Several times we talked about turning back but we persevered and made it all the way up. We remember how windy it was at the top.

Jesus climbed a mountain with some of his disciples. They never forgot it (Mark 9:2-8 / Second Peter 1:16-18). My mountain adventures with friends and family were very special too. Let me encourage you to climb a mountain *this year*. Make a plan and make a memory with your family or friends. You will be glad you did and they will too.

January 8
Three Cheers for the French

I know we often make fun of people from different nationalities. For many years people made fun of the Polish people with "Pollock Jokes". Some people made fun of the stuffy British with their tradition of afternoon tea. Sometimes I heard people say the French people are not friendly to foreigners. One author wrote a book that characterized us as "The Ugly Americans" who were loud and obnoxious.

However I would like to express my appreciation to some people my wife and I met during a trip to Paris a few years ago. When we took the train from the international airport into Paris we got off at the station near the hotel where we had reservations. Unfortunately we exited the subway with our luggage and began to walk in the wrong direction.

After walking several blocks we realized we were lost and didn't know which way to go. We stopped and asked an older woman if she could tell us where our hotel was. She spoke English and gladly offered to help. She told us we were going in the wrong direction. She insisted on walking with us until we found our hotel. We might still be walking the streets of Paris if we didn't have her help and guidance.

On another day in Paris we had trouble buying a Subway ticket. It was a small station near the Eifel Tower. But they only had automated machines. There were no employees at this station only the ticket machines. But the machines would not accept my credit card. Soon there was a small crowd of impatient subway riders lined up behind us waiting for us to purchase our tickets. Finally a man stepped up and used his own credit card to purchase our two tickets. We offered him some cash but he refused to accept it.

These two encounters gave us a new impression of the French people. Both were very helpful and very kind. You may have had similar experiences as you traveled to various countries around the world. I wonder what visitors to our country think of us. Would they say Americans are friendly and helpful? Or would they say we are unfriendly and not helpful?

There is a verse in the Bible that says, "Be kind to aliens and foreigners" in your country (Deut. 24:19-22). Let me encourage you to be ready to help someone *this week* who is a guest in your country. Help them find their way. They will be glad you did and you will too.

Do You Have a Passport?

There were several things we looked for when we were considering a new person to serve in a leadership role at our church. Did they attend church services regularly with their family? Were they involved in a week night small group or Sunday morning Bible study class? Were they respected by others in our church?

Another question we asked was, *"Do you have a passport"*? This may seem like an unusual requirement to qualify to serve on a leadership team. But it was an important requirement because we expected them to be involved in our short-term mission program.

One of the things our church valued was missions. The Bible teaches every follower of Christ has the privilege and responsibility to tell others about Jesus. Our mission statement was, *"To Know Jesus and Make Him Known"*. We wanted our leaders to be committed to our mission.

If they wanted to be on our leadership team they needed to participate in a short-term mission trip at least once during their three year term of service. This could be a close as going to Mexico or as far away as Europe or Asia. We frequently sent teams for a weekend south of the border to build houses or work with children's programs. We also sent teams for longer two-week trips as far away as Russia or China.

By participating in our mission projects these new leaders were able to experience life and ministry in a foreign country. They got to work alongside missionaries who were supported by our church. They gained an appreciation for the work and sacrifice missionaries make as they share Christ in other parts of the world. If they wanted to serve on our leadership team they needed to have a passport.

There are two passages in the Bible which detail the some of the qualifications for church leaders. The Apostle Paul wrote, "If anyone wants to provide leadership in the church, good. But there are preconditions. A leader must be well-thought-of, committed to his wife, cool, collected, accessible and hospitable (First Timothy 3:1-13 The Message Bible). A similar list is found in Titus 1:6-9.

Let me encourage you to be willing to serve in leadership at your church. It is not an easy roll to fill. And make sure you have a passport!

Like a Good Neighbor

My wife and I purchased our first home when we moved to Tucson many years ago. We had lived in several apartments and a mobile home but this was the first time we had ever owned a house. It was brand new with three bedrooms and two baths and about 1200 square feet with a single carport.

When we moved into this new subdivision we met a number of neighbors. Several families had young children. There were a few empty nesters and we had a widow living right across the street. Our young son was less than a year old when we moved in. But in the following years we added three beautiful girls to our family.

We learned it was nice to have neighbors. It was nice to be able to borrow tools and have an extra hand doing new home owner projects. We also learned it was nice to have neighbors like a teenager named Alaine to baby sit when we went out and a widow named Bernice who provide child care when my wife was teaching at the preschool.

One of the other neighbors we got to know was Lorraine. She was the one we called every time we went to the hospital to have another baby. Night or day she was always ready to come stay at our house and watch our kids while we rushed off to labor and delivery. I wonder how well you know your neighbors.

Jesus said one of the greatest commandments in the Bible is, "*Love your neighbor as yourself*" (Mark 12:31 / Romans 13:9-10 / Leviticus 19:18). Now we live in Southern California. And we are still grateful for our neighbors. Instead of child care and babysitting, now we text our neighbor Kenny to ask him to put out our garbage cans and bring in the mail when we are traveling or away from home. We are thankful for his help and glad when he asks us for help too.

Let me encourage you to express your love and appreciation to the neighbors who have lived around you for many years. And, let me encourage you to get to know the new neighbors who have moved in on your street. You may be able to provide child care or babysitting for them just as our neighbors did for us many years ago. And, you may be able to help put out their garbage cans or collect their mail for them. They will be glad you did and you will too.

Music (Part One)

It is interesting how music has such an influential role in our thoughts and emotions. Our daily lives are filled with music on the radio in our car, over the PA system at work and in our own homes. We often talk about how music is so important to teenagers but it is also enjoyed by young children and older adults too. Music is played in shopping malls and in elevators. It is heard at clothing stores, grocery stores and restaurants. Golfers now play music in their carts on the golf course. Music is heard in warehouses and tea rooms, movie theaters and the dentist office. It is everywhere.

Recently a popular singer was performing at Sofi stadium in front of a sellout crowd for six nights in a row. The new stadium holds over 50,000 people and hosted the Super Bowl. Ticket prices were hundreds of dollars. Many fans paid much more to attend this event.

Music effects our mood. It can be a calming presence in a funeral home or it can stir our patriotic spirit at a baseball game. It can be a welcomed wakeup call in the morning or set a romantic mood at the end of the day.

My wife Susan introduced me to a musician named Mantovani. I do not remember hearing his music when I was growing up. But he was well known for his arrangements of many popular songs. His full orchestra played songs from musicals like *Sound of Music* and *Man of La Mancha*. He also played music from some of the sound tracks from movies like *Camelot* and *The King and I*. Mantovani's music provides a relaxing atmosphere in our home. Instead of listening to the news on TV we enjoy hearing songs performed by his orchestra.

There is a passage in the Bible where King Saul struggled with depression and anger. He was on an emotional roller coaster. One of his aides suggested they find a musician who could calm the king's heart. They found a gifted man named David who played the harp. One verse says, "When David played his harp relief came upon King Saul and he would feel better" (First Samuel 16:23-24). Let me encourage you to fill your home with good music that is comforting to your heart and soul. Fill your mind with relaxing songs. Turn off *"Talk Radio"* in your car and listen to some pleasant music on the stressful freeway. You will be glad you did.

Music (Part Two)

In my last story I shared about how music effects our mood. This is true for people of all ages from new born children to teens and adults. Parents often quietly play some relaxing music when they put their baby to bed at night. Working adults enjoy a variety of music at the end of the day too.

But music can also stir the soul to action. I used to listen to the theme song from the "*Superman*" movie as I drove to church on Sunday morning. It got me fired up and ready to preach in the church service.

I have heard coaches use music to motivate their team for the big game. Teachers use music in the classroom to prepare their students for the day's lesson. My son Tim used to play his guitar when he was a new high school teacher. I don't know how much his students learned but I do know they loved his English class.

It is interesting how different people like different types of music. Some prefer Country Western while others prefer Classical music. Some enjoy Hard Rock while others like Rap music. Some prefer Rock N Roll and others prefer songs by Frank Sinatra and Bing Crosby.

Now with Apple iTunes and Amazon Music every type of music is available at our finger tips. I can ask Alexa to play Ricky Nelson or the Beach Boys and she has it ready to go in an instant. Apparently Alexa keeps track of my musical preferences and anticipates what songs I want to hear.

Many people may not realize music was a big part of the lives of people in ancient times. There are 150 different Psalms in the Bible. These were songs set to music to help people remember the lessons they contained. Our children's ministry used songs to help the kids remember their Bible lessons. Teens and adults express their adoration and worship to God with music in the Sunday church service. There is a verse that says, "Let the word of Christ dwell within you with all wisdom, teaching and admonishing one another with *psalms, hymns* and *spiritual songs, singing with thankfulness in your hearts* to God" (Colossians 3:16). Let me encourage you to listen to music which draws your heart and mind to worship God. And lift up your voice to honor Him. You will be glad you did and He will too.

Singing

I have shared some of my thoughts about music in our culture today and what was written and sung in Bible times 3,000 years ago. But there is a big difference between listening to music and hearing a choir perform than there is when you actually sing a song yourself.

Sometimes I will stand next to one of the men in our church service and tell them I want to hear him sing. Women seem to be more comfortable singing out loud than men. I tell my wife I love to hear her voice when we sing worship songs together in church. But most of the men sing quietly and most of the women sing loudly.

There is something powerful and personal when we actually sing along with other people. One voice can be beautiful but there is strength in many voices singing together in a church service or public gathering.

I vividly remember the first time a group of men from our church went to a Men's Retreat at Forest Home Conference Center. There were about ten men from our church and we arrived late. We quickly took our sleeping bags and duffle bags to our cabin and then hurried to join the evening meeting in progress in the Chapel. When we opened the door we were amazed to hear almost 500 men singing together. It was a powerful moment.

The same thing was true when a larger group of guys from our church attended the Promise Keepers gathering at Angel stadium in Anaheim. There were over 20,000 men at the weekend event. It was amazing to hear so many men singing contemporary praise songs and old hymns like *Amazing Grace*. It was so encouraging to hear men singing boldly with their voices from their heart.

There is a passage in the Bible which says, "*Sing songs from your heart to Christ. Sing praises over everything. Use any excuse to sing a song to God*" (Ephesians 5:19 – the Message Bible). Let me encourage you to sing with confidence and conviction. Sing hymns and praise songs at church so your spouse and children can hear you and follow your example. Proudly sing the National Anthem at the baseball or football game too. Don't be a silent spectator. Be a proud participant as you raise your voice in song. You will be glad you did and your family will too.

Home Sweet Home

Sometimes when we watch an old movie or TV show we notice things which give a hint when the movie was made. For example if you are from that era you might see a '57 Chevy like the one I owned parked in the background of a movie set.

I love the movie series "*Back to the Future*" which portrayed life in America in the 1950's. The buildings are from a Hollywood set in Universal Studios. And the cars and trucks are too. The café or diner looks just like those we remember when we were young.

The architecture is also designed to look like life in past decades. The movie "*Seabiscuit*" is set in the era of the Great Depression. The cars and trucks and clothes all reflect that generation which suffered terrible economic times.

Recently I saw an old house in a movie which had some distinctive windows in the front door. The small panes of glass were in a diamond shape. We had those on the front door of my house when I was a teenager. They were called "*Diamond Pane Windows*". They looked stylish in the 1960's but look old fashioned now. You still see them on some homes in older neighborhoods from the sixties and seventies.

Another unusual feature I saw on an older home was called "*Weeping Mortar*". Normally when brick masons built a block wall they cleaned off the excess mortar between each row of blocks. But some builders left the excess mortar on the wall. That is why they called it "*Weeping Mortar*". That was how our first home in Phoenix looked when we moved there in the 1950's.

Archeologists look for similar clues when they excavate historical sites. They watch for small details in the construction, architecture and other things which reveal the age of their discoveries. Archeologists are usually dealing with sites which are hundreds or thousands of years old. Many historical events and locations confirm the reliability and accuracy of the biblical record. Little details reveal a lot.

Let me encourage you to watch for small details which provide a clue to the age and era of a movie or TV show *this week*. Watch what is in the background and see if you recognize anything familiar.

The Pioneers

One day when my car was in the repair shop a friend offered to drop me off at the *In N Out Burger* in Walnut so I could have lunch while I waited for the estimate from the mechanic. As I stood in line to place my order I noticed two men who looked familiar. After I ordered my usual cheese burger and fries I walked back to say hello. They invited me to sit down while I waited for my order to be ready.

Both of these men had worked in the local school district where my wife taught and where all of our children had attended. One of these men had been the principal at Diamond Bar High and the other was the dean of the Math department. Both of them were part of a nine-member committee that launched Diamond Bar High in the 1980's. It was fascinating to hear them share about some of the challenges and opportunities involved in opening a new high school. Diamond Bar High was a spin off from Walnut High. The community was growing rapidly and Walnut High did not have enough room for more students.

About one half of the faculty for Diamond Bar High came from Walnut High. The other half of the teachers and staff came from other schools both inside and outside the district. These men shared how much they enjoyed being part of the new high school. The faculty and administration bonded together as they made recommendations for the new school's mascot and school colors. They were in a unique position to develop new strategies for both the classrooms and the extracurricular activities.

They talked about the success of the athletic program at Diamond Bar High and the school's success against other schools in the area. They won numerous CIF titles in sports like football and baseball. The school became well known for its athletic accomplishments. The same was true in the classrooms with many students excelling in academics. I could have sat and listened all day to the history they shared about the high school where all my kids attended and where my son got his first teaching job. Many of the things they shared were familiar because my wife and I were students at a brand new high school in Scottsdale, Arizona in the 1960's.

Let me encourage you to learn more about the history of the school your children attend. Ask some of the older faculty and staff about their experiences. They will be glad you did and you will too.

Why I Believe the Bible

There are many references in each of my books to verses in the Bible. Many of my readers have church backgrounds and are familiar with the people and events in the scriptures. But many other readers may not have been raised in a faith and do not know much about the Bible.

As a pastor my sermons were always based on passages in the Bible. After I graduated from college I went on to study at Dallas Seminary for four years. We studied every book in the Bible. I learned Hebrew and Greek which are the original languages the Bible was written in. We discussed many theological issues and biblical history. We had classes on preaching, counseling and leadership. It was an intense season of study and learning.

There are four reasons why I believe in the Bible. First - the **internal claims**. The Bible claims to be the word of God. The authors of the Bible claim to be writing and speaking words from God. From start to finish the authors say things like, "God said this", "God did this", God promised" and "God predicted". The authors believed they were being led and guided by God to record the events in the Bible and to record His words. One author wrote, "All scripture is inspired by God" (First Timothy 3:16-17).

Second - the **external confirmations**. Many people, places and events recorded in the Bible are confirmed by archeology and history. Often critics express their doubts about the accuracy and reliability of the Bible. But research and discoveries continue to confirm things written in the Bible are historically accurate.

There is a small book titled, "*The Bible in the British Museum*". It was written to guide visitors to specific exhibits which display items which provide confirmation of things recorded in the Bible. One of my favorite is the *Cyrus Cylinder*. This small clay object recorded a decree by the Persian King Cyrus allowing exiled people to return to their home lands. It confirmed what was recorded in the Bible (Second Chronicles 36:20-23 and Ezra 1:1-4). It was discovered by archeologists in 1879.

The Bible isn't just a collection of myths and stories. It is a remarkable account of real events and real people in recorded history. Over and over again archeology and historical writings confirm the reliability and accuracy of the Bible. (Continued)

Why I Believe the Bible (Part Two)

In my earlier story I explained why I believe and trust what is written in the Bible. First are the **internal claims**. The authors of the Bible claimed they were recording God's words and God's works. Second are the **external confirmations**. Archeology and history continue to confirm the accuracy and reliability of the people, places and events recorded in the Bible.

The third reason I believe in the Bible are the **predictions** which are **fulfilled**. Prophets predicted specific events would take place and they did. They claimed God revealed things to them and sent them to warn and inform people of coming events.

One of my favorite examples was God's prediction the Israelites would be defeated by the Babylonians and be taken into Exile away from their homeland. But the prophet Jeremiah predicted they would return *seventy years* later (Jeremiah 25:1-14 / 29:4-12). And they did! The discovery of the Cyrus Cylinder in 1879 confirmed this event in history.

The fourth reason I believe the Bible is how **practical and personal** it applies to my life. The Bible is filled with memorable events and biographies about real people living real life. It is not a fairy tale which starts with "*once upon a time*" or science fiction which says, "*Long ago in a galaxy far far away*". It is real people living in recorded history.

There are instructions for parents and married couples sharing their lives together. There are words for widows and single mothers. Words for young and old. There are words of wisdom for life and warnings about living without God. There are amazing accounts of faith and tragic examples of moral and spiritual failure. The Bible is not a book about perfect people living perfect lives. It is a practical book with endless accounts of God's love, mercy and forgiveness. One verse says, "God is gracious, compassionate, slow to anger and abounding in love and kindness" (Psalm 103:8). The Bible says God became a man and dwelt among us in the person of Jesus so whoever believed in Him would find forgiveness and have eternal life (John 1:14 / 3:16). Let me encourage you to read the Bible yourself. Don't start on page one. Start in the book of Mark. Read a chapter-a-day. Then read John, Acts and Romans. Read Old Testament books like Genesis, Exodus, Psalms and Proverbs too. Ask God to reveal himself to you through his word – the Bible. You will be glad you did and I will too.

Costco

One of the remarkable success stories in retail sales is Costco. It ranks as one of the top five most prominent retail businesses in the world. They have over 500 stores in the United States and another 105 in Canada. They are also located in eleven other foreign countries included the United Kingdom, Japan, Taiwan, China and Iceland.

My daughter and her family live in Portugal. Recently she called to tell me about their trip from Lisbon to Seville, Spain to shop at Costco. It was a four and one half hour drive to Seville. But they we were excited to shop at their closest neighborhood Costco.

She saw Pumpkin Pies for sale at the Costco in Spain. They were giving out free samples trying to convince European shoppers to find out what pumpkin pie was all about. They also sold rotisserie chicken just like they do in our country. She said it was amazing to see a Costco store in Europe. It was very similar to what we have here in the USA.

However they didn't have Costco in Bible times. Shopping was very different 2000 years ago when Jesus walked through the streets of Jerusalem. Jesus sent two of his disciples into the crowded city to purchase food and prepare a place for them to celebrate the Passover. Peter and John went into Jerusalem on a secret mission (Luke 22:7-12). They met a man carrying a pot of water on his head who led them to a large upper room where they prepared for the Passover (Mark 14:12-16). Men did not normally carry the water so that was how the disciples knew who to follow.

Another passage explained Judas carried the money for the group (John 13:29-30). He would normally be involved in shopping for food and preparing a meal but he was dishonest and not trusted to go on this clandestine assignment (John 12:4-6).

I'm sure you have done your share of shopping over the years. You may be a member of Costco or Sam's Club. You may shop in smaller stores like Trader Joe's or Sprouts. We are very blessed to have so many choices when it comes to shopping. I always say thanks to the workers. I tell them we can't eat without them. Let me encourage you to express your appreciation *this week* to the employees who work so hard to make your shopping possible. And give thanks to God who provides for all your needs.

Writing a Book

I published my first book, *"Let Me Encourage You"* in 2019 and my second book, *"Let Me Encourage You More"* in November, 2022. It took hundreds of hours to write and edit 365 stories for each book. I decided to include a few black and white pictures in the second book to enhance the content. Self-publishing has some advantages. I found a wonderful printer on the internet named **DiggyPOD** which stands for *Digital Printing On Demand*. They are a small company in a small town in Michigan. Their staff have been so helpful.

I am able to print a limited number of books at a time. I usually order my books in batches of 100 copies. This is cost effective and includes the shipping. One hundred books weigh over 100 pounds. The printer sends me updates on the publishing process and estimated shipping date. I love to track the shipment on the internet as my books thread their way across the country from rural Michigan to urban California.

One of the other benefits of self-publishing is it enables me to correct mistakes and improve the quality of each new batch. When I read the first copies of my newest book I discovered spelling errors and spacing problems. For example one story was about a Mexican food restaurant that served all you can eat dinners for $1.49. I wasn't sure how to spell the name of the restaurant. Was it *Pancho's* or *Poncho's*? A friend explained to me one spelling is a personal name while the second spelling is something you wear. So the first 100 copies of my book are spelled one way and the next 100 books are spelled the other way.

Printing is not cheap. My first book was listed at $20 per copy. My second book is listed at $25. But one of my best marketing strategies was to offer two books at a lower price. I sold two copies of the first book for $30 and two copies of the second book for $40. My goal was not to make money. My goal was to get as many books into the hands of as many people as possible. I also gave away a lot of books. I am humbled when someone buys a book for themselves and honored when they buy a book to give to a friend or neighbor. Let me encourage you to consider writing a book. Make the effort to put your thoughts and ideas on paper. Consider printing some copies to sell or to simply share with others. I highly recommend DiggyPOD for your printing needs. You will be glad you did and your family and friends will too!

January 20
The First Bible

I was a senior at Saguaro High School in Scottsdale, Arizona when I was looking around a local book store. A younger student I knew came in with several girlfriends. Her name was Gena. She wanted to buy a Bible for herself.

She asked me what version of the Bible I would suggest. Don't misunderstand – there is only one Bible. But there a number of different versions and translations. The King James Bible was popular in the 1960's but it was rather difficult to understand because it was written in English that was spoken in the 1600's. There were more recent translations like the Revised Standard Version and the American Standard Version. One of the more modern versions at that time was the *Phillips Bible*. It was easier to read and helpful for people who had not read the Bible before. She seemed to like that one.

After she left with her friends I bought a copy of the Phillips version and gave it to her at school a few days later. She was very surprised and very thankful for this simple gift. I have seen Gena and her husband Larry a number of times over the following decades. They became influential leaders in Young Life ministry and several local churches in Scottsdale. Every time I see them she thanks me for the Bible I bought for her when she was a freshman at Saguaro High.

I wonder if you own a Bible. I wonder if you have ever read the Bible. It is the bestselling book in history. Many people have never read the Bible for themselves. It seems so big and intimidating. But I remind them it is a library of 66 books. Don't try to read it from front to back. I suggest they select one book in the table of contents and read one chapter-a-day. If you follow this plan you can read the whole Bible in three years. I always recommend starting in the book of Mark since that is my name. If you simply read one chapter each day you will read the book of Mark in half a month. Put a check mark in the table of contents to remind you what you have read. Then select another book like John or Acts. Slow and steady – one chapter-a-day and one book at a time. Try a book from the Old Testament like Genesis and Exodus.

There is a passage in the Bible that says, "Your word is a lamp to my feet and a light to my path" (Psalm 119:105). The Bible is God's word written for us to read and follow. Let me encourage you to find a Bible and read a chapter-a-day. You will be glad you did and I will too!

On Eagles' Wings

The 1960's and 1970's were a turbulent time in America's history. At the same time America was landing astronauts on the moon our nation was also deeply divided over the war in Viet Nam. In addition Russia had divided Europe after World War Two with the Iron Curtain which prolonged tensions between east and west. The Middle East was also an unstable region with the fall of the Shah of Iran and the new leader's imposition of Islamic Law in that country. People from many western countries fled Iran but two employees from a computer company called Electronic Data Systems (EDS) were not allowed to leave. Their company was accused by the new regime in Iran of cooperating with the Shah's secret police. The two employees were thrown into prison.

The owner of EDS was a man named Ross Perot. He was a graduate of the Naval Academy and later worked for IBM. Eventually Perot created Electronic Data Systems which became very successful. When he learned his employees had been imprisoned in Iran he launched a determined effort to rescue them. Perot hired retired Army Colonel Arthur Simons to go to Iran and rescue his employees. A Hollywood movie called, "*On Wings of Eagles*" is the true story describing the successful rescue effort based on the book written by British author Ken Follett. It was a remarkable experience for Simons and other EDS employees who freed the two prisoners Paul Chiapparone and Bill Gaylord.

There is a similar escape from prison recorded in the Bible. The Apostle Peter was arrested and thrown into prison in Jerusalem by King Herod Antipas. The king had already arrested and executed another Apostle named James. Antipas planned to do the same thing to Peter. But people prayed and God moved in a remarkable way to free Peter from prison only hours before his scheduled execution. You can read it for yourself (Acts 12). There are several other accounts in the Bible which describe how God rescued Joseph (Genesis 41), Daniel (Daniel 6), the Apostle Peter (Acts 12) and the Apostle Paul (Acts 16) from similar situations.

Jesus predicted his followers would face persecution and even death because of their faith in him. Some were rescued but many others were not. There are millions of Christians facing persecution for their faith in many parts of the world right now. Let me encourage you to *pray* for them *today* and look for ways to encourage them.

January 22
The Greener Grass

Every year in southern Arizona, landscaping companies trim the permanent Bermuda grass very low and over seed with Rye grass seed. The Bermuda grass goes dormant in the cooler weather and the winter Rye grass provides a rich, dark lawn during the cold winter season. Golf courses, green belts and bike trails are covered with Rye grass seed which attracts hungry birds. Recently I was walking along one of the bike trails when I came upon hundreds of doves feasting on the Rye seed. They looked fat and content as they ate at a rapid pace. There were also thin blades of Rye grass growing up in the cracks and expansion joints in the cement sidewalk. It was obvious some of the Rye grass seed had been scattered on the hard concrete as well on the prepared soil.

This scene looked very similar to what Jesus described in the parable of the *Sower and the Seed* in Mark 4:1-20. In that passage Jesus said some of the seed fell on hard soil, some fell on rocky soil and some fell on soil filled with weeds. But some seed fell on good soil and it produced an enormous crop.

Jesus used parables to teach valuable lessons to his followers. Someone said parables are earthly stories with a heavenly lesson. They were word pictures people could easily grasp and remember. In the parable in Mark Chapter 4 Jesus said the seed represented the Word of God. The different kinds of soil represented the hearts of men. Just like some of the Rye grass fell on hard ground and on concrete and was eaten by birds, Jesus said His words fell on the hearts of some people who were hardened and unreceptive to His teaching.

I think he was also preparing his disciples to understand some people would be receptive to His words but others would be unresponsive. That is still true today. As you tell people about Jesus and what He has done in your life – some will be open and receptive while others will be indifferent and even resistant to what you tell them. One verse says, "When the council saw the boldness of Peter and John, they realized that they were unschooled ordinary men and took notice these men had been with Jesus" (Acts 4:13). Let me encourage you to boldly tell your classmates, co-workers, neighbors, friends and family members about your faith in Jesus. Some may be resistant but others will be responsive to His words and your words. You will be glad you did and they will too.

Moss on the Mail Box

One of the few things I remember from my Boy Scout days was how to find your way home if you get lost on a hike or an outing. It is easy to get lost in a thick forest of trees or dense underbrush. One of the first things you need to do is get yourself oriented. Figure out which way is north and which way is south. We were taught the sun comes up in the east and sets in the west.

We were also told moss grows on the north side of a tree. The reason is obvious. The north side of a tree receives less sunshine and retains moisture longer. The same is true of a ski slope. They are usually built on the shady side of the mountain where the snow will not melt as quickly as on the southern side which receives more sunlight.

Recently when I went to check my mail box I was surprised to see a slight amount of moss growing on the north side of it. I don't ever remember seeing moss on my mail box. But we have had a ton of rain in Southern California this winter and more is on the way. Lawns are saturated. Hillsides are covered with a carpet lush green grass and big weeds. The local mountains are topped with a fresh layer of snow. Everyone is talking about the unusual amount of rain. Some are complaining but most are thankful for the abundance of rain and snow after several years of drought.

There are a number of places in the Bible where people suffered during times of drought. Elijah was one of the prophets in the Old Testament who predicted it would not rain in Israel for three years (Frist Kings Chapters 18-19). Streams dried up and fields were parched due to the lack of rain. Everyone from the king to the common people were impacted by the severe drought. I'm sure there was no moss on their mail boxes. The rain finally did return after three years as the prophet predicted. It was a welcomed sight.

There is a verse in the Bible that says, "God has provided evidence of his kindness by giving you rain from heaven and crops in their season. He provides you with plenty of food and fills your hearts with joy" (Acts 14:17). Rain is a simple reminder of God's care for us. Let me encourage you to give thanks to God for things like rain and snow that provide the essentials for the food we eat and the lives we enjoy. You will be glad you did and He will too.

January 24
Oh My Aching Back

As a church pastor I often visited people from our church who were in the hospital. It was an honor to pray with them and encourage them. I did not stay very long. It was usually a short visit to learn about their condition, treatment and how their recovery was going.

Sometimes it was hard to find people in the hospital. Older facilities are not easy to navigate. I wrote a story in my first book about how I got lost in a hospital looking for a patient's room and how a helpful employee escorted me to my destination.

On other occasions my visit might be interrupted by a doctor who was checking on patients in the hospital. Sometimes the patient from our church would ask me to stay and listen to what the doctor had to say about their recovery and progress.

Sometimes a therapist would show up to work with the patient while I was in the room. There are physical therapists, occupational therapists and speech therapists in every hospital. They also have respiratory therapists who help both infants, children and adults with breathing problems. I usually finished my visit with a short prayer and then departed to make way for the therapist.

One day I visited a patient who was recovering from back surgery. It had been pretty extensive and the recovery would take time. As I listened to the physical therapist address different aspects of the recovery I was surprised to hear them mention a booklet was available for a small fee. I don't remember the title of the publication but it provided important information about sex after back surgery.

I think the patient was surprised too. However he had left his wallet at home and did not have any money with him. I knew he was interested in learning more so I offered to pay for the book myself. I think he was a little embarrassed but very grateful his pastor was present to purchase the helpful pamphlet. There is an interesting account in the Bible when Jesus visited Peter's home near the Sea of Galilee. Peter's mother-in-law was very sick with a fever but Jesus healed her and she was able to resume her activities (Mark 1:29-31). Let me encourage you to visit a friend or family member in the hospital. I recommend you not stay too long but I do recommend you bring your wallet in case the patient needs to purchase an informative book!

The Quilt

When we made the difficult decision to leave the church we served in Tucson, the people at the church gave us a wonderful celebration. It was a fun filled evening where people shared stories and memories of our 13 years at the church.

In addition they presented us with several gifts. One of the most memorable gifts was a quilt. The quilt was a large bedspread with a collection of squares made by individual families. We kept the quilt in a large trunk for many years.

Recently I came across the trunk and was delighted to see the quilt again. It had been over 30 years since we were given this thoughtful gift. I took time to read many of the squares and was deeply touched by the messages people shared.

Just reading the names of families and individuals brought smiles to my face. I was reminded of many adventures we shared together. We raised our children together and built church buildings together. We went on campouts and marriage retreats together.

I was reminded of individuals who came to faith in Christ during our years at the church. I smiled as I reflected on memorable moments like weddings and the births of children. The names on the quilt and the creative designs were helpful reminders of God's blessing in our lives and theirs. A number of missionaries were also included on the quilt.

In his second letter to the Christians in Corinth the Apostle Paul referred to the people in the church as "*living letters*" who reminded him of what God had done through his ministry with them (Second Corinthians 3:2-3). *They were living proof of a loving God.*

The squares on the quilt were visible reminders of how God had touched people as we served together at the church. There were older adults who were like grandparents to our young children. There were young couples who were raising their children just as we were. Each square told a different story. Let me encourage you to write a letter or send an email *this week* to some people who have touched your life and family in the past. You may want to add an old photo that reminds you of adventures you shared together. They will be glad you did and you will too.

Grief

My wife died about a year ago. She had fought a long journey with Breast Cancer. Although I have peace knowing she is in heaven, my children and I still feel the impact of her death every day.

Grief takes many forms. Some people withdraw and want to be left alone. Other people feel angry and express their anger in a variety of ways. Some may want to talk and vent their frustration with words. They just need people to listen as they verbalize their grief.

One of my sons-in-laws shared an article with me that he found on the internet. It was written specifically to fathers who had lost their wife. It was filled with some helpful ideas of how a dad can help his children as they grieve the death of their mother. The author emphasized even adult children who have lost their mother experience grief and loss. They may have a family of their own but they still feel the impact of the death of one of their parents. They can find comfort from their spouse and their own children but they still grieve the death of their mother.

At the same time their father is dealing with his own loss. My wife and I were married for fifty years. As a husband I experienced the reality of my wife's death every day. I came home to an empty house and I slept in an empty bed. I ate meals alone and had no one to talk with about the day's events.

The article reminded me I needed to be more alert and attentive to the grief my own children were experiencing. So I began to call them more often and was more intentional listening to their thoughts and feelings about their mother's death. I started meeting weekly for dinner with my son. I was more consistent calling my three daughters to ask how they were doing and listen to their grief.

One of the best questions I used was "***How are you doing today***?" Every day is different but it gave them an opportunity to express their feelings and frustrations at that time. Some conversations were short and others were longer. I think we all benefitted from those conversations. If you or your children have experienced the death of a loved one let me encourage you to listen to them carefully. Ask them ***how they are doing today***. Share your thoughts and feeling as well. They will be glad you did and you will too.

Coyote Encounter

My wife and I live in a suburb of Los Angeles. We live in the city of Diamond Bar about thirty miles east of downtown. We have schools and shopping centers and parks and walking trails. A large amount of open space was preserved by city planners and was not developed into homes, apartments or businesses.

According to the 2020 US Census about 55,000 people live in our city. In addition, a lot of animals live here too. There is an active population of wild life within the city of Diamond Bar. We see rabbits eating in our front yard and we used to see a lot of skunks too. We used to see deer from time to time and we have seen some large snakes too. I have also seen coyotes trotting down my street in the early morning hours.

A few years ago I saw a helpful sign in a neighborhood in Costa Mesa advising residents how to respond if they encounter a coyote in their community. I haven't seen the sign in Diamond Bar but I may send a letter to the City Council requesting one for my neighborhood.

The title on the small street sign read, "*Coyote Encounter*". Below these words were a number of recommendations on how you should respond if you are confronted by a coyote. *Don't Run. Don't Approach. Be Large. Back Away Slowly.* The last words on the sign were sobering – If Attacked – Fight Back!

I think these suggestions could apply if you are confronted about your faith by antagonist. Maybe you should respond in a similar fashion.

Don't Run - Be willing to engage a person in a respectful conversation.

Don't Approach - Don't pick a fight or act in an aggressive manner.

Be Large - Stand up for your faith. Don't be intimidated.

Back Away Slowly - End your conversation on a good note.

There is a verse in the Bible which says, "Always be ready to give an answer to anyone who asks you about the faith in you with gentleness and respect" (First Peter 3:15). Let me encourage you to share your faith in Jesus with the people around you. Do it in kind way holding to the convictions of your faith. You will be glad you did and they will too.

January 28
Freedom

Peter Marshall was a Scottish-American pastor of the New York Avenue Presbyterian Church in Washington, DC. He was later appointed the Chaplin of the United States Senate in 1947. His wife Catherine Marshall wrote a biography about Peter's life and ministry in the book titled, "*A Man Called Peter*". It was made into a Hollywood movie by the same name. Peter suddenly died of a heart attack two years later. He was only 46 years old.

After Peter's death his wife Catherine developed a career as a writer publishing more than 200 books. Many of them included Peter's sermons and some of her own inspirational books. The best known book was a best-selling novel titled, "*Christy*" inspired by her mother's account of her early teaching in a poor community in Appalachia.

During his brief time serving as the Senate Chaplin Peter Marshall included these words in a prayer at the opening of a session of the Senate in 1947. He prayed, "*May we think of freedom, not as the right to do as we please, but as the opportunity to do what is right*". This has been quoted many times by many people.

We take our freedom for granted. Our country gained its independence from England almost 250 years ago. The US Constitution and the Bill of Rights guarantee freedom of speech, freedom of the press, freedom of assembly, freedom of religion and the right to petition the government.

Often people demand their personal rights to do as they please. But Peter Marshall urged people to use their freedom as an opportunity to do what is right.

There is a verse in the Bible which may have been the basis for Pastor Marshall's words. The Apostle Paul wrote, "It is absolutely clear that God has called you to live a free life. Just make sure that you don't use this freedom as an excuse to do whatever you want to do. Instead use your freedom to serve one another. That is how freedom grows" (Galatians 5:13 - The Message Bible). Let me encourage you to use the opportunities you have *this week* to help and serve other people. Don't focus only on your own needs and wants. Focus your time and energy to serve others. You will be glad you did and they will too!

Friday Night Fun

I wonder what you remember about your childhood. What were some of the traditions and routines that were part of your family's life when you were growing up?

I remember my father telling my brother and me how his family went for a Sunday drive when he was growing up in Colorado the 1920's and 1930's. His parents took him and his siblings to church on Sunday morning and then loaded up the family car and drove up into the beautiful Rocky Mountains outside of Denver on Sunday afternoons.

When I was young I remember driving to my grandparent's house on Christmas Eve when we lived in Scottsdale, Arizona. The peaceful desert was illuminated by Christmas lights decorating the homes on both sides of the road. The air was crisp and the stars were bright as we went to celebrate Christmas with Grandma and Grandpa Halliday.

I have four grandchildren who live near Lisbon, Portugal. They have a fun routine on Friday nights. They do *Pizza and a Movie* with their parents at home every Friday evening. This may sound a little boring but actually the kids and the parents really enjoy it.

They order pizza from a local shop and have it delivered to their house. The menu is pretty simple. Each of the grandkids get the kind of pizza they like. Mom doesn't have to cook and the cleanup is easy.

In addition, they get to watch a movie while they enjoy their tasty food. Popcorn is included with plenty of butter. It sounds delicious and must be very healthy too. The kids take turns selecting which movie to watch along with the pizza and popcorn.

One of the best known traditions in the Bible is the Jewish Sabbath which goes from sundown Friday evening to sunset on Saturday evening. The details are listed in Exodus 20:8-11. It is one of the Ten Commandments. God instructed the Jewish people to enjoy a day of rest and to set apart time for worship every week. I don't think it included pizza and popcorn.

Let me encourage you to develop some routines and traditions with your family which your children and grandchildren will remember and pass along to their children. They will be glad you did and you will too.

Locked Out

I drove to the Dollar Tree Store to buy a birthday card for my favorite daughter-in-law and stopped at the bank to get some cash to put in the envelope. I was planning to leave the card and cash for Christine at their house when I stopped by to check on their dog Moose. He stayed indoors while Tim and Christine were at work.

However, when I arrived at their house I realized I forgot the key to their house. I didn't have time to drive back to my house to get the key because I needed to be in Costa Mesa to pick up two granddaughters after school. I called Tim and Christine to see if they had a hidden house key I could use to let Moose out for a few minutes and leave the birthday card. No luck - there was no hidden key.

I left their house in Glendora and drove about an hour to the grandkid's school in Costa Mesa. The weather was unusually hot as parents and grandparents waited to pick up their young passengers. After I found Emily and Janie we drove from the school to their house. I used the code to open their garage door but we discovered the door from the garage to the house was locked. I called my daughter to see if they had a hidden house key. No luck - we were locked out of their house too!

The grandkids were hot and tired and wanted to get into the house. I decided to take them to a local Frozen Yogurt shop to cool them down. However, the Yogurt shop was really warm from all the Yogurt machines running in the building. We ended up eating our melting Yogurt on an outside picnic table.

Their mother was a teacher at BIOLA University in La Mirada. She was able to leave her school early and drive home to let us into the house. When she arrived we were glad to finally cool off in their air conditioned home. It had been an eventful day and they were glad to be home.

There is a verse in the Bible where the Apostle Paul said he learned to be content in any and every situation (Philippians 4:13). I'm sure this would include a hot and humid September day when you are locked out of the house with no hidden keys nearby. Let me encourage you to follow Paul's example to be content in whatever circumstance you find yourself *today*. You will be glad you did.

Something is Missing

I have an old Hewlett Packard lap top computer. Actually I don't know how old it is but the Microsoft Word program is dated 2013. I think that means it is like an antique in the computer world. I like to use it because it is familiar and I enjoy using it to write stories. I suppose it is like an old pair of shoes. They provide a comfortable and familiar feeling when I go for a walk. My lap top is comfortable and familiar too. I can usually figure out how to make corrections and solve problems using my old HP laptop computer.

My father was a writer. He worked for a number of employers during his career. For many years he used an old manual typewriter to craft articles and stories for Valley National Bank in Phoenix. I could hear the rhythm from his typewriter. It was like someone playing the piano.

Later he graduated to an electric typewriter and eventually had an IBM typewriter with the interchangeable ball with different fonts to choose from. I remember how excited he was when they introduced computers at the bank in the 1980's. He could type on the keyboard and view the text on the computer screen. This was revolutionary for a man who learned to use Morris Code and the telegraph in World War Two.

We have come a long way from the days when I used a manual type writer in Typing class in high school. However some things have not changed. One problem I have with my old HP is some letters on the keyboard don't always work. My latest problem is with the letter "U". When I am crafting a sentence I notice some words are missing the letter "U". It is frustrating to have to stop and go back and correct the mistake. Sometimes my spell check catches the mistake but often it does not. A sentence may not make sense when one letter is missing.

The Apostle Paul emphasized every part of our human body is important. He wrote, "We have a body with many parts, each its proper size and proper place. The way God designed our bodies is a model for understanding our lives together as a church. Every part is dependent on every other part" (First Corinthians 12:12-26 – The Message Bible). God designed us to be part of a family and part of a church. We need one another. When someone is missing it is like a letter on the computer key board is missing. Every person is important just like every letter is essential. Let me encourage you to connect with a church near you *this week*. You will be glad you did.

February 1
Making New Friends

Many years ago my family and I moved from Tucson, Arizona to Southern California where I became the new pastor at the Evangelical Free Church of Diamond Bar. There were about 100 Churches in our denomination from Santa Barbara to San Diego. Pastors from these churches met once-a-year at a beautiful resort along the coast in Oxnard. Three pastors were assigned to a room. The early guys got their own beds and the late arrival got to sleep on the pull out sofa bed.

This three day conference included some general sessions with a guest speaker. There was also time for recreation including early morning basketball games at a nearby church gym and an optional round of golf in the afternoon. The conference allowed pastors to reconnect and to share about their ministries and families.

I always remember the first time I attended the District Conference in 1988. I had driven by myself and was late getting to the hotel so I was the one who got the pullout bed in the living room. When I went downstairs to the first meeting I was struck by two thoughts. I realized I didn't know anyone in the room and I felt like all of the other pastors looked a lot younger than me. However I was glad I came. I got to know several men at the basketball games before breakfast and I got to know some other guys on the golf course. I also enjoyed spending some time with the District leader Wally Norling. He would provide me with some helpful wisdom and timely support in the years ahead.

There is a passage in the Bible where Paul became a follower of Jesus. When he came to Jerusalem he did not know the leaders of the early church. But a man named Barnabas personally introduced Paul to the other Apostles (Acts 9:28-31).

I never imagined I would continue to serve at our church in Diamond Bar until I retired in 2018. I attended the annual pastor's meetings and enjoyed getting to know more men in the years ahead. I was determined to watch out for pastors who were new to the district. I intentionally sought them out and invited them to share a meal or dessert. I wanted to make sure they felt included and connected with other pastors. Let me encourage you to attend some of the conferences and training sessions in your profession. Make an effort to get to know others working in your field and make sure you welcome the new people. They will be glad you did and you will too.

February 2
Rescuing the Lizards

Moving is always a challenge. There are so many boxes to empty and so many decisions to make. What things should you keep? What things should you get rid of? What things should you donate to charity or a local thrift store?

One time when we were making a major move we had boxes and boxes piled up on our back patio. I put some of the cardboard boxes on a wood pallet above the concrete surface. I also covered the pile of boxes with a blue plastic tarp to keep them out of the rain.

It seemed like a good idea until one day when I noticed some droppings nearby. I realized that I had created a haven for some four-legged critters. At first I thought they were mice but later determined they were rats. I had not only provided shelter for the cardboard boxes but shelter for some neighborhood rodents too.

I went to our local Home Depot and purchased some rat poison and some rat traps. I also purchased some sticky pads that could stop a mouse or rat on the pad and prevent the intruder from getting away. It seemed like a good idea until I discovered the sticky pads trapped two large lizards. I felt so bad when I found them stuck and unable to escape.

At first I thought they were dead. They were motionless and unresponsive. But when I took a closer look I noticed one tail moving very slightly. So I quickly found a flathead screw driver and gently tried to pry them loose. I was concerned I might injure them during my rescue effort but slowly and carefully I began to lift them out of the sticky surface one leg at a time. Gradually I was able to free both of them without injuring them. Success! If you have read my other books you know I have rescued more lizards in the past.

There is a passage in the Bible which says God loves us, cares for us and rescues us in our times of trouble. It reads, "I waited patiently for the Lord. He heard my cry and lifted me out of the slimy pit, out of the mud and mire. He set my feet upon a rock and gave me a firm place to stand" (Psalm 40:1-2). Let me encourage you to read and memorize a few verses that can be helpful reminders of God's love and care for you. Call on Him in prayer in times of trouble. You will be glad you did and He will too.

The Old Trunk

It has been interesting to see how suitcases have evolved over the years. When I was young most people packed a suit case with their socks, shirts, pants and underwear. They were usually made of leather or other durable material. Over the years suitcases were made of metal or a hard plastic shell. There was a memorable TV commercial showing an ape playing with an unbreakable *Samsonite* suitcase. Other developments included the addition of wheels to make it easier to transport the suitcases through airports and train stations. Prior to the dawn of aviation, many people transported their clothing and other belongings in trunks. They have been used for centuries. We see them in movies where pirates are looking for trunks filled with gold coins, jewels and other valuable treasures. We have an old trunk in our family. It is made of wood with metal bands holding it together. It has metal braces on each corner and strips of wood reinforcing the flat sides and curved top. A friend replaced some of the leather handles many years ago and lined the inside of the trunk with shelf paper. The trunk also has a lock on the front. It has been used to store blankets, bed spreads and a quilt in our home for many years.

We believe it was used by my Swedish ancestors when they came to America in the 1800's. They took a ship from Sweden to America and then traveled by train and a horse-drawn wagon to get to their relative's farm in Iowa. I'm sure the trunk has many adventures to tell if it could speak. Who knows the places it has gone and the cargo it has carried. I wonder who made it and how much it cost when it was new. I wonder how many owners it has had and what it is worth today. I know there are many stories of pioneers crossing America with covered wagons filled with furniture, stoves and farming tools. They also brought dishes and pots and pans. Sadly many of these things were discarded along the Oregon and Santa Fe trails as pioneers struggled to cross the prairie and climb the Rocky Mountains. There is a passage in the Bible when the Pharaoh sent wagons to bring Joseph's family from Canaan to Egypt (Exodus 45:16-28). It was a remarkable journey that saved the Israelites from the famine which consumed the world at that time. I wonder if they had any old trunks to carry their belongings in.

Let me encourage you to share some of your family history with your children and grandchildren. Tell them where your ancestors were from and how they got here. They will be glad you did and you will too.

The Old Trunk (Part Two)

I shared in a previous story about the old wooden trunk that we have had in our family for many years. I have asked my brother what he knows about the trunk but we really know very little. We do know it is old and we think it belonged to our ancestors from Sweden. It is fairly well preserved and a friend did clean it up and replace some leather straps a few decades ago.

It is fun to speculate where it came from and some of the places it might have been. I imagine a skilled craftsman built the wooded trunk in the 1800's in Sweden. We do know that my ancestors came to America from Linkkoping, Sweden in the 1840's. They settled on a farm in Iowa. My grandmother Marie (Sherman) Halliday was born in Boone, Iowa in the1890's. Her father (my great grandfather) Wesley Bartine Sherman was born in 1845 in Iowa. He later fought in the Civil War.

I imagine one of my ancestors purchased the trunk in Sweden and filled it with clothes and other essentials for its journey to America. The trunk was probably loaded onto an ocean going vessel to cross the Atlantic Ocean to America. I assume it arrived safely with its owners in New York or Boston after a long journey.

The trunk was probably loaded on to a train on the East Coast and followed the rail road tracks to Chicago or St. Louis. Eventually it arrive in Des Moines and was met by helpful relatives and taken by a horse drawn wagon to their farm in eastern Iowa. I wonder what things the trunk contained. I envision it had clothing and fabric that would be used to make more clothes in the future. It may have contained a few family heirlooms, pictures and jewelry. I'm sure that it was a prized possession and a valued addition to the family's new home.

As the years passed the trunk may have been used for storage and the safe keeping of jewelry, money, guns and ammunition. It may have been used to serve as a dresser or closet for clothing and sleep ware. I know my mother and my wife used it to store blankets and bedspreads. It is still in our house to this day. I wonder if there are some things in your house that have a story to tell. Let me encourage you to tell your children and grandchildren about some of your possessions that have come down to you from your ancestors. They will be glad you did and you will too.

February 5
Dead Battery

Many years ago we owned a two-door Dodge Dart with a slant-six engine. I think it was a pretty reliable car but not very practical with two young children in the back seat. We took several family vacations in that two-door car including a trip from Arizona to Colorado in 1977. Members of the Hopper family were gathering in Denver for my Grandmother Hopper's 75th birthday. We decided to stop at some campgrounds along the way to enjoy the beauty of the Rocky Mountains and to reduce spending money on hotels.

I attached a roof rack to the top of the car to help transport the tent, ice chest, sleeping bags and other camping supplies. The trunk was filled with luggage and baby supplies for our new born daughter Trisha. We looked like the *Beverly Hillbillies*.

When we got everything and everyone loaded into the car we asked a neighbor to take our picture before we departed. However when I turned the key I discovered we had a dead battery. A neighbor got his car and battery cables to try to jumpstart our car. No Luck.

After we got the kids out of the car I removed the old battery and drove to JC Penny's to buy a new one. A regular battery in those days was about $35. But they also offered a more expensive battery with a *lifetime warranty* for about double the price. In a weak moment I selected the more expensive option. I bought the lifetime battery. It was one of the best investments I ever made. In the years ahead I think JC Penney's replaced that battery at least three or four times! I certainly got my money's worth. Eventually Penny's stop selling car batteries.

I don't think many companies offer a lifetime warranty on their products anymore. But I actually did when it came to marriage. I told couples in premarital counseling they could come back for help as long as I was still alive on this earth. I promised to be available to meet with them when they had problems. I am convinced God can heal and restore marriages if couples are willing to follow His instructions and willing to *make changes in their own life*. If you are going through difficulties in your life or your marriage, let me encourage you to get help now. Begin with your own life. Jesus said, "Before you try to take the speck out of your brother's eye, remove the log from your own eye" (Matthew 7:3-5). I guarantee this will help you! And read "*The Man in the Mirror*" in my second book "***Let Me Encourage You More***" (p. 41-42).

Women are Always Right

I saw this phrase while I was looking for the restroom at a restaurant in Phoenix. The words were painted on the wall between the entrance of the Men's and Women's restrooms. Actually the complete sentence was – "*Men to the left because women are always right*". I told my wife she needed to see the words on the wall between the Men's and Women's restroom too. She smiled when she returned to our table. She said she agreed with the statement! I suppose most women do!

The Bible says God created both men and women. Adam was distinctly different than Eve (Genesis Chapter Two). God designed us to be different. Men are different than women both physically and emotionally. Our preferences and priorities are usually different. Our interests and intuition are different. Our perspectives and pursuits are often different too.

These differences can be a source of frustration or fulfillment. I have observed most people tend to marry someone who is different than themselves. I often asked couples these questions. Which one of you is the neat one and who is the messy one? Who is the sleeper and who is the getter upper? Who is the spender and who is the saver? Who is more social and who is more reserved?

Most couples know the answer to these questions. In fact in many ways they were drawn to each other because they saw these different qualities and characteristics in their future spouse. Often during the dating process one spouse is willing to put up with or participate in something the other one enjoys. But often after marriage the spouse will lose interest in the things the other spouse likes to do. For example a woman might be willing to go camping or fishing with her future spouse even though she doesn't really enjoy it. But after they get married she would rather stay at a nice hotel and eat at a nice restaurant instead of camping and cooking in the forest.

There is a verse in the Bible which says, "With humility, gentleness, patience and tolerance keep the unity of the spirit in the bond of peace" (Ephesians 4:2). In marriage we need to think of others first and be patient and tolerant of our differences. Let me encourage you to watch for an opportunity to demonstrate these qualities in your relationship *this week*! Your spouse will be glad you did and you will too.

Two Really Are Better than One

Recently I have been involved in a number of projects to add more storage space in our house. One of the most challenging was assembling and mounting some large steel storage racks on the ceiling in the garage. I have seen them in the garage of several friends.

The purchase was easy. I went online and discovered the storage racks were on sale at Costco. Two 4X8 racks were only $299. I decided to buy four of them since we really needed more storage space. They arrived a few days later in two heavy card board boxes.

I soon discovered the installation was not as easy as the purchase. I realized I needed help if there was any hope of getting the large heavy metal racks out of the boxes and onto the ceiling of my garage. So I phoned some friends.

Actually I sent a text to a few guys who might be willing to help me. A phone call seemed like an indication of desperation. A text seemed more informal and made it easier for a friend to decline my request. But to my surprise everyone I asked responded with a firm – yes! They would be glad to help me. And so it began. One or two guys at a time came over to help during the next few days. None of us had assembled storage racks before. We read the directions and watched a helpful video several times on You Tube. It took several days and many hours to install all four of the storage racks in the garage. The first one took a number of hours but it got easier with each new one.

The key to our success was the men who helped me. I could not have done this without their help. My wife helped too. Clearly it was a team effort. It really did confirm the passage in the Bible that says, "Two are better than one" (Ecclesiastes 4:9-12). The author said two can help each other with work and help defend each other when threatened. Two can keep each other warm in the winter and assist one another when injured.

I know for some of us it is hard to ask people for help. But there are times in life where we cannot accomplish our goals or complete a project without the help of others. Let me encourage you to send a text or phone a friend and ask them for help. And let me also encourage you to be willing and ready to help others when they call or text you. You will be glad you did and they will too.

Two Really Are Better than One (Part Two)

In my last story I shared how thankful I was for the men who helped me install the storage racks on the ceiling of my garage. I could not have installed these heavy metal frames without their help.

But there is more to the story. We not only needed storage space in the garage. We also needed more storage space in our bathroom. I had built the room addition shortly after we bought our house in Diamond Bar in 1988. I installed a fiberglass bath tub, a toilet, a vanity and a sink in the new bathroom. A few years ago I made some improvements and replaced some of these.

But my wife was frustrated by the lack of drawers and cabinets to store towels, hair dryers and other bathroom essentials. We went to IKEA and Home Depot and purchased a new mirror with a medicine cabinet. We also purchased a small cabinet to hang on the wall above the toilet and we got a tall free standing cabinet to provide more storage too. However, each of these required installation. And the five foot tall cabinet required assembly before installing it. So I made a few calls and sent out a text asking a few guys if they could help me with this project. I was thankful several guys responded including Jerry, Dave, Paul, Mark and Al. They came on different days to lend a hand.

They not only assembled pieces of the cabinet and held the mirror up while I attached it to the wall, they also helped me read and understand some of the instructions that came with each item. It was very helpful to have someone else in the room to figure out which side was up or down and which nut and bolt went where as we built the tall cabinet. In other words – *two brains were better than one*. They not only helped me assemble the parts with their hands but they also helped me understand how and where things fit together with their minds. It was very helpful to have another pair of eyes reading the directions and studying the diagrams that came in the boxes.

One Bible verse reminds us of the value of consulting with others when you are looking for a solution to a problem. It says, "Refuse good advice and watch your plans fail – take good counsel and watch them succeed" (Proverbs 15:22). Let me encourage you to be willing to ask others for help and wisdom not only when you are doing repairs and improvements around your house but also in mending and improving relationships too. You will be glad you did and they will too.

February 9
Where to Find a Guy

When I was a seminary student in the 1970's my wife Jeanne and I led the High School ministry at Northwest Bible Church in Dallas, Texas. We liked working with the students and enjoyed getting to know their parents as well. I was studying full-time at Dallas Seminary and Jeanne was a full-time Special Education teacher at a nice elementary school in the northern part of the city. Working, studying and leading the high school program kept our schedule busy.

In addition we led a mid-week small group of adults at the church. This growing church had a Wednesday night pot-luck dinner and a variety of classes and programs for children and adults. The small group provided me with an excellent opportunity to improve my skills leading and teaching adults in addition to relating to the teenagers.

Most of the adults in the group were married couples. However I was surprised to see three young women join our group too. They were college graduates who were working in different professions in the Dallas area. They had just started attending Sunday services and wanted to get to know other adults at the church.

One of the questions everyone wanted to ask these three friends was why they started going to our church and why they joined a small group. Their reply was memorable. Each of them was hoping to find a man they could marry. Their reason was insightful. They had been going to bars and other social settings for adults their age hoping to find *Mr. Right*. But they soon realized they weren't likely to find the kind of man they hoped to marry in those places. It finally dawned on them the best place to find a man to marry was in a church not in a bar.

Remember the internet did not exist in the 1970's. There were no online dating sites in those days. Once you graduated from college it became harder to connect with single adults your own age. I know at least one of those women did eventually meet and marry a sharp young man whom she met at Northwest Bible Church. There is a verse in the Bible which says, "Do not be unequally yoked to an unbeliever" (Second Corinthians 7:14). In other words don't marry someone who does not share your values, priorities and faith in Christ. One of the best places to meet your future mate is at a church. Let me encourage you to start there! You will be glad you did and I will too.

Serve Don't Search

Today there are all kinds of dating sites for singles to choose from as they look for a life partner. I know a number of people who have used the internet to find someone they might marry. I'm sure there are a number of pro's and con's to this approach.

But I am convinced the best way to find someone to marry is not by searching for them but by serving God and helping people. One author said "We don't find happiness by searching for it. We stumble over it in the path of duty".

I know several couples including my daughter Trisha who met their future spouse while they served together at a summer camp. When you work at a camp or at a job you meet a variety of people. You get to observe how they handle themselves and how they treat others. You discover if they are lazy or a hard worker. You see how they handle stress and success.

There are many passages in the Bible which emphasize the importance of service. Jesus said He did not come to be served but to serve others and give His life for them (Mark 10:45). The Apostle Paul urged his readers to follow Jesus' example and serve people (Philippians 2:5-11). The Apostle Peter urged followers of Jesus to use their time and talents to serve others (Frist Peter 4:10).

When we are busy helping and encouraging other people God delights to bring someone across our path who could be a wonderful life partner. When you are dedicated to serving and too busy to be searching, God may surprise you by bringing a spouse into your life.

This is why I encourage young and older adults to find a place to serve. Invest your time and energy as a volunteer at a local church, school or hospital. Watch what God will do while you are busy serving.

There is a movie titled, "*While You Were Sleeping*" staring Sandra Bullock. She met the man she wanted to marry when *she saved his brother* from a fast moving commuter train. I think we could use a similar title, "*While You Were Serving*" to illustrate one of the best ways to find a mate. It is not by searching websites but by serving God and volunteering your time. That is be the best way to find a mate for life. You will be glad you did and they will too.

Counterintuitive

We became Los Angeles Angels Baseball fans after we moved to Southern California in the 1980's. We had seen the stadium at a distance as we drove up the freeway to Disneyland on summer vacation but we never actually attended a game in person. I always dreamed we would get to go to a major league baseball game at the stadium someday. My dream came true as we began to attend some games in the early 1990's. During the first decade of the new millennium the Angels won the American League Western Division five times in ten years! They were the team to beat on the west coast. We actually bought season tickets for three of those years in the early 2000's. It was fun to see them win.

But the Angels have not done very well over the past few years. Even though they have two of the best players in baseball – Mike Trout and Shohei Ohtani – they have not even made it the playoffs. They changed managers several times but with little improvement. One of the more memorable managers in recent years was Joe Madden. He had been an assistant coach with the Angels during the previous decade when they had dominated the west. He also led the Tampa Bay Rays and the Chicago Cubs to World Series Championships.

Joe was not afraid to try unusual things to win games. One time he told his pitcher to intentionally walk a batter even though the bases were loaded. In case you are not familiar with baseball this meant you were giving your opponent a run instead of trying to get the batter to make an out. It was unheard of to give the other team a free run but that is exactly what Joe told his pitcher to do. It was counterintuitive. It didn't make any sense. But that is what they did. Joe didn't want to pitch to the opponent's best batter so he walked him. The Angels were able to get the next batter to hit into a double play to end the inning. Later the Angels got some additional runs and won the game but sports writers criticized Joe Madden for walking a batter with the bases loaded.

There are some interesting examples in the Bible where leaders were led by God to do some unusual things. God told Joshua to march his army around Jericho once-a-day for seven days instead of attacking the city's defenses. On the seventh day they shouted and the walls fell down (Joshua Chapter Six). Let me encourage you to consider some counterintuitive things to address problems you may be facing. The Bible calls it faith. Live by faith and watch God work.

The Candle

Ken Poure served as the Director of Hume Lake Christian Camp for many years. In addition he was a popular speaker and was in high demand during his career. My brother Steve suggested I invite Ken to speak at our Men's Retreat. Ken had retired in Palm Springs and our Men's weekend was being held at a camp in the mountains near there.

Steve gave me a helpful suggestion. We should have Ken come and speak at our church on a Sunday morning so the men could get an idea of what a good communicator Ken was. I liked Steve's idea. Ken came and spoke at our church a few weeks before the Men's Retreat. He did such a good job that some of the wives asked if they could come to the Men's event too!

Ken's messages were filled with humor and memorable illustrations. He told the men he started every day with a prayer. He got out of bed, stood at attention and told God he was *reporting for duty*. In other words he was ready to do whatever God called on him to do every day.

Another memorable story he shared at the Couple's Retreat involved a candle in his bedroom. Ken often traveled around California and to different parts of the country. Sometimes he returned home late at night after his wife had gone to bed. He told us he and his wife had adopted a simple signal to communicate with each other after he had been away. If she wanted him to wake her up when he got home she would leave a candle burning in their bedroom. That small candle signaled her desire to welcome him home after a long trip.

One of the most vital components in marriage is clear communication. Husband and wives need to be willing to share their thoughts and ideas and also listen intently to what their spouse is saying (James 1:19). Their words need to be filled with encouragement and not criticism (Ephesians 4:29). Husbands are instructed to live with their wife in an understanding way (First Peter 3:7). As one author said, *husbands need to become a lifelong student of their wife*, listening and learning what her needs are and striving to fulfill them every day. Let me encourage you to strive to improve the communication in your marriage. Ask your spouse good questions. Listen to their response. Share what is on your heart and listen when they share what is on their heart. Determine to encourage and not criticize each other. You will be glad you did and they will too. And don't forget the candle!

February 13
Youth Ministry

When I was a student at Dallas Seminary my wife and I led the High School ministry at Northwest Bible Church. We enjoyed working with these active students but some of them were not very enthusiastic about our leadership. One of the ways we tried to strengthen our relationship with some of the less enthusiastic teens was to spend a weekend together at a lake house owned by a church family. We made meals together, studied the Bible together and enjoyed outdoor and indoor games together.

However, a couple of the seniors didn't come with the group but drove by themselves in their own car. I was surprised when they arrived and a little apprehensive about how they would conduct themselves on the weekend getaway. I specifically told them if they wanted to be part of the retreat they needed to stay with the group and they were not allowed to drive into town. My philosophy was come together, stay together and go home together. They had already violated rule number one. I was concerned they might brake rule numbers two and three.

On Saturday evening they left the lake house in their car and drove into the nearby town. When they returned later in the evening I asked them where they had been. They admitted they had gone into town without my permission. I decided to send them back to Dallas. They knew the rules and intentionally broke them. They had an uncooperative attitude and cast a sour mood over the whole group. I drove my car behind them to make sure they obeyed my directions and got them home safely. I drove back the next day and finished up the weekend with the rest of the students.

Did I mention one of the students was the son of the president of Dallas Seminary? I was called into the president's office the following week to explain why I had sent his son and the other student home from the retreat. I explained the behavior of the two teens and why I sent them home. He seemed to understand why I took action but I don't think he agreed with my decision. Working with students should be fun and rewarding but that isn't always the case. In the Bible there were leaders like Moses and Joshua who had to deal with uncooperative people who challenged their leadership and defied their rules (Numbers 16 / Joshua 7). Let me encourage you to teach your children to cooperate with their pastors, coaches and school teachers. The leaders will be glad you did and your children will be better prepared for life too.

February 14
Are Two Better Than One?

Greeting cards have been part of our nation's culture for many generations. Email, texting and other social media provide new alternatives to the more traditional Christmas, Easter and Mother's Day cards. But it seems Valentine cards will never be outdated. Store shelves are filled with cards and gifts that express love on Valentine's Day. Boxes of chocolates and flower bouquets are popular gifts too.

I try to buy my Valentine cards early each year. Too often in the past I found myself shopping with other desperate men who were trying to find just the right card when most of the good ones were already gone. More recently I have tried to purchase my Valentine cards four to six weeks before the actual day. It lessens the stress level and provides a greater variety of cards to choose from.

I faced a new problem this year. I bought a few nice Hallmark cards at the Dollar Store about a month before Valentine's Day and hid them in a safe place where they would not be seen by my wife. The price was right and I found several very nice Hallmark cards. However, as Valentine's Day approached I could not remember where I hid them. I searched all over the house but could not locate them. Finally I decided to buy some more cards to make sure I had something to give my wife. I signed the cards and put them out where I knew she would see them.

The day before Valentines I found the original cards in my car. Since I didn't want to waste the cards I signed them and added them to the growing collection on the dining room table. My wife was surprised to see so many cards waiting for her on Valentine's Day. However, when she started opening and reading the cards she noticed two of them were identical. I had bought the same card at the same store a month earlier and again a few days before February 14th! And I had written virtually the same note on both cards too!

There is a verse in the Bible that says, "Two are better than one" (Ecclesiastes 4:9-12).This verse is often quoted at weddings in reference to the marriage of a man and a woman. But this verse doesn't seem appropriate when it comes to Valentine's cards! I don't recommend giving your wife or sweetheart two of the same cards. Let me encourage you to shop early to find the best selection of Valentine cards but make sure you read them again before you give them to the one you love. She will be glad you did and you will too.

51

Engaged

Recently I met a young man who was excited to share the news he was engaged to be married. But I sensed he was a little overwhelmed by the prospect of married life. When he learned I was a pastor he asked me for some sage advice for marriage. I shared with him what I tell every couple in premarital counseling. There are *two things* which cause problems in marriage – a *selfish attitude* and a *critical attitude.*

We are all *selfish* by nature. From the time we were young children until we become grown adults, we tend to think of ourselves first. You can hear it in our conversation and see it in our actions. We say things like, "I like this. I don't like that. I want to do this. I don't want to do that".

The Bible teaches us to do the opposite. *Don't be selfish. Be a servant.* Put the needs of others ahead of your own. One verse says, "Don't just look out for your own needs but think of others also" (Philippians 2:5). Jesus modeled this in his earthly life. "He did not come to be served but to serve others" (Mark 10:45).

The second problem I observe in many marriages is a *critical attitude.* We focus on the faults of others and don't notice the faults in our own life. Before we get married we tend to overlook things we don't like in our future spouse. But after we get married we become frustrated and irritated by some of the things they do and don't do.

A wife may expect her husband to help around the house and expect him to buy flowers and thoughtful cards. A husband may expect his wife to light some candles and plan a romantic evening. But when those things don't happen a husband or wife can become frustrated and disappointed. They begin to focus on their spouse's imperfections instead of their positive qualities.

Let me encourage you to use more compliments and less criticism. Focus on your spouses' good qualities. And work on the areas in your own life which need to be changed (Matthew 7:1-5). Look in the mirror. Ask yourself what changes do you need to make in your own life? Don't be selfish – serve. Watch for opportunities to serve your spouse. And don't tear people down – build them up (Ephesians 4:29). Focus on their good qualities not their faults. You will be glad you did and they will too.

Love and Marriage

I conducted many wedding ceremonies during my career as a church pastor. I married young couples and older adults. I did weddings for couples whose spouse had died and they decided to get married again. And I had the honor of marrying one couple who had been through a divorce and later decided to remarry their former spouse.

Different cultures have different ways of uniting a husband and wife in marriage. My wife and I attended the wedding of her former sixth grade student who was from India. The groom rode up to the gathered guests in the resort parking lot on a beautiful horse. It was a lavish ceremony with a lot of guests. We also attended an Armenian Orthodox wedding. At one point the priest instructed the man and woman to put their foreheads together as he wrapped a rope or necklace around them. It was a visual expression of their love and commitment to one another.

One of our former neighbors was from India. He shared with me how his marriage was arranged by his parents and the parents of the bride. I was surprised to learn this was still practiced. But when we were on a tour in Israel we noticed several young couples meeting privately in the lobby of a large hotel. Our tour guide explained the parents of these young couples had hired a *Match Maker* to introduce their son or daughter to a potential marriage partner. The couples were meeting for the first time. The *Match Maker* was watching from a distance while these couples got acquainted. There are several examples of arranged marriages in the Bible. One wealthy man named Abraham sent his trusted servant hundreds of miles to find a wife for his son Isaac (Genesis Chapter 24). Jacob's marriage was arranged by Laban the father of Rachel and Leah (Genesis Chapter 29).

I like the words from my neighbor from India. He explained, "*In America first you fall in love and then get married. But in India, first you get married and then learn how to love one another.*" I'm sure most American teens and young adults don't agree with this concept. They want to find a husband or wife through dating and searching the internet. But most parents know their children well and understand their temperament and strengths. I'm sure every parent prays for their children to find a spouse who shares their values and would be a good match for their child. Let me encourage you to seek the guidance and wisdom of your parents and friends and ask God to lead you to a life partner. You will be glad you did and your parents will too.

Hot and Cold

After the death of my wife from breast cancer, I eventually married a wonderful widow in our church. We were thankful for the opportunity to start a new journey together. We knew each other's spouse and we had been part of the same church for many years.

But it is interesting trying to blend two households into one. I already had a houseful of furniture, beds, linens and so much more. My new wife did too. We had two refrigerators, two washing machines and two dryers. We had two sets of pots and pans. We had two ironing boards, two step ladders and two kitchen tables. The list went on and on.

When the moving truck arrived at my house with all of my wife's things it filled our two car garage and the back patio. We unpacked boxes for weeks as we worked together to blend our things into one house. It involved a lot of patience and understanding as we decided together what things to keep and what things to give away. One example involved the appliances. Since Susan's washer and dryer were newer and bigger, we agreed to give mine away. A young couple with young children was thrilled to get my washer and dryer. They brought their pickup truck and hauled them away. The movers were able to install and hook up Susan's washer and dryer. It was a win-win.

However, over the following weeks Susan began to notice the clothes were not coming out as nice as they had at her old house. She thought the clothes came out of the washer feeling warm even though she washed some loads with only cold water. Finally after a few weeks we figured out the movers had connected the water lines incorrectly. We discovered the hot and cold water lines were on the wrong connections on the back of the washer. We switched the hoses and laundry began to come out better. It was an easy fix.

It has been an interesting journey blending two houses into one. There is a verse in the Bible where the Apostle Paul wrote, "Do all things with humility and patience, pouring yourselves out for each other in acts of love, alert at noticing differences and quick to mend fences" (Ephesians 4:2 – the Message Bible). These are helpful reminders for newlyweds and for those who have been married a long time. We need God's help to blend our lives together as married couples. We need to demonstrate patience, humility, tolerance, love and forgiveness every day. You will be glad you did and your spouse will too.

February 18
A Memorable Birthday

My brother Steve was born on February 18, 1948. He is my favorite brother. Actually he is my only brother. After we finished school and got married we didn't see each other very often. He and his wife Sharon raised their three kids in Northern California. My wife Jeanne and I raised our kids in Southern Arizona and Southern California. But we did get together from time to time. One of our favorite memories was spending a week with Steve and Sharon and their kids at the Mount Hermon Conference Center near Santa Cruz, California. One year we camped nearby at the Henry Cowell State Park. They had a tent and we borrowed a popup trailer. It rained most of the week but we enjoyed the speaker and seminars and our kids enjoyed the camp activities with their cousins. In later years we rented cabins for the week and enjoyed meals in the dining hall at Mt. Hermon.

Another favorite memory was surprising my brother for his 50th birthday. Our mother had died from a heart attack in 1989. Our father lived by himself in Phoenix. My family and I lived in Diamond Bar. Steve and Sharon lived in Grass Valley, California. I suggested to my dad we should do something special for Steve's 50th birthday. I asked him to fly from Phoenix to the Ontario airport near me. Then we flew together from Ontario to Sacramento. I shared my plan with Sharon to enlist her help surprising Steve.

My dad and I rented a car in Sacramento and drove to the town of Auburn near Grass Valley. Sharon agreed to meet us at one of their favorite restaurants for dinner. We got there first and found a table in the back of the restaurant. But when Steve and Sharon arrived the parking lot was pretty full and Steve suggested they go eat somewhere else. Thankfully Sharon was able to persuade Steve to at least go inside and see if there were any tables available. He was very surprised to see us waiting at a table for him! I still smile when I recall that memorable birthday with my brother and our father. After dinner we drove back to their house and spent a few more days together. I wonder if you have surprised a friend or loved one for their birthday. I wonder if you have been surprised yourself on a special occasion. Let me encourage you to make a plan to surprise someone for their birthday or anniversary *this year*. They will be glad you did and you will too!

Pastor of the Day

My brother Steve served as a pastor in several different churches during his career. He graduated from Dallas Seminary in 1974 and accepted a position as an Associate Pastor at the First Baptist Church in Davis, California. He enjoyed leading the Christian Education program at the church. He also mentored several young couples who were doing graduate work at the University of California in Davis. One of those students became a lawyer and eventually worked with the Attorney General in Sacramento.

Steve also served as the lead pastor of a church in Grass Valley, California for ten years. Then he accepted an invitation to serve as an Associate Pastor at the First Evangelical Free Church in Austin, Texas. It was located in downtown Austin near the University of Texas campus. Again his focus was primarily in Christian Education. He also enjoyed mentoring young professionals who were doing graduate studies at the University.

Steve had a unique opportunity while he was at the church in Austin to do the invocation at a session of the Texas House of Representatives. He was invited to be the **Pastor of the Day** which included praying for the assembled representatives as they carried out their duties serving the people of the state of Texas. Steve has a framed certificate thanking him for his service as *Pastor of the Day* on August 8, 2003.

There are many examples in the Bible where men and women had important opportunities to advise and influence Kings and rulers of government. Joseph was an adviser to the Pharaoh of Egypt (Genesis 41). Daniel was a trusted advisor to the Persian King Nebuchadnezzar (Daniel 1-6). Esther and Mordechai influenced another Persian King (Book of Esther) and Nehemiah was a personal advisor to another King and Queen in the book of Nehemiah (Chapters one and two).

My brother didn't get to advise or speak to the Governor of Texas but he did have the opportunity to pray for the leaders in the Texas government. The Apostle Paul reminded followers of Jesus to pray for the emperor and others in authority in the Roman Empire (First Timothy 2:1-2). You may never have the opportunity to pray in the halls of government but you can certainly pray in your own home or office for those in leadership in your city, state and nation. You will be glad you did and they will too.

The Commencement Speaker

My nephew Matt Hopper graduated from Pepperdine University in Southern California in 1996. My wife and I and our four children (Matt's cousins) attended the ceremony in Malibu, California. It was a long drive from our home in Diamond Bar. But we were glad to celebrate Matt's graduation with his parents and his two sisters.

The speaker was the governor of one of the larger states in our country. I remember his opening comments when he shared with the graduates and their guests that he did not remember who spoke at his college graduation. And he suspected most of those attending the ceremony would not remember him either.

As I reflected on my own college graduation from Arizona State University, I did not remember who the commencement speaker was. The ceremony was on the football field at ASU in June, 1971. There were several thousand students graduating that evening. In fact they did not even read the names of all the graduates. We were simply invited to stand with our fellow students as each college was recognized. Actually they only read the names of students receiving a Master's or Doctorate degree. It was a very impersonal experience.

When I graduated from Dallas Theological Seminary in 1975 it was a very different experience. There were only 125 students receiving their Master's Degree and another dozen were awarded their Doctorate's degree. I remember walking across the stage, shaking hands and receiving my diploma from Dr. John Walvoord the school's president. But I do not remember who spoke at my graduation either.

I wonder if you can remember the name of the commencement speaker at your college graduation. I suspect most students don't really care who the guest speaker was. Students are ready to get their diploma, get a job and get on with their life.

In the case of my favorite nephew, it was a memorable experience because the speaker would become the President of the United States a few years later. After serving as the Governor of Texas, George Bush was elected President in 2000 and served two terms in the White House. I suspect most of the students who were at the commencement ceremony at Pepperdine University in the 1996 will never forget who spoke at their graduation.

February 21
Driving Safely

I always wondered why male teenage drivers paid higher insurance rates than female drivers. An insurance agent explained to me that almost every male teenage driver would be in a car accident by the time they were eighteen years old. Female drivers had a lower accident rate so they also paid lower insurance premiums. I was thankful to not be in an accident when I was a teenager. I was so excited to start driving when I was sixteen. I actually got my driver's license on my sixteenth birthday. I was not in a car accident until I was in my 20's when another car slowly slid into my car on an icy road in Dallas, Texas.

However, there have been a few times in my driving career when I didn't exercise good judgement. When our children were young my wife and I found a way to change drivers in our Dodge Van without coming to a stop. We knew if we stopped the vehicle it might wake up sleeping kids. So we figured out a way for one of us slip out of the driver's seat while the other one slipped in while driving at 65 MPH. Looking back this probably wasn't a very responsible way to drive.

Another time I used poor judgment when my wife and I were driving with her parents to attend the Rose Bowl Game on January 1, 1987. I was driving her parent's car from Arizona to California. We were driving on Interstate 10 near Palm Springs. It was a warm winter day as we crossed the desert and I was wearing a sweat shirt. The sun was beating in my side window. Instead of getting off the freeway I decided to pull the sweatshirt over my head while driving at 65 miles an hour.

It was only a spit second but it was not a smart thing to do. My father-in-law firmly expressed his alarm and displeasure with me taking off my sweatshirt as we sped down the freeway. Looking back I have to admit I was wrong and put all of us in danger. Thankfully we did not have an accident and we did get to the Rose Bowl Game safely. By the way the ASU Sun Devils defeated the Michigan Wolverines 22-15.

There are many examples of people making poor decisions throughout the Bible. I'm sure there are some examples in your own life where you made a poor decision or acted foolishly. Thankfully we have a God who loves us and is willing to forgive us for our mistakes. Let me encourage you to be willing to forgive others as you hope they will forgive you too (Ephesians 4:32). You will be glad you did.

February 22
Never Leave without a Kiss

There is a line in a popular movie that I like. When someone asked the main character how long he was married to his wife he replied, "*Not long enough*". My wife and I were married for over 50 years. She died from breast cancer when she was 71 years old. We were married for many years but it was not long enough.

After she died, I married a widow from our church. She had been married to her husband for 49 years. We had attended the same church for a long time. I knew her husband and she knew my wife. We went to baseball games together and enjoyed dinners together. We attended many of the same church activities and shared friendships with some of the same people. We never dreamed both of us would lose our spouse and one day get married again.

It has been a wonderful experience joining our lives together and starting on a new journey. But it has also been a learning curve. We have brought old habits and routines into our new relationship. We are learning to adapt and adjust to each other. We are learning to be patient and kind with one another.

One thing I have learned is to not say goodbye without a kiss. I am sure I did this in the past but now I realize how important this is every day. *Don't leave without a kiss*. Recently my wife was getting in her car to go to a hair appointment. She was a little frustrated trying to find her car keys and get out the door. Finally as I watched her back the car down the driveway and on to our street, she stopped her car and ran back to the house. I thought she had left something behind in the house. She had actually left the car in the street with the engine running. I asked her what was wrong.

Susan realized she had left without kissing me goodbye. She had forgotten one of our fundamental agreements – *never leave home without a kiss*. So she left the car running in the street while she dashed back up the driveway to properly say goodbye. I still smile at that simple gesture. There are many passages in the Bible where people greeted each other with a kiss and said goodbye with a kiss (Acts 20:36). It is a simple way to express our love and appreciation for another person. Let me encourage you to take time *today* to express your love for someone with a simple kiss. They will be glad you did and you will too.

February 23
Check the Oil

I mowed my own lawn for many years. I enjoyed the exercise and I saved money doing the work myself. The biggest problem was finding the time to get the yard work done. The grass kept growing year round and even faster in the hot summer days.

I have mentioned in other stories that I had Bermuda grass in my yard. It is drought resistant and requires less water than other types of grass. It is frequently used on golf courses and requires a special lawn mower to cut the grass properly. It was called a *McLane Seven Blade Mower*.

These mowers can be very expensive to purchase. However they do last a long time and you can frequently find a used one at a reasonable price. My old *McLane Seven Blade Front Throw Mower* burned a lot of oil. I usually checked the oil level each time before I mowed the lawn but I must admit I was negligent from time to time.

One time when I tried to start the mower, the pull cord would not move. I pulled and pulled with all my strength but it would not budge. I thought the pull cord might be caught in the pulley. I took the mower to the repair shop hoping they could fix it quickly so I could get back to cutting the grass.

However, when the repairman called me the news was not good. He said the mower had overheated and seized up because the engine did not have any oil in it. The engine was ruined. It could not be repaired. I would need to replace the engine or buy a new mower.

How did this happen? How did the oil get so low? I was careless to not check and see if the oil level was adequate. There was a big bright label on the mower that said, "*Check oil before each use*". I had failed to take this warning seriously. Now the mower was ruined.

At the end of the Sermon on the Mount, Jesus said people who heard His words and followed them were like a wise man who built his house on a rock. But people who heard his words and did *not* follow them were like a foolish man who built his house on the sand. When the floods came the house of the wise man stood firm but the house of the foolish man was washed away (Matthew 7:24-29). I was a fool for not following the instructions. Let me encourage you to do what you read and learn from the Bible. *Don't just read it live it*. And check the oil too!

David and Goliath

Some of my favorite memories of my father-in-law are the times we spent playing golf together. I had never played golf until I married my wife many years ago. A common scenario in those early years was my wife and her sisters would go shopping and have lunch with their mother. The men in the family would usually go play golf. My father-in-law Walt and his son Walt Jr were good golfers. One of the other sons-in-law Steve was a very good golfer. The other sons-in-law Pat and Jim were not golfers. And then there was me.

When the women decided to go shopping and have lunch the golfers usually made a tee time at a local course. They would look at me and ask if I wanted to come too. They were hoping I would say "no" but I always said "yes"! Sure I would love to play a round of golf with them! It was usually a painful experience for them. I didn't play very well. I hit my ball in the water and in the weeds and slowed down the whole group. My father-in-law would tell me to hurry up and pick up my ball because we were holding up the golfers behind us. Instead of discouraging me this actually motivated me to learn how to play golf better. It took many years but I finally beat my father-in-law in a round of golf when he was over 70 years old.

I really did enjoy playing golf with him in Arizona, California and even in Hawaii. But we did have one very unpleasant experience that I have never forgotten. We were playing on a public course in Phoenix when a golf ball hit him in the forehead just above his glasses. It wasn't a bouncing ball on the ground but a hard shot in the air with no warning. He fell to his knee and groaned with pain. It was terrible.

I didn't know what to do. I offered to help him get into the golf cart and take him back to the Club House to get some medical attention. But he refused. He wanted to keep playing and finish the round even though he had a golf ball size bump on his forehead. I'm thankful it did not hit his glasses and shatter in his eye. We did finish but I knew he was in pain. There is a passage in the Bible where a young man named David took a golf ball size stone and used a sling to throw it into the forehead of the giant Goliath (First Samuel 17). David killed his enemy with one stone. I'm thankful my father-in-law was not seriously injured or killed. Let me encourage you to spend time and make some memories with your father-in-law. And watch out for stray golf balls coming your way. You will be glad you did and he will too.

February 25
The Mystery of the Dark Spot

I heard a friend share an interesting story about an unsolved mystery in their home. One evening Nancy noticed a black spot on their kitchen tile. She hadn't seen it before and wasn't sure what had caused it. She tried to wash the spot away with some cleaning solution but it didn't help. However, the next day it was gone. How did that happen? She clearly saw it the previous day but now it was gone. A few days later she saw the large spot again. She told her husband and he couldn't figure it out either. Since their custom home had been built on the slope of a hill in Tucson, he suspected there might be some moisture or other material under the floor causing the dark image to appear on the surface of the clay tile.

Another curious feature was the dark stain was only seen at night. And even though she washed it with a number of cleaning agents she could not remove it. But when she checked the next morning the spot was gone. They also wondered why the spot was only on one of the sixteen inch square tiles and not on any other. Maybe it was a manufacturer defect or something was wrong with this specific tile that made it different than the others.

Since her husband was in the construction industry, he consulted with a couple of friends asking what they thought might be causing this dark image on just one tile. Most speculated there was a leak under the floor. But Lothar knew there were no water lines under the kitchen floor. This truly was a mystery. A dark image on only one floor tile that did not respond to cleaning and scrubbing. And it only appeared at night and was gone in the next day.

Finally it dawned on Nancy and Lothar there was a small potted plant on the kitchen counter which cast a shadow on the floor when the kitchen lights were on at night. The spot or stain was actually just the shadow caused by a small plant sitting on the kitchen counter! When they moved the plant the spot moved too! They laughed as they shared this story with us. The mystery was solved and life went back to normal. There are several passages which refer to shadows in the Bible. One author described God's protection as a shadow covering and protecting us in the *Shadow of the Almighty* (Psalm 36:7 / 91:1). Let me encourage you to thank God for His love and protection. And make sure you move the plants before you start scrubbing the stains on the floor.

A Fun Movie

Recently my wife and I watched an enjoyable movie titled, *Mrs. Harris Goes to Paris*. It was a delightful tale of a humble widow who dreamed of going to Paris to purchase the dress of a lifetime. The setting is in the 1950's when famous dress makers like Christian Dior and Louis Viton held private events for wealthy buyers in France's capital.

Mrs. Harris was neither wealthy nor part of the upper society in France but she was determined to fulfill her dream of buying one of those exclusive dresses for herself. She was a widow who lost her husband in World War Two. She had a limited income from cleaning homes and private apartments in London. But through a variety of unusual circumstances she gathered enough money to fly to Paris and purchase a beautiful and stunning dress.

But the underlying theme of the movie wasn't about purchasing a designer dress for herself. It was about helping people. Mrs. Harris cleaned apartments even though some of her clients were late in paying her. She encouraged the dress maker's employees when it looked like they would be laid off from their jobs.

She loaned her expensive dress to a younger woman who had an important appointment which could open the doors for her future career. She encouraged a widower who had lost his wife. Every time she had the opportunity she set aside her own interests in order to help other people.

Mrs. Harris Goes To Paris is not a Christian movie. It is just a fun tale of a determined widow to fulfill a lifelong dream. But the lesson it teaches is very important. Make it your goal in life to encourage and help people around you. There is a verse in the Bible which says, "Use the gifts and abilities God has given you to serve others" (First Peter 4:10). Jesus modeled this for us when He washed the feet of His disciples (John 13:2-15) and when he stopped to help those who were helpless (Mark 10:46-52).

Let me encourage you to make it a priority in your life to help and encourage others. Don't just focus on your own wants and needs. Watch for an opportunity to help someone *this week*. They will be glad you did and you will too.

Stop and Smell the Roses

My wife and I try to go for a walk every day. Sometimes we walk through a park but most of the time we simply walk through our neighborhood. We enjoy greeting other people walking along the streets and sidewalks. We also like to see the different houses along the way and admire the lawns and landscaping.

We have noticed more and more people have removed their lawns and installed artificial grass. It looks very nice, doesn't require water and needs very little maintenance. Other homeowners have replaced their lawns with crushed granite and succulent desert plants. These look very nice too.

However the thing which really caught our attention this spring were the number of neighbors who had roses blooming in their yards. I never really noticed how many homes had roses. There were an endless variety of roses with different colors and the blossoms which seem to be unusually large this year. Some of them were huge.

The rose bushes had dark green leaves and looked very healthy. We thought it may have been the result of the heavy rains we had last winter. The precipitation must have enriched the soil and produced a bumper crop of beautiful roses.

One day when we were walking we saw a woman trimming back some of her rose bushes. We slowed to admire them and commented on how wonderful they looked. The woman said she appreciated our words and promptly gave us a handful of fresh cut flowers.

We carried those with us on the rest of our walk and put them in a vase when we got home. I am looking at these beautiful flowers in our family room as I type this story. It has been amazing to see how large the blossoms have become and the colors are spectacular. We are thinking about going back and asking for more on our next walk!

There is a verse in the Bible which reminds us God created the heavens and the earth. He created an endless variety of plants, animals, sea creatures and birds for us to observe and enjoy (Genesis Chapter One). Let me encourage you to *stop and smell the roses* in your neighborhood this spring. You may want to plant some more at your house too. You will be glad you did and your neighbors will too.

Entertainment at *In N Out Burger*

We enjoy eating dinner at our local *In N Out Burger* restaurant. It is one of our favorite places for fast food. The food is great and the prices are affordable. *In N Out Burger* has become a legend in California and has spread to other states including Arizona, Nevada and Texas.

In N Out Burger is family friendly with children, teens, adults and grandparents too. Recently we observed a mother and her young son enjoying their visit. We were surprised to see the mother allow her young four year old son to help with her dinner. After they placed their order they found a table across from where we were sitting. Then the mother asked her young son to get some ketchup from the condiment area. He dashed off and proudly returned fulfilling her request.

Then she asked him if he wanted to get their soft drinks. He gladly went to the self-serve soda area and filled two cups with their favorite flavor. We wondered if the little guy could carry them back to their table and not spill. To our surprise he did great.

He also spotted another child in the restaurant with an official *In N Out* hat. His mother suggested he go back to the service counter and ask an employee if he could have one too. Sure enough he walked over by himself and asked the employee if he could have a hat. They were glad to fulfill his request. When he got back to his table the mother asked him if he had said "*Thank You*". I guess not because he hurried back by himself and personally thanked the employee.

When their order was ready his mother sent him to collect the food and bring it back to their table. Again the little guy confidently picked up the plastic tray filled with burgers and fries and delivered it safely to their table. It really was quite entertaining to see this young four year old boy handle his assignments so well.

There is a passage in the Bible which instructs parents to raise up their children in a responsible way (Deuteronomy 6:6-9). Other passages emphasize the importance of preparing our children spiritually and practically to enable them to live a life pleasing to God (Proverbs 22:6). Let me encourage you to train your children well, not only in regards to their faith in God but also developing confidence in their own ability to make wise choices and live responsible lives. Give them some opportunities to fulfill some tasks *this week*. They will be glad you did!

A Familiar Route

Many years ago a number of men from our church drove to Phoenix, Arizona to attend a Promise Keepers event. Thousands of men from around the Southwest gathered for a weekend of encouragement and training in this beautiful city. I not only enjoyed the PK conference but I also enjoyed getting to know more men on deeper level.

Most of us traveled together riding in two church Vans. A few guys drove their own cars and one man flew in a private plane. When the conference was over Dave asked me if I would like to fly back with him to California. Which would you choose - six hours in a crowded church van or two hours in a comfortable private plane? I chose the plane.

We left Phoenix around sundown. The sky was clear and the wind was calm. I wore a headset so I could talk with my friend the pilot and hear his conversation with the tower in Phoenix and others along our route. Dave flew the small plane in a capable and professional manner.

As the sky darkened I was able to identify some familiar landmarks along the way. Our course followed Interstate 10. I recognized the Palo Verde nuclear power plant west of Phoenix. It was brightly lit and easy to see. I knew when we flew over the Colorado River near Blythe, California. It is a small town surrounded by farm fields fed by the river water. Palm Springs was a bright oasis in the California desert. The whole Coachella Valley was easy to identify as Interstate 10 threaded through this growing community. The final leg of our flight continued to follow the freeway until we reached our destination at Brackett Field near the LA County Fair Grounds in Pomona.

It was fun to recognize so many sights as we flew over them in the night sky. Dave encouraged me to keep an eye open for other aircraft in our path. Our flight went smoothly and I enjoyed my flying adventure. There are several verses in the Bible which describe how God leads and guides our lives. David wrote, "Even when the way goes through Death Valley, I am not afraid when you walk by my side" (Psalm 23:4).

I don't know what fears you are experiencing in your life. But let me encourage you to put your trust in God. He is like a good shepherd who will lead and guide and protect you on your journey. The path may not be smooth and the obstacles may be many but he will never leave you or forsake you if your faith is anchored in Him (Hebrews 13:5-6).

The Contractor

My wife taught sixth grade in the local school district. She taught Language Arts and Social Studies. She loved teaching sixth graders. They were old enough to discuss the subject matter and still young enough to be respectful and helpful to their classroom teacher.

Language Arts involved developing the students writing skills. I can still see her sitting on our family room couch grading papers night after night. She wanted to make sure spelling was correct and the children were improving their ability to express their ideas on paper.

The Social Studies curriculum for sixth graders included ancient civilizations including China, India, Egypt, Israel, Greece, Rome and the Fertile Crescent. She was able to blend their history studies with their reading and writing skills. However some students were frequently late getting their homework done on time. They were late completing their assignments and were not completely honest when explaining why their work was late again. She came to the conclusion that most sixth grade boys who didn't get their school work completed on time grew up to be *building contractors*.

I served as the lead pastor at our church in Diamond Bar for over 25 years. We went through several building programs during those years as the church grew. We did some of the work ourselves but we also hired building contractors for the larger projects. Expanding and improving the facilities was stressful and frustrating at times. One man in particular did not meet goals and deadlines. The quality of his work was questionable and the cost of the project frequently increased with change orders. He made excuses why the work was behind schedule.

It finally dawned on me this contractor was one of those students my wife often referred to during her teaching career. Don't get me wrong. I'm sure many contractors do complete their projects on time and many sixth grade boys do get their homework done on time. But some contractors do resemble the sixth graders my wife described. There is a passage in the Bible that says, "A good reputation is more valuable than gold" (Proverbs 22:1). Let me encourage you do be a person who is reputable and honest regardless of your occupation. Get your work done on time whether you are a sixth grade student or a building contractor. You will be glad you did and your teacher and your clients will be too.

Flags

I typically see a number of people walking through my neighborhood during the day. As the days get longer it seems like more people are out walking. It is nice to greet one another and catch up on family or neighborhood news. Recently I put some small flags in my yard. These were not little American flags to show our patriotic spirit on the Fourth of July. And they were not small banners celebrating a specific season like Easter or Thanksgiving. These small bright flags were attached to a thin metal wire. They were scattered all over my front yard. I was surprised by how many people stopped and asked why I had put these little flags in my lawn.

I explained I was using these colorful flags to identify the location of the sprinklers in my lawn. I had scheduled a gardener to use a large machine called a "*Lawn Comb*" or "*Lawn Thatcher*" to thin out my Bermuda grass. I mentioned in another story how gardeners plant Rye Grass seed in lawns in Arizona when the Bermuda grass goes dormant in the winter months. Now that spring was coming it was a good time to thin out the Bermuda because it grows so thick during the summer months. This was an opportunity to thin out the thick grass so it will have more room to grow in the months ahead.

Some people seemed satisfied with my explanation while others seemed a bit skeptical. Why was I really putting these flags in my yard? I was tempted to manufacture a better story to satisfy the unconvinced in my neighborhood. Maybe I should have told them I was marking the location of the hidden treasure in my yard or the places where goffers hide underneath my grass. But the truth of the matter was they were simply marking the location of the lawn sprinklers so the gardener would not break or damage them when he used the machine to thin out the grass.

There is an interesting individual named Samson in the Bible. God gave Samson great power and physical strength to overpower his enemies. His opponents used a variety of tricks to attempt to learn the source of his strength. Samson told his enemies several stories to confuse and mislead them (Judges Chapter 7). Let me encourage you to be ready to give a clear explanation when someone asks you about where you find peace and hope in this crazy world (First Peter 3:15). You will be glad you did and your friends and neighbors will be too.

A Helpful Habit

When I was a teenager I was busy with school, sports and a part-time job. My days were full of activities and responsibilities. I stayed out late with friends on weekends and got up early to deliver a hundred newspapers every morning. I'm thankful for that season in my life. I was new in my faith and anxious to learn and grow in my relationship with God. I enjoyed going to church and attending Bible studies and other activities with the teens in our church. Sunday sermons helped me to learn more about the Bible and I loved sharing with others what I was learning myself.

One thing I was encouraged to do was read the Bible. I love history and biographies and the Bible was full of both. But it was difficult to find time to read a chapter from the Bible in addition to all of the other things in my life at that time.

I developed a routine of reading the Bible when I went to bed at night and when I woke up in the morning. I had watched our youth pastor do this when we were backpacking in the Grand Canyon and when I traveled with him when he was the guest speaker at a youth camp. I always saw my friend Sherrill reading his Bible before he went to bed at night and when he woke up in the morning. So I put my Bible on the table between the lamp in my bedroom and my bed. I had to reach over the Bible to turn off the light. This was a helpful reminder for me to stop and read a chapter every morning and every night.

President Jimmy Carter shared in an interview he also read his Bible every night before he went to bed and every morning when he got up. I was encouraged to learn even the President of the United States made time in his busy day to spend a few quiet minutes with God reading the Bible every morning and every night.

There is a verse in the Bible which says, "Early in the morning while it was still dark Jesus got up and went out to a lonely place to pray" (Mark 1:35). This was a priority even after some of the busiest days of His earthly life. Let me encourage you to start a new habit in your life this week. Dust off your Bible and begin to read one chapter a day. Or you might want read one chapter in the morning and another chapter at night. Read from a contemporary version like the *Message Bible* or *Living Bible*. Don't start on page one. Start in the book of Mark. You will be glad you did and I will too.

The Power Sprayer

We have a nice patio in the back of our house. It is a perfect setting to entertain guests and visitors. It also provides a pleasant place to simply relax and enjoy a cup of coffee or ice tea.

It was also useful as a place to store stacks of boxes when my new bride moved into our house. The movers piled boxes upon boxes on the patio as they emptied the delivery truck. Many more boxes went into the garage. It took weeks to bring boxes into the house one by one and find the best place for their contents. Several times we had to cover the boxes on the patio with large blue tarps to protect the corrugated boxes from heavy rains that drenched Southern California. Thankfully the contents of most of the boxes survived the rainy season. Gradually the piles were reduced and the patio became visible again.

I actually squeezed the last few boxes and some plastic storage tubs into our garden shed so we could clean up the patio for an upcoming BBQ. I used a small power washer to hose down the patio surface and the two large glass patio doors. It was a remarkable transformation from the piles of storage boxes to the clean clear cement surface and the glistening glass doors. Suddenly we were able to see the plants and flowers in the back yard. The afternoon sunlight flooded into our family room. It was amazing how clean and nice everything looked. The guests at our BBQ had no idea how different the patio looked only a few weeks before. I'm convinced the power sprayer was one of the keys to cleaning off all of the dust and dirt and making the windows look so nice. It really was a transformation.

There are several passages in the Bible which describe how God changes and transforms our lives (Romans 12:1-2 / Ephesians 4:17-32). And just like the power sprayer washed away the dust and dirt, the Bible says Jesus can wash away all of our spiritual dirt and sin (Isaiah 1:18 / First Peter 1:13-16).

If you are looking for a way to clean up your patio or clear the dirt off the stucco on your house, I recommend you buy yourself a power sprayer. And if you are looking for a way to clean up your life and clear away your sins, accept God's offer of forgiveness and new life through faith in Jesus (First Peter 2:24-25 / 3:18). Start with a simple prayer to God. Confess the sins of your past and ask Him to transform your life as you follow Jesus. You will be glad you did.

Plumbing Problems

When we bought our first home in Tucson, Arizona in the 1975 I knew very little about home repair and maintenance. I didn't know how to trouble shoot or repair electrical and plumbing problems. But I learned a lot in the next few years. One of the first steps was to gather some basic tools like screw drivers and a few wrenches. I bought some Teflon tape for the plumbing and black electrical tape for connecting wires and replacing light fixtures. I got a hand saw to cut wood and replace baseboards. These tools were essential in maintaining our house.

I was pretty cautious with electrical matters. I knew it was important to connect the black wires to the other black wires and white with white. I knew the green wire was the ground wire. Plumbing was easier to understand but often more difficult to do when it came to repairing or replacing a toilet valve or a water line. I knew I needed to check for drips and leaks before the project was done.

One day I took my handy tool box and set out to replace the brass rings in the bathroom faucet. Tucson was known for its hard water and sometimes a tiny pebble would get stuck in the small brass ring under the handles of the faucet. This prevented the small rubber gasket from completely fitting into the brass ring resulting in a small constant drip. There was a special tool to help remove and replace the old brass ring.

I launched into my project confident I could do this simple repair. But when I removed the faucet a geyser shot up covering the bathroom floor. I forgot the first step in any plumbing project – *turn off the water* supply under the sink or at the main valve outside the house. I dashed out the door and closed the main valve. What a mess. I had a small lake in the bathroom that was inching toward the adjoining bedroom. Thankfully the damage was minimal and I was able to mop up the flood quickly with some bath towels. It was a careless mistake and a lesson I did not forget in the future.

We all make mistakes in life. None of us are perfect. There is a chapter in the Bible where David confessed his sin and asked God for forgiveness (Psalm 51). Let me encourage you to learn from your mistakes. If you have offended or hurt someone ask for forgiveness and don't do it again. And if you are doing plumbing make sure to *turn off the water* supply before you begin! You will be glad you did!

A Palm Tree and A Pine Tree

I have shared in previous stories about how much I enjoy playing golf. A golf course is like a giant park with trees and green grass. The trees are filled with a variety of birds who make their home and raise their families in this peaceful setting. Migratory birds like Canadian Geese fly thousands of miles to enjoy the warmer climate for the winter. They love to hang out on golf courses. Other wildlife also abound on a golf course including deer, skunks and ground squirrels. Even the courses in the desert are beautiful with natural vegetation and wildlife like snakes, coyotes and tortoises.

Recently I was playing golf with some friends at a local golf course and saw something unusual. As we were walking back to our golf cart I noticed a palm tree growing in a pine tree. This was not the first time I had seen this but I did stop to view this remarkable phenomenon. There was a space in the pine tree about eight to ten feet above the ground where a tree branch and the trunk formed a "*fork*" or "*Y-shaped*" space. Apparently pine needles and dirt had accumulate in this space. It is likely a bird left a seed there and it took root in the soil and needles. With some moisture from our recent rain the seed from a palm tree started to grow.

I had actually seen this phenomenon before on a different golf course. A palm tree was growing in the saddle of two branches of a tall pine tree. In Southern California it is not uncommon to see a small palm tree sprouting in the crack of a sidewalk. A tiny seed can start to grow in the smallest of spaces. Over time these little trees grow and become a problem damaging walkways and driveways.

Sometimes people are skeptical of unusual events recorded in the Bible. Some think these may be natural phenomenon like a storm on a lake or food provided by birds in the desert. But there are many accounts of miracles in the Bible that cannot just be explained by natural causes like feeding 5,000 people with only five loaves of bread and two fish (John 6:1-14) or raising a dead child back to life (Mark 5:35-43). Let me encourage you to read the Bible yourself. The Bible is a library with sixty six books. Read about the remarkable things Jesus said and did. Read it not as a skeptic but with an open heart and mind. Marvel at the message and the miracles recorded in those pages. You will be glad you did and I will too.

Inflation

I enjoyed a recent conversation with some college students about the health of our economy. Two of them were majoring in Business studies so I asked them what can be done to address the runaway inflation in our country. It was interesting to hear their responses. Some were not concerned about inflation. Others said they had not really discussed inflation in their business classes. None of them were aware of the causes and the impact of inflation in their lives.

You don't have to be an economics expert to know things you buy today are more expensive than they were a year ago. That is basically what inflation is. It takes more money today to purchase food at the grocery store than it did a year ago. Prices have gone up but your paycheck has probably not kept up. Retired people living on a pension or Social Security have not kept up either.

One of the areas where I have seen inflation is at my local donut shop. I attend a Bible study with some men at our church every Friday morning. We take turns bringing a box of donuts to share with the other guys. In 2017 a dozen donuts typically cost $10.00. By 2020 the price had risen to $10.50 a dozen. But in 2022 inflation drove prices up dramatically. A few weeks ago I paid $16.00 at the same donut shop for the same number of donuts. That is what we call inflation. It takes a lot more money to purchase the same items.

There are several reasons for inflation. For example when the cost of raw materials like flower and sugar go up the price of the finished product goes up too. When the price of fuel for the trucks that deliver the raw materials goes up the finished product goes up too.

One way to deal with inflation is to stop buying donuts. They are not essential. We might call them a luxury. But there are many items which are essential like milk, eggs, meat and produce. The price of a head of iceberg lettuce used to be under a dollar. Now I am spending almost two dollars for the same head of lettuce. I don't need donuts but my wife and I do need food and other essentials. There are a number of passages in the Bible which remind us to be content in whatever circumstances we find ourselves (Philippians 4:10-19). Many things in life are out of your control. Let me encourage you to be content with what you have as you deal with runaway inflation. Trust in God to supply all your needs (Matthew 6:25-34).

Inflation (Part Two)

I shared in my last story about the runaway inflation we are facing today. The federal government reported that prices food and energy increased over 10% from 2022 to 2023. Although they reassure us inflation is decreasing in reality it is still the highest since the 1970's. You may be too young to remember high inflation in the 1970's. The root cause was the increase in the price of oil. Arab nations attacked Israel in 1973. When the United States sent weapons and ammunition to support Israel the Arab nations cut off oil supplies to our country and other nations like England and France who supported Israel.

The oil embargo caused a shortage of gasoline. Gas was rationed and the amount you could purchase was restricted. The price of gasoline skyrocketed. There were long lines of drivers waiting to put gas in their cars all across the country. In California you could only purchase gasoline on the odd or even number days that corresponded with the last number on your license plate. In Texas gas stations rationed how much gas they could sell in a day. We always bought gas first thing in the morning because some stations would stop selling by mid-day.

The leaders of our nation promised to not let this happen again in the future. We determined to produce enough of our own oil and gasoline so our country would not be held hostage by other nations. Exploration for new oil was launched in parts of Alaska, offshore in the Gulf of Mexico and on the west coast. But now here we are again dependent on foreign oil to fuel our cars and commercial trucks. Although more drivers are buying electric cars there are not nearly enough to impact the price of gasoline.

Foreign governments have raised the price of oil and natural gas and we are paying the price with huge increases for gasoline, diesel fuel, heating oil and natural gas. People in California were shocked to see their natural gas bills triple from the previous year. The price to heat my home in the winter of 2021 was about $100 a month. In the winter of 2022 the price was over $300 a month - a 300% increase! You may not care about the cost of donuts but you probably do care about the higher cost of driving your car, heating your home and feeding your family. Let me encourage you to not lose hope during these uncertain economic times (Philippians 4:19 / First Timothy 6:17). Be wise in how you spend your money and be ready to share with those in need. You will be glad you did and they will too.

Listening to Two Veterans

Recently I had lunch with two men from our church. We talked about a number of things including their service in the military during the war in Viet Nam in the 1960's and 1970's. I did not serve in the military and did not go to Viet Nam. I received a high lottery number in the 1969 draft and was able to stay in school and finish college. It was interesting to hear them share about their experiences and reflect on those tumultuous years. Both men served in the US Army. Paul was an engineer and spent most of his time building bridges and destroying booby traps set by the Viet Cong. Gary was in the infantry and was stationed in various places in Viet Nam. His job was to try to avoid the booby traps and protect Army installations in the country.

Their conversation included some humorous stories about their time in Viet Nam. Some of the things they saw and did were funny and unusual. Other things they saw were very serious and sad. Both shared how difficult it was to know who to trust. Often it was difficult to know who was a friend and who was a foe. The North Viet Nam army wore uniforms but the local Viet Cong did not. The enemy blended in with local villagers and were difficult to identify. Both men experienced fear while serving in an active combat zone. Gary mentioned how frightened he was manning a fox hole by himself on the perimeter of his unit. Night time was especially difficult watching for an enemy incursion. Paul said he experienced fear as well when they passed through villages not knowing if the enemy was waiting for them.

Another thing they both shared was how difficult it was to come home after their service in Viet Nam. Our nation was divided about the war and many young people protested against the war. When soldiers returned to the USA they were frequently harassed and greeted with disrespect. Soldiers in uniform reported being spit upon in airports and other public settings. One of the men I talked with said he actually wore a wig when he went to Disneyland so people would not know he was serving in the military. There are many passages in the Bible recording wars and stories about serving in the military. Three of David's older brothers served in King Saul's army (First Samuel Chapter 17). Later David became the leader of the army of Israel. Let me encourage you to express your appreciation to the men and women who serve in our military today and to those who have served in the past. You will be glad you did and they will too.

Overcoming Obstacles

Two of my favorite books are about gigantic construction projects that looked impossible to most people. Author David McCullough wrote a book about the building of the Panama Canal titled, "*The Path Between the Seas*". He provided vivid details about the huge undertaking to build a canal through Panama and create a passage for ocean vessels.

Another book with a similar theme recorded the building of the railroad across our country from Omaha, Nebraska to Sacramento, California. The author was Stephen Ambrose and the title is, "*Nothing Like it in the World*". He believed the construction of the Transcontinental Railroad was essential to unite our nation. Previously it took up to 200 days to sail from New York to San Francisco around the tip of South America. Building the railroad reduced the trip from 6-7 months to 6-7 days. Both books provided vivid descriptions of the challenges and hardships people experienced completing these huge projects. It took ten years (1904-1914) to build the Panama Canal and it took six years (1863-1869) to construct the railroad which connected the eastern and western halves of the United States.

Both projects looked impossible with many challenges and obstacles to overcome. Knowledgeable engineers, skilled craftsmen and common laborers were successful in constructing both the canal and the railroad. Massive amounts of earth had to be moved and huge locks had to be created to complete the Panama Canal. Tunnels had to be dug through mountains and bridges built over many rivers and canyons to complete the Transcontinental Railroad.

There is a similar project on a much smaller scale in the Bible in the book of Nehemiah. The author volunteered to leave his position of influence in the Persian capital to lead an effort to rebuild and repair the fortress walls around the city of Jerusalem. The city had been burned by the Babylonians over 100 years before Nehemiah got involved. The people were defenseless and the city was in disrepair. The project looked impossible but Nehemiah believed it could be done with the God's help. He faced opposition from local leaders and lacked support from some of his own people. But Nehemiah overcame the obstacles with prayer and persistence (Nehemiah Chapters 1-6). Let me encourage you to ask God to help you with challenges you may be facing in your own life. Nothing is impossible with God (Luke 1:37).

Water Conservation

When we bought our home in Diamond Bar, California in 1988, it already had a sprinkler system for the lawn. The original owner had put sprinkler pipes in the front and back yards before planting the grass. I was thankful for the hard work he had done although I have replaced a few valves and a lot of sprinkler heads over the years. However the flower beds did not have valves, pipes and sprinkler heads to water the flowers and shrubs. I had good intentions to lay some pipe in these peripheral areas over the years but I never got it done. As a result we often had to ask a friend or neighbor to water the outdoor plants a couple of times a week when we were traveling.

Finally I decided I had procrastinated long enough. I went to Home Depot and purchased some PVC pipe and the needed sprinkler heads. I also bought some PVC glue and various elbows, unions and parts to assemble the pipe. I was able to tap into the existing sprinkler system and extend the pipes into the flower beds. I used a drip system to conserve water and give individual plants and shrubs better coverage.

It was a lot of work expanding the outdoor water system. I was always bending over or getting down on one knee to assemble the pipes and install the risers and drip caps. I started in the back yard and got a feel for how far I should space the sprinkler heads. Then I pressed on to the front courtyard. Slowly the new system took shape. It took several days to cut and glue the pipe and to add the risers and drip caps. It also took several trips to Home Depot and my local Ace Hardware store to finish the job.

My wife was thrilled to have water supplied to all of the flower beds and landscaping along the block wall in the back yard. She has been ready to plant new shrubs and flowers for a long time. I'm glad to finally have all of the yard and plants on an automatic watering system so we don't need to bother neighbors and friends to do the water the plants when we are traveling.

There is a passage in the Bible which says, "One plants and another waters but God causes the growth" (First Corinthians 3:1-10). Let me encourage you to plant some flowers and vegetables in your yard *this month*. Get busy and fix the leaks and add some new soil so you can enjoy the bounty of your garden and the beauty of flowers in your yard. You will be glad you did and your neighbors will too.

Gleaning

The fruit on our orange tree usually ripened at the end of the year. This sturdy tree produced wonderful oranges year after year. They were tasty and juicy. I usually picked the first ones in early January. It was a great way to start the New Year.

However I noticed someone else was enjoying the Navel Oranges at our house. It took a while to solve the mystery. One day I saw a squirrel carrying a large orange in its mouth as it scurried along the top of the block wall in our backyard. The fruit was almost as big as the thief. The hard working neighborhood squirrel was eating my oranges.

At first I was pretty unhappy to see my precious oranges being stolen by this crafty critter. But then I remembered a story in the Bible in the Book of Ruth. Both Ruth and her mother-in-law Naomi were widows. Their husbands had died and the two women moved back to Naomi's hometown in Israel. It was called Bethlehem.

One of the ways a widow could provide for her needs was to glean in the farm fields after the workers had harvested the crops. The Israelites were instructed to leave some of the crops on the edge of the fields and leave some fruit on the trees so widows, orphans and foreigners could forage for food (Leviticus 19:9). Ruth went out to the fields and picked grain that was left over after the workers harvested the crops. She did this to support herself and to share with her mother-in-law (Ruth Chapter Two).

I realized I should be willing to share some of the bountiful orange crop with other residents of my neighborhood – including the squirrels. They need food to survive and feed their young too. Gleaning is a very practical way to help feed those who are lacking food. It is a good way for those who have plenty to share with those in need. And it is a good way of those in need to retain their dignity and pride by working with their own hands to feed themselves and their family.

I have seen advertisements on TV which report almost 10% of families in our country are food challenged. Many organizations collect and distribute food to people in need in your community. My Rotary Club sponsors a canned food drive in partnership with local schools to collect food for families during the holidays. Let me encourage you to share with those in need. You will be glad you did and they will too.

The DMV

Recently I went with my wife to the *Department of Motor Vehicles* to help her renew her driver's license. It is an interesting experience to see how this whole process works. There were dozens of employees at work but one woman stood out among them all. The first challenge was finding a parking place. The lot was full and spaces were scarce. The DMV recommends you make a reservation to schedule a specific day and time to go to their office. There were two lines as we stepped through the front door. The longer line was for Walk-in's. The shorter line was for people who had an appointment. Thankfully my wife had an appointment.

The nice lady at the front door examined the documents my wife had brought and directed her to the area where she could fill out an application form on a computer screen. The lobby was packed with people. The number of chairs were limited and many people were standing while they waited for their number to be called. After completing the application form we waited about 20 minutes until her number was called to go to window number nine. She passed the vision test and paid for her new license.

Then she was instructed to get her picture taken by following the yellow line. The woman at the photo window was happy and cheerful. She stood out above all the other employees. She had a warm and friendly personality which took the edge off of the slow process. She took time to make sure every person smiled for their photo.

The final step was passing the written driver's test. This was on the green line. Susan took the test on a computer screen and passed! What a relief. The agent assured my wife her new driver's license would arrive in the mail in about two weeks. We walked out of the crowded DMV office with a sigh of relief. It was a slow and sometimes confusing process but the deed was done – success.

As we reflected on our time at the DMV we both commented on the woman taking the pictures. Other people were working hard but the woman at the photo window was so positive and encouraging. There is a verse in the Bible which says, "Do your work with all your heart" (Colossians 3:23). Let me encourage you to be the kind of person in your office, campus or construction site who encourages others. You will be glad you did and your clients, customers and coworkers will too.

March 15
The Lonely Shoppers

Online shopping has changed our lives. Millions of people use their computers and smart phones to purchase everything from groceries to garage doors, from clothes to car parts and from office supplies to beauty supplies. However, I still prefer to go to the store to do most of my shopping. I like to interact with the employees and receive personal assistance when I can't find something. I like to get their suggestions when I am buying a new appliance or electronic device. Maybe it sounds a bit old fashioned but I still like to shop in person rather than online.

Recently my personal shopping didn't go too well. My wife and I went to a large big box store looking for a DVD player. I'm sure just the idea of buying a DVD player sounds out-of-date. Who buys DVD players? Every movie in the world is now available through one of the many streaming services like Netflix and Prime. But we still own dozens of DVD's and want to be able to watch them without paying an online fee.

We drove over to one of the giant retailers and asked for directions to the electronics department. It took a while to get there and find the DVD players. There was a nice selection with many at a reasonable price. However, they were all kept in a locked glass display case. It seemed unnecessary to have these locked up. The one we were looking for was less than $40. Some were more expensive but they were not anything as valuable as a diamond ring at a jewelry store.

Unfortunately we could not find a sales person in the electronics department. We asked a couple of employees for help but they said only two people had the keys to unlock cabinets in this area. One said the employee we needed had left early to attend a friend's graduation. Another employee said they would call a supervisor and get someone to help us but no one came. After waiting for about 15 minutes we left the store without a DVD player. It seemed so sad. We were shoppers ready to spend money and there was no one around to help us with our purchase. I suppose this would never happen if we were shopping online. Maybe you have had a similar experience. Stores and malls do not have enough employees and they are losing business.

If you work in sales at a local store or shopping mall, let me encourage you to do all you can to help the customers who walk through your door. They will be glad you did and you will too.

The Water Filter

One of the problems with our water is the high mineral content. A lot of the water we drink and use in Southern California is imported from the Rocky Mountains and the Sierra Nevada Mountains. Aqueducts transport this water hundreds of miles in a network of open canals and stored in large reservoirs before arriving in our local communities. Even though the water goes through a treatment process at regional facilities it is still considered "hard" water when it comes out of the kitchen faucet or shower head.

Hard water can cause a film to build up on your shower glass door and bath tub. It can clog water pipes over time. It doesn't taste as good or feel as good as filtered and bottled water. There are many companies offering different products to filter the water in your house. Even our refrigerator has an expensive water filter which needs to be replaced every six months. Filtered water is better water for cooking, cleaning, bathing and drinking.

The woman who does my wife's hair recommended a water filter that attached to the bathroom shower. The hair dresser said the water filter would be better for my wife's hair. I was a little skeptical but we did buy one from Lowe's. It was easy to install and I must admit the water feels much better than it did without the filter. It is called a "*Sprite*". It works.

Another thing that needs a filter is our conversation and vocabulary. I am amazed at the volume and amount of foul language included in our public and private conversations. Adults, teens and children are using words and phrases which were unacceptable only a few years ago. The media has contributed to this in movies, TV sitcoms and online websites. It is amazing to hear the profanity used in conversations between actors and actresses. In addition new words, phrases and acronyms continue to be introduced into our vocabulary which are unhealthy and misleading.

These is a verse in the Bible which says, "Watch the way you talk. Let nothing foul or dirty come out of your mouth. Say only what helps" (Ephesians 4:29). "No more lies, no more pretense. Tell your neighbor the truth. When you lie to others you end up lying to yourself" (4:24) (The Message Bible). Let me encourage you to watch your words. Clean up your vocabulary. Speak the truth. You will be glad you did and your friends will too.

Getting Married Again

My wife and I were married for 50 years. We met at Scottsdale High in the 1960's. We were married in 1971 after I finished college at ASU. She died after 16 years fighting breast cancer. We had four children and ten grandchildren. I'm very thankful for our lives together.

The months following Jeanne's death were very lonely even though I received the support and encouragement of many friends and family members. It was a strange uncharted journey to go on living without your life partner. Coming home to an empty house and sleeping in an empty bed after 50 years of marriage was unimaginable. I missed Jeanne's touch and our talks together. I missed traveling with her and I did not like making important decisions without her. Nothing can prepare you for living without your life partner.

Gradually I began to consider dating other women. This alone was a strange concept. It was unfamiliar territory to actually have lunch or dinner with another woman. There were a number of widows in our church and they had experienced the death of their life partner too.

My children and other family members were uncomfortable when I told them I had begun dating a widow from our church. I believe adult children find it difficult to see their father or mother with another person. It just looks and feels strange. Gradually I began to consider getting married again. It was unfamiliar territory for me and my family and my friends. As a pastor I had done a number of weddings for couples who had lost their spouse. I spent time with them considering the pros and cons of their decision. Most of those marriages have done very well.

Eventually I asked Susan to marry me. She had been married to her husband for 49 years before he died after open heart surgery and a stroke. We dated for many months going for walks at a local park and enjoying some new adventures together. This was unfamiliar territory for both of us. Were we ready to be married again after the deaths of our spouse? How would this effect our own families and our future? There is a verse in the Bible that says, "It is not good for the man (or woman) to be alone" (Genesis 2:18). I believe God designed us for companionship. He intended us to share life's journey with others. I'm thankful God brought Susan into my life to be my wife as we began this new journey together.

Family Reunions

One of the things we intended to do after our children started getting married was to bring our family together on a regular basis. Our first reunion was in Estes Park, Colorado in 2005. Hondo and Trisha were the hosts and they called themselves the "FRC" – *Family Reunion Committee*. We shared several days together including a round of golf for the men and shopping and tea for my wife and our three daughters.

At the first reunion we told our children and their spouses we had purchased a Timeshare in Maui. We agreed to schedule a week in June for our next family reunion in 2007. We were able to reserve a second condo and gather our family together for a week in Hawaii. This trip included a day trip to Honolulu to visit Pearl Harbor and the Submarine Museum. My father-in-law served in submarines during World War Two and was stationed in Pearl Harbor and Midway Island.

Our next Family Reunion was in Ljubljana the capital of Slovenia for Christmas in 2009. Our daughter Teri and her husband Jacob were not able to join us. Trisha and Hondo were the FRC Committee. It was a special time with our young grandchildren Caleb, Katie and newborn Carly. We enjoyed the Christmas decorations and the outdoor shops.

Another memorable family reunion was in Lisbon, Portugal for Christmas 2013. Traci and Jonathan were the FRC. Our whole family came. We remember going to the Lisbon Zoo and getting a family photo taken with some colorful birds and grandkids holding maps.

A few years later we were able to get our whole family together for a few days in the mountains above Los Angeles. Our friend Al Smith climbed up a tree limb to get a family photo. We enjoyed swimming in Lake Gregory and hiking in the woods. We also experienced a significant earthquake on that July 4th weekend.

Our most memorable Family Reunion was in Maui in June, 2021 to celebrate our 50th wedding anniversary. We reserved four condos at our Time Share resort. Each family had their own unit and Jeanne and I used a guest house nearby. You can read more about this reunion in my second book. One of the most emotional Family Reunions in the Bible is in Genesis Chapter 48 when Joseph was reunited with his family. Let me encourage you to make a plan for a family reunion. You will be glad you did and your family will too.

Getting Back to the Gym

We have access to a gym near our house. It is one of many fitness centers that have replaced grocery stores in older communities. The one in our neighborhood is called "*Crunch Fitness*". It seems to be busy with a lot of cars in the parking lot and a lot of people inside.

I used to have a regular routine of going to the gym three mornings a week. But after my wife died I found myself less motivated to get out of bed and get to the gym on a regular basis. I did miss the connection with the older people at the gym and when I did go I was greeted enthusiastically by my peers.

However I did begin to do more walking in the months following my wife's death. I took my cell phone along with me and listened to Audible books and podcasts while I got some exercise. It was a good use of my time and I slept better at night when I walked during the day.

Recently I went back to the gym for the first time in months with my new wife. Susan provided a little push to get me back to gym. We enjoyed walking together but we both realized we needed to add some other exercises to strengthen our arms and core muscles.

It was a small start but it did feel good to go to the gym. It was also more fun to go together. I wasn't very motivated to go alone but it was more fun to go with someone else. That is probably true in many areas of life including hobbies and other special interests.

That is also true when it comes to going to church. It is hard to get motivated to get out of bed on Sunday morning by yourself. But you may be more inclined to go with a friend or family member. And you may find it more meaningful when you are greeted by fellow church goers. There is a passage in the Bible that says, "Do not forsake assembling with others to worship God" (Hebrews 10:25). Pastor Rick Warren used to say, "*We are better together*". We are more motivated to do something when we do it together with other people. That is true of physical exercise and spiritual worship too (First Timothy 4:8). Let me encourage you to get off the couch and back to a gym in your neighborhood. Let me encourage you to get out of bed and to back to a church too. Your family will be glad you did and you will too.

The Volunteers

I shared in one of my previous books that my father served as a volunteer at a hospital in Arizona after my mother died. He did not have any medical experience. He actually worked as a writer for a large bank in Phoenix for many years. My mother died of a heart attack a few years after he retired. Instead of sitting home alone he decided to get busy by volunteering some of his time at a local hospital.

My friend Chuck did something similar. After Chuck sold his business he and his wife joined our church staff working with our senior adults and overseeing the church facilities. Chuck and Jackie were the *dynamic duo* helping and encouraging widows and older adults. He was also very helpful solving computer problems at the church.

But after Jackie died he decided to volunteer with the California Highway Patrol. He had served in the military many years ago but he did not have any official law enforcement experience. It was a long journey going through the application process including interviews and a background check. But almost two years later he was finally approved to serve as a volunteer with the Highway Patrol. Chuck helped at the office in Baldwin Park a suburb of Los Angeles. He did a variety of things including sorting and organizing paperwork from the citations officers had issued during the previous week. He told me they handed out over 2,000 tickets during the Memorial Day weekend. It was a record high for their office.

He also got to drive a patrol car from time to time. As a volunteer he was not allowed to issue citations but his presence on the freeways helped to slow traffic when drivers saw a CHP cruiser behind them. Chuck and other volunteers also helped with sobriety check points to catch people driving under the influence of alcohol. They also directed traffic at major events and helped with road closures when there was a wild fire or mud slide near a major highway. Chuck enjoyed getting to know the people who served in the office and on the highways. He liked to help and encourage them. Law enforcement has become very stressful and highly criticized. His goal was to lighten their load and encourage them in the difficult work they did. A verse in the Bible says, "Encourage one another" (First Thessalonians 5:11). Let me encourage you to volunteer your time at a school, church or other organization. As you encourage others you will be encouraged too!

Traci

Your mother and I always remembered the day you were born on March 21, 1978. We lived in Tucson at that time and had gone to Phoenix to visit my Grandmother Marie Halliday who was in poor health. She died a few months later. On our drive back to Tucson mom went into labor. We did not have a clock in our car or a cell phone to monitor the contractions so we drove 60 miles an hour (each mile was one minute) to calculate how far apart the contractions were.

We called the doctor when we got home. I always remember he asked if we were a drinking family. I said we did not drink but wondered why he asked. He said sometimes wine could slow or stop labor. We told him we did not have any wine in the house so he recommended we come to the hospital. You were born a few hours later at 4:00 AM in the morning. You were about 6-8 weeks early and very tiny. The doctor requested an ambulance to rush you to a larger hospital in Tucson that had an Intensive Care Unit for new born babies. You spent the next four weeks in the NICU before coming home.

You have always been a special part of our family. Your laughter and energy are infectious. It is clear you love God and love people. It was fun to watch you and your sister Trisha grow up during your teen years. I remember one morning when both of you were washing your cars in front of the house. You drove the tomato and Trisha drove the potato. You were active in the Color Guard at Diamond Bar High and invited many friends and classmates to the youth program at our church. You and Trisha developed a heart for missions while serving children during Easter break in Mexico. Later you traveled to the Dominican Republic and Spain to work with missionaries in those countries.

We are thankful you found Jonathan after you graduated from BIOLA. You two make a great team serving as missionaries and raising four kids in a foreign country. I enjoy watching you interact with people in their language and how hard you work as a mother of four kids. You have become a wonderful wife, mother and a mentor to younger women. I love your pioneer spirit. You are just like your mother. We are very proud of you. Happy Birthday!

Let me encourage my readers to write a letter to your children. Tell them how much you love them. Share with them some of the positive qualities you see in their life. They will be glad you did and you will too.

March 22
Share You Experience

There is a man in our church who is a Metallurgical Engineer. He is a graduate of the famous *Colorado School of Mines*. For many years he worked for companies with foundries mixing various metals to make castings and parts for the aerospace industry. I had no idea it was so difficult mixing and shaping metals for use in aircraft engines and other vital airplane parts. These castings have to be strong enough to withstand the extreme stress on a jet engine or the weight on the landing gear of a Jumbo Jet. The quality and care in manufacturing is critical to the safety of the passengers and crew in the thousands of planes in the air every day.

During his career, Paul was often called upon to solve problems in the foundries where he worked. He was the *Jedi Master* that employees in the office and on the foundry floor went to for solutions and suggestions when they had manufacturing problems. Even after he retired his company hired him to be a consultant to help them with some major production projects.

One of the highest compliments he received was an invitation to teach some classes to new incoming engineers. His former boss asked Paul to share his experience and insight with these new college graduates. These young employees had engineering degrees from colleges around the country. But many did not have much experience working in foundries which actually produced the final products that go into airplanes and other applications. These young engineers were attentive and eager to learn from this older veteran.

There is a passage in the Bible where the Apostle Paul told his young disciple Timothy to teach other people the things Paul had taught him (Second Timothy 2:2). Timothy had traveled with Paul throughout the Roman Empire. He had heard Paul teach and saw how the Apostle faced opposition, responded to false teaching and endured persecution. Paul instructed Timothy to teach other believers the things he had seen in Paul's life and heard from Paul's heart.

Let me encourage you to share your knowledge and experience with younger members of your family and younger employees at work. You have the knowledge and experience that can help them succeed. They will be glad you did and you will too.

Night and Day

We have been doing a lot of projects around our house over the past few months. We hired a painting crew to paint the interior of our house and a gardener to make improvements to the outside of the house. It feels good to see the progress and enjoy the results of all this work.

One area that needed attention was the back patio. I had rebuilt the roof over the patio a number of years ago but it suffered from some leaks during the winter rainy season. In addition the shade screen had deteriorated and the exterior patio lights were dirty and dim. I finally threw them away.

The result was bright sunshine poured into the family room from the west facing patio. The sun reflected off the patio surface and the interior tile floor. We started eating dinner in a different room to avoid the bright light and hot sun in the family room.

Finally we went to Home Depot and purchased a new sun shade and a string of new exterior patio lights. Some friends helped me put the new shade screen up and I installed the new patio lights. The benefits were immediate. We could easily lower the shade screen in the afternoon to eliminate the heat and the bright sun light flooding the family room. And the new lights have enticed us to spend more time on the patio in the evening too.

I was surprised what a difference these small improvements made. The patio was more pleasant and inviting and the family room was more comfortable. We enjoy seeing the new patio lights coming on at dusk and we are glad the bright afternoon sunlight was no longer a problem.

There is an unusual passage in the Bible in the book of Jonah where the prophet was discouraged by the hot sun and long days. God provided him with shade and food while Jonah waited to see what God would do to the city of Nineveh (Jonah Chapter 4). Let me encourage you to get busy and deal with some things in your life and around your house that are keeping you from enjoying the things God has given you. Don't put it off. *Do something this week.* You will be glad you did and your wife and family will too.

Logistics

I shared in an earlier story how several friends helped me install some overhead storage racks in my two-car garage. These metal racks were anchored to the ceiling and hung down about 18 inches. This provided much needed extra storage space and still allowed for my car and my wife's SUV to be parked under them.

When the movers delivered the cardboard boxes and plastic storage tubs with my wife's things they put some of the storage containers on the new racks in the garage. Many more boxes and tubs were stacked on the garage floor and on the back patio. The garage looked like the warehouse at the end of the movie, "*Raiders of the Lost Ark*".

We unpacked the boxes on the patio first and put the contents in kitchen cupboards and closets in the house. Then we worked in the garage. Eventually we cleared enough space to get one car in. The ultimate goal was to get both cars back in the garage again.

Recently I brought down most of the containers from the racks in the garage so we could confirm what was in each box or tub. Susan looked through each one and identified which contents could be brought into the house and which ones needed to go back on the storage racks.

I knew I needed help lifting some of the heavier boxes and plastic containers. So I called my friend Phil and asked if he had time to help me lift these up onto the storage racks. He was glad to come. Phil turned out to be a good call because he is not only strong but he was also in the logistic business with the Nestle Corporation. He managed several hundred employees at their distribution center in Mira Loma. He knew how to load and unload large trailers and he could visualize what storage boxes and containers could fit on my garage racks too.

Phil was not only helpful with the logistics and organizing the boxes and containers but he was also available. He was willing to change his schedule and come right away to help me get the things off the floor and onto the storage racks again. There is a passage in the Bible that says, "A friend loves at all times" (Proverbs 17:37). Let me encourage you to be ready and willing to respond when a friend or family member needs help *this week*. They will be glad you did and you will too.

Aquila & Pricilla

The first time I met Al and Bev was on the patio of our church. I noticed this good looking couple walking up the steps and introduced myself to them. We were meeting in the Fellowship Hall in the 1990's.

I was impressed with their friendly personality but didn't realize the names Al and Bev would become a regular part of our vocabulary over the next three decades. Bev became a close friend with my wife and Al became a faithful friend to me. One of the things Al and I shared together was golf. We played many rounds on many golf courses.

Al was not only a close friend but he also was very helpful serving on the leadership team at our church. He provided insight and wise counsel over the years. He always found a way to encourage me even during difficult times.

He was also handy. He helped me with many projects at my house as well as at our church. He also climbed up in a pine tree to take a photo of our family reunion near Arrowhead, California. He was a hard worker and was available to put up Christmas decorations and help build props for Christmas programs at church.

Al was a natural leader. He served as the chairman of our leadership team on several occasions and led some of the capital campaigns when we raised money to expand the facilities at our church. He also had a passport and participated in some of our short-term mission teams in Russia and Romania.

He was a man of faith. He was a faithful follower of Jesus and loved to share his faith with others. We spent many evenings together visiting homes of people who had visited our church. He had good insight and thoughtful answers to questions people asked.

There is a couple mentioned several times in the Bible who were faithful supporters of the Apostle Paul. Aquila and Pricilla met Paul in Corinth when Paul was experiencing a difficult time in ministry. They encouraged Paul and other leaders in the early church (Acts 18:1-3 / 24-28). Al and Bev were some of those people to me and my wife. Close friends and people of faith who loved God and served others. Let me encourage you to say thanks to the special people God has brought into your life. They will be glad you did and you will too.

A Phone Call from the Past

Recently I was sitting in church waiting for the service to begin when I received a text on my phone. It was from some friends from Texas. They had been career missionaries in Guatemala. At first I decided to ignore it until after church. But then I wondered if there was something wrong. So I responded to their text and told them I was in church and I would get back to them later. I also asked if they were okay.

My friends replied it wasn't urgent but it was important. Could I talk for a few minutes? So I walked out to the patio and sent another text telling them I could talk now if they wanted to call. A few moments later they called me on *Face Time*.

To my surprise Glen and Judy were not calling from Texas. They were calling from South Africa. They were visiting old friends Eric and Susan who are missionaries in Hilton, South Africa. It was 8:00 PM where they were calling from and 8:00 AM where I was in California.

Eric and Judy were in the high school youth ministry that my wife and I led at Northwest Bible Church in Dallas, Texas in the 1970's. After college, Judy married Glen and Eric married Susan. These two couples served with different missionary organizations in different parts of the world. Both of them knew and loved my wife Jeanne who died from breast cancer about a year ago.

I was honored they wanted to call me and share some of their memories of the years we were together at the church in Dallas. Eric and his wife Susan also served as summer interns at our church in Tucson. I have seen both couples at various times over the years. They have been so kind to check up on me. I enjoyed hearing about their families and their ministries too.

If you read some of the letters the Apostle Paul wrote to various churches around the Mediterranean world you will discover he often expressed personal greetings to individuals in the different churches. He was thankful for their faithful service and steadfast commitment to Christ (Colossians Chapter Four / Romans Chapter Sixteen). Let me encourage you to keep in touch with your former pastor and other Christian friends. *Why not call or send a text this week* and thank them for the influence they had in your life and faith. They will be glad you did and you will too.

Don't Touch the Gold

Two of my four children serve as career missionaries in Europe. Traci and her husband Jonathan serve with *Reach Global* in Lisbon, Portugal. Trisha and her husband Hondo serve with *Josiah Venture* ministries in Maribor, Slovenia. Most of my grandchildren have been born overseas and most of them have learned a foreign language.

In their early years serving in Europe there were not many American made products available. They learned to shop and cook using local meat and produce. They learned how to bake cakes and cookies using the metric system instead of measuring with tablespoons and ounces.

One of the things I missed when I visited them was the taste of American made chocolate and candy. I tried to bake some chocolate chip cookies using their ingredients but it never tasted like it did back home. Eventually I learned to bring a bag of Nestles chocolate chips so I could bake a batch of cookies for them to enjoy.

In the past twenty years many American made products have become more available in Europe. I continue to see more European products in our grocery stores too. However that wasn't the case on our early visits to see our children and grandchildren in Portugal and Slovenia. American candy and baked goods were pretty rare and very expensive. They were like gold.

On one of our early visits to Slovenia we met an American college student who was serving as a summer intern with Josiah Venture. He was working with Trisha and Hondo for ten weeks. One day my wife noticed there were some *Reese's Peanut Butter Cups* in the refrigerator. Just as she was about to indulge the intern stopped her. He explained the interns had been instructed to never eat any of the American made candy in a missionary's refrigerator. It was like gold and not to be touched.

There a several passages in the Bible where people were warned to not touch certain things that we considered holy and set apart for God (First Samuel 21:1-6). You may have instructed your children to not touch things that are sharp or food that could be harmful to them. Let me encourage you to ask before you indulge in someone's candy or cookie jar. Ask before you eat. You will be glad you did and your host will too.

March 28
Let There Be Light

One of the darkest places in my house is the garage. There is only one light fixture which holds only one light bulb. The garage door opener also has a light but it goes off in about two minutes. We try to not linger in the garage for very long knowing the light will go out quickly.

I suppose I could replace the original one-bulb light fixture which was installed by the home builder in 1979 but it doesn't seem to be a high priority. We have survived with the original light fixture this long. Why not keep using it until it stops working. *Don't fix it if it is not broken.*

However during our recent home consolidation project it seemed like we were spending more and more time in the garage. Maybe it was time to do something about this dimly lit room. Maybe we should buy one of those fancy motion sensor light fixtures. We could step into the garage and not need to find the light switch. The light would come on automatically. But I'm sure those motion sensor lights were expensive.

My wife had a helpful suggestion. Maybe we should purchase a more modern light bulb for the old light fixture. Why didn't I think of that? We were using an old incandescent light bulb because it still worked. But when we purchased one of the new LED bulbs it illuminated the whole garage. Wow! We were amazed when we saw what a difference one LED light bulb made in our garage.

There are many passages in the Bible regarding darkness and light. One passage says, "In the beginning God created the heavens and the earth and God said, *Let there be light*" (Genesis Chapter One). Those few words and that one act of God changed our universe from darkness to light in an instant. Light flooded the universe.

I was impressed how one light bulb could change our dimly lit garage into a comfortable safe setting. Jesus told His followers to be lights in the world (Matthew 5:13-16). One of the best ways to do this is by serving and helping people.

Let me encourage you to be a light of hope and encouragement in the lives of the people around you. Help the helpless. Encourage the discouraged. Feed the hungry. Care for the widows and orphans. You may not be able to help everyone but you can *help someone this week.* One small light bulb can make a huge difference in a dark place.

Santa Catalina is Waiting for Me

Dave and Lisa directed *Campus by the Sea* on Catalina Island off the coast of Long Beach, California. They lived on the island and were in charge of the programs and facilities of the center. On one occasion my wife and our three daughters spent a week at the camp providing child care for one of the groups meeting there.

Public schools also rented the facility to enable students to study and experience marine life for a few days. Some of my children spent a week on the Island studying the ocean and the sea life with their classmates when they were in middle school.

The only way to get to from the mainland to Catalina Island was by boat or private plane. As the familiar folk song said, *"Twenty-six miles across the sea, Santa Catalina is waiting for me."* The boat ride took about 60-90 minutes depending on the size of the ship. When they lived on the island, Dave and Lisa actually took their children to school every morning not in a car but in a small motor boat around a cove to the public school on the island.

I visited the island with a man from our church to do some maintenance on one of the camp buildings. It was the first time I had ever been to Catalina. Getting to the Island by boat went smoothly. We enjoyed spending a couple of days helping Dave with some projects.

However getting back to the mainland was a little more challenging. As we boarded the ferry boat in Catalina we noticed the water was pretty choppy. The white capped waves did not look like your usual calm and peaceful excursion. Once we left the shelter of the island our boat began to rock up and down in the growing swells. Passengers we getting sea sick and using plastic trash bags provided by the management. It was a miserable boat ride back to Long Beach.

When we finally reached the mainland we heard the ferry captain announce this was the last boat of the day due to the bad weather and stormy seas. I wondered why they didn't make that decision before we departed from the island. It was a boat ride I have never forgotten. There is a passage in the Bible when Jesus calmed a storm on the Sea of Galilee (Mark 4:35-41). His disciples never forgot it either. Let me encourage you to enjoy an ocean adventure with your family but make sure you fasten your life jacket just in case!

Shoes and Books

When my brother and I helped our parents move from their house in Scottsdale to their new home in Gilbert, Arizona, we discovered our mother had over 100 pairs of shoes. I don't know how many more because we stopped counting at 100. This was extraordinary. How can someone have so many shoes? Who has the time and money to purchase and store all of these?

I have since learned most women have lots of shoes. I don't know why. Maybe they were taught in their Home Economics class in high school to buy a lot of shoes. Maybe women are just trying to keep up with the changing fashion trends which requires new shoes. If I could do it over again I think I would have bought stock in companies that manufactured women's shoes. It seems like a sound investment strategy.

On the other hand I don't think I would invest in companies that made shoes for men. I have seven pairs of shoes in my closet. Three pairs of nice shoes for work and a pair of shoes for taking walks and a pair of sandals for going to the beach. I also have a pair of golf shoes in the trunk of my car with my golf clubs. I do have an old pair of shoes in the garage which I wear when I do yard work. I also have one pair of hiking boots that I wear in bad weather or traveling to cold climates.

I might buy some stock in companies like Nike or Adidas who make shoes for sports like basketball and track. I saw a movie that portrayed how Nike created *Air Jordan* basketball shoes. They have sold well.

In Bible times most people wore sandals. They were usually made with a leather bottom and fastened to their feet with strips of rope or leather. People removed their sandals and washed their feet before entering a house to reduce the amount of dirt that gets carried into the dwelling.

John the Baptist said he was not worthy to untie the sandals Jesus wore (Mark 1:7). The Old Testament records the Israelite's clothing and shoes did not wear out during the Exodus from Egypt to the promised land (Nehemiah 9:21). Let me encourage you to take care of your feet and your shoes. Be willing to share some of your extra shoes with people who do not have any. Don't hoard them – share them. You will be glad you did and those who need them will too.

March 31
Shoes and Books (Part Two)

In my last story I shared when my brother and I helped our parents move from Scottsdale to Gilbert, Arizona we discovered our mother had over 100 pairs of shoes. We were amazed. We had no idea there were so many shoes in her bedroom closet.

But I thought I should give equal time by sharing our father had several hundred books too. While our mother's shoes were concealed in her bedroom closet our father's books could be seen all over the house. He had books on shelves and table tops. He had some stacked on the floor and boxes filled with books too.

Since our father's career revolved around writing I think he loved to read books to learn from what other authors had written. Sometimes he would purchase a new book just because of the title or the picture on the cover. His sister Aunt Betty scolded him for buying so many books. Why didn't he just borrow them from a local library instead of filling his house with books?

Both my brother Steve and I also had many books that we purchased during our days at Dallas Seminary. Some of the books were required reading for a specific class. We also purchased other reference books and Bible commentaries for use in preparing future Bible studies and Sunday sermons. It was back breaking work to pack up our books when we moved to a new church or into a new home.

There is a passage where the author says Jesus did many more things than are actually recorded in the Bible. He wrote, "There are so many other things Jesus did. If they were all written down, each of them, one by one, I can't imagine a world big enough to hold such a library of books" (John 21:25 – The Message Bible). The Bible is the bestselling book of all time. Let me encourage you to read it for yourself. But don't start on page one – start in the book of Mark since that is my name. It will encourage your heart and instruct your mind. Take your time. Just read a chapter or two a day. Read and reflect on the words and works of Jesus.

And let me suggest you not count the shoes in the closet or the books on the shelves. Don't hoard them or hide them. Enjoy them and be willing to share both your shoes and your books with others. You will be glad you did and they will too.

The Easter Bunny

I heard Pastor Rene Schlaepfer tell a remarkable Easter story. He was the lead pastor of Twin Lakes Church in Lake Tahoe, California. Since their own facility was small he was looking for a venue that could accommodate a larger number of people on Easter Sunday.

He got the idea of holding an Easter Sunday service in a ballroom in one of the Casinos in Lake Tahoe. The church Elders were not very enthusiastic about the idea. However he received a phone call from one of the Casino managers who had heard about Rene's inquiry. The manager expressed his willingness to have an Easter service at their facility to make it easier for guests and employees to attend.

Rene convinced the church leaders to give it a try. He had no idea how many people might attend the Easter Sunday service at the hotel but was excited about the possibilities. The manager of the Casino gave a lot of help and support to Rene and his team. Hotel employees were glad to help set up chairs and sound equipment for the church service.

Over 1,000 people came on Easter Sunday! Rene was surprised and amazed. Some were from the church but many more were hotel guests and employees. People from other hotels also came. They filled the large banquet room.

One guest Rene did not expect to see was the Easter Bunny! A Casino worker who wore a Bunny costume on Easter asked his supervisor if he could take his morning break and attend the church service. His boss said the employee could not take off the head of the costume. He didn't want young children to see a headless Easter Bunny. So the worker kept his head piece on and walked into the Casino Ballroom wearing his full costume as Rene was giving his sermon. Rene was surprised to see the Easter Bunny sitting in the back of the room!

The real Easter story is not about a cute bunny and colored eggs. The real Easter story is found in the Bible in Matthew Chapter 28, Mark Chapter 16, Luke Chapter 24 and John Chapters 20-21. It is the day Christians around the world celebrate the resurrection of Jesus from the dead. The Bible says Jesus died on the cross and rose from the dead to pay for your sins and purchase a place for you in heaven. Let me encourage you to read these passages for yourself. Examine the evidence and put your faith in Jesus today.

Teri

Your mother and I always remembered the day you were born in Tucson, Arizona on April 2, 1981. We had always planned to have four children but after your sister Traci's premature birth in 1978 we wondered if we should be content with three kids. After your mother's three week trip to Germany in 1980 we both agreed we would always wonder who was missing if we didn't have number four. We checked with the Obstetrician and the Pediatrician and both felt it was safe to try for another baby. We are thankful we did.

Your mother did go into early labor again but the doctors were quick to respond with medication which enabled you to go full term. You were the fastest delivery and the largest of our four kids at birth. You came home to a house full of kids with the Chicken Pox but you did not get sick.

I smile as I remember how much joy and fun you brought into our family. Your older siblings loved to make you laugh. Your sisters allowed you to play with them if you would be the cat and just lay around until they needed you. You came to faith in Jesus when you were five years old at the *Trail Ride* campout in South Dakota. You were in second grade when we moved to California. Your high school years were busy with Color Guard and school musicals like *Joseph and the Technicolor Dream Coat* and *Guys and Dolls*. You were also involved in the Youth Group at church and on short-term mission trips.

We are thankful you attended BIOLA University and later became a Professor in Speech Pathology there. We are grateful you are training future Speech Therapists. We observed your kind and professional care for Grandpa Ballenberger when he had his stroke in Arizona. We are thankful you married Jacob and have two beautiful children named Emily and Janie. You are a remarkable daughter, wife and mother. We are so proud of you and all you have accomplished. Happy Birthday!

The Apostle Paul wrote a letter to encourage his young disciple Timothy (First Timothy 3:14-17). Let me encourage my readers to write a letter to your children and grandchildren. Share some memories with them. Tell them about the strengths and positive qualities you see in their lives. Encourage them. They will be glad you did and you will too.

April 3
Home Security

Some teenagers broke into my friend's home a few years ago. Chuck had an alarm system and thought his home was pretty secure. However he did not anticipate how a group of teenagers managed to break into his house. They used a younger sibling to squeeze through the doggy door in the back of the house to get into the kitchen.

My wife felt very strongly we needed a home security system at our house. I know many friends and neighbors have them. I chose an alarm system which is designed for the homeowner to install himself. It is completely wireless and works off the internet equipment already in your home. My friend Al had installed the same system in his house so he came over to lend a hand. We put sensors in every window and on every door. We called the company help line and a technician walked us through each step as we installed the security system.

The alarm company also recommended we purchase a monitoring plan so we would receive a phone call if our alarm system detected some activity when were not home. Unfortunately there can be false alarms. Many years ago I remember a family abruptly left our church service. I wondered if I had said something in my sermon that offended them. I talked with them a few days later and they explained they had received a security alert during the church service. They spoke to the monitoring company as they hurried home. It looked like someone had broken into their house. The operator asked them several questions about their house. Did they have any pets that might have triggered the alarm? No. Did they have any guests staying at their house? No. When they got home their house was undisturbed. Then they noticed the air conditioning system was blowing some balloons in the house which were left over from a birthday party. The motion sensor detected movement in the house and triggered the alarm.

Jesus reminded his followers to not put their hope in the uncertainty of material things where thieves can "break-in" (literally dig through the mud walls) and steal your valuables (Matthew 6:19-20). Jesus said we should store up wealth in heaven not on earth. The Apostle Peter said our inheritance in heaven is secure (First Peter 1:3-4). Let me encourage you to do what you can to secure the safety of your house and your loved ones. But don't build your life on the uncertainty of material things which thieves can steal on the internet and from your home. Build your life on the certainty of heaven through faith in Jesus.

Number One Again

One of my favorite fast food restaurants in Southern California is the *In N Out Burger*. There are 267 in California, 41 in Texas and 34 in Arizona. They have expanded into Nevada, Utah, Oregon and Idaho.

I have written a number of stories about *In N Out Burger* in my previous books. Their food is great and their service is excellent. They hire good employees and they go out of their way to make your dining experience enjoyable. They have a simple menu with burgers, fries and shakes. They also offer a grilled cheese sandwich and Gluten Free burgers for people with special dietary limitations.

One time I took some of my grandkids to *In N Out* Burger to get them out of the house on a rainy day. I didn't know they offered free hot chocolate to children on rainy days. So they not only got to enjoy the burgers, fries and shakes but they were given small cups of delicious hot chocolate to warm them up on a cold winter day. They loved it.

A typical *In N Out* restaurant will sell several hundred meals a day. When you place your order at the front counter they hand you a receipt with a number on it. They also give you some cups for your beverages. When your meal is ready they call your number and guests walk up to the counter to pick up their food.

On a recent visit to *In N Out Burger* with my grandchildren I placed my usual order of a cheeseburger with extra lettuce, light tomato and no spread. I also ordered my wife's meal which included a cheese burger Gluten Free with grilled onions, no spread - Protein style. My wife also wanted fries well done. I requested regular French fries. We both asked for a cup of water. The employee repeated my order and the price - $12.61. I used my debit card to pay for our food. Then the employee handed me my receipt and told me I was **number one**! This has only happened to me one other time in 35 years of eating at *In N Out Burger*. I plan to save my receipt and frame it for posterity.

It is not often when someone says to you – **you are number one**. Let me encourage you to tell someone you know they are *number one* in your heart. Why not send a card or make a call *today* and tell your parent or grandparent, spouse or sibling, friend or neighbor they are *number one* in your life. They will be glad you did and you will too!

April 5
On the Phone with the IRS

My wife and I were careful to file our annual federal and state income taxes before the April deadline. We filed our income taxes separately. My wife had to pay some additional taxes but I had overpaid and got a nice refund. She filed online with the help of her CPA. I filed online using Turbo Tax. It is always a great feeling getting taxes done on time. However that wasn't the end of the story. On June 8th my wife received a letter from the IRS informing her that she owed more money. We dug out a copy of her tax return and realized the amount due was already paid with her Visa Card on the date she electronically filed her taxes.

We called the IRS and waited about 20 minutes to speak to someone. While we waited we looked up her VISA statement and confirmed she had paid the correct amount with her credit card. The payment was actually made to a third party – a company that charges an additional fee to collect electronic payments for the IRS. When we finally talked with the IRS agent on the phone she explained the computer did not have a record of my wife's payment. The credit card statement showed the payment was made but the IRS did not have it in their system.

The woman on the phone was the most helpful and professional IRS representative I have ever dealt with. She worked with us for over an hour trying to find the missing credit card payment. She politely asked several times if we would wait on the phone for 5-10 minutes while she searched various records trying to find the missing money. My wife suggested we pray while we were on hold and we did. The agent was persistent and relentless. One key item was missing from the Visa payment and the IRS letter. Neither had a confirmation number. Finally she stumbled on the missing payment. Someone had recorded it under "10407". The number "7" should not have been with the "1040". That one additional number confused the computer. Problem solved! Wow!

There are several references to tax collectors in the Bible. They were hated because they worked for the occupying Roman forces. Jesus was criticized for spending time with sinners and tax collectors (Matthew 11:18-19 / Mark 2:13-17). Jesus went out of his way to show love and forgiveness to those who were tax collectors. Let me encourage you to be kind and patient with government employees including the IRS just as God is kind and patient with you and me. And let me encourage you to pray before you call. You may get the agent who was so helpful to us!

What Happened?

There has been a sudden and swift change in the spelling and vocabulary in the American language. I'm not sure you have noticed but there are two letters which have been dropped from our writing and grammar. The two letters are "*ly*". We used to say "Come here quickly". Now everyone says, "Come here quick".

When we studied grammar in grade school we were taught words which ended with "*ly*" were called "*adverbs*". Adverbs helped intensify or modify verbs. We used to write "He laughed loudly". Now we write "He laughed loud".

Maybe writers and publishers are trying to save paper. By eliminating "*ly*" at the end of a word they can reduce the number of trees that are cut down every year to produce pulp for the paper industry. Or maybe news reporters are trying to shorten broadcasts by omitting "*ly*" from their breaking news stories.

We may never know the reason for this radical shift in our vocabulary and written language. We used to say, "They lived happily ever after". Now I suppose you just say, "The lived happy ever after". Somehow it just doesn't sound the same. It feels like something is missing.

One author told me she attended a writer's workshop where they were told to not use "*ly*" any more. It was no longer needed and if they continued to use "*ly*" their writing would look old and out dated. I'm sure no author wants to look like they are old fashioned.

However, I think it is time to start a movement to reinstate "ly" into our writing and speaking. We could circulate a petition online and gather millions of signatures to demand "*ly*" be restored to the American language. We could demand school text books be revised to include "ly" in their printed materials. "*Ly*" should be given equal consideration with other changes being forced upon us by book editors and publishers.

Please let me know how you feel about this important issue. This is a serious matter. If we let this trend continue other changes will soon be made to our written and spoken language. We had better act quick before it is too late!

The Coyote

Southern California is a sprawling metropolis with hundreds of suburbs and communities linked together by a ribbon of freeways. There is very little undeveloped land between Santa Barbara and San Diego. Millions of people live here and most of them drive cars that fill our freeways.

It may sound strange but coastal California actually has a desert climate. Our annual rainfall is often less than what falls in the aired landscape of the Arizona. California may look like a paradise because we get water from the Colorado River and northern California. Our green lawns and lush landscape are deceptive. Without the imported water Southern California would look a lot like Arizona. We already have Prickly Pear Cactus on the hillside above my home.

We also have wild animals who live with us in our suburban cities. We hear reports on the news of bears and mountain lions who have wandered into bedroom communities which border the San Bernardino Mountains. We also have skunks, opossums and coyotes in my neighborhood. These resilient creatures have adapted and survived in the expanding suburbs all over Southern California.

I was reminded of this recently as I pulled my car into the driveway of my home one evening. I noticed out of the corner of my eye something moving in my neighbor's front yard. At first I thought it was a stray dog but when I looked more closely I realized it was a coyote. Its slim silhouette and casual trot confirmed it was not a local pet. It was a crafty predator looking for food.

This wasn't the first time I have seen a coyote in our community. I have seen a number of them in the past. I have also heard them howling to celebrate a kill on the hillside above my home. It is not uncommon to hear a neighbor share how their dog or cat was killed by a coyote.

People had to contend with predators in ancient times. David said, "When I was watching my father's sheep and a bear or a lion carried one off, I went after it and rescued the sheep. When it turned on me I seized it by the hair and killed it" (First Samuel 17:34-37). Let me encourage you to be watchful as you coexist with wild animals in your community. Teach your children about the wild life in your area. Please respect their habitat and keep your children and pets safe.

Porch Pirates

There has been a growing problem with people stealing packages from the porch or front door of homes in residential neighborhoods. This happens even more during the holiday season. When Fed Ex, UPS and Amazon drivers leave packages on the doorstep thieves like pillaging pirates take what rightfully belongs to someone else.

This has become a nationwide problem in suburban neighborhoods across our country as more and more people order items online and have them delivered to their home. One friend shared with me the Amazon delivery truck stops at her house almost every day including weekends. This provides thieves plenty of opportunities to steal your stuff.

Recently another friend shared his story about a package that was stolen from his front porch. My friend Gary had ordered a book online and was pleased to get a notice on his cell phone that it had arrived. However, he was working in the backyard and didn't respond right away to the notification. When he finally went to the door less than an hour later the package was gone. Someone had stolen it from his front door in broad daylight. He suspected the villain had been following the delivery truck and just waited until the van was out of sight to run up to the house and steal the book he had ordered.

Local law enforcement officials say there is very little they can do to prevent porch pirates from stealing things from your door step. Crime is at an all-time high in in many communities. Police do not have enough officers to patrol every street and neighborhood in your city.

Fortunately for my friend the item which was stolen could be replaced. The book was not very expensive and he already had another copy. He had simply ordered a new book with larger print to make it easier to read. The book he had ordered was a *new Bible*. We laughed as we listened to his story. Several speculated what the thief might have thought we he or she discovered what they had stolen. Several said they hoped the pirate would read the Bible and repent of their sin. There is a verse in the Bible that says, "Stop stealing, start working so you can provide for your own needs and have something to share with others in need" (Ephesians 4:29). Let me encourage you to do the same. Stop stealing, start working and share with others. You will be glad you did and they will too.

You're a Fool

As a pastor one of my responsibilities was to hire new people when there was an opening on our church staff. We listed the job opening in the Sunday bulletin and online. We also posted the position with some local Bible Colleges and Seminaries. My job was to interview several candidates who looked qualified for the position and then recommend one of them to the church Elders for their consideration. In addition, I often called some of the references people listed on their resume.

One time we had an opening for a new position to lead the Women's Ministry. Several women from our church submitted applications along with a few others online. I reminded each applicant I could only hire one person even though many of the applicants seemed to be well qualified for the position. After sifting through the applications and going through the interview process I was tasked to recommend one person to fill the position.

The woman who looked like the best person to lead the Women's Ministry was Linda. But before I had time to make all of the phone calls to get references about her, the principal from a local elementary school spoke to me at a church event. I will always remember her words – "*If you don't hire Linda you are a fool*". That was a pretty strong endorsement! Linda had served as a volunteer at the school leading the parent – teacher organization. She was a good organizer and enlisted many other adults to volunteer at the school. The principal had seen Linda in action and did not hesitate to recommend her to fill the opening at our church.

There are many verses in the Bible in the book of Proverbs which describe different characteristics of a fool. The author wrote fools don't listen to the wisdom of others (Proverbs 1:7). Fools are characterized by poor use of their time and resources (Proverbs 13:20 / 14:24). Fools are also known to repeat their mistakes (Proverbs 26:11).

I was grateful for the wisdom the school principal shared with me. Linda did become one of our most effective staff members leading the Woman's and later the Children's Ministry at our church. Let me encourage you to listen to the wisdom and advice of others. *Don't be a fool*! You will be glad you did and they will too.

Stamps

When I was young my brother and I collected postage stamps. We could purchase old stamps through the mail. A company in New York City sent a few stamps each month "*on approval*". We would look at them and select a few to buy and then send the rest of the stamps and the payment back to the company. We still have some of those stamps.

The world has changed and stamp collecting has become a lost art. Most people use email and other electronic media instead of stamps and envelopes. However, both my wife and I still use postage stamps to send birthday cards and pay some bills the old fashioned way.

I have also learned men and women view the value of stamps in different ways. When I go to the Post Office to mail a package and buy some stamps I usually request ones with the American Flag on them. I use the same stamps for sending birthday cards and paying bills.

On the other hand, my wife buys a variety of stamps for use on different occasions. She likes to use postage stamps which have the word "*Love*" when she sends a card to a newly married couple. She may use a different stamp when she sends a sympathy card. Another stamp has different colored bubbles with the letters "*Celebrate*" for birthdays, graduations and anniversaries.

I think most men view stamps as a simple necessity to get a card, letter or payment to someone on time. They don't expect the recipient to even notice what stamp comes on the envelope. But I have learned most women take time to admire how the stamp goes with the color of the envelope and the content of the card inside. This is just another reminder of how men and women are different. I believe God designed it this way.

I'm not sure there are any examples of stamps in the Bible but there are a number of passages which record the use of a seal or signet ring which was used on mail and decrees sent throughout the kingdom by Joseph (Genesis 41:41-43) and Mordecai (Esther 8:8).

Let me encourage you to not get stressed over stamps. It is the thought that counts. Send a card or text to someone *today* and let them know you are thinking of them. They will be glad you did and you will too.

Customer Service

My wife and I planned to spend two weeks at our Time Share in Maui. Our non-stop flight from Long Beach went smoothly and arrived on time. However, the rental car agency struggled to provide cars for dozens of travelers. After waiting over an hour at the airport we finally got our luggage and my golf clubs loaded into the rental car.

After a stop at the Costco near the airport we drove to our Time Share in Kihei on the west side of the island. We picked up the keys at the front desk and unloaded our suitcases and groceries into our condo. We noticed the unit wasn't very cool. I checked to see if the AC was working and then we left to find dinner and walk along the ocean to watch the sunset in the long summer evening.

It seemed like a perfect end to a long day of travel. But when we returned to our condo our perfect day began to unravel. The AC was still not working very well. One of the toilets wouldn't shut off and the rubber seal on the dishwasher was hanging off of the appliance door. In addition the towels and linens did not smell fresh and a lock on the patio door had a piece missing.

I called the front desk and expressed my concerns but they informed me the maintenance department was closed for the day and they could not help us until the next morning. So my wife and I tried to sleep in the guest bedroom with an uncomfortable mattress. I told my wife I felt we had checked-in to Motel Six instead of our comfortable Time Share.

The manager called the next morning and asked about our situation. He promised to address each of our concerns. He sent an employee to look at the AC and toilet. He also fixed the dishwasher gasket. Soon a repairman came to deal with the AC, door lock and toilet. Then a woman brought us fresh linens and a new bathroom floor mat.

The manager called several times to check up on the repairs. I thanked him for all the help and explained we were on our honeymoon. Later in the day another employee arrived at our door with a box of chocolates and a package of Hawaiian cookies. Our spirits were lifted by this exceptional customer service. Jesus said He came to serve others and give His life for us (John 10:45) Let me encourage you to go out of your way to serve and help someone *today*. You will be glad you did and they will too.

LA County Hospital

People in our church in Diamond Bar had a variety of vocations. Many were school teachers. Others were in financial and investment roles. There were also a number of people who worked for city, county, state and federal governments. The list was endless.

At least two people worked at the Los Angeles County Hospital near downtown. Paul was a medical doctor treating patients at the County medical center and at the new USC Teck Hospital. He was also on the USC faculty training future doctors and other medical professionals. His specialty was infectious diseases. He treated many AIDS patients during the 1980's and 1990's. I had lunch with Paul on a number of occasions while he served as the chairman of our Elder team. I appreciated his help at the church and enjoyed touring the hospital with him as he checked on patients and students.

Another person from our church who also worked at the LA County Hospital was Ricca. She was a Physician's Assistant and primarily worked in the Emergency ward. She often worked all night on the weekend shift. I was amazed she had the strength to attend church on Sunday morning after working Saturday night in the busy emergency ward. I actually got to see Ricca in action on a Saturday night when I went to visit someone from our church who was in an accident and taken to the County Hospital. She did not personally treat the person from our church but I was able to track Ricca down in the crowded emergency room.

One of my favorite people in the Bible was a doctor named Luke. He is mentioned several times in the New Testament (Colossians 4:14). He was a respected historian who wrote two important books which provide helpful information on the life and ministry of Jesus in the Gospel of Luke and details about the growth of the early church in the book of Acts.

Let me encourage you to express your appreciation to your doctor and the other medical professionals who serve in our health care system. They work long hours to keep us healthy and to help us when we need emergency care. Send a note and express your thanks for all they do to support you and your loved ones. They will be glad you did and you will too.

April 13
Running the Bases Backward

I have been a baseball fan all my life. When my brother and I were young our grandfather took us to Spring Training baseball games in Scottsdale, Arizona. In those days Arizona did not have a major league team. But a number of well know baseball clubs played their preseason games in sunny Arizona. We got to see some famous players like Ernie Banks and Willie Mays.

Both Steve and I played on Little League baseball teams when we got into grade school. I was selected to play on the Little League All-Star team two years in a row. Both of us also played some baseball when we attended Scottsdale High.

When we got involved leading the Jr High youth ministry at Scottsdale Bible Church we looked for fun ways to attract students to the program. We had swim parties in backyard pools and took them to Farrell's Ice Cream Parlor for some tasty treats. We also met at a local park for a fun evening of games and food.

One popular game was Kickball. It was similar to baseball and softball but easier for students to play and it did not require special equipment like bats and gloves. The pitcher simply rolled a large inflated rubber ball to the batter who kicked it as hard as they could and then ran to first base just like in baseball. The kids loved it.

One day we got the idea to have the batter run the bases backwards. In other words when the batter kicked the ball they were told to run to third base, then second, then first and finally home. It took a while for them to remember to run the bases in the opposite direction. It was a lot of fun but there was some frustration too. A student who ran in the wrong direction had to retrace their steps and go back to home plate and then run in the other direction.

We are all creatures of habit. We tend to do things the same way day after day, week after week. It is hard to break old habits and adopt new habits. Change can be frustrating but the results can be beneficial. I wonder if you have some old habits and routines that need to be changed. Do you need to get off your computer and spend more time talking with friends? Do you need to stop watching TV and get out of the house and start a new exercise routine? Let me encourage you to try running the bases backward *this week*. You will be glad you did!

Nice Hat

When I was growing up in Arizona I rarely wore a hat. I did wear a baseball cap when I played on my Little League team but I don't remember wearing a hat from day to day. However as I got older and my hair got thinner I noticed it was uncomfortable sitting in the bleachers at my son's track meet or at our daughters band competition. I also began to wear a hat when I mowed the yard and washed my car.

At a recent appointment with my dermatologist the doctor admonished me to be more careful about exposure to the sun. He reminded me it was important to use sunscreen more consistently and to wear a hat. He recommended I wear a broad rim one to shade more of my face and ears. The baseball cap didn't provide adequate protection.

I found an attractive straw hat on a shelf in my closet. It had a wider rim and did shade more of my face. It was light weight and comfortable. And there was a distinctive logo that looked like a fish on the front. As I began to wear my hat to the store and the bank I received a number of complements from the employees. Friends noticed my hat too. I began to feel like a celebrity as I wore my hat around town. However the distinctive logo was unfamiliar to many people. Several times people asked me if I liked fishing. At first I didn't understand why they asked until I realized they were referring to the fish on my hat.

Finally I began to explain the aquatic emblem on my hat was used by a famous professional golfer named Greg Norman. He was from Australia and had a successful career winning a number of major golf tournaments in his day. His nick name was *The Shark*. Recently I was on a trip with my wife when a salesman commented on my hat. He said he owned one just like it. He explained he was a golfer too and he knew the hat and the logo were from Greg Norman.

I wonder what people think when they see the clothes and hats you wear. Do they elicit a positive response and recognition or do they stir up questions and criticism? There is a passage in the Bible which says, "Do not judge people by the clothes they wear" (James 2:1-7). Let me encourage you to not form opinions of people by the clothes or the hat they wear. Listen to their words and observe how they treat other people. Get to know their heart. And don't forget to wear a hat and use plenty of sun screen too!

Discovering My Roots

Both my brother Steve and I served as pastors of different churches over a span of 50 years. We both graduated in the 1970's from Dallas Theological Seminary which was a non-denominational graduate school. People often ask us why we both became pastors. The short answer is our mother responded to a message by Billy Graham at the Arizona State University football stadium in 1964. She went down on the football field and met with a counselor who told her about Scottsdale Bible Church. Our family started attending the church and began to learn about the Bible from the young pastor Dr. Jim Borror who was also a Dallas Seminary graduate. Steve and I had opportunities to serve in the youth ministry which strengthened our desire to study and teach the Bible and become a church pastor.

But there is more to this story. Our great-grandfather Fredrick Hopper came to America in the 1880's to help launch YMCA's in Illinois, Nebraska and Colorado. In those days the YMCA (Young Men's Christian Association) was an evangelical ministry providing housing and Christian education to young men who were moving from rural communities to large cities in England and America. An American evangelist named Dwight L. Moody worked closely with the YMCA in England and America. I wonder if our great-grandfather was influenced by Moody to leave his home in London and start YMCA's in America.

In addition our great-great-grandfather Niles Swanson came from Sweden in the 1840's to settle near Boone, Iowa. Niles attended an evangelical church in Sweden. He carried a letter of reference from his pastor in Sweden to his new church in Iowa. Dwight L. Moody's crusades in England also had an impact in countries like Denmark, Norway and Sweden. Although Moody did not personally visit those countries his message "spilled over" to them too. Some immigrants from Scandinavia brought their evangelical faith to America. The Evangelical Free Church of America was organized in Boone, Iowa in the 1800's. Steve and I both served in different EFCA churches in our career. Steve and I were indirectly influenced by the preaching of famous men like Moody and Billy Graham. We are pastors today because of our mother's prayers and the ministry of men like Moody and Billy Graham and pastors like Dr. Jim Borror and Sherrill Babb. Let me encourage you to express your thanks to the people in your life who taught you the Bible and encouraged your faith in Jesus. And ask God to use you to encourage others on their faith journey too.

Men in Action

I was grateful my friend Bruce agreed to lead the Men's Ministry at our church in Diamond Bar many years ago. His philosophy was men should do things with other men that they don't often get to do. He certainly encouraged men to be connected in small groups for Bible study and prayer. But he also wanted men to build bonds through shared adventures and activities they rarely got to do.

One of our memorable events was kayaking around one of the Channel Islands off the coast of Santa Barbara. We took a charter boat out to one of the islands and rented two-man kayaks to paddle in the open water. We were given specific instructions and special equipment by professional guides to make sure this was a safe experience. The men really liked paddling the kayaks along the coastline and exploring some sea caves. It was a memorable time for the men.

Another adventure the men enjoyed was white water rafting on the Kern River about an hour outside Bakersfield, California. We drove up on Friday night and stopped at an "*All You Can Eat*" buffet restaurant near Porterville. The men loved it. Later that night we slept on the pews and the floor of a small church. The next morning the men gathered along the Kern River for a white water adventure. Experienced guides gave us helpful instructions on how to navigate the raging river. We were warned about tree branches that were nearly invisible under the water. Rafts could be overturned or pulled under by these unseen obstacles. Winter rains had swollen the Kern River and the water was running high and fast. It was another memorable time for the men.

There is something special about a shared experience. When men do things together it creates a common bond. They have something to talk about and reflect on in the months and years ahead. They enjoy remembering adventures like a kayak trip or white water rafting.

Jesus shared many memorable moments with his twelve disciples. He probably laughed with them when he reflected on mistakes they had made and lessons they still needed to learn. He said to them, "Don't you remember?" (Mark 8:14-21). Let me encourage you to make a plan and set a date for you to do something memorable with some other men in your life. Go camping or fishing together. Participate in a service project together. Build some bonds and make some memories together. They will be glad you did and you will too.

April 17
How to plan a Memorial Service

One of my responsibilities as a pastor was to help families through the death of a loved one. I was honored to be asked to lead the service. I always met with family members to learn more about the person who had died and to hear their ideas for the memorial service. I hope this information can help you in the future when you lose a loved one.

Survivors – Who are the living survivors? This may include a spouse, children, grandchildren and great grandchildren. Are any parents or siblings still alive?

Speakers – Who is planning to speak at the service? I encouraged any people who were planning to speak to write their thoughts down. It can be difficult and emotional for people to speak in front of a group. Do you want an open mike where other people can get up and share in the service? I also offered to read something for someone if needed.

Slides – Is someone preparing a video or slide presentation which will be shown at the service? I always encouraged that person to coordinate with the tech people at the church or mortuary to be sure it was in a format compatible with the AV equipment.

Special Music – Does the family have any songs they would like to include in the service? Almost any music is available online.

Scriptures – Are there any specific Bible verses they would like me to include in the service? I often use passages like Psalm 23, Psalm 103 and John 14:1-6. There are many other passages to choose from.

I also asked a number of questions to learn more about the life of the one who died. Where did they grow up? How did they get to California? What did they do for a career? What were some of their hobbies and interests? Did they serve in the military? The mortuary can schedule a military honor guard. I also asked surviving family members to share some words which describe their loved one. Then I asked them to explain why they think of those words.

The death of a loved one can be very difficult for the surviving family. There is a passage in the Bible where Jesus shed tears at the grave of his good friend Lazarus (John 11:22). Let me encourage you to help a friend or family during this difficult time. They will be glad you did.

113

April 18
Doing Damage

My wife and I love to walk around our neighborhood early in the morning or later in the day after dinner. We always seem to notice some new things and improvements as we stroll along the streets. We also love to see new landscaping neighbors have added and to admire beautiful flowers blooming in season.

However one thing we don't like to see is the damage tree roots have done to sidewalks and driveways in our neighborhood. You probably see examples of this where you live too. People planted young trees in their front yard years ago. Over time these little saplings grew into large sturdy trees.

But along with the strong branches and shady leaves came roots which spread under the street and into the yards of neighbors. It is both amazing and alarming how much damage tree roots can do.

Recently we saw a large concrete driveway cracked and broken by the roots of a large tree in the front yard. We also noticed a block wall and a sidewalk at another house which were damaged by the roots of a nearby large tree.

Roots are essential to provide nourishment and provide stability to the tree. But they can also do significant unintended damage to nearby sidewalks and structures.

One author used the image of tree roots to illustrate how they capture water to sustain the life of the tree. He wrote "Like a tree planted by living waters" (Psalm 1:3). The Apostle Paul expressed his desire to see followers of Jesus deeply rooted in their faith. He wrote, "I pray that you will be rooted and established in love" (Ephesians 3:17).

However another author warned "*roots of bitterness*" can do much harm in a person's life and in their relationship with others. He wrote, "See to it that no root of bitterness grow up and cause trouble and injure many" (Hebrews 12:15). Just as tree roots can cause a lot of damage to your home, driveway and sidewalks so bitterness can cause a lot of damage in your marriage and family too. Let me encourage you to keep an eye on the roots of trees and plants around your house and let forgiveness not bitterness get rooted in your heart (Ephesians 4:31-32). You will be glad you did and they will too.

Trisha

Your mother and I always remembered the day you were born on April 19, 1977. We had just finished a picnic lunch with Pauline when mom's water broke. When we got home we called the doctor and he recommended we come to the hospital. But as the day progressed mom's labor slowed down. We stayed at the hospital overnight.

The next morning the doctor said you were breach and he needed to do a C-section. We were surprised and not prepared for these developments. They did not let me come in to the delivery room as I had with your older brother but we were glad you were born safely.

You have been a wonderful daughter. You have strength and courage. I remember when we dropped you off at Chaparral Middle School on the first day of school in Diamond Bar. The school looked so big but you bravely got out of the car and walked confidently onto the campus.

Your high school days were filled with friends and activities. You joined the Color Guard with your friend Inez and performed with the Diamond Bar High band at football games, in field competitions in the spring and in several parades including the Fiesta Bowl parade in Phoenix.

You are just like your mom with a love for Jesus and a heart to serve people. You were part of some mission trips to Mexico and served on the summer staff at Pine Summit Camp in Big Bear. All of these things prepared you for your life of service as a missionary in Eastern Europe.

We are thankful you found Bryan while both of you worked at Pine Summit Camp. You were the first of our four kids to get married. We are thankful for your children Caleb and Elizabeth. You are a wonderful wife and mother. You are so clever with new games to play and you are an excellent writer too. You have done an amazing job learning a new language and living in a foreign country. You have used your teaching skills in Oregon, Colorado, at home and on the road. We are so thankful for you and your family. We love you. Happy Birthday!

Let me encourage my readers to write a letter to your own children and grandchildren. Remind them of their strengths and encourage them for their future. They will be glad you did and you will too.

April 20
Walking the Dog

My wife and I enjoy going for walks in our neighborhood. Some people walk in the early morning before the sun comes up. It is fun to greet them as we walk up and down our street. Many other people walk in the early evening before the sun goes down. I think the evening people outnumber the morning people.

In addition to the people our age we also see young parents walking with their young children. I think the parents like to get the kids out of the house on a pleasant evening before they get them ready for bed. We also see a few serious runners who keep up a fast pace as they enjoy exercising outdoors.

Recently we saw something new. As we walked in one direction we noticed a man and woman pushing a baby stroller coming in the other direction. We assumed they were taking a grandchild out for an evening walk. But when we got closer we realized this couple did not have a baby in the stroller. They had a small dog. Yes, they were taking their dog for a walk but not in the traditional sense.

I know people love their pets. We did too. We've had several puppy dogs and a couple of cats in the past. But we decided to not get another pet to make it easier to travel and not have to arrange for pet care.

We do see more and more people bringing their small pets on airplanes and mass transit. We also notice more people bringing their pets to places like Home Depot and the local shopping mall. Apparently people feel more secure with a furry companion.

But we had never seen people taking their pet for a walk in a stroller. In fact I'm not sure you can define it as a "*walking the dog*" when the dog is actually *not* walking. It could be the animal had some health or mobility problems. I'm sure there was an explanation. The owners may be getting some exercise but the dog was not.

There is a passage in the Bible where the Apostle Paul said "Physical exercise is of some value, but spiritual exercise is even more important" (First Timothy 4:8). Let me encourage you to get out for a walk in your neighborhood *this week* and take your furry friend with you. But let me also encourage you to get some spiritual exercise by reading the Bible and going to church. You will be glad you did.

You Never Know Who Is Watching

Many years ago people dressed up for church. I remember my father wearing a coat and tie on Sunday morning. My mother insisted my brother and I also wear something nice to church. The same was true of air travel. Women wore nice dresses and men wore suits and ties when they got on an airplane.

When I attended graduate school at Dallas Seminary all of the men were required wear a coat and tie to class. When I became a pastor I always wore a suit on Sunday. Most of the older adults also dressed up for church. It was unusual to see someone without a coat and tie.

But times have changed. Most adults and kids dress more casually on Sunday morning. More men have replaced the long sleeve shirt and tie with T-shirts and collared sport shirts. Many women are wearing a blouse with slacks and jeans instead of a dress. I must confess I no longer wear a coat and tie to church either. I usually wear slacks and a dress shirt. No one seems to notice.

I know all of us want to dress appropriately and we want to look nice when we go to church or other gatherings. I wonder if my hair is straight and if my shirt and pants match. I was never very good at selecting the matching shirt, pants, belt, shoes and socks.

Recently my wife and I were sitting in church when we noticed a woman who was straightening her hair and her dress before coming into the service. The windows were tinted and she looked at her reflection to check her appearance. But the woman did not realize people inside the building could see what she was doing. Everyone in church could see her fixing her hair and straightening her dress.

Thankfully she didn't do anything wrong or embarrassing. But it was a reminder that people may be watching what we are doing when we are not aware of it. There is a passage in the Bible which reminds us God knows and sees everything we say and do (Psalm 139). He sees what we do and hears what we say in public and in private. Let me encourage you to say and do things which are pleasing to God all of the time. And make sure you look in the mirror at home before you come to church so you don't use a tinted glass door to inspect your hair and clothes. You will be glad you did and your friends will too.

April 22
Hats

How many hats do you have in your closet or bedroom shelf? I was surprised to discover I had over 20 baseball style caps. Several of them had the *Los Angeles Angels* logo on them. We collected these when we had season tickets to the Angels' games for three years. During the season the team gave away a number of free items including several different style Angels' baseball caps.

One hat I found in the closet has the words *"Living Proof"* on it. This one is from the new church we started in Eastvale, California. They want their people to be *'Living Proof of a Loving God"*. The hat is a reminder to church members to live out their faith in their community every day. Vantage Point Church started in 2008 and they now have over 2,000 people coming to their new campus each week.

I found at least four hats from *Maui*, Hawaii. These bring a smile to my face when I reflect on our vacations in Hawaii with our family and friends. One hat has a turtle emblem on it. Another hat reminds me of the lesson I learned – *"Sometimes it is better to receive than give"*. I wrote a story about it in my previous book.

There was a hat with the logo from the *Tesla Owners Group*. These hats are only given to people who owned a Tesla electric car. I don't own a Tesla but a friend who sold them gave me a hat. A cab driver in Paris noticed my hat and was excited to hear about Tesla cars.

I also had a hat with the logo from the *Apollo 13* mission. It was a gift from Cape Canaveral in Florida where they launched the lunar space missions in the 1970's. I hope to visit the cape in the future. One hat I miss was from the USS Teddy Roosevelt nuclear aircraft carrier. It was a reminder of the cruise on the carrier with my son Tim and his wife Christine and her son Landon. I gave the hat to my grandson Jonah.

I wonder if there are some hats or other things around your house which remind you of adventures with your family or a gift from a friend. There is a verse in the Bible which says, "A gift opens the way for the giver and ushers him into the presence of the great" (Proverbs 18:16). Let me encourage you to call someone who gave you a hat and thank them for being part of your life. Do it *this week*. Thank them for their thoughtful gift which reminds you of their love and friendship. They will be glad you did and you will too.

Relaxing in Hawaii

I am writing this story while I am sitting on the lanai at a condo in Maui. The view is terrific overlooking the ocean and there is a cool breeze in the air. I'm on the shady side of the building which provides protection from the warm sunshine.

My wife Susan and I are enjoying two weeks in Hawaii. It has been relaxing and restful as we take a slow pace. Our days have been filled with good conversations and thoughtful reflection. We manage to blend some sightseeing with shopping in some of the local stores.

We usually start our day with an early morning walk along the street overlooking the beach. Sometimes we stop at the local cinnamon roll shop and bring home a tasty treat to add to our breakfast. It has been so nice to eat our food on the porch overlooking the ocean. My wife enjoys a cup of coffee and I enjoy a cold glass of orange juice.

Some of the highlights of our time in Maui have included snorkeling in the clear blue water and just relaxing under a shady tree on the beach. I played a round of golf at the Maui County Course which has numerous holes right on the water. The price is right and the views are spectacular.

We have also enjoyed some nice meals at Cheese Burger in Paradise and Kimo's restaurant on Front Street in Lahaina and Taco Tuesday at Fred's in Kihei. We have made several meals at our condo with some delicious steaks we purchased at the Costco near the airport.

There is a verse in the Bible where Jesus encouraged his disciples to get away from the crowds and enjoy some rest after a busy season of ministry to the multitudes (Mark 6:30-31). Jesus also made time to withdraw and spend time alone with His heavenly Father (Mark 1:45).

Let me encourage you to make a plan and mark your calendar so you can enjoy some time to relax with your loved ones and friends. Don't let all the demands on your time steal the joy in your life. Every day is a gift. We don't know what tomorrow will bring (James 4:13-15). You will be glad you did and your loved ones and friends will too.

Men, Meat and a Movie

Several men from our church began to meet together for lunch in a parking lot during the Covid19 pandemic. Most of the restaurants and Fast Food places closed their indoor dining rooms but continued to serve customers with take-out food or drive through access.

We met once-a-week for fellowship and encouragement. We brought our own lawn chairs and met under a shady tree in the parking lot. These men came alongside to help me during my wife's cancer journey. We talked and laughed and prayed together while we enjoyed some good food from *In N Out Burger* or *The Hat Deli*.

This small band of men continued to meet with me after my wife's death. They offered support and encouragement in the months following her passing. I appreciated spending time with them regularly during the unfamiliar journey of living alone after 50 years of marriage.

At some point along the way one of the men suggested we get together for a BBQ at his house. Bob had a BBQ Smoker and loved to prepare various meats like ribs and brisket. We enjoyed our first meal so much we agreed to do it again in a month or so. We agreed to let Bob do the cooking and we would pitch in to pay for the food. It has now become a regular routine.

In addition to the great food we agreed to watch a movie too. Bob had a huge flat-screen TV with surround sound. He suggested a movie guys would enjoy and the result has been our men's "*Meat and Movie Night*". We actually invited our wives to come and enjoy dinner with us on one occasion. The evening went well but most of the wives agreed it was better if it was just the men. I guess they didn't enjoy it as much as we did.

There are many passages in the Bible which remind us of the value and importance of men spending time with other men. One verse in the Bible says, "As iron sharpens iron so one man sharpens another" (Proverbs 27:17). Friendship and fellowship are essential in the lives of men just as they are for women. Men need to spend time with other men. Let me encourage you to join the Men's ministry or a men's small group at your church. Or why not start a "Men, Meat and a Movie" group with some other guys. They will be glad you did and you will too.

Lost and Found

Our church is located on Diamond Bar Boulevard which is the main street running through the city. A Shell gas station and an AM/PM store are located a short walk from our offices. Often some of the staff would take a morning break and walk over to the AM/PM store to get a snack or soda.

One day several of us were walking through the AM/PM's parking lot when I saw what looked like a dollar bill crumpled up on the ground by the front door of the store. When I reached down to pick it up I discovered it wasn't a dollar bill – it was a *one-hundred* dollar bill! Someone had dropped the money as they were entering or leaving the mini market.

My first thought was someone had a bad day and had lost a lot of money. They may have been paying for gasoline or buying some food or lottery tickets. Either way I was confident someone was missing one hundred dollars.

I wasn't sure what to do. I went inside and explained to the store employee what I found. Had anyone come back looking for the lost money? He suggested I talk with the manager and explain the situation to him. The manager offered to hold on to the money and see if someone did come back looking for their missing money. I explained I worked right across the street and gave him my contact information.

A week later I went back to the store and asked the manager if anyone had come to claim the money. The answer was no. So he handed the one hundred bill back to me. I was thankful for his honesty. He could have easily lied and said someone did come back to get their money but kept it for himself.

There are passages in the Bible which tell us about people who were honest with money and who lived with integrity (Ezra 8:24-34/ Nehemiah 7:1-2). Let me encourage you to be known as trustworthy and honest especially in the area of money. Greed and dishonesty can ruin your life. Ask God to guard your heart and guide your decisions especially when it involves money. You will be glad you did and He will be too.

Keeping Memories

When my wife Susan and I got married we spent several days in a small beach town on the central coast of California. Cambria is a cozy spot with a number of small hotels and a lot of shops which sell attractive items to tourists.

We had fun looking through the local stores and saw many interesting things. One shop sold a lot of older items like old magazines and comic books from the 1950's. It also had some old vinyl records with songs from the fifties and sixties.

Another store had a variety of more modern things for home decorations and kitchen supplies. One item which caught my wife's attention was a unique plate for making and serving tacos. It was about the size of a dinner plate but the rim was shaped with curves that could hold eight taco shells. Each hard or soft taco could fit neatly along the rim of the plate with a space in the center for salsa or guacamole. It looked perfect for making and serving tacos.

The taco plate was decorated with bright colors and had a festive Mexican pattern on it. My wife and I had never seen something like this. It was both helpful and practical. Every home should have one. A few months later we saw some similar taco plates at our local Walmart store for about half the price. I guess the small tourist shop had a larger markup than the giant Walmart store. We purchased two more plates in case we have guests at our house for Taco Tuesday.

We have actually used the Taco plates on a number of occasions. They really do help when you are making the tacos and they provide an attractive way to display and serve them too. We always smile when we use these festive plates. They are a visible reminder of our special time in Cambria.

There are a number of examples in the Bible when the Israelites were instructed to pile some rocks (Joshua 4:1-9) or build a structure to serve as a reminder of God's faithfulness (Nehemiah 8:13-19). Let me encourage you to take a photo or purchase a souvenir to help you and your family remember a special time in your life. You will be glad you did and your family will too.

April 27
The Gideon's

Many hotel rooms have a copy of the Gideon Bible in a desk or dresser drawer. Don't misunderstand, the Gideon's did not write the Bible. They are a non-profit organization who place Bibles in hotels and resorts for guests to use and enjoy.

On a recent vacation we found a Gideon Bible in the bedroom dresser drawer of a condo we were using. I had heard the story of the Gideon's from several people in the past. But it was helpful to read in the introduction how the program got started and how large it has become.

It had a small beginning when two traveling businessmen met in the fall of 1898 in a Wisconsin hotel. They discovered they were both committed Christians and talked about ways to point other travelers to Jesus. One idea emerged from subsequent meetings. Why not get permission to place Bibles in hotels and motels across the country. This would enable men and women to read the Bible for themselves while they were away from home.

That small beginning led to the creation of an organization which has placed Bibles in many different languages in more than 170 countries around the world. They also distribute Bibles to school students, hospitals and people serving in the military.

In 1974 I met a farmer in El Centro, California who was actively involved with the Gideon's work. His name was Henry Worthington. He had personally traveled at his own expense to South America to distribute Spanish Bibles in several Latin American countries. He was not a traveling salesman. He was a humble, hard-working farmer. He gave his own time and money to make the Bible available to others.

I have read a number of accounts where people were alone in a hotel room dealing with depression or addiction. Some were contemplating suicide. But they found some verses in the Gideon Bible which gave them hope and help at a critical moment in their life. The goal of the Gideon's is to point people to Jesus. The tool they use is the Bible which reveals God's love and forgiveness through faith in Christ. Let me encourage you to read the Bible in your home or in your hotel room. Start in the Book of Mark. Read about Jesus' love and compassion. Discover how there is a hope and a future for you. Invite Jesus to come into your life today. You will be glad you did and He will too.

A Memorable Dinner

When I meet people from Austin, Texas I often tell them I had dinner with Robert Duval at the *Salt Lick Restaurant* on the outskirts of the city. Texans from Austin are very familiar with the *Salt Lick*. It is famous with celebrities and new comers too. Duvall was one of many Hollywood movie stars who dined at the *Salt Lick*. The truth is I didn't actually sit at his table but I was eating at the same restaurant when the actor walked by our table on his way to a private dining room.

However, my father really did attend a dinner with President John Kennedy in the early 1960's. Kennedy was giving a speech at an event at the Westward Ho Hotel near downtown Phoenix. My father was not a guest but he was covering the speech as a representative of Valley National Bank.

I remember my dad sharing some of the details of the event. He described how the Secret Service made sure doors were locked and no unauthorized people were allowed into the banquet room. He shared how young the President looked. My father was impressed by what Kennedy had to say. It was an evening my dad always remembered.

You probably have a similar story. You may have been a guest at an event with a famous political or media personality. Maybe it was a fund raising event for a local charity. Maybe it was a political speech during an election campaign. Maybe it was a banquet or celebration with some family or friends.

I'm sure many of you remember the dinner setting where you proposed to your wife and asked her to marry you. The setting was perfect and the meal was expensive. It was a moment you will never forget.

There are several memorable meals recorded in the Bible. Jesus' last supper with his disciples is recorded in all four of the Gospels (Matthew 26 / Mark 14/ Luke 26 / John 13-15). It was an evening they never forgot. Another meal was in the home of Lazarus with Jesus and his disciples (John 12:1-3). Let me encourage you to set a date and make a plan *this week* to share a memorable meal with your spouse and loved ones. They will be glad you did and you will too.

Calendars

How do you keep track of appointments and other important dates? Today most people use their smart phones to organize their schedules and avoid overbooking. However some people like me still prefer to use an old fashioned paper calendar and day planner.

For many years my daughter Traci made a paper calendar with family photos on each page. It also highlighted birthdays and anniversaries for each of our family members. I found this calendar to be very meaningful and helpful. It was especially useful to remind me of upcoming birthdates for my children and grandchildren.

My paper day planner is especially valuable when I need to schedule various activities and appointments. In the past I purchased an annual preprinted planner with a page for every day of the year. It usually cost $30-$50 a year. More recently I have been buying a blank day planner at the Dollar Store. It usually costs one dollar.

To conserve paper and save trees I actually write two dates on each page. Then I write in doctor and dentist appointments months ahead. I also schedule breakfast or lunch plans with friends and date nights with my wife. I also write down dates and times for a wedding, funeral and other ministry commitments. The older I get the more dependent I am on my old fashioned daily planner.

I'm sure you have a system which works for you. If the smart phone works best then use it. If the paper calendar works well then stick with it. The most important thing is to use a system that works for you.

However, there is a passage in the Bible which reminds us we don't even know what tomorrow will bring. The Apostle James wrote, "You do not even know what will happen tomorrow. Your life is very brief. Instead you should say 'If it is the Lord's will we will live and do this or that' (James 4:13-16). He told his readers to commit their lives and their plans to God. We can and should make plans for the future but remember we don't know what tomorrow will bring.

Let me encourage you to keep track of your plans and appointments. Use your time well. Every day is a gift. Commit your life and your time to honor God and love others. You will be glad you did and they will too.

Jonathan

We are thankful you married Traci and became part of the Hopper family. Your wedding on January 18, 2004, was a memorable day. It was filled with laughter and joy with so many family members and friends attending the ceremony and reception. We will always remember the words of wisdom your father shared at the rehearsal dinner. He quoted a verse in the Bible which said, "Moses listened to his father-in-law and did everything he told him" (Exodus 18:24).

You have been a wonderful husband and father. You and Traci make a great team as you raise your family in a foreign country. We are thankful you love our daughter and thankful you make time to support and encourage one another.

We are thankful you have shared adventures with your four kids. They loved going camping with you when Traci was traveling. They loved other adventures like driving across Europe to attend a conference or to visit their cousins in Slovenia. They love their dad. We're grateful you encouraged Traci to spend time with her mom and sisters. We enjoyed visiting your home in Portugal at different times of the year. We enjoyed the food and culture too.

We are also thankful for your faithful ministry in a foreign country. It is fun to hear you preach and interact with people in their language. You and Traci have done a great job raising a family and serving churches in this beautiful country.

It has been exciting to see you pursue further education and serve as a professor at the Bible College in Lisbon. We are glad you and Traci are sharing your knowledge and experience with younger missionaries who are learning how to live and serve overseas.

Thanks for encouraging us to invest with your former employer. We are grateful this helped us establish college investment accounts for each of our grandchildren. Thanks for being a great son-in-law. We pray for you and your family every day.

To my readers – Let me encourage you to write a note or make a call *this week* to express your love and appreciation to the men and women who married one of your children. They will be glad you did and you will too.

A Dinner to Remember

One of the nicest restaurants in Maui is *Mama's Fish House*. It has a reputation for good service and great food. However it is almost impossible to get a reservation because people could make them up to three months in advance. We were already on the island and only staying in Maui for two weeks.

However I called anyway and to my surprise someone answered the phone. I simply asked if they had any times available today due to a last minute cancelation. The employee said the only thing they had was at 8:30 PM. I knew that was past our bed time so I thanked them for their time and said goodbye.

But before I could hang up the person said they did have several cancelations for tomorrow July 4th around 6:00 PM. Would I be interested in one of those openings? I responded with an emphatic "Yes"! I would take the six o'clock time. I couldn't believe it. Suddenly my wife and I had a reservation for two at 6:00 PM at one of the most popular restaurants in Maui.

I called Susan immediately to ask her if she would like to go to a nice dinner at *Mama's Fish House* tomorrow night. Her answer was an emphatic "Yes"! This was unbelievable. She asked how I got a reservation at one of the nicest places in Maui so I told her the story.

When we got to the restaurant the next day I expected our table-for-two would be in the back of the dining room since we were a last minute addition. But I was very surprised when the hostess led us to one of the best tables in the restaurant next to an open window with a beautiful view of the ocean. I was amazed and Susan was impressed.

We had a lovely and memorable dinner together. The service was outstanding and the food was excellent. During the meal one of our servers even walked us outside to take our picture on the sand at sun set before we returned to our table to enjoy dessert. It was a wonderful evening we will remember for a long time. It was the highlight of our two weeks in Maui. Let me encourage you to do something special with your spouse or family *this month*. And ask your favorite restaurant if they have any last minute cancelations. You will be glad you did and your wife and family will too.

The Oldest Alumni

The Evangelical Free Church of America holds a national biannual conference every two years. This year the gathering was held at a large church in Fullerton, California. It was only fifteen minutes from our church in Diamond Bar. Several staff members from our church went to the three day event. Over 800 church leaders from across the country and around the world attended the conference.

In addition to the general sessions they also had smaller seminars and discussion groups on a variety of topics on the schedule. Lunch was also provided each day. The California weather in early June was great and many delegates from other parts of the country enjoyed eating lunch on the outdoor patio areas.

One day I attended the lunchtime gathering for Dallas Seminary alumni. About twenty men and women and some of their spouses came to the lunch meeting. We heard updates about the school from the seminary's alumni director. He told us about the growth of the Dallas campus and other satellite sites in Texas and Washington, DC. He also shared information related to online learning and professional development classes available to alumni.

Near the end of the meeting our host invited each of us to introduce ourselves and tell the group what year we graduated from Dallas Seminary. Some were recent graduates while others had been out of school for thirty to forty years. I graduated in 1975 – almost fifty years ago. When we finished introducing ourselves I realized I was the oldest alumni in the room.

I am very thankful I was able to study at Dallas Theological Seminary many years ago. It was a rigorous four year program which included studying theology, biblical languages and every book in the Bible. My wife worked full-time as a school teacher so I could go to grad school full-time. We both learned so much during our days in Dallas.

The Apostle Paul wrote, "Do your best to present yourself to God as a workman who does not need to be ashamed and who accurately handles the Word of truth" (Second Timothy 2:15). Paul emphasized the importance of being well grounded in our faith and in our knowledge of the Bible. Let me encourage you to dust off your Bible and start reading a chapter every day. You will be glad you did!

New Neighbors

When we moved our family to Diamond Bar in 1988 our youngest child started second grade and our oldest child started high school. The two girls in the middle started fifth and sixth grade. Several neighbors had kids in the same grades. As I look back I realize those were good days.

Fast forward 35 years and those young kids are now married with children of their own. Now they have kids in elementary, Junior High and High School. How times have changed.

Now we have new neighbors on both sides of our house with young children who are in preschool and elementary school. We hear them playing in their backyards. We notice parents driving children to and from school. Those parents are busy.

One day I was walking along the side of our house when I noticed a young girl looking out a second story window. Her name is Charlotte. She just learned to walk in the past few months. She is shy but does respond when we wave and call her name. She has an older brother named Logan. He is in kindergarten. He seems busy and active.

We don't spend a lot of time with these young neighbors but we are thankful to have them next door. When my wife and I travel, the father helps pick up our mail and put out our garbage cans on trash day. He has helped me move furniture and loaned me some garden tools when I couldn't find my own. His wife is a surgeon at a local hospital.

Regretfully we don't know our new neighbors as well as we knew our old ones. Some neighbors are the same age we are. Their kids are grown and some of them are married and have kids of their own. Other neighbors are younger than we are and have children who are in college or have started a career of their own.

There are several passages in the Bible which instruct us to love our neighbors (Mark 12:31 / Romans 13:9-10 / 15:2). Good neighbors are hard to find. Let me encourage you to take the initiative to get to know some of the new neighbors on your street *this week*. Make a batch of cookies and go knock on their door. Introduce yourself and invite them to your home. Be a good neighbor. They will be glad you did and you will too.

A Changed Life

Recently I was asked to lead a memorial service for a man named Charles Biller. He was the father of a friend who attended our church. I did not know Charles well but I had enjoyed the time we spent together and was honored to be asked by his family to lead his service.

I like to spend time with a family to learn more about their loved one. So I spoke with some of Charles' children in person and with others on a conference phone call. I learned he was a strong and determined individual with an interesting past. He was a fighter literally and figuratively too. When he was growing up he often got in trouble at school for fighting with classmates. He was also an amateur boxer. This seemed so out of character for the gentle man I knew.

His children explained that Charles' life was dramatically changed by Jesus Christ. On a cold rainy night he was drawn to a church where he heard about God's love and forgiveness. He learned Jesus had died on the cross and rose again to pay for his sins and give Charles a new life. It was a turning point. He changed from being an angry young man who was fighting his way through life to a man of faith who found peace and hope.

Charles's life turned in a new direction. He began to attend church and enrolled in a Christian College. Eventually he became a church pastor. Over the following decades he pastored several churches. He was hard working and constructed several church buildings. Later in his life he led the ministry for older adults at a large church in Covina, California. When he retired the church gave him a Shepherd's Staff to acknowledge his shepherd's heart for the people he served.

Don't misunderstand, Charles was not perfect. He had his faults and shortcomings just like the rest of us. But his life was dramatically changed from a fighter to a man of faith when he believed in Christ.

When each of his four sons spoke at Charles's memorial service, they all talked about his love for them and for their sister and their mom. And they spoke about Charles' love for Christ. There is a verse in the Bible which says, "I have fought the good fight, I have finished the race and I have kept the faith" (Second Timothy 4:7). God is in the business of changing lives. He loves you and will change your life too if you humble yourself, admit your sins and put our faith in Jesus today.

Happy Mother's Day

Erma Bombeck was an American humorist who achieved great popularity for her newspaper humor column from 1965 to 1996. She also published 15 books – most of which became best-sellers. She was born in 1927 and died in 1996. Her first book was a compilation of her early columns and was titled, "*At Wit's End*".

She wrote over 4,000 newspaper columns. She used humor to describe the ordinary life of a Midwestern suburban housewife. By the 1970's her columns were read twice a week by 30 million readers in 900 newspapers across the United States and Canada.

I came across an article in a file which was titled, *Thoughts for the Millennium – from Erma Bombeck*. I don't know where it was published but I liked some of the thoughts she shared near the end of her life:

"If I had my life to live over, I would have talked less and listened more."

"I would have sat on the lawn with my children and not worried about grass stains."

"I would have invited friends over for dinner even if the carpet was stained and the sofa was faded."

"I would never have insisted the car windows were rolled up on a summer day because my hair might get messed up."

"When my child kissed me impetuously, I would never have said, 'Later. Now go get washed up for dinner."

"There would have been more "*I love You's'* and more *'I'm sorry's'* but mostly – given another shot at life I would have seized every minute and looked at it and really see it and lived it and never give it back."

There is a verse in the Bible which reminds us life is short and we don't know what tomorrow will be like. "You do not know what tomorrow will bring. What is your life? You are a mist that appears for a little while and then vanishes" (James 4:14). Let me encourage you to read the list again. Look for an opportunity to put one of them into practice *this week*. Life is short. Every day is a gift from God. Enjoy every day to the fullest. You will be glad you did and your loved ones will too.

Bait and Switch

My wife Jeanne was a Middle School teacher who taught Social Studies and Language Arts. In California the curriculum for sixth grade covered ancient civilizations including China, India, Greece, Rome, Israel and Egypt. She always dreamed we would be able to personally visit each of those countries and eventually we did.

Our trip to Egypt was fascinating. We not only saw the pyramids near Cairo but we actually climbed inside of the largest one and saw the Pharaoh's burial chamber. We saw many other remarkable things in Cairo and in the Valley of the Kings. We also visited the Cairo museum where many ancient artifacts were on display.

We stayed at a nice hotel in Cairo. The staff was attentive and helpful. There were a number of gift shops on the property selling many interesting items. One day while my wife was resting I went down to the lobby to visit a shop which was selling golf shirts. I tried a few different shirts and sizes and finally decided on a nice white shirt made with Egyptian cotton.

The salesman said he had the same shirts in the back that were not opened and offered to get one for me. It seemed like a good idea. I used my credit card to pay for my purchase and he handed me a white golf shirt. After we got home from our trip I pulled out the unopened shirt and realized it was not nearly as nice as the ones I had tried on. They had given me a similar looking golf shirt which was clearly inferior to the ones I had tried on at the hotel shop. It was a bait and switch sale and there was nothing I could do about it.

I suspect you may have experienced a similar moment when you were misled by a car salesman or a home repair contractor. Maybe you purchased something online but the item you received was inferior to the thing you thought you were getting. There is a saying in the business world which says, "Buyer Beware". The Bible teaches us to be honest in our business dealings. One passage says, "Do not use dishonest standards when measuring length, weight or quantity. Use honest scales and measurements" (Leviticus 19:35-36).

Let me encourage you to be honest when you buy and sell. Treat other people the way you would like to be treated. Live a life of integrity. You will be glad you did and the people you do business with will too.

The Hitchhiker

One day when my wife and I were driving together we saw a middle aged woman hitchhiking along a two lane road in Maui. In the past it was not uncommon to see people with their hand out hoping to catch a ride. But in recent years with Uber and Lift we rarely see people by the side of the road asking for a free ride from a stranger.

A few generations ago it was not uncommon for men and women in uniform to try to catch a ride by holding their thumb out beside the road. During World War Two members of the military who were on leave looked for ways to get home before reporting for their next assignment.

One day a man named Dawson Trotman picked up a sailor who was hitchhiking in Southern California. Trotman had a ministry in the Long Beach area with servicemen who were assigned to naval ships there during the war. As they rode together Dawson told the young man about Jesus. The sailor was excited to put his faith in Christ. However, a few months later Dawson gave another ride to the same sailor. He was disappointed to learn the young serviceman had not grown in his faith. His vocabulary and conduct were unchanged. Trotman realized it was not only important to tell people about Jesus but to help them grow in their new faith too.

One of the ways Dawson did this was by gathering a group of men on the same ship to meet together regularly for Bible study and prayer. In addition he also began to meet with men one-on-one to train and equip more men how to study the Bible and how to share their faith. Today we call this *discipleship*. One man training another man who will in turn train another man. The goal was to multiply the number of men and woman who were spreading the good news and helping new followers of Christ to grow in their faith and share Jesus with others. This strategy was the foundation of the ministry called the *Navigators*.

There is a passage in the Bible where the Apostle Paul wrote, "Take the things you have heard from me and commit them to faithful men who will teach others also" (Second Timothy 2:2). Let me encourage you to tell more people about Jesus. And when someone decides to follow Christ ask them to meet with you on a weekly basis so you can personally help them grow in their faith. And invite them to go with you to a Bible teaching church. They will be glad you did and you will too.

The Lost Sunglasses

In addition to the popular resort locations like Lahaina, Wailea and Kapalua there are a number of small towns on the Island of Maui. Makawao is known for its annual rodeo and popular art galleries upcountry in a cooler part of the island. The winding road to Hana leads to a more tropical part of Maui along its eastern coast.

We were less familiar with the town of Paia which is on the north shore. It is known for wind surfing and was a popular a hippie hang out in the 1960's. The famous *Mama's Fish House* restaurant is also in Paia.

One day we decided to drive across the island and spend some time and money in Paia town. We looked through some shops and bought three casual long-sleeve T-shirts with images of sea turtles and other designs to remind us of our time in Maui.

We also found a small restaurant with casual dining in Paia. We were seated quickly and enjoyed some good food at this popular spot. The waitress was very helpful as we placed our orders. When she came back with our beverages we asked her how long she had lived on the island. She said she had lived in Maui all her life and loved it. She also told us she was a science teacher at the local high school and performed in some local theaters. In fact she was getting ready for her part in a musical opening the next night.

We were one of the last of the lunch crowd to leave. We thanked her for her excellent service and for telling us about her life. We gathered up our leftovers and went out to do some more shopping. We waited at the street corner for the light to change and then walked to the other side of the street. Suddenly we heard someone calling to us. When we turned around we saw the waitress with my sunglasses in her hand. I had left them on our table at the restaurant. Fortunately she saw them and ran after us to return them. She saved the day.

I was amazed the waitress went the extra mile to help us. She could have easily put them in lost and found and let us drive back across the island to retrieve the glasses. Instead she acted quickly and made sure the sunglasses were returned to us. There is a passage in the Bible where Jesus told his followers to "*go the extra mile*" (Matthew 5:41). Let me encourage you to do the same *this week*. Watch for an unexpected opportunity to help someone. You will be glad you did.

Friends Are Friends Forever

Michael W. Smith began composing and singing songs in the 1980's. He has written many popular Christian songs including, "*Open the Eyes of My Heart Lord*", "*Awesome God*" and "*Draw Me Close*". He is still writing and performing his music today. He has written over 35 number one songs and has received three Grammy Awards. He has sold more than 15 million albums.

He also wrote the music to the song "*Friends Are Friends Forever*". His wife Debbie wrote the lyrics. They wrote the song because a close friend was moving away. They wanted to express their love and appreciation to him. It was a last minute idea to write a song for the going away party later that night. Debbie sat down and wrote the lyrics in 30 minutes. Michael sat down at a keyboard and wrote the melody in three minutes. They sang it for their friend at the party later that night. Everyone cried.

When our ministry partners Dennis and Barb announced their decision to leave our church in Tucson in 1985, we made plans for a going away party for them. They had served at our church for over five years and decided to become missionaries in West Africa. That was a long way from Southern Arizona.

The evening was a special time to encourage them and to celebrate their ministry at our Tucson church. There was a lot of laughter as a number of people shared fun stories about Dennis and Barb. And there were a lot of tears when we concluded the evening by singing the song by Michael W. Smith "*Friends Are Friends Forever*". The lyrics are:

"Friends are friends forever if the Lord's the Lord of them.
And a friend will not say never because the welcome will not end.
It is hard to let you go, but in the Father's hand we know,
A lifetime's not too long to live as friends"

My wife and I attended a Michael W. Smith concert with some long-time friends in 2018 in San Antonio, Texas. It was a timely reminder of the value of these dear people. I believe God did not intend for us to go through life alone. He brings people into our life who become friends to encourage us and for us to encourage them. Let me encourage you to send a note or make a call *this week* to express your love and appreciation to a friend. They will be glad you did and you will too.

The Cowboy Chuck Wagon Dinner

My wife and I raised our family in Tucson, Arizona. Three of our four kids were born there. We were part of a church in this desert community with a number of young families. We didn't have a lot of money but we do have a lot of wonderful memories of Tucson.

We had grown up in the Phoenix area about two hours north of Tucson. From time to time our parents would drive down to visit and spend time with their grandkids. Whenever we had visitors we felt a responsibility to show them something new in Tucson.

One time we got the idea to take Jeanne's parents to a popular tourist venue. It was a Cowboy Chuck Wagon Dinner. It included a typical western dinner and an entertaining stage show. We weren't sure how they would feel about it but thought it was worth a try.

Things started off a little rocky. The seating arrangements were long wooden picnic tables. We were surrounded by total strangers. People were nice but it wasn't what we expected. The traditional Chuck Wagon dinner consisted of meat, beans, half of a canned peach and corn bread on a tin plate. We were warned the plate would be very hot and we should hold our plate under the canned peach. It was the only cool spot on the hot plate. They also served strong cowboy coffee in a tin cup. My father-in-law was not impressed.

The stage show included ballads and traditional cowboy songs. The servers were also the entertainers. They mixed in some humor and a few cowboy stories. It turned out to be a nice evening for our family and my in-laws. It was an expensive evening and stretched our budget. But it was a conversation piece for many years to come.

There are several passages in the Bible that provide insights into the type of food people enjoyed and how they served it in Bible times. (Mark 14:17-20 / John 12:1-3). Israel is actually an Asian country with a very different culture than what we experience in the west. However many eastern restaurants are available in our country today.

Let me encourage you to enjoy the variety of foods and customs available in your community. You will be glad you did and your guests will too. And if you eat a western Chuck Wagon dinner make sure you hold your hot tin plate under the cool peach!

Making the Right Decision

I hate canceling a scheduled event or meeting. I prefer to stick to the plan and not have to reschedule it for a later date. One of the hardest things I had to do as a leader was to decide whether to postpone or cancel an event. Our church held an annual event every summer in Tucson. We reserved a local water park west of the city for a church family night. Parents and children loved to race down towering water slides and splash their friends in the large swimming pools at *Water World*. We also included a baptism service as part of the evening.

However, Tucson is known for its summer thunderstorms. The sky could be clear on Sunday morning but cloudy and threatening to by late afternoon. Dust storms often accompanied the powerful monsoon rain. The park would close the pools and the water slides if thunder and lightning were threatening the area. On several occasions we wrestled with the dilemma. If the weather reports predicted rain and thunderstorms should we keep the event or cancel? People had invited guests and it was impossible in those days to notify everyone if we decided to cancel the family water park event. What would you do?

We faced similar situations in the winter. We typically held a marriage retreat for couples during the winter months. But snow was a real possibility in the mountains above Tucson. Sometimes roads were closed or access was limited due to a large amount of precipitation. One time we were able to drive up Mt. Lemon but we discovered the road off the highway was closed. We parked our cars along the main road and actually carried our sleeping bags, luggage and food supplies through the snow to the cabin we had reserved. The men thought it was fun but the women were not as enthusiastic. Every winter we wrestled with the same decision. If we heard a storm was coming should we reschedule the retreat or stick to the plan?

There was a pivotal moment in World War Two. The Allied forces were poised to invade France to liberate Western Europe from German occupation in June 1944. General Eisenhower postponed the invasion for one day but then made the decision to go. On several occasions King David asked God whether he should launch an attack on his enemy (First Samuel 23:1-6). Let me encourage you to take time to pray and consult with other leaders before you make an important decision. You will be glad you did and they will too.

137

Searching for Gold

There was a man in our church in Diamond Bar who loved to go looking for gold. Terry was a pharmacist and directed the pharmacy department at a local hospital. But he also loved searching for gold. He had actually found small flakes of gold in the streams and riverbeds in the mountains above Southern California.

Terry and his friend Warren came up with the idea to go to Alaska and search for gold in a remote area of the state. They researched where gold had been found in Alaska. They looked at remote sites which were only available by airplane. They searched for sites which had specific characteristics of gold country.

After a year of planning they flew to Alaska to begin their adventure. They took a commercial flight to the state and hired a local pilot to take them to their target area. After being dropped off at remote air strip they used an inflatable raft to reach their desired destination.

They spent two weeks panning for gold in this remote region. They pitched a tent and cooked their own food while they searched for the precious metal. They saw huge herds of Caribou and other wildlife. One time a small curious fox walked into their camp to meet these strangers. Then they used the raft to reach a prearranged pick up site. It was an exhausting and exciting adventure. They found about 18 ounces of gold. In the 1990's gold was worth about $400 an ounce. By 2023 it was worth almost $2000 an ounce.

There were two men in the Bible who shared some similar interests. They loved the outdoors and served in the military together. Jonathan and David became life-long friends (First Samuel 18:1-4). I wonder what hobbies and interests you have. Do you love star gazing or scuba diving? Do you enjoy horseback riding or rebuilding old cars? Do you like to work with wood or repair old radios? The list is endless.

One of the benefits of a hobby or special interest is the connection you have with other people who share the same passion. One of the best ways for men to connect with other men is sharing something in common. Let me encourage you to share some of your hobbies with other men. Ask them what they are interested in and tell them about things you like to do. They will be glad you did and you will too.

A Plane Full of Children

My wife Susan and I celebrated our honeymoon by spending two weeks in Hawaii. We enjoyed a quiet restful time eating breakfast on the lanai at our condo and discovering new restaurants for lunch and dinner. We also did a lot of cooking at the condo and enjoyed eating some delicious steaks from the BBQ grill.

We used a rental car to visit a variety of places on Maui and to purchase some souvenirs and gifts. It was fun to discover some new places and beaches that neither of us had been to before. We continue to smile as we remember our time together in Hawaii.

However our air plane flight home brought us back to reality. We flew my favorite airline Southwest non-stop from Long Beach to Maui. Our return flight was also non-stop back to Long Beach. But unlike our outbound flight the trip home was very different.

Both flights were full but the plane ride home was filled with over 40 children. There were a large number of families with little kids. It wasn't as bad as it could have been but it was a noisy active group on our flight. Some babies and little children struggled with the change in air pressure. It was difficult for some to sleep. The cabin was filled with the cries of infants who were tired and uncomfortable.

Parents tried so hard to comfort and quiet their little ones. Some parents walked up and down the aisle of the plane to try to settle their child down. Others tried electronic toys and video screens to keep their kids quiet. Some were successful and some were not.

Eventually we arrived safely in Long Beach. It was a long flight. I'm sure those kids were happy to be back in their own beds. The parents are probably reconsidering their plans for their next trip to Hawaii. I suspect they may wait until their young children are teenagers.

There is a passage in the Bible which illustrates Jesus' love for little kids. He scolded his disciples for preventing young children from gathering around Him. He opened his arms and welcomed them to his side (Mark 10:13-16). Let me encourage you to be patient and understanding when you are in a room full or a plane full of young children. And you may want to ask your airline to schedule your next flight with fewer kids on board. You will be glad you did.

The Best Meal on an Airplane

I'm sure all of us have our own individual tastes when it comes to food. And I suspect there are a few special meals you still remember which you enjoyed at an upscale restaurant. Your mother probably made some of your favorite meals or desserts for your birthday or for a holiday that are memorable too.

Recently I enjoyed one of the best meals I have had on an airplane in a long time. The quality and volume of food served on airlines has declined in recent decades. Many airlines including my favorite Southwest only serve prepackaged snacks and sweets. Other companies offer food for sale but usually it isn't very good.

I enjoyed every bite on my recent flight. The reason is my wife Susan packed some sandwiches, chips and a chocolate chip cookie. The sandwiches were actually small sliders made from Hawaiian rolls we bought at Costco. She used some leftover steak we had cooked on the BBQ and some leftover chicken we had purchased at Costco too. She packed some fresh lettuce which I added to the sliders with a little mayo and it tasted great. How often do you get a steak sandwich on an airplane made with real slices from a fresh ribeye steak?

In addition she packed some kettle style potato chips in a zip lock bag. They added a salty taste and a crunchy texture to my delicious meal. She included the homemade chocolate chip cookie we bought at a bakery in Maui. It was the best meal I have enjoyed on an airplane in a long, long time.

I forgot to mention the midflight snack she included. There is an old grocery store upcountry on Maui in the town of Makawao. It was opened in the early 1900's to serve the large Portuguese community which was recruited to work on the cattle ranches in Maui. They still make and sell a Portuguese pastry called a Malasada. It is similar to a small glazed donut but better. It is served on a wooden stick. People line up to buy them at the store in Makawao. My wife managed to put a few in my backpack for a delicious treat during the flight.

It really was some of the best food I have eaten on an airplane in a long time. Let me encourage you to pack some good food and tasty treats for your next flight. You will be glad you did.

Aristarchus

The first time I met Richard was at a park near our church in Tucson in the 1970's. He had just finished playing tennis with a few friends and I asked him if they might have room for another player. They already had their usual foursome but eventually he invited me to fill in when one of the regulars could not be there. I never dreamed this would be the beginning of a life-time friendship.

Richard and Karen had three kids and we eventually had four. Our wives and children became good friends too. They began to attend Chapel in the Hills and became actively involved. Later Karen would teach in the new preschool and Richard became part of our leadership team. We enjoyed attending church together and camping together. We remember playing table games together after the kids went to bed.

One of the other things Richard and I enjoyed was golf. We played with other men like Tom and Randy on a number of different courses in Tucson. Later we started our Golf & Shop getaways with our wives where the men golfed and the wives shopped. Even after we moved to California we continued to meet annually for 30 years in places like Las Vegas, San Diego, Park Cities, San Antonio, Phoenix and Hawaii.

Richard and I helped each other build room additions on our homes. We worked together on the facilities at our church too. He led the effort to construct the worship center at Chapel in the Hills. His career with the Tucson Electric Power company made him very helpful and knowledgeable in the construction trades.

When we made the difficult decision to leave the church in Tucson and move to California, Richard insisted on driving the U-Haul truck to get us and our furnishings to Diamond Bar. Later Richard worked with other church leaders to relocate Chapel in the Hills and merge with another church in the community. This was a slow and deliberate step of faith which resulted in a larger, stronger church with new facilities in a prime location in Southwest Tucson. Richard was like a man named Aristarchus in the Bible who faithfully helped the Apostle Paul (Acts 19:29 / 20:1-5 / 27:2 / Colossians 4:10 / Philemon 24). Like Aristarchus, Richard was a faithful friend who believed God could do great things in the lives of people and in building a church. Let me encourage you to express your appreciation to some special people in your life *today*. They will be glad you did and you will too.

Tips

A unique feature in American culture is leaving a tip at a restaurant. Most customers will add a specific amount to the bill to express their thanks to their waiter or the people serving them. I was surprised to learn this is not the case in restaurants in other parts of the world.

One common question is how much you should tip your waiter and the staff. For many years customers tipped 10%. If your meal cost ten dollars you gave your server one dollar more. Over the years the cost of eating out has skyrocketed. The price of a meal at a typical restaurant is easily $20 these days. It can be considerably more in upscale resorts and fine dining establishments.

Restaurants frequently suggest an amount for your tip. They used to recommend a ten, fifteen and twenty percent tip at the bottom of the bill. Now some start at 18% and suggest even larger tips up to 25% or more for you to consider. Where will it end?

When it came to leaving a tip at a restaurant I must admit I stuck to a specific percentage in the past. You probably know what that was. But as I have gotten older I think I have been giving more generous tips to the employees at restaurants and the coffee shops.

One thing I do which irritates my wife is round up the tip so the final bill ends up with a whole number. In other words if a bill for dinner is $42.00 I round up the tip so the final payment is an even amount. A fifteen percent tip on the bill would be $6.30. The total payment would be $48.30. But I like to round it up to the next dollar and make the tip $6.70 for a total of $49.00. I know it sounds a little crazy but I like to see even numbers on my credit card statement.

There is a passage in the Bible which condemns a stingy man but commends someone who is generous in their dealings with people. There is a verse in the Bible which says, "A generous man will proper. He who refreshes others will himself be refreshed" (Proverbs 11:25).

Let me encourage you to error on the side of generosity. Don't be stingy when dealing with people or leaving a tip for the waitress or waiter who served you. They will be glad you did and you will too.

Laughter is the Best Medicine

One of the things I noticed was laughter – lots of laughter. I'm talking about the atmosphere around Christians. Their conversations were full of laughter. Their countenance was joyful and happy. They smiled a lot and seemed to enjoy being together.

For example, when I played sandlot baseball with other kids in my neighborhood there were a lot of disagreements and arguments. There were disputes over little details like did the runner tag up on a fly ball or did the second baseman tag the runner sliding into the base. We got lost in the details and lost the joy of playing the game.

But when I started playing on a church slow-pitch softball team I noticed there was a lot more laughter and a lot less arguing. People were just having fun playing the game with friends. There was no trophy at stake. It really didn't matter who won.

When I played a round of golf with my buddies there was a lot of laughter too. There may have been be some moans and groans over a missed putt or a lost ball but there was a lot of laughter too.

I also heard laughter in the hallways on Sunday morning and in the worship service too. People greeted one another warmly and with a kind word. They genuinely seemed glad to see each other. People were polite in the parking lot and no one argued over a parking space.

There is a letter in the New Testament where the Apostle Paul wrote to a group of new Christians in city of Philippi in northern Greece. Paul used words like *joy* and *rejoice* more than a dozen times. He remembered his time with these people and wrote a letter (Philippians) to encourage them. Paul was writing from a prison cell in Rome and yet his theme was positive and upbeat. I realize there is a difference between laughter and joy. But I think one of the ways we express joy is through laughter.

I wonder if there is much laughter in your life. Are you going through a difficult time right now? I don't have any simple solutions to your present circumstances. Let me encourage you to read Paul's letter to the Philippians. Ask God to bring some good people and joy into your life and some laughter too. I hope you will share the joy He brings into your heart with others. Laughter really is the best medicine.

Camping & Picnics

I pastored only two churches over a span of 40 years. It was a privilege to lead and serve these two congregations. There were many memories of marriages and new babies. We celebrated the completion of several buildings and participated in many missionary experiences.

But one of the favorite things I remember were the church picnics and family campouts. Picnics at a local park were always a lot of fun. There were games to play for children and adults. Typically the food was potluck although in later years it was easier for the church to provide the food and have people just bring desserts to share.

Family campouts were also wonderful times. In Arizona we camped on Mt. Lemon high above Tucson and also in the White Mountains near the border of New Mexico. In California we camped near the beach above Santa Barbara and in the desert at Calico near Barstow.

It was so relaxing spending a week or a weekend with other church families. The kids played, the dads fished and the mothers talked. I liked getting to know people better in this more personal setting. It was interesting to see family dynamics in a less formal atmosphere. Some people drove large motor homes or pulled travel trailers. Others like my family used a Coleman tent, a Coleman stove and a Coleman lantern and slept in sleeping bags.

I also liked to watch people make new friends at picnics and campouts. Most attended the same church but many attended a different church service. Camping people were usually friendly people. Introductions and conversations were the seeds which blossomed into lifelong friendships. Singing songs around the campfire were memorable too.

One of the most famous books of the Bible recorded a forty-year long camping experience. The book of Exodus records the journey of the Israelites from slavery in Egypt to freedom in the promise land. As you read it yourself you will see many similarities to a church picnic or a church campout.

Let me encourage you to make a plan and set a date for a picnic or a campout with some church members, your own family or some friends. You will be glad you did and they will too.

The Refrigerator Repairman

It is not a good sign when you are on a first name basis with the man who comes multiple times to fix your refrigerator. But like it or not we have seen the same repairman many times over the past eight years.

It all began when we purchased a brand new Frigidaire refrigerator when we remodeled our kitchen in 2015. We bought a very nice model with French doors on top and freezer pull-out drawer on the bottom. It had a stainless steel finish to match the other appliances in the kitchen. They looked very nice.

However less than a year later we had our first problem with the new refrigerator. It was not cooling properly. Milk and other beverages were not as cold as they should be and the ice cream in the freezer was soft. We discovered this only a week before the one year warrantee expired. The repairman worked for several hours replacing a critical part which regulated the temperature in the refrigerator and freezer.

We were advised to purchase an extended warrantee to cover repairs in the future and we were glad we did. Two years later we began to have problems with the ice maker. Different repairmen came on numerous occasions to replace parts to get it working again. The ice maker continued to break down or freeze up. I believe we have had an average of one service call a year. One year we actually had three service calls in nine months. Our confidence in new appliances has declined to record lows.

Our latest problem occurred this week. After a two week trip we came home to find a sheet of ice on the bottom of the freezer. Our repairman Ulysses came to our rescue again. He is a certified factory trained technician. Other repairmen have come at different times but we now know him on a first named basis. He explained why the freezer had a thick layer of ice even though the water had been shut off at the front of the house. He corrected a couple of things and pronounced our refrigerator ready to use.

There is a passage in the Bible where two men repaired their nets after fishing in the Sea of Galilee (Mark 1:19-20). It is a reminder that appliances, cars, clothes and fishing nets all wear out with time. Let me encourage you to not get attached to material things. They don't last. Put your hope in God who is eternal. You will be glad you did.

Building a New Community

In 2003 I was invited to help start a Bible in a community called Eastvale. It was about 20 miles east of where our church was in Diamond Bar. Several people from our church had moved to this area where new homes were more affordable and new neighborhoods were popping up like weeds. This small study group eventually became a church under the leadership of Mark Lee and Tom Lanning which twenty years later has over 2,000 people attending each week.

Two of the couples who came to the new Bible study were dairy farmers. They had relocated their dairies from urban Los Angeles to the Corona Valley in the 1960's where there was plenty of land to raise dairy cattle. These two families shared how dairy farmers built a thriving community.

First they started a *new church*. Their ancestors were Dutch so they started Dutch Reformed churches in the area. Churches were important to a new community. They provided a moral and spiritual foundation. Second they started *a bank*. They knew a bank would be vital for farmers and all of the businesses related to them like truckers, feed supply, equipment sales, etc.

Third, they started *a school*. Children would need an education. There were some public schools in this rural area but the farmers wanted to provide a Christian school option for those families who preferred a private education.

Fourth, they opened a *Thrift Store* which could collect donations and make used clothing, furniture, appliances and other things available to anyone in the community. They wanted to give back and share with others who might be in need.

I was impressed with the foresight of these dairy farmers. They wanted to establish a community which would support their businesses and provide a healthy environment to raise a family. In Bible times Jewish families provided spiritual and moral foundations for their communities. The Synagogue was the center of daily life (Mark 1:21-22). I wonder if these priorities are missing in many communities today. Life is more than building houses and starting businesses. We need biblical values too. Let me encourage you to support local businesses and attend a church in your community. You will be glad you did.

On Your Hands and Knees

I have great respect for men and women who work in the building trades. These hard working people use their brains and their bodies to construct houses and hospitals, streets and schools and so much more. They are plumbers, electricians, carpenters and carpet layers. They get up every morning and put in a hard day's work to provide services essential to your community and mine.

Many years ago my wife Jeanne and I got the idea to replace some dark evergreen colored carpet in our house with new bright white ceramic floor tile. It sounded like a good idea but I had no idea how hard it would be. We went to Bedrosian's tile warehouse in Anaheim and purchased boxes of heavy tile. We also purchased the cement mix needed to install it on the floor in the kitchen, family room and part of the living room leading to the front door.

It was expensive to purchase but even more exhausting to install. First we had to remove the old evergreen carpet. Then we had to remove the tack strips which held the old wall-to-wall carpet in place. Then we needed to patch some of the holes left from the tack strips and seal the cracks in the concrete.

The next step was to snap a chalk line to create a starting point to lay the tile. Most rooms are not completely square so you don't normally start along a wall. It is better to snap a line and work from there to install the full tiles first and then cut tiles to fill in along the edges of the room. The full pieces go in pretty fast but measuring, cutting and installing the pieces along the edges is very slow and time consuming.

Did I mention all of this work is done on your hands and knees? It really is back breaking work. You are bending over all of the time spreading the adhesive and installing the tile one piece at a time.

There is a description in the Bible of the hard labor the Israelites were forced to do in Egypt. It was unimaginable back breaking labor as they built cities and monuments along the Nile River (Exodus 1-2). The Bible instructs owners to treat their workers well and for workers to do their work well (Ephesians 6:5-9). Let me encourage you to do your job well. Be an example others can follow. And if you are planning some home improvements projects this year you may want to join the local gym first to get your back, knees and body ready for hard work.

Pouring a Backyard Patio

When my parents moved from Scottsdale they bought a nice three-bedroom two story patio home in Gilbert, Arizona. It was one of many new suburbs popping up around the Phoenix area. They were glad to get out of the older four-bedroom house and into a smaller brand new house. However, the contactor only put in a small slab of concrete outside the rear patio sliding door. Clearly the builder was saving money by not including a patio in the back yard.

I had learned how to do concrete work while serving as the pastor of a church in Tucson. With the help of a contractor we constructed a classroom building and a large auditorium. Church members did a lot of the work themselves as a cost saving measure. We did the wood framing, installed kitchen cabinets, painted the interior and poured concrete sidewalks too.

When I saw my parent's backyard I offered to put in a patio for them. I went to the local building supply store and bought some wood to make a form for the concrete. I used a pick and shovel to level and compact the dirt. I hired two young college students to use wheelbarrows to move the concrete from the Ready Mix truck in the street into the back yard. The wet cement was very heavy. It was hard work.

After pouring the concrete I started the finishing process. Again this is back breaking work. First I used a tool to tamp down the concrete so the rocks would be below the surface. Then I used a flat tool on a long pole to smooth out the surface of the cement. As the mix began to harden I used a smaller trowel to smooth out the surface and create a nice finish on the top. The finishing process required a lot of time on my hands and knees.

The final product looked good. I was glad my parents had a new patio to use and enjoy. There is a verse in the Bible which reminds us to do our work in a way that is pleasing to God (Colossians 3:23). Let me encourage you to lend a hand and help a neighbor or family member with a home improvement project. Use your experience and skills to help others. They will be glad you did and you will too.

The Jesus Revolution

A new movie came out in 2023. It was written and produced by Greg Laurie who is the pastor of a large church called Harvest Fellowship in Riverside, California. The title of the movie was *The Jesus Revolution*. Although the movie is about Greg Laurie's life and faith, the broader focus is on the *Jesus Movement* which swept our nation in the 1960's.

Greg was a teenager and young adult when Hippies and Surfers began to fill the beaches and communities along the west coast including San Francisco and the LA area. Some of them began attending churches when they realized drugs did not provide a real sense of peace and contentment they were seeking.

One of the churches where Hippies began to gather was Calvary Chapel in Costa Mesa in Southern California. The pastor was Chuck Smith. While some churches were unfriendly toward these young visitors Chuck welcomed them. Some older adults at Calvary Chapel were uncomfortable too. When someone expressed concern the beach people would destroy the new carpet, Chuck personally washed the feet of everyone at the front door before they walked on the carpet. Later he suggested the church simply remove the new carpet and hold the worship service using folding chairs on the bare concrete floor hoping this would address the objections from the older members.

Attendance continued to grow. More and more Hippies were coming to faith in Jesus. Chuck personally baptized many new believers at a place called *Pirate's Cove* in Corona Del Mar near Newport Beach. We used the same beach to do baptisms for people from our church many years later. It is still a popular place for public baptisms today.

Greg Laurie was a teenager during this remarkable time. He came to faith in Christ and became deeply involved at Calvary Chapel. Chuck Smith saw the potential in Greg's heart and life and encouraged Greg to become a church pastor. God opened a door for Greg to become the founder and leader of Harvest Fellowship Church in Riverside.

In the Bible the Book of Acts describes the remarkable growth of the early church. Many people became believers and followers of Jesus. You can read it for yourself. Let me encourage you to watch the movie *The Jesus Revolution*. And let me encourage you to become a believer and follower of Jesus too. You will be glad you did!

Hospitality

When I married my wife Susan I didn't realize all of the extra benefits that came with my new bride. She came with a nice car and two flat screen TV's. She brought all of her kitchen dinnerware, silverware and cooking pots and pans. She had a tool box and several battery operated power tools for home repairs. She is amazing.

However, one of the nicest things she brought into our relationship was some comfortable patio furniture. Previously I only had a rectangular glass patio table with six metal chairs and six cushions. These had served my family well for many years.

Recently one of her daughters was moving out of her house and asked Susan if we could store and use a number of pieces of patio furniture. It seemed like a good idea. My patio furniture was old and rusted. We could certainly use some newer and nicer stuff. We had a sneak preview a few weeks before it arrived and it did look very nice.

When the delivery truck arrived it was filled to the rim. It included one large heavy square tile table with eight large cushioned chairs and an umbrella. There were two lounge chairs with thick covered cushions and comfortable head rests. There was also a large three piece couch with thick cushions and a matching smaller *Love Seat*. There were also several attractive end tables and at least four foot rests. In addition she also brought a beautiful gas KitchenAid BBQ grill.

As I gaze out the patio door this morning I am amazed at how many pieces of patio furniture we now have at our house. A few months ago our patio was piled with cardboard moving boxes. Now the boxes are gone and the patio looks beautiful and ready to entertain. We hope to welcome guests into our home and on to our patio in the days ahead.

There are several passages in the Bible which remind us to show hospitality to friends and strangers. The word in the New Testament means "*a love of strangers*" (*philos xenos*) (Romans 12:13 / First Timothy 5:10 / Hebrews 13:2 / First Peter 4:9). Let me encourage you to open your home to friends, neighbors and strangers. You don't need to have expensive furniture and a fancy BBQ grill. You just need an open heart. Set a date and invite some people over *this month*. They will be glad you did and you will too.

Can You Believe in Jesus and Budah

One of the things I enjoyed doing as a pastor was getting to know new visitors who came to our church. Usually I left the service during the final song so I could be on the patio ready to greet people as they left. I felt like a hockey goalie trying to catch new people as they walked out the door. I not only wanted to meet new people but I always tried to introduce them to other people their age or in their stage of life.

Another way I got to meet new guests was by going to their home during the week. We actually had a home visit ministry where we sent out 2-3 small teams of adults to follow up on our recent guests. Each team brought a box of cookies to express our thanks to the people who had visited our church. Most people were surprised and pleased we came and invited us into their home for a short visit.

We loved to get to know more about our recent visitors and we loved to tell them a little more about our church. We usually gave them some printed information and asked if they had any questions. I will always remember the time a thoughtful woman asked me, "Can I believe in Jesus and Budah?" I don't think she wanted to argue about the different faiths. I believe she was very sincere. She had been brought up as a child believing in Budah but now she was considering becoming a follower of Jesus. Could she believe in both?

I was surprised and pleased she would ask. It is a very good question that many other people have probably asked. I used the analogy of marriage to explain why I thought the answer was "no". I asked her if she could be married to two different men. Would she accept her husband having another wife? I realize some cultures accept polygamy but most people believe marriage involves one man and one woman. She knew she did not want two husbands.

The same is true with Jesus and Budah. Each person must decide for themselves. Will you follow Budah or follow Jesus? The thing which sets Jesus apart from all other religions is His death on the cross and His resurrection from the dead (First Corinthians 15:1-20). There is a verse in the Bible which says we can only serve one master (Matthew 6:24). The context is actually about money but the principle is the same regarding our faith in Jesus. I think the woman understood my answer. Do you? Let me encourage you to put your faith in Jesus. Decide to believe in Him alone. Follow and serve Him. You will be glad you did.

In Over Our Heads

As our church in Tucson grew in the 1970's and 1980's we needed more parking space and more classrooms. God provided a man with a road grader to clear out some undeveloped land on our property. He literally went past our church driving his huge earthmoving equipment on a Sunday morning after church. I jumped in my car and chased him down and asked him if he could help us clear some of our land so we could park more cars. He was happy to help.

We had a building campaign to raise some money and also took out a small loan to finance the construction of a new classroom building. We did a lot of the work ourselves and completed it in January, 1980. The structure also met Arizona's building requirements for a preschool which we opened after the final inspection and approval.

The biggest step we took at the Tucson church was to construct a large *Family Worship Center* so more people could attend church services and provide additional restrooms and classrooms. The new auditorium was about the size of a Jr. High gym with a twenty foot high ceiling surrounded by classrooms, restrooms and a large kitchen. It was over 7000 square feet of floor space. It was a big building.

We agreed to not borrow money but to build as donations came in. We did a lot of the work ourselves but hired a contractor to pour the floor and lay the block walls. I will always remember the day someone came to the work site to see what we were doing. His words stuck in my mind when he said, "*You are in over your heads.*" In some ways he was right. This was a big tall building we were trying to construct. How would we pay for it? Would we be able to complete the job? With God's help we did and opened the doors without any debt. It was amazing.

There was a man in the Old Testament named *Nehemiah*. He recorded the challenges and obstacles he faced leading the effort to rebuild the walls around the city of Jerusalem. I wonder if he felt he was *over his head* undertaking the massive project. Let me encourage you to read his personal diary in the Bible with his name on it. He did a lot of praying and he saw God's hand many times in the process (Nehemiah 2:18 / 6:15-16). The walls of Jerusalem were completed with God's help just as we completed the Worship Center in Tucson with God's help too. I hope you will be willing to step out of your comfort zone and watch for God's hand and help in your life. You will be glad you did.

Twenty Years Ago

Recently my wife and I had dinner with a delightful couple who joined our church staff in Diamond Bar 20 years ago. When they came to our house for dinner during the interview process they brought their six month year old son Nathan with them. He was their first child. We enjoyed our dinner and conversation. A few weeks later Mark was invited to join our church staff. He and his wife Andrea and their son Nathan were a valued addition to our leadership team.

Mark's role was pastor to young families. We wanted him to connect with young parents already attending our church and attract more families in the community. Mark developed a new ministry on Sunday morning which was popular with these young parents and other young adults.

A home Bible study had started in Eastvale in the home of Greg and Carol Crawford in 2003. A few years later in 2006 we began to dream of launching a church in that growing community. At first Mark was not enthused with the idea but gradually sensed God might be leading him to accept this unique opportunity. Eventually Mark and our worship leader Tom decided to work together to start a new church in Eastvale, California. The Diamond Bar church provided financial help. In addition to the people attending the home Bible study, a large number of other families and individuals from Diamond Bar joined the effort.

We prayed for three things – A l*eader*, a *location* to meet and **land** for a future building site. God provided two leaders – Mark and Tom. God opened a location for these pioneers to begin monthly church services at a Middle School in the fall of 2007 and weekly services in February 2008. Later as their numbers increased they were given permission to use the auditorium at Eisenhower High School. They eventually purchased ten acres of land and built a 600 seat auditorium.

Today Vantage Point Church has almost 2500 people attending each week. The leaders and the people have worked very hard to impact their community. The journey continues today. We marvel at how God provided and all the lives and families who have been impacted. It continues to be a journey of faith. There is a verse in the Bible which says, "The hand of God was on us" (Nehemiah 6:11-12). By the way did I tell you little Nathan is now 20 years old and going to college?

A Hawk in Our Backyard

We have lived in our home in Diamond Bar, California for 35 years. Diamond Bar was a cattle ranch until it was sold in the 1960's to an investment group. They subdivided the land and sold parcels to a variety of developers and home builders. The slogan they attached to this new community was "*Country Living*". There was a lot of open space and a variety of wildlife including deer, coyotes, rabbits, skunks and snakes too. It was common to watch hawks glide freely above the area looking for breakfast or dinner.

Over the years the wildlife population has declined as new homes and shopping centers were built. The number of hawks hovering in the sky has diminished too. But we still see them from time to time. I like the hawks because they help limit the number of rabbits who feast on my front lawn. But the number of rabbits has increased as the number of hawks has declined.

Thankfully there is a new hawk in our yard. He is tall and slim with a penetrating gaze. No rabbit or human would want to tangle with him. Actually it is not a real hawk. It is a statue carved out of wood. It looks very real with its life-like features. You can't help notice his menacing presence.

We have learned there is a good side and a bad side to having a hawk in your yard. We have seen fewer rabbits since the hawk found his new home. But on the other hand we are also seeing fewer birds in our yard and in our trees. Apparently the smaller birds are intimidated by our new feathered friend.

Hawks are mentioned in the Bible (Job 39:26-30). God used Ravens to provide food for the prophet Elijah (First Kings 17:1-7). The Bible says there were all kinds of birds on Noah's Ark (Genesis 7:1-15). Birds add to the sounds we hear every morning when they announce to the world they are awake and think you should be too.

Let me encourage you to enjoy the sights and sounds birds bring to our daily lives. We love to see a new family of birds building a nest in one of the citrus trees outside our kitchen window. Give thanks to God for His marvelous creation. And if you are having problems with other critters eating your lawn I recommend you hire a hawk!

The Upside Down Airplane

The United States Post Office printed a new stamp in 1918. The stamp featured a picture of the JN-4 Curtis Bi-plane. A bi-plane had two wings one above the other. The purpose of the stamp was for sending a letter by air mail. The price was twenty four cents.

The stamp was rushed into production without anyone noticing it had a flaw. The Curtis Bi-plane was printed upside down. It became known as the "*Inverted Jenny*". No one noticed this mistake until the first sheet of 100 stamps was sold. It became the most famous and most valuable stamp ever produced by the US Post Office.

Stamp collectors have paid considerable amounts of money to own one of these stamps. Eventually the sheet was broken up so that the stamps could be sold individually. Over the past century Philatelists have paid more and more money to add this rare stamp to their collection. Recently a single "*Inverted Jenny*" stamp was found in a safe deposit box and sold at auction for $2 Million!

I shared this story with a group of men from our church. I had given away a half-dozen of my books at a weekend retreat. I told the men they would probably find some mistakes and flaws in this first edition. Even though I had read and re-read my newest book I knew readers would find some spelling errors or other mistakes. For example the words "*our*" and "*out*" are very similar and the letters "*r*" and "*t*" are next to each other on the key board of my computer. I found this mistake several times in the first edition but I'm sure I didn't find them all.

Then I told the men the story of the "*Inverted Jenny*" postage stamp. I explained the mistake on the stamp actually made it more valuable! If my book ever became a *New York Time's Best Seller* the first edition of my latest book even with all its mistakes could be very valuable too!

All of us make mistakes in life. Things we have done and words we have spoken may have offended or hurt others. We need to admit our mistakes and ask for forgiveness from the people we have offended. And let me encourage you to forgive those who have offended you. There is a verse in the Bible which says, "Be kind and compassionate to one another, forgiving each other just as God in Christ has forgiven you" (Ephesians 4:32). And if you find some mistakes in this book please send me a note so I can correct them before the next edition!

Hummers

I have written several stories in my previous books about how much we enjoy the birds at our house. We love to watch a pair of sparrows or doves make a nest in the citrus tree outside the kitchen window. We enjoy observing them sit on the eggs until they hatch. We like hearing the chirping of hungry new hatchlings as they lift their heads to get some food from their mother or father. Birds are amazing creatures.

Recently my wife Susan added a new bird feeder in our backyard for Hummingbirds. She mixed a small bottle of nectar and hung it on a tall pole so the birds could find and enjoy the liquid contents in the feeder. We became a popular stop for Hummers looking for food.

I did not know Hummingbirds migrated from Alaska and Canada to Mexico every year. They fly over 3,000 miles. I think the ones in our yard decided to skip the migration this year and simply enjoy the California cuisine.

They feed on the nectar from local flowers and also eat insects. They love sugar water with about four parts water to one part sugar. Some experts believe the clear mixture is better for the birds without red dye. One article I read about Hummingbirds said they flap their wings over 1,000 times per minute. They believe Hummers have better eye sight than humans and they can capture small bugs in the air.

I did not know they typically live 3-5 years. They build their tiny nests with twigs and bind the nest together with spider webs. The mother does most of the work feeding and caring for the little ones. Hummers are also territorial and don't like to share their bird feeder with their friends. However they can be social and fly or rest near humans.

It is amazing to observe these remarkable creatures. The Bible says God created the heavens and the earth. And He created all of the plants, animals and the fish in the sea and the birds in the air (Genesis Chapter One). Let me encourage you to enjoy the feathered friends around your house. Take time to ponder the beauty of God's handiwork. Watch the details of their color and their character. You will be glad you did and I will too.

Special Delivery

When I was in High School I used to deliver newspapers early in the morning seven days a week. I rode my bicycle up and down the streets in my neighborhood to deliver about 100 papers every day including weekends and holidays. It didn't pay a lot but I did save enough money to buy a '57 Chevy when I turned sixteen.

I have shared in my previous books that I was selected the "Newspaper Boy of the Year" by the Arizona Republic in 1968. I also received a $1,000 college scholarship from the newspaper when I graduated from Saguaro High School.

A lot of things have changed since those days. Instead of a teenager riding a bicycle, now a man driving a car delivers the newspaper in our neighborhood. Instead of going door-to-door to collect the sixty cent weekly fee, now it costs sixteen dollars a month and subscribers pay their bill online! In the past most people in my neighborhood got the Arizona Republic delivered to their house. Now very few home owners get the LA Times delivered in our neighborhood. Most read it online.

At least one thing which hasn't changed is the delivery method. When I delivered newspapers I tossed them from the sidewalk over flowers, shrubs and lawns hoping to land it on the front porch. The guy driving the car today tries to do the same but with far less accuracy. I was able to hit the porch nine times out of ten from the sidewalk. I must admit I did break a few milk bottles over the years. But the guy in the car barely reaches the driveway from the street. I did a lot better than he does.

My wife Susan and I usually go for a walk early in the morning. We often see the newspaper guy racing up and down the streets in our neighborhood delivering the LA Times or the Orange County Register. I know he is in a hurry and I think he does the best he can. But the newspaper is usually far from the front door. Sometimes we see people walking out to the driveway in their bathrobes to retrieve their precious paper. There is one house in particular where we pick up the newspaper on the driveway and take it to their front door when we walk by. We call this our *special delivery*. The neighbors know who we are and always thank us when they see us. There is a verse in the Bible which says, "*Go the extra mile*" (Matthew 5:41). Let me encourage you to *go a few extra steps* to help some people in your neighborhood *this week*. They will be glad you did and you will too.

Thirty Five Years

I began my new job as the Pastor of the Evangelical Free Church of Diamond Bar 35 years ago on June 1, 1988. As I reflected on that eventful day I was struck by how much of an impact that decision had on our whole family. Our children were young. Tim was 13, Trisha was 11, Traci was 10 and Teri was 7. My wife Jeanne and I were only 37 years old. We were a young family moving to a new community in Southern California. It was a new world and a new adventure for us.

In the fall the kids started attending new schools in the area. They made new friends and adapted to our new church. I know it wasn't easy for them but they handled the change pretty well. Little did we know that one day Jeanne would become a teacher in the local Middle School and later Tim would become a teacher at the local high school.

We bought a new house. It was smaller than our home in Tucson with only three bedrooms but we were able to add a fourth bedroom and a third bathroom to accommodate our growing family. Tim and Teri shared a room for a year. Trisha and Traci shared a room too. It took about twelve months for me to complete the room addition.

Our move to California and Jeanne's teaching job opened the way for our son to attend Azusa Pacific University in Azusa, California and for our three daughters to attend BIOLA University in La Mirada, California. These Christian schools had a significant influence on all of our children and on their future careers. The schools also connected some of them indirectly to their future spouse.

Moving to California also opened doors for my wife and I to travel to parts of the world we never dreamed of. We led short-term mission teams to places like Russia, China and India. Jeanne also traveled with other women to serve missionaries in Irian Jaya, Turkey and Croatia. Two of our four children became career missionaries in Central and Western Europe. Most of our grandchildren still live there.

There is a passage in the Bible where Abraham and his family moved from Ur of the Chaldees to the land of Canaan (Israel) (Genesis Chapter 12). His decision to move his family had a big impact on his family but he was willing to go even though he did not know what lay ahead. Let me encourage you to be willing to step out in faith and follow God's leading in your life. We were glad we did and you will too.

Honor the Flag

I was a history major at Arizona State University and earned my teaching credential in secondary education. I enjoy reading about American history and ancient history too. Recently I read a book titled *Caesar's Legion* by Australian author Steven-Dando Collins. He is an expert on the history of the Roman Legions who fought under various Roman Emperors. *Caesar's Legion* follows the story of the 10th Legion which was the favorite of Julius Caesar. They carried him to victory in many famous battles during Caesar's lifetime. After his assassination they went on to help suppress the Jewish rebellion, conquer Jerusalem and capture the fortress of Masada in 70-73 AD.

One of the things I learned from reading some of Collin's books on the history of the Roman Legions was how seriously they valued their flags. Each Legion had a unique flag to distinguish it from other Roman troops. And each of the smaller units within the Legion also had flags or banners which they carried into battle.

It was a great honor among the troops to be the flag bearer. A soldier would give his life to protect their unit's flag and prevent it from falling into the enemy's hand. Roman Emperors went to great lengths to recover a banner or flag seized by their enemies.

As we approach Flag Day on June 14th I wonder if military and civilians respect and value the flag of our nation like the Romans did in the past. My generation was shocked when protesters burned the United States flag during the Viet Nam war. Our nation was offended when foreign nations burned our flag during the Iran hostage crisis in the late 1970's.

I wonder if you even own an American Flag. Is there a flag on your children's school campus? Is a flag on display in their classroom? Do you display the American flag on you house on national holidays? Do you know the proper way to display the flag and the proper way to dispose of it? The Boy Scouts will retire a flag for you when it gets tattered and worn. Let me encourage you to fly the American flag on your house. Treat the flag with care and respect. Help your children understand the history and significance of the Red, White and Blue. They will be glad you did and you will too.

Make Your Bed

Admiral William McRaven wrote the book titled, "*Make Your Bed*". It was a New York Times best seller. The book was based on his commencement speech to the graduating class of the University of Texas at Austin. In his address he shared ten lessons he learned from his Navy SEAL training.

One of my favorite lessons in his book was, "*It is not the size of the flippers – it is the size of the heart*". They always work in pairs in SEAL training. Each team was given challenging assignments to complete. Many of them involved underwater demolition and other covert operations. Navy SEALS do a lot of swimming above and beneath the water.

Most people would assume the bigger men in the training class would out-swim the smaller guys. But to their surprise it was the little guys who often came in first on a long swim. McRaven concluded it was not the size of the swimmer or their flippers but the size of their heart. They worked harder and swam faster because of their competitive spirit and determination.

There is a lesson here regarding our faith. Jesus said, "If we have faith the size of a mustard seed we could move mountains" (Luke 17:5-10). One author wrote, "A mustard seed is very small, but has great potential to grow. A small amount of genuine faith in God will take root and grow. The amount of faith is not as important as its objective and its genuineness. Faith is total dependence on God and a willingness to do his will" (The One Year New Testament on July 17 by Tyndale House Publishers).

Admiral McRaven said it is not the size of the flippers but the size of the heart in Navy SEAL training. Jesus said it is not the size of your faith but the attitude of your heart centered on Him. Let me encourage you to trust God to guide you and lead you in everything you do. Trust Him to provide for your needs and help you in times of uncertainty. Trust Him to answer your prayers and to protect you and your family. Trust Him to deepen your faith and rely on God every day. You will be glad you did and He will too.

Driving through the Desert

One of the biggest mistakes of my life was selling my '57 Chevy and buying a VW Bug. The Chevy was my first car. I bought it before I was sixteen and couldn't wait to drive it by myself. I had to have an adult ride with me until I got my license on my 16th birthday. I loved that car.

The '57 Chevy with a four barrel carburetor was a gas guzzler. I was planning to live at home and commute to ASU after I graduated from high school. I decided to sell my Chevy and purchase a gas saving VW Bug. Looking back I should have kept the '57 two door Belair and found a way to pay for the thirty-three cent a gallon gasoline.

One thing I didn't know about Volkswagens was they were air cooled. It didn't have a radiator to cool the engine like most cars. It had a small rear engine with an oil cooling tower. Later Volkswagen would build newer cars with a radiator to cool the engine but not mine. The Arizona desert was not a good place to drive an air cooled Volkswagen.

When I was in college I led a summer youth camp near Prescott, Arizona. It was a good place for teens to get out of the summer heat. When I drove my VW to Prescott with two other guys my car overheated on Interstate 17 north of Phoenix. It started to make a terrible sound and finally stopped on the side of the road. We did not have cell phones in the early '70's but we finally got a ride to the camp and called someone to help tow my VW to a repair shop in Prescott. When a mechanic examined my car he said the engine had overheated and the pistons wouldn't move. The engine was ruined.

I know this has happened to other cars crossing the hot Arizona desert. The options were to replace the engine or find another car. I chose the first option. It was expensive to replace the engine even in those days. But no one was hurt and we had a wonderful week at the Junior High camp.

There is a verse in the Bible which says, "You can be sure that God will take care of everything you need" (Philippians 4:13 The Message Bible). I don't remember how I was able to replace the engine on my small summer intern salary. I believe a few generous people helped. Let me encourage you to trust God to provide your needs. I also recommend you skip the old VW and drive a car with a radiator!

A Picture is Worth a Thousand Words

Recently I was walking through a hallway at a local hospital when I saw a wall covered with photos of the medical staff. Actually the pictures were of all of the doctors currently working at that facility. There were faces of probably 30-40 men and women on the wall.

One of the things I noticed was how young most of them looked. Some could fit right into a high school year book. I know they were all college graduates and all of them had earned degrees in medicine. But they sure looked young. I remember the first meeting my wife and I had with her cancer doctor many years ago. Dr. Park looked so young. But don't let their youthful appearance concern you. Someone told me the new young doctors have learned the latest information and research in the world of medicine.

Another thing that impressed me was the number of women serving at the hospital. The women doctors clearly outnumbered the men. This was a reminder of the valuable impact women continue to have in the medical profession. I hope more little girls and young women will fill the needs in all levels of medical care. My daughter Teri is a Speech Pathologist. She helps children and adults with speech and swallowing problems and is a college professor training new speech therapists.

I also noticed all of the people filling the wall were smiling. I realize the photographer probably encouraged them to smile. But their faces and appearance really gave the impression these doctors liked what they were doing and enjoyed helping people with their medical needs. There is a passage in the Bible where the Apostle Paul write, "Don't just do the minimum that will get you by. Do your best. Work from the heart" (Colossians 3:22-24).

Let me encourage you to express your appreciation to the people who help deal with your medical needs including the doctors, nurses, therapists, technicians, clerks and janitors. Medical care is a team effort involving many people with different skills and training. And, let me encourage you to consider joining the medical field yourself. There are not enough people to fill the ranks today. God has given you skills and abilities to serve Him and help others. You will be glad you did and He will too.

The Ponderosa

There was a popular series on TV from 1959 to 1973 called "*Bonanza*". It involved a large family with a father and his three sons. Lorne Green was Ben Cartwright, Michael Landon was "Little Joe", Dan Blocker was the big fella "Hoss" and Pernell Roberts was Adam.

It was one of the most popular shows on television for over a decade. Viewers tuned in each week to see what challenges the Cartwright family faced and to watch how their favorite member of the family handled different situations.

Many years ago Jeanne and I met with some other couples for our annual "*Golf & Shop*" gathering. The agenda was very simple. The husbands played golf for three days and the wives shopped for three days. We met in San Diego, Park City, Phoenix, Las Vegas and other locations. It was a wonderful tradition we kept for thirty years.

One year we met at Lake Tahoe. We learned about a pancake breakfast and tour of the Ponderosa Ranch – the location for the TV series Bonanza. A lot of the filming was done near Lake Tahoe and the producers had constructed a house and other buildings for filming. We enjoyed the breakfast and the tour. It was interesting to learn how the actors and producers recorded both outdoor and indoor scenes. At the end of the tour each of us received a small tin cup with a picture of the Cartwright family on it. We also took our own group photo. I still have the cup and the photo from our time at the Ponderosa.

There is a passage in the Bible where the Apostle Paul reflected on the time he spent with new believers in Philippi in northern Greece. His brief visit was filled with wonderful memories of what God did in changing the lives of several people in that city. In his letter he wrote, "Every time you cross my mind, I break out in exclamations of thanks to God. I find myself praying for you with a glad heart" (Philippians 1:3-4 - the Message Bible).

My wife and I felt the same way when we saw that small tin cup on a shelf at our house which we received at the pancake breakfast at the Ponderosa Ranch. It brought a smile to our faces when we remembered our time with our dear life-long friends. And it reminded us to pray for them with a glad heart. Let me encourage you to pray for your friends as you remember special moments you shared together.

My Wonderful Wife

Susan is a wonderful woman. She was married for 49 years before her husband Harold died. She has two adult daughters - Cathy and Susie and five grandchildren – Alexandra, Morgan, Cate, Jake and Addison. She also has two big sturdy sons-in-law – Pat and Chuck.

Susan loves Jesus. Although she had a traditional church background she did not come to a personal faith in Christ until she was 38 years old. She loves to study the Bible and share her faith with everyone she meets. She became a co-leader in our Women's Bible study program and has been active with the Stone Croft ministry which hosts a monthly luncheon outreach to women. She has a heart for prayer too.

She loves people. She had a successful career as a flight attendant with American Airlines for over 30 years. She flew many miles all over the country and also to Europe and Asia. She easily connects with strangers and became good friends with many of her co-workers.

Susan loves to help others. She is very compassionate and caring. She has a shepherd's heart. She has provided transportation for widows and visited the sick. She did shopping for shut-ins during the Covid19 crisis and cooked meals for people in need.

Susan and her husband Harold began attending our church in Diamond Bar after they moved from San Diego to Orange County in 2006. They got connected with an adult Bible class on Sunday morning and Harold became one of the teachers.

My wife Jeanne and I enjoyed getting to know Harold and Susan. We enjoyed dinners and went to baseball games together. I was honored to lead the memorial service when Harold died in 2016 after heart surgery and a stroke. My wife Jeanne died after a long journey with Breast Cancer in 2022. We had been married for 50 years.

There is a verse in the Bible which says "It is not good for a man or woman to be alone" (Genesis 2:18 / First Timothy 5:15). Susan and I were on an unfamiliar path as single adults. We began to talk and pray about getting married again. And we did. Let me encourage you to come alongside friends and family members who have experienced the loss of a loved one. Offer your help and support to those who are living alone. They will be glad you did and you will too.

A Good Name

I met Mark when my wife Jeanne and I were leading the High School ministry at Northwest Bible Church in Dallas, Texas. I was a student at Dallas Seminary and enjoyed the opportunity to work on the staff of this growing church. Mark was a senior in high school when he came to the youth group with a friend. I liked him right away because he had a good name.

Our relationship grew over the next few years. He and other students came to our apartment for breakfast and a Bible study. Jeanne fed these hungry guys and she told them embarrassing stories about me. Mark was also one of guys who came to play basketball and study the Bible on Saturday mornings at the church. We also shared a memorable canoe trip down the Brazos River where we were almost swept away by the rising water in the middle of the night when we camped on an island in the middle of the river. Mark visited us when we lived in Tucson. He spent a day at our house on his way to his next military assignment after he enlisted in the Air Force.

A number of years passed until we reconnected after my family moved from Tucson to Southern California. Mark and his wife Beverly were living nearby. But his life was busy and mine was too. However I was surprised and pleased when he came to the memorial service after Jeanne died. He went out of his way to speak to me after the service and it was an opportunity to renew our relationship.

We began to meet for coffee and catch up on his life and family. Mark has a wonderful wife, two daughters and a number of grandchildren. He retired from his civilian job and enjoys restoring old radios and he plays a guitar in a Blue Grass Band. He has undergone treatment for cancer with good results so far. We continue to meet for breakfast.

There is a verse in the Bible which says, "A friend loves at all times" Proverbs 17:17). I'm thankful I met Mark over 40 years ago. I'm thankful he reached out to me after my wife's death. We have been making more of an effort to stay connected and keep in touch.

Let me encourage you to reach out to an old friend, co-worker or family member *this week*. The years go by quickly. Life is short. They will be glad you did and you will too.

How to be a Christian without being Religious

Author Fritz Ridenour wrote a book with the above title in the 1960's. According to an online article the book has sold over four million copies. It is a helpful and thoughtful book based on the book of Romans in the Bible. Ridenour's book provides a helpful perspective on how to be a follower of Jesus without being burdened by a lot of religious rules and regulations.

The introduction on the back cover says, "Do you sometimes feel trapped into playing a game called "church" when you are going through the religious motions in order to please a God who probably isn't very happy with you anyway?" It continues, "The Christian life is a rich relationship with God, not a religious treadmill."

The book includes sketches to illustrate some of the truths the Apostle Paul shared with the believers in Rome as they began their journey following Christ. Some of the illustrated topics include – "Even a religious man cannot reach high enough to meet God's standard", "No baseball player bats a thousand (1.000)", "On parole or fully pardoned?" and "Grace is like getting a warning ticket when you deserve a suspended license".

I know pastors who have preached on the book of Romans for several years – Sunday after Sunday. It is a remarkable letter authored by the brilliant Apostle Paul. But you can get a helpful overview of Romans by simply reading this small paperback book. Fritz Ridenour takes some of the complex concepts of Paul's writing and makes them simple and easy to understand. You can find it on Amazon.com.

The Bible was written for us to understand. I believe you can learn so much by reading the Bible by yourself. And you can certainly benefit from the study and teaching of pastors and Bible teachers. Faith in Christ and living as Christian isn't difficult or complicated. It starts by simply admitting you are a sinner and believing Jesus died on the cross and rose again to pay for your sins and to purchase a home for you in heaven. You can put your faith in Jesus today with a simple prayer. Let me encourage you to pray right now. Here is a suggestion, "Lord Jesus I know I am a sinner. But now I believe you died on the cross and rose again to pay for my sins. I invite you into my life right now. Change my life and help me to live by faith to please you". If you pray that prayer please contact me *today* at *markh@efreedb.org*. Thanks!

June 10
Trail Ride

In July, 1985 our family loaded up our Dodge Van and drove from Arizona to South Dakota where I was the speaker at a camp. This annual church event was called *Trail Ride* and met at a state park near Deer Lick in the Dakota Badlands. People drove motor homes and pulled travel trailers. And they brought their horses too.

This week long event included games and activities for children and adults. There was a community breakfast in the morning and a camp fire in the evening. I taught a series of messages from the book of Nehemiah. It was a fun week getting to know this group of friendly church people. One of the families were our friends Ray and Margaret Redmer. They attended our church in Tucson in the winter but had a farm and many friends in North and South Dakota.

One of the main attractions for the week was horseback riding. Every day people saddled up their horses and rode along trails in this beautiful country. My wife and I and our kids were invited to participate. The problem was I had never ridden a horse before. This was a new and uncomfortable experience for me.

Two things I discovered about horses – they did not have a steering wheel and did not have a brake pedal. I had a hard time figuring how to steer and how stop the horse I was riding. In addition I learned horses are pretty tall. When you get up on a horse and sit in the saddle you are six to eight feet off the ground. It looked like a long way down.

My daughter Trisha had a frightening experience with one horse. She asked if she could sit on a horse which was tied up by a fence. When she got on, it began to express its displeasure. It bucked and rose up on its back legs. I was standing next to her and tried to calm the horse but it continued to fight and struggle. Finally an experienced rider came to her rescue and got the horse to settle down. It was a scary moment.

There is a vivid description in the Bible when Egyptian horses and riders were swept away when the Israelites escaped through the Red Sea (Exodus 14:28). Until the invention of the railroad horses were the fastest means of transportation. Let me encourage you to introduce your children to horseback riding when they are young. Let them experience these beautiful creatures God created for us to enjoy. And make sure you fasten your seatbelt. You will be glad you did!

June 11
The Iao Valley

I enjoyed sharing some new adventures in Hawaii with my wife Susan. She had been to most of the islands but she had not been to the Ioa Valley (pronounced EE-yow) on Maui. This beautiful setting is nestled in a canyon north of downtown Kahului.

This popular tourist location provides helpful insight into the history and culture of the Hawaiian people. It was the site of a major battle between the two competing groups populating the Hawaiian Islands in the 1700's. King Kamehameha's victory over the Maui fighters in the 1790 completed his conquest of the islands and united the islands under his rule.

The Iao Valley has been designated a National Park to protect and preserve farming and living areas in the valley. It reveals how the Hawaiian people raised different crops like Tao and pineapples by terracing the land and using the steady water supply to grow food. The sophisticated water system was an example of how the local inhabitants maintained themselves over several centuries.

There are examples of how early people lived on the island and the type of housing they developed. It also showed how the Hawaiian people defended themselves against raiders and enemies from other Polynesian groups.

We also learned about the work of early missionaries who came to the Hawaiian Islands in the late 1800's and the important role they had developing literacy and creating a written language for the indigenous people.

It was interesting and helpful to see how proud the Hawaiian people are of their history and culture. We gained a new appreciation and understanding of what daily life was like on the islands. Today Maui is a bustling community with thousands of tourists filling the streets and shops. But Hawaii has a remarkable past too.

The Apostle Paul often referred to the history and culture of local people as he visited different cities and countries in the Roman Empire (Titus one / Acts 14 & 17). Let me encourage you to learn more about the history and culture of the people who live in your community. You will be glad you did and they will too.

June 12
It is a Dry Heat

My wife and I decided to fly to Arizona to visit some family members and friends. I'm not sure why I selected the month of July but the plane tickets were on sale when I made the reservation in January. I did not foresee the possibility of mid-July being one of the hottest weeks on record in Phoenix.

Before our trip we watched some of the weather forecasts and it did not look very good. There was a high pressure system over the four corner states which was preventing the normal summer thunderstorms from bringing any rain or relief to the Southwest.

When we stepped off of the airplane we immediately felt the heat. It was over 100 degrees at 8:00 PM. When we exited the terminal the full force of the heat hit us like a hammer. It never got below 90 degrees that night and the weather man predicted it would be even hotter the next day. It was clear this was not the best time to enjoy Phoenix.

The next day I went out to the parking lot where our car was stored. I could feel the heat increasing after the sun came up at 6:00 AM. When I started the engine and turned on the air conditioning I only felt warm air. The air conditioning was not working. I had not used the AC over the past few months but I didn't expect it would completely stop producing cold air during one of the hottest weeks ever in Arizona.

My wife Susan and I drove the car to find some breakfast nearby but the AC was only blowing hot air. After breakfast we did some grocery shopping and went back to the condo. We didn't want any food to spoil or ice cream to melt. It became more and more uncomfortable every time we used the car. Finally I got the name of a reliable mechanic and called to make an appointment. To my surprise they encouraged me to bring the car right in. Now I am sitting in the office of the car repair shop holding my breath and waiting to hear how much it is going to cost to cool my car. Today's forecast for Phoenix is 119 degrees.

There is a passage in the Bible where a man named Jonah complained about the heat he endured as he looked over the great city of Nineveh. He complained to God about his discomfort (Jonah Chapter Four). I know we all complain at times but let me encourage you to thank God for every day of life. And if you visit Arizona in the summer make sure you drink plenty of water!

We Are Having a Heat Wave (Part Two)

I shared in an earlier story about our recent trip to Arizona. The intense heat we experienced on the trip to Phoenix made life miserable. The local meteorologist explained there had been a record number of continuous days with temperatures over 100 degrees in Phoenix. This was also the case in a number of other cities across the Southwest including Las Vegas, El Paso and Tucson. In the midst of all of this the air conditioner in our car was not working. My wife was glad to stay in our condo and not venture out in the hot weather.

What do you do with the hot weather and the AC not working in your car? The first step was to get the air conditioner fixed. I wasn't sure who to trust or where to take my car. I made an appointment at the local Firestone Tire store but the earliest they could look at my car was the next day.

However when a friend called me about meeting for lunch I asked him if he could recommend a reliable car mechanic. He told me to call the place where he got his car serviced – *Thompson Automotive* near Hayden Road and Indian School Road. I found their number online and called to see if I could get an appointment. The nice lady on the phone said I could bring my can in now – no appointment necessary! It was only 15 minutes away. They checked the AC system, added Freon and changed the cabin filter. Success! The air conditioning is working great so far. Now my wife is willing to leave the condo!

Another way to get relief from the heat is to go shopping. Our first stop was the local Costco store. We got there just as it opened. When we walked in the front door we were engulfed by fresh cool air. We took our time shopping going up and down every aisle. I discovered the best place to cool off was the Dairy section. It was a separate room filled with eggs, butter and other dairy items. It was at least 10 degrees cooler than the rest of the warehouse. I noticed a lot of customers lingering longer than usual selecting eggs and other items there.

We also discovered spending time in the local shopping mall was another good place to cool down during a record heat wave. We also planned to go to a movie theater. Let me encourage you to get creative as you look for places to cool off during the next heat wave. You will be glad you did and your family will too.

Can't you fix it?

One day my wife and I went shopping for some things at Home Depot. We wanted to exchange some light bulbs which were the wrong wattage and replace them with new bulbs to match the other ones in the fixture at our condo in Arizona. We also found a small part for the kitchen faucet too.

While we walked up and down some other aisles we noticed some new modern kitchen faucets which might look nice in our home in California. The current one had a steady drip and didn't work properly. The faucet at our house also had a pull-out flexible metal hose. This enabled us to wash large pots and pans and clean the corners of the kitchen sink too.

I am not a fan of this type of kitchen faucet. It seems like every time I installed one it eventually had a problem. I always vowed to never purchase another one again. But at a weak moment I agreed to allow the kitchen remodeling company to install the flexible hose, pull-out model in our new kitchen. Now, a few years later the pull-out kitchen faucet does not work properly.

As I tried to explain to my wife why I didn't like that kind of faucet, she said in a firm voice, *"Can't you fix it – can't you fix it?"* She thought a new washer or some adhesive would be able to stop the drips.

We did not realize a customer nearby overheard our conversation. He started to laugh when he heard what Susan said. The emphatic tone of her voice and the way she repeated her words implied any husband should be able to *"fix it"*. That is what husbands do. They fix things!

Then we both started laughing too. The customer had covered his face as he continued to laugh at the words Susan had spoken to me. Maybe his wife had said the same words to him.

If you are a husband you have probably heard these words before. If you are a wife you have probably said these words to your husband too. There is a verse in the Bible which says, "Love is patient and kind" (First Corinthians 13:4). Let me encourage you to do whatever you can to help each other and fix the things in your own life and around your home. Be patient and understanding with each other. You will be glad you did and your spouse will too.

Epaphroditus

I met Tom and his family one day when I was riding my bike through our neighborhood in Tucson. Tom and Barb had three young boys. He was a civil engineer and loved to solve problems and find efficient ways to develop land for residential and commercial projects.

Tom volunteered his time and skills to help us while we were building the new worship center at our church. We were thankful to have his help and to have him and his family coming to church.

One of the ways I got to know Tom better was meeting with him early in the morning before work. Once a week we met at his office to study the Bible and pray for our families. It was refreshing to watch Tom grow in his faith in Christ.

We kept in touch with Tom and Barb after we moved to California. They were part of the "Golf & Shop" friends who met annually to spend a few days together. The men golfed and the women shopped. We were able to attend some of the weddings for their sons and they attended some of the weddings of our kids too.

Tom had a sensitive heart and cared about people. He also had an engineer's mind and often offered solutions to challenges we faced at church and in our own families. Tom and Barb helped their older parents and family members. They welcomed a single mother and her children into their home for several years. They encouraged my wife and me during Jeanne's journey with breast cancer. And they continued to provide support and encouragement to me after she died.

There is a passage in the Bible which says, "A friend loves at all times" (Proverbs 17:17). There was a man in the Bible named Epaphroditus who was from the town of Philippi in Northern Greece. He was a model of a servant leader (Philippians 2:25-30). He faced some serious health problems but faithfully provided help to the Apostle Paul when Paul was in prison in Rome. Tom was a man like Epaphroditus who gladly helped and encouraged other people. I'm thankful God brought Tom and his family to our church in Tucson. He has been a faithful friend for many years. Let me encourage you to express your love and appreciation to some of the friends who have supported and encouraged you. They will be glad you did and you will too.

June 16
Have a Good Flight

We often fly to Phoenix from Southern California. We have friends and family members there and it is a short one-hour flight from the Ontario airport to Sky Harbor in Arizona. Susan and I tried to find someone to take us to the airport so we didn't have to leave our car in the long-term lot. It can cost over $20 a day and I don't like to leave the car in the hot sun and exposed it to all the residue from the jet air planes.

But one time we were not able to find anyone to take us to the Ontario airport. We know people are busy. We understood. So we drove our own car. I dropped Susan off at the terminal with our bags and I parked in the $20 a day plus tax long-term lot. We carried our small suitcases and got through security quickly with our TSA-Pre passes. We were at our departure gate in plenty of time for our flight.

However the airline asked for volunteers to take a later flight. They needed to get an extra flight crew on our plane so they could get to Phoenix for their assignment. They offered $700 flight credit to each person for future travel. We offered to give up our seats and take the next flight three hours later. Future travel here we come!

What could we do for the few hours until the next flight? We thought about taking our car back home and calling a friend at the last minute to see if they could take us back to the airport. Yes – they would be glad to help. So we left the airport, stopped at In N Out Burger for an early dinner and drove our car back to our house. I did have to pay the $20 a day parking fee for the one hour I used the long-term lot but that was better than the estimated $160 for a whole week. Our friend picked us up at our house and drove us back to the airport in plenty of time for our flight which was only half full. We got to Phoenix later that evening. It was an interesting adventure!

By the way – did I mention my wife wore two different shoes to the airport? She didn't discover her error until we got to the gate the first time. I think this was an added incentive to go back home and get the matching shoes. There are some interesting travel stories in the Bible. The Apostle Paul and his companions survived a huge storm and shipwreck (Acts 27). Paul had prayed for God's protection. Let me encourage you to be flexible and thankful when you travel. Ask God to protect you and your fellow passengers. And make sure to check your shoes before you leave the house.

173

Vantage Point

Recently my wife and I flew from Ontario, California to Phoenix, Arizona. It was late in the afternoon and we had a clear view of the ground beneath us as we took off. The airplane banked to the left to turn east and then leveled off as we gained altitude. I was sitting in the window seat and saw something that brought a smile to my face.

Twenty years ago a couple from E Free Church in Diamond Bar moved to a new community called Corona Valley. Hundreds of homes were being built on land that had been used to raise dairy cattle. Greg and Carol Crawford sold their home in Diamond Bar and purchased a home in this new development. This area became known as Eastvale.

One day Carol called me and asked if I would help them start a Bible study in their new home. I was glad to help. The first gathering was in early 2003. Greg and Carol invited neighbors on their street and other people they knew in the area. About 10-15 people came the first night. Soon there was a sense we should do more than have a weekly Bible study. We should start a new church in this growing community.

Leaders at the Evangelical Free Church in Diamond Bar adopted the proposal. We prayed for three things – a leader, a location for the church to meet and land for a future church site. Two men on the Diamond Bar staff offered to lead the new church. Mark Lee and Tom Lanning were able to find a Middle School in Eastvale to start Sunday services in 2007. The Diamond Bar church started a three year fund raising campaign and eventually raised $650,000 to help buy land for a church site.

Weekly church services began in February 2008 with 200 people attending. The church continued to grow and moved services to Roosevelt High School. They were able to purchase ten acres of land and construct their first building on Archibald Road. Today there are almost 2,500 people attending Sunday services. We are very thankful for what God has done at Vantage Point Church in Eastvale, California.

Let me encourage you to look out the window of your plane if you fly out of Ontario airport. Watch for a parcel of land along the Santa Ana River on Archibald Road with a 600 seat church and a big parking lot. It is Vantage Point Church. It is a remarkable reminder of a small Bible study that grew into a mega church. It will bring a smile to your face.

Expensive Car Repairs

Cars can be expensive to maintain and repair. We own a total of four cars right now and we only have two drivers. However most of the cars are older and there is some peace of mind when you have a backup in case one dies or is not reparable.

The newest car I drive is a 2012 Toyota Camry. It already has over 100,000 miles on it. The 2006 Toyota Highlander has 180,000 miles and my 2004 Camry has 170,000 miles. My wife's car is a 2017 Hyundai Tucson. It has about 40,000 miles on it. You can see we tend to keep our cars a long time.

There are some advantages to owning older cars. All of them are paid off. We have no car payments. All of these cars have good driving records and have a reputation for lasting a long time. However, repairs and maintenance can be expensive. I spent $1200 at my local repair shop recently to replace the valve cover gasket and for a major tune up. I must admit the car is running well and the engine is clean and looks like new.

One time things didn't look so good. My car was driving erratically. It felt like there wasn't much power when I pulled away from a traffic light. I suspected it was the transmission. I expected it would be expensive. My trusted car mechanic and his assistant raised the car on a lift and looked under the engine and transmission. They didn't see any leaks. The mechanic suggested flushing out the old transmission fluid and putting in new fluid. He was surprised this resolved the problem. It ran like new and accelerated like it should. Who would have thought changing the fluid could make such a difference?

The cost of the repair was far less than having to fix or replace the transmission. The mechanic was glad it solved the problem and I was thrilled by how much less expensive it was than I had expected. Sometimes the solution to the problem may be easier than you think.

There is a verse in the Bible that says, "Don't worry about tomorrow. God knows what you need even before you ask" (Matthew 6:25-34). Let me encourage you to trust God when you face problems and uncertainty. Ask for His help and watch how He works. You will be glad you did. And don't forget to change the fluid in your car's transmission.

June 19
A Man With A Gun

Some friends shared this remarkable story about an incident they were involved in several years ago. Margaret and her adult daughter Cathy lived together in a condo in Scottsdale, Arizona. One night Margaret was awakened by frantic pounding on her backyard patio door. A neighbor was pounding on her sliding door demanding she let him into her condo. It was the middle of the night. She yelled at the man and told him to go away and leave them alone. But the neighbor was relentless. He said some people were after him and trying to kill him. They learned later the man was high on drugs and hallucinating. He had a high powered gun in his hand.

Cathy quickly got her mother out of the room. They hid behind a bed in Cathy's room and called 911. By that time the man with the gun had broken into the condo and was actually firing his gun at the imaginary pursuers. The police later confirmed the man had fired more than 50 rounds inside their condo. Thankfully the neighbor went out the front door and walked down the street fleeing for his life. The police arrived and were able to arrest the man before he could hurt anyone or himself. It was a terrifying experience for both mother and daughter.

As Margaret and Cathy reflected on those unbelievable minutes with a man with a gun in their house they expressed their thanks to God for His protection and for saving their lives. Both of them could have been killed by this confused neighbor. Cathy said she had an unusual calm trying to protect her mother and talking on the phone with the 911 operator. She believed God watched over them amidst the chaos.

After the police arrested the man, they came through the front door to search the condo and see if Margaret and Cathy were alive. The SWAT team members looked frightening with their helmets and special protective gear. The police were concerned there might be other armed people hiding in the condo. When they knew it was safe they escorted Margaret and Cathy outside.

There is a verse in the Bible which says, "Even when I walk through the valley of the shadow of death I will not fear for you are with me" (Psalm 23:4). Let me encourage you to thank God for His protection as you go about your daily life. And say thanks to those who serve in law enforcement and public safety who risk their lives to protect you. They will be glad you did and you will too.

A Badge of Honor

There is a scene in the World War Two series *"Band of Brothers"* where an older soldier confronts a new replacement because of a small badge. The older man had parachuted into Normandy, France with the 101st Airborne Division on June 6, 1944. The younger soldier joined the division months later.

The small pin was a Unit Citation recognizing the critical role the 101st Airborne Division had played on D-day. The older veteran told the younger man he had not earned the badge because he was not part of the Normandy invasion. The younger replacement took off the pin.

When we see men and women wearing these small medals and pins on their uniform we don't really understand how significant and important they are. But those who earned them and wore them did.

We have a small pin which belonged to my grandmother. It was called a military service pin. Mothers and fathers who had a son or daughter in the war were welcome to wear these small blue pins. It was one way to honor their family member who was serving in the military.

We also have my Grandfather Gail Halliday's Dog Tag. Everyone in the military was required to wear a Dog Tag under their uniform on a chain around their neck when they went into combat. It would help people identify them if they were killed in battle. It was a sobering reminder of the danger and risk of serving in the military.

It was not uncommon to see older men in Russia wearing their military pins and medals they had earned during World War Two. These old veterans were proud of their service and sacrifice to save their country when it was invaded by Germany. I sensed younger generations were not impressed and did not fully appreciate the service and sacrifice of the older generation.

Let me encourage you to ask your parents and grandparents about their military experience during wars like Korea, Viet Nam, Iraq and Afghanistan. Express your thanks to them for their service. They will be glad you did and you will too.

Why this Movie

Years ago when our children were young my wife and I visited her parents in Albuquerque, New Mexico. One of the things Jeanne liked to do was have lunch and go shopping with her mother. They loved to wander through stores and find things for themselves and for our kids. They really enjoyed shopping and lunch *without* the children.

I offered to take our four kids to a movie. I noticed in the newspaper the Disney movie *Dumbo* was playing at a nearby movie theater. This seemed like a good way to keep the kids entertained so my wife and her mother could shop and enjoy lunch.

However, when we arrived at the movie theater I noticed the name of another film on the marquee. It was titled, *Raiders of the Lost Ark*. I had not seen the movie but I had heard a number of people say they really enjoyed it. So I asked my kids which movie they wanted to see. Did they want to see *Dumbo* or *Raiders of the Lost Ark*? I knew they had seen *Dumbo* before and I knew none of us had seen the Indiana Jones' movie. I am not sure which movie they voted for but I made an executive decision to watch *Raiders of the Lost Ark*.

After we bought our tickets and got some popcorn we settled into our seats ready to see this new movie. I don't know if you remember the opening scene when Indiana Jones carefully enters a cave searching for an ancient gold treasure. As he cautiously probed through cobwebs a number of large tarantellas crawled on Indiana Jones' back. It was a scary scene.

Right at that moment I heard my young daughter ask, "*Daddy – why did you bring us to this movie*?" I still smile when I recall that moment. I tried to reassure Trisha it would be okay. The movie would get better. Actually it had a lot more scary scenes but we stayed until the end.

I suppose *Raiders of the Lost Ark* was not the best choice for a young audience. There is a verse in the Bible which says, "Fathers do not exasperate your children or they may become discouraged" (Colossians 3:21). I really enjoyed the movie and I can still her the timid voice of my young daughter in that dark movie theater. Let me encourage you to make some memories with your children. And make sure to select some age appropriate forms of entertainment. You will be glad you did and hopefully they will too! ***Happy Father's Day***!

June 22
Sheet Metal

Our church sent teams to New Orleans for almost ten years to help with rebuilding the city after Hurricane Katrina. We usually sent a team of young adults over the Christmas holidays and another team of teens and adults during the hot summer months. The teams worked in a low income area known as the *Lower Ninth Ward*. We painted the outside of homes, repaired roofs and replaced damaged floors inside homes. One time we sent a small team to work on a special project creating an internet center where students and adults could access the web if they did not have the internet in their home.

We always reminded our teams we were there not only to repair damaged buildings but to also encourage discouraged residents. Often people in the community would come by and ask where we were from and what we were doing. We always stopped our work so we could talk with them and listen to their stories.

There is a book in the Bible which records the efforts of Nehemiah and the people of Israel to rebuild the walls of Jerusalem. They worked side by side with the local residents to restore the city and encourage the people (Nehemiah Chapters 1-6). At the end of one trip we decided to do a free BBQ to encourage the adults and kids in the neighborhood. One of the men on our team knew how to build a temporary BBQ grill using concrete blocks, sheet metal and a wire grill top.

However, when we were ready to dismantle the grill I cut my leg on a corner of the sheet metal. I didn't see the corner sticking out and got a deep cut on my leg. It started to bleed heavily. Our team leader wanted to rush me to an emergency room but Jim pulled out a first aid kit. He sat me down and opened the wound in my leg. It was a deep cut. He washed it with a bottle of water and poured in an antiseptic. Then he poured in a dark powder that looked like saw dust. It was called *Wound Stop*. Then he put a warp around my leg and the bleeding stopped.

I went to my urgent care center when we got back to LA. They examined my leg and left the bandages on it. They gave me a tetanus shot and a prescription for an antibiotic. I'm thankful my leg healed up without complications. It was an unexpected adventure at the end of our week in New Orleans. Let me encourage you to volunteer to help others in need. Take time to listen to their stories and be willing to lend a hand to help them rebuild their homes and their lives.

179

June 23
Still on the Shelf

Recently my wife Susan and I attended a Sunday service at the church my parents attended when my brother and I were in high school. We started coming to Scottsdale Bible Church in the 1960's when the church met in a rented facility on Scottsdale Road. Later the church purchased land and constructed their first building on McDonald Drive. In the 1970's they moved to a larger site and built a beautiful new campus on Shea Blvd in north Scottsdale. The new facility includes a book and gift store and coffee shop.

I was thankful the church was willing to put my first book "*Let Me Encourage You*" on the shelf in the book store. When I completed my second book, "*Let Me Encourage You More*" they were willing to put a few copies of my newest book on the shelf too.

After the Sunday church service Susan and I walked over to the Book Store to see if there were any copies of my two books left on the shelf. I was sure they had become best sellers and thought the manager would need additional copies. It took us a while to locate my books. They were on the very bottom shelf. They looked kind of lonely. I was sad to discover no copies had been sold over the past few months. The number of books with my name had not changed.

It is humbling to realize my books were not flying off the shelves. Maybe this was because they were on the bottom shelf. I have heard businesses fight to get their product on the eye level shelves at a grocery store to increase sales. Maybe sales are slow because of the book covers. The first one has an images of two stick figures. The second book has a picture of my smiling face. Maybe I need to hire an experienced artist to improve the covers of my two books. Maybe I need to hire a publisher and an agent to promote my books.

On the other hand I was glad to know some books were still there. I could easily direct people to the SBC bookstore if they needed a copy of either book. I am thankful the bookstore manager allows me to have my books on display along with some well-known Christian authors. The Apostle Paul instructed his disciple Timothy to bring the books and parchments Paul used for reading and study (Second Timothy 4:13). Let me encourage you to make a habit of reading books written by respected Christian leaders. You will be glad you did and they will too.

June 24
The Lost Wallet

The annual back pack trip to Havasu Canyon began when I was in high school. A small group of teens from Scottsdale Bible Church went with Pastor Jim Borror and a few other adults to hike into Havasu Canyon. It was a long hot *drive* from Scottsdale to the rim of the Grand Canyon and a long *hike* from the rim to the bottom where we camped near the towering Havasu Falls. The last trip from Scottsdale was when I graduated from college and married Jeanne in June, 1971.

We renewed the annual trip to Havasu Canyon when I became the pastor of Chapel in the Hills Church in 1975. I led a group of five high school guys with another adult on our first trip from Tucson. However we adopted a new strategy. We usually left Scottsdale early in the morning and got to the rim at the hottest part of the day. But from Tucson we decided to drive through the night and start our hike in the coolest part of the day. Every trip had some memorable moments.

We typically stopped in Phoenix as we drove north during the night to get some snacks, stretch our legs and use the restroom. I remember one year when I was having some tummy problems. I needed to use the bathroom several times before we got back on the road. When we got back in the cars I realized I didn't have my wallet. It must have fallen out of my pocket while I was in the restroom. We frantically looked for it but no luck. Maybe a stranger had found it and taken it.

We left my contact information with the employee on duty and asked him to call me if my wallet showed up. We continued our drive north and arrived at the rim of the Grand Canyon at sunrise. After the long drive and the long hike we enjoyed several days swimming under the beautiful waterfalls. One day some of us hiked the extra eight miles along the Havasu Creek down to the ragging Colorado River.

During our trip one of our campers quietly told me a guest in our group had my wallet. I confronted the student and he acknowledged he found my wallet in the restroom. The money was gone but at least I got my driver's license and credit cards back. There is a similar story in the Bible where King Saul went into a cave to go to the bathroom and David stole a piece of the King's robe. David confessed his sin too (Frist Samuel 24). If you find someone's wallet or money, let me encourage you to return it to the owner. And if you stop to use the restroom hold on tight to your wallet or purse. You will be glad you did!

Gate Change

The number of people traveling by airplane has skyrocketed since the end of the Covid19 Pandemic. Airports are bursting with passengers and airlines are struggling to keep up. One of the problems facing the airlines is a shortage of personnel. There are not enough pilots, flight attendants and ground crews to keep the planes in the air.

One of the things which often happens are gate changes. The airline usually includes the number of your departure gate on your boarding pass or e-ticket. This helps passengers navigate through the endless number of terminals and gates at the airport.

But sometimes airlines change the departure gates at the last minute. Passengers may not be aware of the change and are at risk of missing their flight. This happened to us recently. Friends dropped us off at the Phoenix airport in plenty of time for our flight to Ontario. We moved through security quickly and found the gate number printed on our boarding pass. We were over an hour early. There wasn't the usual crush of passengers in the waiting area. It was a nice time to relax before boarding our plane.

However I noticed the sign over the gate door read *San Diego*. I thought this was referring to the flight which had just departed. I looked at the gate number on our ticket to confirm we were in fact at the correct gate. But there was only a small number of people sitting in the waiting area. Finally I went to the airline desk and asked about our flight to Ontario. The employee told me the departure gate for our flight had changed and we needed to go to another terminal. Thankfully we still had plenty of time. We walked for about 10 minutes to the new gate and there was a crowd of passengers waiting to go to Ontario.

Things worked out fine but I did manage to leave a treasured water bottle at the old gate. In our hurry to get to the new terminal I think I left the ice cold brown metal bottle at the old gate. I felt like Tom Hanks in the movie *Castaway* where he lost his volleyball friend named *Wilson*. There is a verse in the Bible which says, "Trust in the Lord with all of your heart and don't rely on your own understanding. In all your ways acknowledge God and He will direct your paths" (Proverbs 3:5-6). Let me encourage you to double-check your departure gate when you get to the airport. And keep an eye out for my water bottle if you are in the Phoenix airport. I will be glad you did and the airline will too.

Three Reasons

There is a story I have heard more than once. It is about a pastor in California who was asked to become the new pastor of a large church in Arizona. After considering the invitation for a few moments he replied, "I think there are *three reasons* why God does not want me to move to Arizona – *June, July and August!*" Most people smile or laugh when they hear this story. But it is true the weather can get very hot and uncomfortable during those long summer months.

I know this from personal experience. My parents moved our family from Denver, Colorado to Phoenix, Arizona in 1956. I grew up there and went to grade school, high school and college there. Summers could be extremely hot. We did not have air conditioning in our home. We only had what was called a *swamp cooler* or an evaporative cooler on the roof of our house. It was a large square box with each side lined with straw. Drips of water made the straw pads wet. The large fan pulled outside air over the wet mats and into the ducts that carried the cool air throughout the house.

This was an old system developed before air conditioning and it worked pretty well in the dry desert weather. But it was not very effective when the humidity rose during the summer monsoon season in July and August. Evaporative coolers only worked well in hot dry weather.

When my wife and I purchased our first home in Tucson it only had a swamp cooler. Every spring I had to climb up on the roof and remove the straw pads. Then I had to scrape off the rust that had developed on the metal frame over the past year. In addition I had to purchase new straw pads to replace the old ones. I usually coated the reservoir at the bottom of the swap cooler with tar to prevent leaks and extend the life of the evaporative cooler. I did not enjoy servicing the swamp cooler each year. It was dirty, messy and sticky.

Over time air conditioning became more affordable and preferable to the old fashioned swamp cooler. Most new homes have modern air conditioners although I have seen a few homes with both. I was thankful the home we bought in California had air conditioning. Let me encourage you to enjoy the comforts of your home. Even when the high electric bill arrives in the middle of summer be grateful not grumpy you have air conditioning. You will be glad you did!

June 27
Just Trying to Help

My wife's parents moved to Arizona in 1959. They bought a nice home in Scottsdale and lived there until most of the kids were grown and out of the house. Later they sold that house and moved to Moon Valley on the north side of Phoenix closer to where my father-in-law worked. The new house was on the Moon Valley Golf Course. In the 1980's they moved to Albuquerque, New Mexico, where he became the manager of a new manufacturing facility for the Sperry Corporation.

When Walt was ready to retire they moved back to Scottsdale. They purchased a nice home with a swimming pool in the McCormick Ranch community. Their final move came in the 1990's when my wife's parents moved to a condo nearby. Unfortunately they moved in the month of August.

All of the family pitched in to help them move from their house to the condo. It was not easy for my in-laws to move from a larger home to a smaller condo. My mother-in-law was frustrated with less closets and smaller storage space. My father-in-law wasn't enthusiastic about moving all of the stuff in the garage including his garden tools and my mother-in-law's Christmas decorations.

I was assigned to the garage. It was at least 110 degrees on moving day and even hotter in the garage with no air conditioning. It was very hot. I think I lost at least five pounds in that steam bath. But I was glad to help. I organized and put things in boxes and carefully labeled things so my father-in-law could find them later. I felt I had made a significant contribution to the family moving event. However, in the coming months and years my father-in-law never stopped complaining because he couldn't find many of the things I had packed and moved from one garage to the other. Even though I had organized and labeled everything he still couldn't find things he was looking for.

Jesus told a parable about a woman who had lost a valuable coin. She searched her house until she finally found it and celebrated her success (Luke 15:8-10). I'm sure my father-in-law was happy to find some of the things I had moved for him too. Let me encourage you to be ready to help a friend, neighbor or family member who is moving. It can be a frustrating and stressful time in anyone's life. They will be grateful for your help. And make sure you label everything carefully. They will be glad you did and you will too.

184

Men in Church

We sent several short-term summer teams to Romania over the years while I served at the Evangelical Free Church of Diamond Bar. A wonderful couple from our church had started a partnership with several churches in Romania and Ukraine. We were glad to serve with Dave and Lisa at summer camps for kids and retreats for married couples. We enjoyed attending church services too. Churches and Christians in both of these countries endured persecution for their faith for 70 years under communism.

I will never forget a statement one pastor made about the health and future of churches in Romania. He said, "The churches are full of women and children. The prisons are full of men". I was stunned and saddened by his assessment of the culture in his country.

I wonder how pastors and sociologists would describe our country today. We certainly have far too many people in our prisons. The daily news reflects growing crime and lawlessness. People feel unsafe riding public trains and buses. The homeless crisis continues with no solutions in sight.

As I look out over the number of people who attend our church services I am very thankful to see a growing number of men. It is great to see husbands and fathers with their wife and children in the worship service. I'm glad when I see men talking with other men and their wives on the patio after church. It is fun to see young children and teens connecting with friends and family members too.

Whenever I have the opportunity I like to seek out some of the young dads and husbands and thank them for coming to church with their wife and children. *I tell them they are my heroes.* I am grateful when men come to church. It encourages their wife and it sets an example for their children. I tell the dads – don't send your children to church – bring them to church with you. Lead by example.

The Apostle Paul reminded fathers to encourage, comfort and challenge their children just as Paul had encouraged them (First Thessalonians 2:11-12). Let me encourage you to be an example your wife and children can follow. Take them to church this Sunday. Be a hero they can look up to. They will be glad you did and you will too.

How Do You Know When to Say No?

There were several times in my career when churches selected the other finalist for their church. A church in Clovis, New Mexico decided they wanted another candidate to be their pastor instead of me. A large church in Arizona hired the other guy instead of me to fill an important staff position. Those were discouraging moments in my life. Why did they hire the other guy and not me?

On the other hand there were several times during my career when I said "no" to some ministry opportunities. A church in Imperial, California asked my wife and me to come and serve as their associate pastor. These were wonderful people who had encouraged us in many different ways when I served as a summer intern at their church. It was difficult to decline their invitation.

There was a church in north Phoenix that I was asked to consider. It was not a formal job offer but a member of their church came to see me in Tucson to ask if I would be interested in applying to be their lead pastor. We had only been in Tucson a short time and it just didn't feel like the right time to leave.

The large church which did not hire me for one position actually offered me a different position on their staff. The senior pastor and two elders flew to Tucson and met with Jeanne and me at the airport. They were looking for someone to launch a new ministry to reach single adults in the community. Jeanne and I did not feel it was a good fit even though it was an opportunity to serve in a larger church as an associate pastor.

How do you know when to say – "No"? How do you know when to stay and when to go? There were several times in King David's life when he faced a similar decision. He prayed and asked God to guide him (First Samuel 23:1-6). I recommend you take a lot of time to pray. Ask God to guide you as you consider an opportunity or invitation.

In addition talk with your spouse. Don't make an impulsive decision. Discuss it with your husband or wife. Talk about the pro's and con's of accepting a job offer and relocating your family. How will this impact your marriage and your children? *When in doubt – don't.* If God closes the door stay where you are. Be patient. Don't be in a hurry when you make a life changing decision. You will be glad you did and your family will too.

June 30
Too Much Stuff

When we walk through our neighborhood early in the morning or later in the evening we notice different things. We see front yards that are trimmed and well kept. We also see lawns which are brown from lack of water and shrubs and plants which are overgrown.

In addition we have been surprised by the number of new cars we see parked on the streets and in driveways. Many neighbors have joined the electric generation with new Tesla cars. Several have two Tesla's in front of their house.

Sometimes we get to peak into garages that are full of stuff. Some are neatly organized with shelves and plastic storage containers while others have boxes piled high and bicycles and extra furniture leaning against each other. Some people may be renting a house or condo and use the garage to store their extra things instead of renting an expensive storage unit. Other people may be the homeowner but can't fit all of their stuff into their house. The garage is full and the cars sit in the driveway or on the street.

As we observed the yards, homes and garages in our neighborhood we wondered what our neighbors notice about our yard and our garage when they walked by our house. Does our lawn look trim? Do we park our cars in the garage or on the driveway? Do we own a Tesla?

Susan and I realized our garage was filled with stuff too. When we got married we worked very hard to combine two households into one house. It wasn't easy. We had two washers and dryers. We had two refrigerators and several TV's. We had a lot of bedroom and living room furniture. We had two sets of dishes, tableware, pots and pans.

There is a parable in the Bible where Jesus addressed the subject of wealth and possessions. When a farmer had no more room to store his crops he decided to tear down his barns and build bigger ones. He kept what he had and did not consider sharing his abundance with others (Luke 12:13-21). But the farmer died leaving his wealth behind. It is a reminder *life is not about keeping what we have but sharing what we have with others.* Let me encourage you to make time *this month* to clean out your garage and give away some stuff to a local thrift store or shelter. You will be glad you did and they will too.

187

A Cool Spot in the Summer Heat

My wife and I both grew up in Arizona. Fall, winter and spring were pleasant but June, July and August were very hot. A recent trip to Phoenix reminded me just how hot it can be in the Arizona desert. The high temperatures were from 115 – 119 degrees during the week we stayed in Scottsdale. And the lowest temperatures did not get below 90 degrees at night. We forgot just how intense the heat could be.

However, I do remember driving my '57 Chevy when I was in high school and there were some cooler places in the Valley of the Sun. My car did not have air conditioning so I usually drove with the windows down. I noticed there were some places which were noticeably cooler.

Jeanne and I lived on the same street but 2-3 miles apart. She lived on San Miguel near Kiva Elementary School and I lived further east at 8649 E. San Miguel near Mohave Elementary School. McDonald Drive was the main road connecting our two neighborhoods.

After dropping Jeanne off at her home after a date, I drove back to my house. As I drove east on McDonald Drive I crossed Scottsdale Road and then went over a two lane bridge crossing one of the irrigation canals which brought water into Phoenix. Just passed the canal the road dropped a little and cut through a large cotton field. It was always cooler as I drove over the canal and down through the cotton field.

I am not sure why it was cooler. It may be the field of cotton absorbed some of the heat in the air. I know plants soak up carbon dioxide and produce oxygen. Maybe this had a cooling effect on the temperature. Or the cooling effect may have been the result of farmers flooding the fields with irrigation water. It may have had the same cooling effect you feel when you walk by a home with the water sprinklers running.

Another place where it seemed cooler on a hot summer night was driving along Lafayette Boulevard where there were many citrus groves. They also used irrigation in those days so it may have been the same effect as driving through the cotton field. The Bible says God created the heavens and the earth (Genesis Chapter One). He wrapped it with an atmosphere where we can breathe and live. The earth spins as it orbits the sun creating the climate we enjoy – both hot and cold. Let me encourage you to give thanks to God for this amazing planet we live on and maybe wait until winter to visit Arizona!

Gardening

My wife and I enjoy working on the various plants in our yard. Susan likes to plant new flowers and decorative plants in our front court yard and in the back yard. My assignment is to make sure water pipes and drips get to all of the flower beds in our yard. It was a big project but it has been encouraging to have water distributed to all of the lawn areas and planters around the house.

Some of the newest additions are some new flowers and two new Avocado trees. The flowers look great but I suspect it will take several years before we see any avocados on our little trees.

There are two sides to gardening. One is the work of planting, watering and feeding the new flowers and shrubs. In addition there is the constant struggle to discourage bugs and insects who want to devour the plants in our yard.

The other side is the enjoyment of seeing beautiful flowers and healthy plants decorating the outside of our home. The variety of colors and the lush green leaves provide a pleasant relaxing atmosphere for us and our guests.

There is a passage in the Bible which describes the Garden of Eden (Genesis Chapter Two & Three). This idyllic setting was intended to be the home God created for Adam and Eve. But after Adam's and Eve's disobedience to Gods' command they were cast out of the Garden. One passage describes the consequences, "Getting food from the ground will be as painful for you as having babies is for your wife. The ground will sprout weeds and thorns. You will get food the hard way planting, tilling and harvesting, sweating in the fields from dawn to dusk" (Genesis 3:17-19 - in the Message Bible).

Gardening is hard work. I have sweat more in the past few days than I have in a long time. Digging up the soil and spreading fertilizer is not easy. Bags of fresh soil are heavy. My arms and back are sore after planting new flowers and vegetables. However the result is both encouraging and rewarding.

Let me encourage you to get off the couch and out of the house and do some gardening this summer. Endure the sweat and sore muscles and enjoy the work of your hands. You will be glad you did!

Celebrate our Heritage

The Fourth of July marks the middle of summer. Kids have enjoyed vacation from school and a lot of summer time activities. Swimming pools are good places to spend some of the hot summer days. I like the Fourth of July.

But it is more than a mid-summer holiday. It is a day to celebrate the founding of our country when the Declaration of Independence was read in public in the streets of Philadelphia on July 4, 1776. It was a bold step for the thirteen colonies to declare their independence from England which was the most powerful nation in the world at that time.

My family visited Independence Hall in Philadelphia many years ago. This was the meeting place where representatives from the thirteen colonies met to draft the Declaration of Independence. The site has been preserved for new generations to visit and understand the importance of this unique event.

Philadelphia was a hot and humid place in the 1700's. No air conditioning in those days. Most residents left the city to avoid the unpleasant weather. But the representatives of the colonies worked tirelessly to create a document which would announce to the world a new nation was born.

The men who signed the document were risking their own lives and fortunes. If they were caught by the British they would have been hanged for treason against the King of England. This was not simply an academic or philosophical exercise. This was serious business. It meant life or death to those who signed their names on the document.

If you read a copy of the declaration you will notice one name stands out above all of the others. It is *John Hancock*. Tradition says he signed his name with large letters so the King of England could read it without his glasses. Another name that caught my attention is Roger Sherman. My ancestors came from a line of Sherman's. My name is Mark Sherman Hopper. I wonder if I am related to the Sherman who signed the Declaration of Independence on July 4th, 1776. Let me encourage you to explain to your children why we celebrate the Fourth of July. They will be glad you did and you will too.

Understanding our History

In recent years there has been a trend to rewrite our nation's story. Authors and academics want to paint a different picture of what our nation was like at the time of its conception over 200 years ago. I'm sure our nation was not perfect then and it is still not perfect today. But let me encourage you to provide a balanced and accurate account of our country's birth to your children and grandchildren.

Books like David McCullough's *1776* and *John Adams* provide a clear and balanced record of the American Revolution. Both books offer helpful information on the life and times in the American Colonies during that pivotal period. Other authors include Ron Chernow's *Alexander Hamilton* and *Washington the Life*. HW Brands' books *Our First Civil War – Patriots and Loyalists in the American Revolution* and *First American – the Life and Times of Benjamin Franklin* are helpful.

I did not realize how much of the American Revolution began in New England before the Declaration of Independence was adopted. The famous Boston Tea Party and the early battles of Lexington and Concord occurred a year before our Independence was declared on July 4, 1776. The famous battle of Bunker Hill and the ride of Paul Revere were also a year before. General Knox's capture of Fort Ticonderoga and hauling the heavy canon from upstate New York to Boston helped drive the British fleet out of the city. This also occurred before the Declaration of Independence was adopted in 1776.

These were significant moments in our nation's birth. I wonder if your children or grandchildren have ever studied some of these important events in their classrooms at school. We take for granted the suffering and sacrifice of those early colonials who banded together to gain independence from England.

There is an interesting passage in the Bible which reveals how many of the Israelites had forgotten how God had given them freedom from slavery in Egypt (Read Exodus Chapters 1-20). God used Moses and many miracles to lead the Israelites from Egypt to the Promise Land. But younger generations had not seen the amazing things God had done for their people (Judges 6:13). Let me encourage you to read a book or watch a video with your children and grandchildren so they will know and understand what the 4th of July and the birth of our nation is all about. They will be glad you did and you will too.

The Franklin Stove

I enjoyed listening to an audio book titled, *"Our First Civil War"* by H. W. Brand who was a history professor at the University of Texas in Austin. The focus of the book was the struggle between the Patriots who wanted independence from England and the Loyalists who wanted America to remain a British colony.

One of the main characters in the book was Benjamin Franklin. I knew about his life and the strategic role he played before, during and after the American Revolution supporting independence. What I did not know was his adult son sided with the British and strongly supported the loyalists.

I also learned Franklin was well known in Europe as well as in the United States. His efforts to understand electricity by flying kites in thunder storms was followed by many scientists. H.W. Brands said Franklin was the best known American of his time on both sides of the Atlantic Ocean.

He made a number of scientific discoveries and invented several things as well. One of those inventions was the *Franklin Stove*. This was different from most of the wood burning stoves of his day. It was made of cast iron and had a flat top for cooking. But it also had doors in the front which could be opened to allow more heat to warm a room.

We actually installed a *Franklin Stove* in the room addition in our house in Tucson. My father-in-law helped me drag the heavy cast iron stove from a truck into the new family room. It was very heavy. I laid some decorative concrete blocks on the cement floor and set the stove on top of them. We ran the chimney through the roof. This provided an ideal way to heat the room addition. We did not use it for cooking but we did enjoy many hours watching the wood burn when we opened the front cast iron doors. It warmed up the family room and provided a pleasant atmosphere on a cold winter night in the Arizona desert.

Benjamin Franklin was just one of many heroes who guided our country during America's Revolutionary War. There are also many heroes recorded in the Bible like Moses, Joshua, David and Solomon who played a strategic role in the history of the Israelites. Let me encourage you to teach your children about America's history and about the history in the Bible too. They will be glad you did.

Don't Forget Your Sweater

These four words were spoken by my mother any time of the year. My brother and I were born in Colorado. But our family moved to Arizona when we were in elementary school in the 1950's. The weather could be pretty cold in Colorado but not so much in the Arizona desert.

I don't remember when this thing with the sweater started. But I remember our mother reminding us to wear a sweater whenever we left the house. Do you remember the slogan the *American Express* Credit Card Company used years ago to promote their product? It was targeted at business travelers and emphasized the importance of having an American Express credit card in your wallet or purse. The tag line was, "*Don't leave home without it*".

That is exactly what our mother said to her two boys. Anytime we were leaving the house she would say, "*Don't forget you sweater*". It made sense when the weather was cold in the winter but it made no sense when the weather was hot in the summer.

It may have been her way of reminding us to be prepared for any unexpected circumstance we might encounter during the day. Remember the Boy Scouts and Girl Scouts had a motto "*Be Prepared*". I still hear people echo those words today. After all you never know what challenges you may face today. Always "*Be prepared*".

Or maybe it was just our mother's way of telling us she loved us. Maybe it was her way of saying "*I love you*" because she said it all of the time no matter what the weather was like. Maybe she wasn't focused on the weather but focused on our relationship.

The Apostle Paul used a familiar phrase in almost all of his letters. He wrote words like these, "Grace and peace to you from God our Father and the Lord Jesus Christ" (Galatians 1:3 / Ephesians 1:2 / Philippians 1:20). It was his way of expressing his love to them and reminding them of the common faith they shared as followers of Jesus.

I'm not sure what words you used when your kids headed out the door. Maybe you reminded them to "*be safe*" or "*call if you will be late*". You may want to add, "*Don't forget your sweater*". You will be glad you did and they will too.

Making Plans

There is a phrase which is often used in Bible. It was frequently written in letters and conversations. It was also used when people were saying goodbye. The phrase was, "*God willing*" or "*If it is God's will*". The Apostle James wrote, "If the Lord wills it, we shall live and do this or that" (James 4:15). When the Apostle Paul said goodbye to the Christians in Ephesus he said, "I will be back, God willing" (Acts 18:21). He wrote similar words to the Christians in Corinth, "I will come to you sooner than you think, God willing" (First Corinthians 4:19).

When we make plans or promises we need to be aware things may not happen the way we want or when we want. I think we saw this happen time and time again during the Covid19 pandemic. People made plans and reservations but when the pandemic began plans were altered and reservations were canceled.

On a much smaller scale we were on an airplane at LAX ready to take off for Paris when the pilot announced the ground crew had damaged the front landing gear and the flight was canceled. It was a mess. We had to be towed to another gate, collect our luggage and make new arrangements to get to Europe. One man shared he was supposed to be the best man at a friend's wedding. Now he would miss the wedding. Another couple said their cruise ship was departing from France the next day and now they would miss it.

Unexpected things happen all of the time. We set a date and make a plan but then something changes and the plans we made are altered or canceled. Everything from a dentist appointment to a Caribbean Cruise may be changed due to things that are out of our control.

There is a verse in the Bible which says, "Many are the plans of a man's heart but it is the Lord's will that prevails" (Proverbs 19:21). God sees the big picture. His plans for our lives may be bigger and different than we can imagine or understand. In another passage God says, "For I know the plans I have for you. Plans to prosper you and not to harm you. Plans to give you a hope and a future" (Jeremiah 29:11).

Don't misunderstand. It is important to make plans and dream dreams. Let me encourage you to not get stressed when plans you made are changed or altered. Be flexible and adaptable. *Trust in God and seek His will* regarding your life and your future. You will be glad you did.

Honor Your Predecessor (Part One)

I only served as the lead pastor in two churches during my 40 year career – 13 years in Arizona and 27 years in California. I am thankful for the men who preceded me in both of those congregations. I was building on the foundation they had laid. Much of my success was due to the labor and dedication of the men who came before me.

There were actually two men who prepared the way for me at Chapel in the Hills in Tucson, Arizona. The first was Gordon MacDonald. He was employed at Hughes Aircraft in Tucson but he was also a seminary graduate with a pastor's heart.

Gordon and his family started a new church in the garage of their home in a growing area of southwest Tucson in the 1960's. When they outgrew their garage they rented White Elementary School for Sunday services. Eventually they purchased property and built a church in the community. A few years later a layoff at Hughes Aircraft forced Gordon and his family to move to Dallas, Texas.

The second man who prepared the way for me to come to Chapel in the Hills was Gayle Bender. He served part-time as the interim pastor at the Chapel. He persuaded the church to set aside money to hire a younger full-time pastor to lead the church. They began a search to find a new pastor. Since Gordon MacDonald was living in Dallas he contacted Dallas Seminary and asked if they could recommend a new graduate to fill the need in Tucson. They gave him my name.

I still remember the hot summer day in Dallas when a stranger named Gordon MacDonald came to our apartment in June, 1975. I had graduated in May but had not found a church to pastor. I was mowing the yard in front of our duplex when Gordon drove up. We had a delightful conversation about the opportunity in Tucson. A few weeks later we visited the church and agreed to be their new pastor.

There is a passage in the Bible where the Apostle Paul wrote, "I laid the foundation and others built upon it" (First Corinthians 3:10). Let me encourage you to honor those who came before you. Acknowledge the work your predecessors did. Express your thanks to them and build wisely on the work they began. You will be glad you did and they will too.

Honor Your Predecessor (Part Two)

There were several men who preceded me at my second church in Diamond Bar, California. District Superintendent Wally Norling had recruited a few families to start a church in this new suburb about 30 miles east of downtown LA. Wally loved to start new churches. He saw the need and opportunity to impact this new growing community.

About 25 children and adults held the first church service in the home of Harry and Jean Anderson on Easter Sunday in 1967. This small beginning continued to grow over the next decade meeting in various locations in Diamond Bar including the YMCA, Evergreen Elementary School and in a building on the original Diamond Bar Ranch site.

Through the efforts of a local realtor named Rainer Key, God provided some land on Diamond Bar Boulevard near Brea Canyon Road. The first building was completed in 1983. Several pastors led the church over those years but my predecessor Steve Campbell was the pastor when they met at Evergreen Elementary and during the construction of the first church building.

I did not know Steve well but we did talk on several occasions. I admire his faithfulness and perseverance to get the church permanently established in the community. I am thankful for the work he did which prepared the way for my arrival. I became the next pastor in 1988.

Wally Norling provided timely encouragement and advice during my early years at the Evangelical Free Church of Diamond Bar. He was the man who had the vision to start the new church and he was glad to spend time with me and other EFCA pastors in the region. We met with Wally once-a-month for lunch, conversation and prayer. He made a lasting impact on young pastors like me in Southern California.

The Apostle Paul used the image of farming to illustrate how God used him and others to plant and grow churches across the Roman Empire. He wrote, "One plants and another waters but God causes it to grow" (First Corinthians 3:5-9). I am very thankful for the pastors and leaders who planted churches in Tucson and Diamond Bar. I am grateful to the pastors who preceded me. I am humbled to have played a small role in the life of two churches. Let me encourage you to honor those who came before you. Take time to thank them for their hard work and faithfulness. They will be glad you did and you will too.

Recycle

We needed additional classroom space for children, teens and adults when our church in Diamond Bar was growing in the 1990's. We had a limited amount of parking spaces and only six classrooms in the two story education building which was filled every Sunday.

Someone in our church heard a large aerospace company nearby in Fullerton was giving away modular mobile office spaces for one dollar. We contacted them and they were willing to donate four of these units to us. But there were some conditions. We had to pay to relocate these large structures, pay for the cleanup of the Fullerton site and pay for preparation of the new site on our property. It would be expensive.

After getting permission from the City of Diamond Bar we pressed ahead to move these commercial units to our church. Several men in our church worked hard to remodel these units into four large classrooms. No plumbing was involved but each unit had an air conditioner to cool and heat them. The crew also built ramps to make the structures handicap accessible. They turned out great.

We estimate the total cost was about $50,000 but they were worth every cent. The mobile buildings doubled the amount of classroom space on our site. They were a timely solution to our pressing need.

During the next few years we were able to construct a new building on our property which included a new worship center on ground level and eight classrooms beneath the auditorium. We were able to remove the mobile units and expand our parking lot.

But what could we do with the mobile classrooms? We learned of a growing Chinese church in a neighboring community which needed more classroom space. We were able to donate the units to them just like the aerospace company did for us. In other our words we *recycled* these large classrooms by giving them to another church.

There is a verse in the Bible which says, "Good will come to those who are generous and lend freely" (Psalm 112:5). We were glad to share with others just as others had shared with us. Let me encourage you to be generous and willing to give just as God has given to you. They will be glad you did and you will too.

197

What is Your Name?

I have mentioned in other stories about our routine of walking every day. My wife Susan and I usually walked early in the morning while the temperatures were cooler in Southern California. But sometimes we got more ambitious and walked at the end of the day too.

We saw a few people walking in the morning but we saw a lot more neighbors walking in the evening especially in the long summer days. It was fun to stop and chat for a few minutes to catch up on their life. But one of the problems was remembering their names.

We had a nice blend of different cultures in our community. People from Taiwan, Macau, Korea, India and the Philippines lived in our neighborhood. Some of them had names which were unfamiliar to us. So we actually began to write down their names on our cell phones so we could quickly access our notes when we saw them again.

Another thing which helped us remember names was using word pictures or associations. We tried to use an image in our minds something that would help us remember. One Chinese woman's name was *Iris* so we thought of a flower to remember her name. One man's first name was *Inder.* He was from India. So when we saw him we used the association of India to remember our neighbor *Inder.*

Sometimes people talked about a recent vacation or adventure. Other people shared concerns about health and family matters. We enjoyed learning more about them and their children and grandchildren. These short conversations reminded us to pray for our neighbors.

I wonder how well you know the neighbors in your community or the people who live on your street. It is more difficult to connect in the winter months when the days are short and most people stay inside. But an early morning walk or a stroll on a long summer evening can provide abundant opportunities to get to know more of the people who live around you.

There is a passage in the Bible which says, *"Love your neighbors"* (Luke 10:25-38). Let me encourage you to get out and go for a walk *this week.* Say hello to some of the people you see on your walk. Stop and chat for a few minutes. Get to know their names. Pray for them as you walk. You will be glad you did and they will too.

Timothy

Phil and Sue came to our church in Diamond Bar when their children were in high school. A school friend invited their son to come to the youth program at our church. So Phil and Sue thought they should go and see what this church was all about.

Gradually they became regular attenders on Sunday morning and got involved in an adult Bible class. After Phil came to a personal faith in Christ he agreed to meet with me once-a-week to study the Bible and encourage one another. We met at a noisy coffee shop for several years and eventually invited some other men to join us.

Phil's wife was a nurse at a local hospital. Her job was to coach new mothers. She helped young mothers including some of my daughters who lived overseas. Phil had a successful career managing a large distribution center in Southern California for the Nestles Corporation. He was a servant leader who cared about his employees. He was effective managing the facility and shepherding the staff.

Phil and Sue also served on a short-term mission team with my wife and me in Romania. We enjoyed teaching a wonderful group of young couples at a marriage retreat. Phil also went with us to India. He and his wife also experienced the death of their daughter. Later they graciously helped other parents who experienced a similar loss in their own family. Phil was one of the men who helped encourage me during my wife's cancer journey.

Phil served on our leadership team at the church in Diamond Bar. He and his wife also made coffee every Sunday for the adult classes meeting on the church campus. They also served as mentors to younger men and women in our College-Career ministry. Phil coached young adults on how to prepare their job resume and how to successfully do a job interview.

There was a man in the Bible who faithfully served with the Apostle Paul named Timothy. He shared many adventures with Paul and learned how to teach the Bible and how tell others about Jesus. Phil reminds me of Timothy. Paul wrote, "Timothy is loyal and genuinely concerned for people. Most people look out for themselves but Timothy is the real deal" (Philippians 2:19-23 - The Message Bible). Let me encourage you to thank a loyal friend in your life *this week*.

A Walk in the Park

There is park in Orange County that has become a special place in my life. It is called *Tri-City Park* and is located near the cities of Brea, Yorba Linda and Placentia, California. It has a small lake and is surrounded by shady trees, grass covered hills and several winding walking trails. There are also a number of large sports fields which are used for baseball, softball and soccer games.

The park provides a peaceful setting for both recreation and relaxation. A number of small benches surround the lake and provide an idyllic setting for older adults to sit, read and relax. Small children enjoy the climbing equipment in the padded play yard as parents and grand-parents keep watch.

Tri-City Park became a memorable setting for me to get to know the woman who would become my future wife. We often spent time there to walk around the lake and sit and talk on one of the park benches. Our conversations included many topics including our faith and families. We talked about our children and grandchildren. We shared the sadness of losing our spouses to cancer and a stroke. We talked about our dreams for the future. We also enjoyed watching the Canadian Geese return to the lake at the end of each day. We loved to admire these large birds as they flew in from different directions to land on the glassy surface of the lake as the day faded into darkness.

There is a much larger lake mentioned many times in the New Testament. It is often referred to as the Sea of Galilee. It is located in northern Israel and was the place where Jesus taught many lessons to the crowds who followed him. He did many miracles on and around the lake where he calmed a violent storm (Mark 4:35-41) and helped his disciples catch a boatload of fish (Luke 5:1-11). The disciples returned to the Sea of Galilee and saw Jesus alive after his crucifixion in Jerusalem (John 21:1-14). That lake provided many memorable moments for Jesus and his followers.

Is there a peaceful place in your life where you have made or continue to make some special memories? It may be a cabin in the mountains or a favorite beach. It may be a local park or even your own backyard. Let me encourage you to find a place where you and your friends and family can make some memories together. You will be glad you did and they will too.

Fixing the Leak

We decided to replace our old washing machine with a newer and larger one. It seemed like a good idea but we soon discovered the newer machine had a water leak. It had been in storage for over four years. The washer was located in the garage so we were able to use some old towels to mop up the leak when we used the washer from time to time. I hoped the leak was not coming from the main water pump inside the machine.

One time when I was searching for the leak I pulled the drain hose out of the pipe in the wall. When I turned the machine on for a few seconds water gushed out of the hose and all over the garage floor. The bottom of many card board moving boxes were soaked with water. I had to stop working on the washing machine to move and inspect a number of boxes to see if their contents were damaged or ruined.

Eventually we determined the leak was coming from the drain hose connecting the washer to the house drain pipe. I worked my hands up and down the flexible rubber hose and finally found the exact location of a small hole. It was probably damaged during the move. We had two options. One was to buy a new hose and replace the old leaky one. Or the other option was to try to repair the hole in the existing hose. What would you do? I chose option number two. I purchased a product my wife had seen on TV called "*Flex Seal*". My wife cut the sticky material and carefully worked the thin strips into the grooves in the rubber drain pipe. Then we added wider strips above the thin ones. I had my doubts. But when we turned the machine on again – it worked! The leak was fixed!

There is a passage in the Bible when King Hezekiah had a much larger water problem. A huge enemy army was advancing toward Jerusalem so the king prayed and asked God for help. He ordered his engineers to dig a tunnel to bring water underground into Jerusalem so they could survive if the enemy besieged the city. And they were told to conceal the source of the water so the enemy could not find it. It worked. His prayers were answered, the city was spared and the water tunnel still exists in Jerusalem today (Second Chronicles 32:1-5 & 30).

Let me encourage you to pray and ask God for help when you face a plumbing problem or something much bigger. He loves to come to our aid and help us with the problems we face. You will be glad you did!

A Memorable Trip

My mother died from a heart attack when she was only 67 years old. My father was alone after 44 years of marriage. My brother and I tried to persuade him to move to California to be closer to one of us. But his house was paid for and he preferred to stay in Arizona rather than move to California.

So Steve and I developed a routine of visiting our father once-a-month. Steve would fly over one month and I would fly to Arizona the next month. The schedule was flexible but we tried to spend time with him on a regular basis.

I smile as I remember those trips to Phoenix. Southwest Airlines had some really low prices back in the 1990's. I could fly to Arizona for $29 each way. You had to stand in line at the airport to get a good seat but it was only a one hour flight.

My dad didn't like driving to the airport so I usually took a bus to Tempe and met him at the McDonalds on Apache Trail and McClintock Road. He loved eating breakfast at McDonalds. I tried to schedule a flight which got me to Phoenix early enough so we could meet at McDonalds before they stopped serving breakfast at 10:00 AM.

When my father was still living in his house I usually did some cleaning and other chores. I always washed his car too. Sometimes we would go to a movie and stop at Starbucks afterward for a snack. He enjoyed analyzing the movie with a cookie and cup of coffee.

Sometimes I would fix him a fancy dinner. I bought a fresh Rotisserie chicken and a package of mashed potatoes at Costco. Then I picked up a jar of gravy and a can of green beans and other items he needed from his local grocery store. There were always leftovers for him to enjoy after I went back to California.

These trips weren't fancy or expensive. It was just nice to spend time with my dad. I smile as I write about those memorable trips to Phoenix. There is a verse in the Bible which says, "Honor you father and mother" (Exodus 20:12). I'm sure I could have done a better job fulfilling those words. But I am thankful for the memories I have of time with my dad. Let me encourage you to do the same. He will be glad you did and you will too.

Prison Ministry

I have written about churches and groups who are making an impact on people who are in prison. I read recently there are more people in prison in America than ever before. Prisons are running out of space for inmates. And there is a shortage of prison personnel too.

It is both a tragedy and an opportunity. The tragedy is the absence of husbands and fathers in millions of homes in our country. Young men and women are growing up without an adult role model in their lives. But at the same time this is an opportunity to encourage people in prisons across our nation.

Recently I had the opportunity to talk with two adults who volunteered to serve in their church's prison outreach. It was interesting to hear their perspective on prison ministries and the world prisoners live in.

This man and woman explained the process of getting into the prison. They had to be pre-approved to gain access into the prison itself. They could not take anything with them inside the walls. They could not take a Bible or any other materials. They could not bring any safety equipment either.

After passing through a series of locked doors they met with a group of prisoners for an hour in a large room. They showed a Bible lesson on video and then encouraged the inmates to discuss it in small groups. They listened to the discussions and interacted with the men who attended the Bible study.

The couple said they usually went to a local restaurant after their visit to the prison to decompress. It was physically, emotionally and spiritually draining to go into the prison and interact with the inmates.

There are a number of examples in the Bible when people were in prison. Joseph, Samson and Daniel were in prison. Some of the early Apostles were kept in prison. The Apostle Paul wrote letters to various churches from a prison cell (Philippians, Second Timothy and Titus).

Let me encourage you to find a prison ministry in your area. Get training and be willing to walk inside a prison. Ask God to give you the strength to help prisoners behind the walls and encourage their families outside the walls too. You will be glad you did.

The Kitchen Faucet

The most important room in your house is the kitchen. You can sleep in different bedrooms and use different bathrooms but there is only one kitchen in most homes. And the most important part of the kitchen is the kitchen sink. You may have an extra refrigerator in your garage. You can use a toaster oven instead of the regular oven. You can take out the garbage if the disposal is out of order.

But there is only one kitchen sink and only one kitchen faucet. The kitchen sink and the kitchen faucet are essential for a family to function. That is why I dread working on the kitchen faucet. Everything comes to a standstill when the faucet is out of action. I noticed an extra drip, drip, drip when I turned the water off in the kitchen. That shouldn't happen. My wife noticed it too. She pointed out the dripping water and suggested I look into the situation.

My first step was to look on You Tube. I found several helpful videos narrated by seasoned professionals. They appeared calm and their words were reassuring as they addressed my predicament. The problem was likely a small washer in the spray nozzle. That sounded simple enough. I removed the part and discovered the small rubber washer was broken. This seemed to be the root of the problem.

I jumped into my car and headed for my local Ace Hardware store hoping to find the small rubber washer. One lesson I have learned from doing home and car repairs is always bring the old part so you can compare it to the replacement part. I brought the spray nozzle and the broken washer with me. It took a while to find an employee to help me but eventually we found a new washer that looked like it would work.

The price was 47 cents including tax. But when I got home I realized the washer didn't go on to the spray nozzle. It needed to fit over the nipple on the supply hose. Unfortunately the washer I bought was too big. I should have purchased several different sizes hoping one would fit. I went back to Ace Hardware to buy 3 different small washers. One of them was the right size. I was able to install it quickly. I ran the water to see if this solved the problem. Success! I think I spent less than three dollars on all of the different washers but it took about three hours to finish the job. Let me encourage you to fix things around your house. You Tube can help you analyze and fix the problem. Buy more parts than you think you will need. And always start with a prayer!

Early in the Morning

I heard a coach tell his athletes if they wanted to be successful in their career the best time to exercise was early in the morning. Yes they could go for a run or go to the gym in the afternoon or evening but the morning was best because they had the most control of their own schedule at that time. Later in the day there might be interruptions or schedule conflicts which might prevent them from getting a good work out. It was less likely things might prevent them from exercising early in the morning.

One of my favorite verses in the Bible says, "While it was still night, way before dawn, Jesus got up and went out to a secluded place and prayed" (Mark 1:45 - The Message Bible). It is clear from this passage and similar verses in the Bible that Jesus made a priority of spending time alone with his Heavenly Father *early in the day*. This was his spiritual work out alone and uninterrupted.

My wife Susan and I get most of our physical exercise in the morning. We try to wake up early and go for a walk around our neighborhood. We compare our schedules for the day and talk about things coming up on our calendars. And we spend time praying together as we walk together. We pray for our adult children and our grandchildren. We pray for people who are going through difficult times in their lives.

There is a small group of men who meet early in the morning in the kitchen of our church. We spend time sharing together and studying the Bible. Some of these men have been meeting every Friday morning at 6:00 AM for more than 20 years. This group started many years ago. At that time most of us had to get up and go to work so why not get up an hour earlier one day a week and meet with some other men for study and encouragement.

Jesus set the example and many have followed it. There is something special about sacrificing a little sleep and spending time alone or with a few other people getting spiritual exercise. Let me encourage you to set your alarm and get out of bed a little earlier *this week*. Use the time to get some physical and spiritual exercise. Join a small group of men or women. You will be glad you did and your friends and family will too.

Griffith Park

I have lived in Southern California for over 35 years. It has many famous attractions like Disneyland, Knott's Berry Farm and Six Flags. It has miles of beautiful beaches and several well-known art collections including the Getty Museum and the Huntington Library. These attract visitors from around the world and are enjoyed by local residents too.

However, one site I had never visited was Griffith Park and the Griffith Observatory. Recently my wife and I decided it was time to go and take a look at this famous Southern California landmark. Griffith J. Griffith was a wealthy business man who made his money in silver mines in Mexico. He purchased a large undeveloped property north of LA in the early 1900's and eventually donated it to the city of Los Angeles. He was impressed by the parks he had seen in major cities in Europe and wanted to give his land to create an urban park in LA.

Griffith Park includes 4200 acres and is the largest urban-wilderness municipal park in the United States. It includes the Greek Theater, a train museum called Travel Town and the Los Angeles Zoo. It offers horseback riding, tennis courts and three golf courses. The famous Hollywood sign is also located near Griffith Park.

We were amazed to see miles of hiking and walking trails in the park. And we were delighted to visit the famous Griffith Observatory and Planetarium perched on a hilltop overlooking downtown Los Angeles. It was opened in 1935 and underwent a major renovation in 2020. The parking was a challenge but some spots opened up just when we drove up the winding road. Our timing was perfect. We enjoyed walking through the planetarium and looking over the LA skyline. The observatory and the planetarium have been included in a number of famous Hollywood movies including the recent musical, "*La La Land*".

The planetarium projects pictures of the stars and galaxies. It reminds us the universe is remarkable and immeasurable. And the planet we live on is amazing. There is a passage in the Bible which says, "The heavens declare the glory of God and the skies proclaim the work of His hands. Day after day reveal His greatness and night after night display his glory" (Psalm 19:1-2). Let me encourage you to visit Griffith Park and the Griffith Observatory. Take time to reflect on the majesty of God who created the universe and our tiny beautiful planet. You will be glad you did.

Our Town

I have lived in Diamond Bar for 35 years. We moved here in 1988 and purchased a house in the middle of town. It is interesting to look back and remember how things were then and what is different now.

For example we used to have a store which sold paint, wall paper and other home improvement products. We were thankful to have things we needed so readily available. However as our town aged and there was little remaining land for new development the store closed and a Big Lots store moved into the building.

Another example was the Armstrong Nursery. It was so convenient to pick out new plants and shrubs. They had fertilizer, weed spray and bug spray. They had knowledgeable employees who offered helpful advice to new homeowners. But over the years their business declined and Armstrong closed. It is now a fruit market. Ironically the Ace Hardware store has managed to stay in business in spite of the presence of the larger warehouse stores nearby.

A number of restaurants have closed or changed. There is a story about the Whole Enchilada restaurant in my second book. It closed about five years ago. It is now a veterinarian's office. Bob's Big Boy closed and a new eatery took over the building featuring Asian cuisine. The Carrow's and Coco's restaurants closed too. Both sites have new restaurants now. But In N Out Burger has remained and several other fast food places have moved into our city.

Grocery stores have changed too. The Ralph's grocery store in south Diamond Bar became H-Mart which is the busiest food store in town. The Ralphs in north Diamond Bar became a Walmart Neighborhood Grocery store. The K-Mart store closed and became a Sprouts market.

There is a passage in the Bible where the prophet Jeremiah told the Israelites in exile in Babylon to, "Build houses and settle down. Plant gardens and eat what they produce. Marry and have sons and daughters. Seek the peace and prosperity of the city where you live" (Jeremiah 29:5-7). Let me encourage you to enjoy the present and embrace the future. Things do change over time but God is unchangeable. Be thankful for your community. Get to know the new neighbors and new businesses. Support the stores that have served you for a long time. They will be glad you did and you will too.

Youth Pastor

When I was a high school kid I enjoyed being part of the youth group at Scottsdale Bible Church. The church was growing and we had a wonderful pastor Jim Borror who taught us the Bible and made it easy to understand. But before the church was large enough to hire a youth pastor they asked a local high school coach to lead weekly events and teach the Sunday morning Sunday School class during the summer.

His name was Nelson Gould. He was a big guy and a respected coach at Coronado High School. The church hired him to lead the youth group activities during the summer while he was not working as a PE and football coach. I think he had a young family and was glad to earn some extra money and encourage students like me too.

Swim parties were a lot of fun. Usually a church family would open their home and invite the high school students to enjoy an evening in their backyard swimming pool. I remember a bunch of us would try to dunk Coach Gould's head under the water. But he was a big solid guy and it was not easy to pull his feet out from under him and get his head wet. I'm sure he earned every dollar wrestling with rowdy high school boys in a swimming pool on a warm summer night in Scottsdale.

I was thankful the church eventually hired a full-time youth pastor while I was still in high school. His name was Sherrill Babb. He was a graduate of Dallas Seminary and he would eventually become the President of a large Christian University in Pennsylvania. But for many of us during our high school years he was a wonderful youth pastor who spent many hours teaching and encouraging us in our new faith in Christ. A number of young men and women from that era eventually became pastors and missionaries through the influence of people like Coach Gould, Sherrill Babb and our pastor Jim Borror.

The Apostle Paul instructed his young friend Timothy with these words, "Take the things I have taught you and share them with faithful men and women who will teach others also" (Second Timothy 2:2). Let me encourage you to pray for the men and women who invest their time, energy and gifts to teach and encourage your teenagers. Express your thanks to the youth pastors and volunteers in your church. They are not just keeping your teens busy. They are raising up the next generation of missionaries, pastors, teachers and Christian leaders. They will be glad you did and you will too.

Wash Your Carrots

The Imperial Valley has become one of the most productive agricultural centers in the country. It is located in the California desert just north of the Mexican border. Thousands of acres of have been transformed from a desolate wasteland into wealthy productive farmland producing fruits and vegetables for export across the country. Crops are grown twelve months out of the year in this isolated valley.

Water from the Colorado River was diverted by gravity down the All-American Canal over 100 years ago and caused the desert to bloom. Many western states compete for water from the Colorado River. The Imperial Valley is one of the largest users of the river water.

One of the major crops grown in the valley are carrots. More carrots are grown in the Imperial Valley and the San Juaquin Valley in central California than in any other place in the country. One of the best known companies growing carrots for many years in California was *Bolthouse Farms*. After harvesting the carrots in Imperial they transported them by truck to Bakersfield for processing.

Eventually farmers noticed the trucks carrying the carrots were also removing a lot of rich top soil from the Imperial Valley. A solution to the problem was to wash the carrots in the valley before trucking them to Bakersfield. This not only preserved more soil but also increased the number of carrots which could be loaded onto each truck.

If you drive south on Highway 111 from Palm Springs to El Centro you will see some truck wash stations along the way. These are not for washing dirty trucks. The wash sites are designed to clean the carrots and remove the soil before they make the long drive to Bakersfield.

Carrots are one of my favorite vegetables because the owners of *Bolthouse Farms* donated a large gift to help with the construction of a new Classroom Building at our church in Diamond Bar in the early 1990's. This timely gift helped us complete the building debt free.

There is a verse in the Bible which says, "My God will supply all your needs according to His riches in Christ Jesus" (Philippians 4:19). God does not promise to provide everything we *want* but He does promise to provide our *needs*. Let me encourage you to pray and trust God to supply your needs. And remember to wash your carrots too!

Moving

Recently I helped my brother and his wife move from Porterville to Atascadero, California. They moved from the east side of the San Juaquin Valley to a town near the Pacific Ocean. They bought a home in Atascadero to be closer to their children and grandchildren. We spent four days loading, driving and unloading a U-Haul truck.

Moving a household of furniture, appliances and clothing is a lot of work. In addition Steve had a lot of books he had collected during his career as a pastor and Sharon had many boxes filled with supplies she had used during her career as an elementary school teacher. They spent weeks sorting and packing to prepare for moving day. It took two days to load the truck and another two days to drive and unload it at their new home. They did hire a professional piano mover to get the piano on the truck and into their new house.

One of the biggest challenges in moving is deciding what to keep and what to leave behind. Almost every item involved a decision from the largest appliance to the smallest table decoration. They donated some things to Goodwill and Salvation Army. Many other things were thrown away. The whole moving process was physically and emotionally exhausting.

There are many examples of people moving in the Bible. One man named Abram packed up his family in the city of Ur along the Persian Gulf and moved to the land of Canaan near the Mediterranean Sea (Genesis 12:1-9). It was a long and difficult journey.

After my wife and I got married many years ago we rented the smallest U-Haul *trailer* on the lot. We filled it with wedding gifts and all of our clothes and belongings and drove a thousand miles to Dallas Texas. It was an emotional journey as we left our families and friends behind. Four years later we moved from Dallas to Tucson with a larger rental *truck*. Thirteen years later we rented the *largest truck and largest trailer* in the U-Haul fleet to move us and our four children from Tucson to Diamond Bar. Every move was exhausting. I'm sure you have your own moving stories. Let me encourage you to be willing to relocate but be prepared for the stress and strain that comes with a major move. Whether you hire a moving company or do the job yourself it is a big effort. Other people are on the move and you can do it too!

Give Them Something to Do

Many years ago I heard a speaker share an idea with a group of pastors which became very helpful for me. He told us to ask leaders to continue to serve even after they completed their term on the church leadership team. He said, *"Give retiring leaders something to do"*,

Even though their official term was completed and they were no longer expected to attend the monthly meetings they still had the experience and skills to help the church. He urged us to let these seasoned leaders know they were still needed. *Find something for them to do.*

Some churches select or appoint leaders for a lifetime. I prefer asking leaders to serve for a specific length of time. In our church in Diamond Bar the Elders served a three year term. After three years each man got time off. This allowed us to bring new people on to the leadership team and it gave the old leaders a much deserved rest.

I also continued to meet with some of the old leaders for breakfast or lunch. I sought out their thoughts and perspective on church matters. I invited them to take on smaller one-time assignments like planning a Men's event or a Couple's retreat.

When someone completes their term and steps away from the leadership team for a while, they may feel left out or unneeded. They may feel out of touch. A wise pastor looks for ways to keep men with leadership experience and abilities involved and active.

There were a number of men who served alongside the Apostle Paul. He continued to give them responsibilities and assignments to fulfill while Paul continued to spread the good news about Jesus. In a letter to Timothy, Paul wrote, "Make every effort to come to me soon. I sent Titus to Dalmatia and I sent Tychicus to Ephesus. Only Luke is with me" (Titus 4:9-12).

Paul continued to use seasoned leaders and disciples even after they had completed their assignment. He knew it was important to give them something else to do. Let me encourage you to do the same with the trusted experienced leaders in your church or organization. Keep them involved. Listen to their wise counsel and suggestions. Give them something to do. They will be glad you did and you will too.

Full Moon Rising

On a recent trip to Arizona we witnessed two spectacular events on the same day. We saw a beautiful sunset in the west followed by a giant full moon rising in the east. It was a moment to remember.

Arizona does have a reputation for beautiful sunsets. The *Arizona Highways* magazine was always filled with photos of memorable sunsets. The variety of mountain lakes and desert sand dunes made perfect places to capture the vivid colors of the setting sun. Some people speculate the colors are enhanced by the dust in the air or by the endless expanse of the landscape. Whatever the reason Arizona is known for its remarkable sunsets.

A rising full moon can be impressive too. The distant mountains and the desert vegetation like the towering Saguaro cactus provide beautiful contrasts to capture the size of a full moon. I remember driving across the Arizona desert many years ago with my wife. We noticed a small bright light on the edge of the dark desert. At first we thought it was a small airplane. But as the light got bigger we realized we were witnessing the rise of the full moon. It looked huge as it rose over the horizon. It was amazing to capture the sun going down in the west and the moon rising up in the east across the desert floor. The timing was perfect.

In ancient times people feared being struck by the light of the full moon. We sometimes hear people referring to being "*Moon Struck*". People were warned to not be outdoors when there was a full moon in the night sky. But the Bible says we do not need to be afraid of the sun or the moon. They have no power over us. God is with us and will protect us. In one passage the author wrote, "God is my guardian, He is at my side to protect me. He shields me from sunstroke and shelters me from being moonstruck" (Psalm 121: 5-6 – The Message Bible).

Let me encourage you to place your trust in the God who created Heaven and Earth. He is our helper and protector. We don't need to listen to ancient folklore or superstitions. He is the one we turn to in times of trouble or uncertainty. You will be glad you did and He will too.

More Inflation

The cost of everything has skyrocketed over the past few years. The cost of food, fuel and other necessities have risen dramatically. The government continues to reassure the public that inflation is slowing and things are under control. But most consumers are skeptical.

I have used the cost of donuts as an example. A dozen donuts at my favorite shop used to be nine or ten dollars. Recent purchases are now sixteen dollars for one dozen! One day I bought a half dozen and it was about the same price a dozen was only a couple of years ago.

Sometimes it is difficult to accurately measure inflation at the grocery store because manufacturers have reduced the quantity of the contents. A breakfast cereal box may look the same but it may contain less cereal. A bottle of orange juice may look the same but the contents have been reduced from 64 ounces to 59 ounces. Now it contains only 52 ounces. Looks can be deceiving. Read the fine print to clearly understand how much orange juice you are getting. Prices have gone up while the contents have gone down.

Years ago the State Department came up with a formula to measure the cost of living for diplomats serving in different countries around the world. They adjusted the salaries of employees based on the how much it cost to live in more expensive cities like Tokyo, Moscow or Paris. They compared the price of a MacDonald's Big Mac burger.

I got the idea to measure inflation by comparing the prices at my favorite fast food restaurant *In N Out Burger.* Several sources I found online confirmed the price of a Double-Double burger in 2022 was $3.95. The price for the exact same burger in 2023 was $4.90. An increase of 24% in one year! The same size with the same ingredients. Some of the reasons cited by various authors were increased wages for workers, the higher cost of transportation and the price of the raw materials for the burgers and fries.

I think most people feel helpless fighting inflation. We need to feed our families and fuel our cars. Prices at the gas pump and the grocery store continue to increase. Jesus said, "Your Heavenly Father knows your needs and will provide for you" (Matthew 6:25-34). Let me encourage you to put your faith in God and not in the government. You will be glad you did and He will too.

A Lizard on the Screen Door

This morning I discovered a new friend at our front door. Actually he was on the screen of the sliding door in the front of our house. I found a small lizard clinging to the outside of the screen door. It looked like his tail was gone so he looked shorter than your typical reptile.

I'm sure he saw me peering at him from inside the house but he remained motionless. He still didn't move when I opened the glass door. Finally I touched the screen which exposed his underbelly but he did not flinch. I wondered if he was dead.

I tried to piece together the situation like investigating a crime scene. I was looking for motive, means and the other things a detective looks for when trying to solve a crime. Since he did not have a tail I postulated he had probably fled for his life from some predator. Maybe a bird had him in its clutches. Maybe he had run for his life from a land based enemy.

The fact he was still on the screen door may indicate he was exhausted and afraid to return to his normal habitat. Maybe the one who threatened his life was still in the area. I didn't think a screen door was a good place to hide but maybe his quick action saved his life.

The next question was what should I do now? What would you do in this situation? I have shared stories in my other books about how I rescued a lizard from some wire mesh on our front gate and when I saved the lives of two lizards when they got stuck on a sticky pad intended to catch mice or rats. I also shared a story about a lizard in our bedroom wondering if I should tell my wife or not.

I finally decided to take action. I planned to go outside with a light broom hoping to safely sweep him off the screen door. I doubt he would like the idea. He wouldn't understand I was trying to help him not hurt him. However, by the time I arrived he was gone. I was glad he was alive and able to resume his daily routine.

There is a verse in the Bible which says, "Joseph's brothers meant it for evil but God used it for good" (Genesis 50:19-21). Let me encourage you to trust God to help you through difficult times. Ask for strength and endurance when problems come unexpectedly. God can use even difficult times for your good when you call upon Him.

Climb Over Chairs

We were glad to have new visitors come to our church. We hoped they enjoyed the worship service and other ministries for teens and children. I always stood on the patio so I could greet new guests. But I not only wanted to personally meet them but I also made an effort to introduce them to other people who were their age or stage of life.

Another way we tried to get to know new people was to visit them in their home. We did these home visits so we could get to know them better and to tell them more about our church. We always brought a box of cookies as a gift for them to enjoy.

We often sent out several teams once or twice a month. At the end of the evening each team returned to the church to report on their visits. It was encouraging to see and hear each team's enthusiasm about their conversations with these new guests.

Before we concluded the night I reminded each team member to do *three things*. I encouraged them to **pray** for the people they had visited. Pray these guests will come back to our church again. Pray for any needs our team members became aware of.

In addition I told the team members to **watch** for these guests next Sunday. Because the team members had made a personal connection with the new guests by visiting their home they had a responsibility and opportunity to help these new guests feel comfortable at our church.

And I told each team member to **climb over chairs** and knock down people to get to their new friends. If they saw the guests across the auditorium or on the patio make sure they personally greeted them and introduced them to more people at our church.

I don't know if anyone really knocked someone down but I think the visiting team members got the message to watch for these new guests and help them feel welcome at our church. There is a passage in the Bible when Andrew introduced his brother Peter to Jesus (John 1:40-42). That was the first step in Peter's life to become a follower of Jesus. Let me encourage you to watch for new people who visit your church and make sure you introduce them to others. Maybe they will become a follower of Jesus one day because you reached out to them. You will be glad you did and they will too.

Mispronunciation

Some people are wired to understand new languages. Their brains process the new sounds and words so they are able to hear and speak in a different language quickly.

My brain does not work that way. I struggled in my Spanish class in college. I failed my first semester of Greek *and* Hebrew in seminary. It was difficult for me to repeat words and sounds in a foreign language.

In addition, I struggled to learn and repeat new names. Sometimes I am asked to lead a memorial service for people I do not know. I am on a call list for one of the funeral homes in our area. If a family has lost a loved one and does not have a church connection, the funeral home may call me or another retired clergy to lead the service.

It is always an honor to lead a service and celebrate someone's life. I'm glad to help the surviving family members during this difficult time. But sometimes I struggle with the name of the person who died.

Some names are easy like Bill, Betty, Bruce or Barbara. But other names like Cirilita or Benito are more difficult. Some of the people are from different cultures and their names can be difficult to spell as well as pronounce. My limited language skills make this part of my job more stressful.

I remember doing a memorial service for a man who was from Italy. He did not attend our church but his adult children and grandchildren did. It was an unusual name. No matter how hard I tried I couldn't get my mouth to say the word properly. I was uncomfortable and the family was frustrated as I kept mispronouncing his name.

There are a lot of unusual names in the Bible too. Have you heard of people named Zerubbabel or Nehemiah? Have you tried to read out loud some names like Jehoshaphat, Hezekiah or Nebuchadnezzar?

Let me encourage you to be patient with your pastor and other people who may have difficulty pronouncing your name or the name of your new born baby or your older loved ones. Help them if you can with little suggestions on how to pronounce the name correctly. They will be glad you did and you will too.

Reflections on the Death of Your Spouse

I don't think anyone can imagine or understand what it is like to lose their spouse. You might talk with a financial planner about how to plan your financial matters. And you would be wise to have a will or Living Trust to provide instructions for your surviving spouse and loved ones.

But when the day comes when your loved one dies few people are really prepared for what is ahead. One immediate result is how alone you feel. Your best friend and companion is gone. You are struck by how lonely you are. Even the best efforts of your friends and family cannot take the place of your spouse.

You sleep in an empty bed. You come home to an empty house. You prepare and eat meals alone. You make decisions by yourself. You make plans and mark your calendar alone. You drive your car by yourself. Your co-pilot is gone.

You miss the familiar voice of your spouse. You miss the laughter and conversation. You miss having another person in the house or walking by your side. You miss the touch of their hand and the brush of their hair. You miss the embrace of their arms and their whisper in your ear. And you miss their visible image. Even though there are photos all around the house and on your cell phone, none of these replace their physical presence and their visual image.

When your spouse dies all of your plans and dreams are changed. Travel plans are canceled. Home remodeling plans are no longer important. Hopes and dreams are dashed.

I have heard some widows say they felt like they lost an arm or a leg. They feel empty and hopeless. They lost the desire to go on. Grief and despair filled their hearts and minds.

There is a verse in the Bible that says, "We do not grieve like those who have no hope" (First Thessalonians 4:13). Our faith in Christ gives us the hope and promise of seeing our loved ones again. It gives us the strength to keep going even without them. Let me encourage you to watch for an opportunity *this week* to encourage someone around you who has lost a loved one recently. There is probably a widow or widower on the street where you live who needs encouragement and help. They will be glad you did and you will too.

Reflections on Remarriage

I have heard men are more likely to remarry than women. And studies indicate men remarry more quickly than women. Men may need the help and support of a wife more than women need a husband. Many widows I have talked to seem more content and confident about living alone than men do.

I certainly wasn't looking for someone to marry during my wife's cancer journey. My priority was to be by her side every step of the way. I was her wing man. I went to every doctor's appointment and drove her to every test and treatment. I slept on a small bed in her room when she was in the hospital. I prepared sermons while I sat next to Jeanne when she received chemotherapy. We were in this together to the end. We were married for 50 years.

After Jeanne died I did not like living alone. I have shared some of my thoughts and emotions in a previous article about life without my wife. Eventually I did begin to date. It was awkward asking a woman to meet me for breakfast or lunch. This was unfamiliar territory for me.

However it was helpful to have someone to talk with and be with. It was nice to have something to look forward to on my calendar. It was nice to have someone to take to the movies or walk with in the park. I got to know a widow in our church who had lost her husband several years earlier. I actually led the memorial service when her husband died. She had a busy life with her children and grandchildren. She was involved in women's Bible study and attended a Sunday morning class at our church. She loved to help other widows.

As our relationship grew the subject of getting married became part of our conversation. She had no plans to remarry. I was more open to the idea. Gradually we came to believe there was another chapter in our lives we could share together. We got married on Valentine's Day.

It has been a wonderful new season for both of us. It has been challenging combining two households into one. It has been an adjustment for us and for our families. But I'm very thankful for my wonderful wife Susan. There is a verse in the Bible which says, "It is not good for man to be alone" (Genesis 2:18-25). Let me encourage you to be ready to help the single men and women in your church or community. And celebrate with those who decide to remarry.

A Trip of a Lifetime

I am working on another tour to Israel. We have about 25 adults who are planning to travel to the Holy Land later this year. I have led several groups in the past and I am excited to be going again.

But you forget how much work is involved planning and promoting the trip. We have worked with the same travel agency since our first tour in 2008. They are located in Pennsylvania and arrange for the flights to Israel. The actual tour company is located in Jerusalem. They provide the hotels, bus and local tour guide. These two organizations put the puzzle together for a smooth and memorable trip.

Promoting the trip is fairly easy. We shared the plans with people in our church and other interested friends and family members. We usually held an information meeting about nine months before the trip to tell people about the date, itinerary and cost of the trip. Individuals paid a deposit to secure their spot on the tour.

Six to eight weeks before the trip we met again to collect the final payments and to prepare people for the journey. We talked about safety and health. We reminded them to bring medicine, eye glasses and other personal items. Keep these items with them on the plane.

We also talked about packing and what they will and will not need. Most people going on a long trip tend to bring too much stuff. Their luggage is limited to 50 pounds max. This is difficult for some travelers. We try to remind them we are going to a modern country with all of the things they might need if they forget something at home. Only one check-in bag and one small carry-on bag are permitted on the plane and on the tour bus.

There is an interesting passage in the Bible when Jesus instructed his disciples to travel light. He told them to *not* pack a large sack of clothes and food. They needed to trust God to provide their needs (Mark 6:8-11). A tour of Israel is a little different. People have paid a lot of money to go on this trip so they are allowed to bring a suit case and carry-on.

Let me encourage you to consider going on a tour to Israel. You will see the places where Jesus walked and taught the multitudes. It is a once in a life time opportunity. You will be glad you did.

Run Forest Run

One of my favorite forms of exercise was running. I ran on the Cross Country team in high school and continued to run after I got married. It didn't required any special equipment like football or baseball and it was something I could do on my own schedule.

I usually ran early in the morning. I woke up and dressed quickly and got out the door. When we lived in Tucson I usually ran through a nearby park and then on to my office at the church. The family could sleep a little longer and I got a little time alone in my study. Then I ran back the house for a shower and breakfast.

When we moved to California I continued my morning routine. But my route was a little different. Arizona was flat. California had hills. I usually jogged through our neighborhood and stayed away from the traffic on busier streets.

One of the hazards of jogging were local predators who were waiting to ambush me. In Arizona there were some huge black birds in the park who always dove at me as I ran by. It was a little scary and unsettling to have several large birds dive bomb me as I ran past their perch. They always approached from behind so I didn't see them coming. I don't know if they were trying to protect their nest or just enjoyed harassing the local athletes.

The hazard in California was different. There were two small dogs in our neighborhood who seemed to take great pleasure pursing me as I jogged past their house. These little guys were aggressive. I don't know why they weren't confined in the backyard. I think their owner was unaware of their misbehavior. But I dreaded being chased and harassed by these two little dogs nipping at my ankles.

The author of the Book of Acts recorded several examples of opponents pursing and harassing the Apostle Paul as he traveled the Roman Empire telling people about Jesus (Acts 17:13-15). I was distracted and frustrated being chased by wild birds and pesky puppy dogs. They drained the enjoyment I found in jogging. Maybe you have someone harassing you at home or at work. Let me encourage you to keep on going and not get discouraged when you face these challenges. Ask God to give you the courage to persevere. You will be glad you did.

What Time Is It

We have been doing some major improvements to the landscaping at our house. I installed new PVC pipes to distribute water to all of the planters and flower beds. I also changed some of the sprinkler heads in the lawn to improve coverage and save water.

We have also planted a number of new plants and shrubs around the backyard patio and in the courtyard in front of the house. We even added a couple of new strawberry plants too.

The expanded watering system has kept the grass and flowers happy. However I have been having difficulty setting the sprinkler timer to run the water at the right time and for the correct length of time. I normally water the lawn in the evening so the water can soak in during the night. I have set each zone to water for five minutes. There are four zones so it takes about 20 minutes to water the lawn, shrubs and flowers.

But somehow I messed up the program on the timer. Instead of watering for 20 minutes the system came on again for an extra 20 minutes. I haven't seen the water bill yet but I'm sure it won't be pretty.

I have watched several videos on You Tube trying to figure out what I did wrong. There are two separate programs on my Orbitz Lawn Sprinkler timer. I think the timer is running *both* program A and program B but I only want the system to water once not twice a day. This has been going on for several days. I have watched a You Tube video several times and made adjustments to the timer but it is still watering twice a day instead of once. Maybe you have some suggestions.

Maybe you are facing bigger problems in your life. You keep trying to change things but nothing seems to work. Maybe you have a strained relationship with your wife or kids. Maybe things aren't going well at work. Maybe you are struggling with a bad habit or unhealthy life style.

There is a verse in the Bible which says, "No test or temptation that comes your way is beyond what others have had to face. All you need to remember is that God will never let you down, He will never let you be pushed past your limit. He will always be there to help you come through it" (First Corinthians 10:13 – the Message Bible). Let me encourage you to ask for His help with the problems you are facing *right now*. You will be glad you did and He will too.

My Grandparents House

My brother and I were born in Denver, Colorado. I was only five years old when our parents moved to Phoenix, Arizona so I don't remember much of Denver. What I do remember was going to my grandparent's house for holidays and birthdays as I grew up in Arizona.

The first house I remember was on St. Joseph Road near 44th Street north of Camelback Road. I remember driving west on McDonald Drive from my parent's home to my grandparent's house just west of Camelback Mountain. McDonald Drive was like a small roller coaster with dips and bumps. It was a familiar way to get to my grandparent's house. We had hot chocolate and warm Ginger Bread and read the Christmas Story on Christmas Eve and dinner there on Christmas Day.

Recently when I was in Phoenix by myself and I went looking for their old house. I located St. Joseph Street and slowly drove through the neighborhood until I found what I thought was their house. I called my brother who lived in California and asked him if he remembered their address. He didn't know the address but he confirmed it was on St. Joseph Street. I sent him a picture on my cell phone and he agreed it did look like our grandparent's house.

When I was in high school my grandparents sold their large home and moved to an apartment. Eventually they bought a house in Scottsdale on Bonnie Rose Drive near Granite Reef Road. It was a small two bedroom house only a few blocks from where we lived on San Miguel. I didn't understand why they moved there until I heard my Grandfather had cancer. Then I understood he wanted Grandma Halliday to be near our family. My mother was Gail and Marie's only child.

Grandpa Halliday died in December when I was a senior in high school. He left a note for my grandmother instructing her to stay in the two bedroom house and find a care giver to live with her. Grandma Halliday had crippling Rheumatoid arthritis. My parent's house had stairs so it was best for Marie to live in her own one story house. I remember many wonderful evenings visiting my grandmother there. She lived ten more years after my grandfather died. The Bible instructs us to care for our parents and grandparents (First Timothy 5:3-4). If your grandparents are still alive let me encourage you to spend more time with them. Watch for ways to help them too. They will be glad you did and you will too.

Hospitality

Recently we had a number of people at our home. It was a lively group of about fifteen adults with plenty laughter and conversation. The purpose of our gathering was to prepare for our trip to Israel. It was a lot of fun to have them in our house. But it was also a lot of work.

I told them how nice it was to have people on our patio because six months earlier the patio was filled with boxes. When Susan and I got married we worked hard to combine our two households. The movers filled our garage and patio with her boxes. It was a daunting task to sort through all of the cardboard boxes. But six months later we were sitting on beautiful patio furniture instead of staring at stacks of boxes.

Even with the moving containers gone, it was still a lot of work to prepare for our guests. We cleaned off all the patio furniture and washed down the concrete surface. Susan set out candles and other decorations to enhance the atmosphere of the patio. It looked very nice. It also took a lot of time to clean the inside of the house too. My job was to vacuum the carpets and mop the floors. Her job was to clean the countertops and dust the furniture. We also cleaned bathrooms and straighten up the house.

Plus there was preparation of the desserts, beverages, plates and cups. When we ate a quick dinner before our guests arrived we agreed it was a lot of work to get everything ready for people to come. Please don't misunderstand. I'm not asking for sympathy or recognition. We were glad to do all of these things in order to welcome our guests. But it was a reminder *hospitality is a lot of work*.

There are a number of passages in the Bible which mention hospitality. One passage says, "Exercise hospitality without complaining (First Peter 4:7). Another says, "Extend hospitality to strangers for some have entertained angels unaware" (Hebrews 13:1-2).

I don't want to discourage you. I want to encourage you to open your home and welcome friends, neighbors and strangers. Don't make excuses because your home or backyard don't look perfect. Don't wait until you get new patio furniture or have your house painted. There are still a few weeks of summer left to invite people to your house. The important thing is spending time together. It does take time and effort but it is worth it. You will be glad you did and your guests will too.

People Are More Important Than Policies

Most organizations have a list of policies and procedures which guide decisions and actions. Often people look at these with skepticism and disdain. Why do we have to follow the rules and regulations? For the most part these policies can be very beneficial. We had some simple guidelines at our church which we expected volunteers to adhere to. For example we wanted to make sure children were in a safe environment while they were on our campus. One guideline was to install windows in the doors of every classroom. We also wanted to have two adults in every children's class.

One time a substitute Sunday School teacher decided to take his students on a field trip to the local donut shop around the corner from our campus. This seemed harmless enough until the parents came to pick up their children after the church service. When they arrived the classroom was empty and no one knew where the teacher and students had gone. It was a tense few minutes until the teacher and children returned with donuts in their hands. After this incident we adopted a policy stating no children were to be taken off the church campus without the prior permission of the parents and the Sunday School Superintendent.

On the other hand we had some policies or practices which were a little too rigid. One time the Women's ministry was having its fall registration. Instead of allowing women to select their preferred class they drew names out of a hat to decide which people would be in which class. This sounded like a nice idea to help people get to know new people. However, one woman wanted to be in the same class with the new guest she had invited. When she heard she could not be in the same class with her friend they both decided to not come. We learned a lesson from this fiasco. We agreed to allow people to be in the same class with their guest. *People are more important than policies.*

There is a passage in the Bible which says, "The Sabbath was made for man. Man was not made to be burdened by the strict rules of the Sabbath" (Mark 2:23-27). In other words be flexible. Don't be locked into rules and regulations and policies. The same is true when you are raising children. Be willing to make exceptions to the rules. It's okay for them to stay up past their bed time once in a while. Remember *people are more important than policies.* They will be glad you did and you will too.

224

Tea Cups

My son Tim and I traveled to Normandy, France to see this historical site. Allied Armies launched an invasion on the French coast to free Western Europe from German occupation in World War Two.

On our way to France we spent a few days in London, England and stayed with my nephew Matt and his wife Sada. Matt was doing research for his doctoral dissertation at the British Library. So while Matt studied, Tim and I enjoyed seeing some of the sites in London.

We used the double decker busses and the subway underground to get from place to place in the city. One day we discovered a Tea Shop. They not only sold a variety of flavored tea but they also sold tea cups. My wife had a large collection of tea cups at home so we decided to get a cup and saucer for her and her three daughters. It was an excellent choice. Tim and I knew Jeanne and the girls would love them.

However I was short-sighted and only purchased four cups and four saucers. The sales person explained the cups and saucers were packaged in boxes of six. He suggested the tea cups would travel better if left undisturbed in the box of six. I wanted to save some money and only bought four. Looking back I wish I had listened to the salesman's advice. It would have been smarter to buy six so my son and I would each have a cup and saucer too.

I wonder if you have made a quick decision too and regretted it later. Maybe you purchased something on sale but realized later you didn't really need it. Maybe you accepted a job offer without talking it over with your parents or spouse and later regretted your decision.

I suspect everyone has done this in the past. Have you made a quick decision without taking time to consider the full ramifications? Have you made a commitment which you later regret? Buying tea cups was not a big deal but other major decisions are.

There is a passage in the Bible which says, "He guides the humble in what is right and teaches them his way" (Psalm 25:9). Let me encourage you to go slow and seek guidance from the Lord and from trusted friends. *When in doubt – don't.* Choose wisely. You will be glad you did. And if you are buying Tea Cups I recommend you purchase the whole package!

Lunch

Recently I had lunch with a couple of men from our church. These two men and several others have invested a lot of time to support me through the months leading up to my wife's death and the months following her passing. They continued to make time in their busy schedules to encourage me on this unfamiliar journey.

It has been a year and a half since my wife died from breast cancer. But these guys have stayed in touch and continue to meet with me for lunch on a regular basis. I can't imagine what it would be like without this small group of friends.

Don't misunderstand. We don't just talk about the death of my wife or about me getting remarried. We talk about their wives and families too. There is a lot of laughter in our conversation. We get along very well and enjoy spending time together.

There are several examples in the Bible where close friends came alongside to encourage and help their friend. When David was on the run from King Saul, Jonathan came alongside David to encourage and support him (First Samuel Chapters 19-20). Even though Jonathan was the son of King Saul and heir to the throne, he did whatever he could to support David during this difficult time.

When the Apostle Paul went through difficult times in his life and ministry, several people came alongside to encourage him. A man named Barnabas took the initiative to embrace Paul even when other leaders were reluctant to do so (Acts 9:26-28). Other friends like Aquila and Pricilla and Timothy and Aristarchus supported Paul too.

Let me encourage you to watch for an opportunity to encourage a friend, neighbor or family member. They may be going through a tough time in their life and God could use *you to help them*. Don't wait for an invitation. Take action. Take the initiative. Call or text them *today*. Invite your discouraged friend to meet you for coffee or lunch.

Commit yourself to sticking with your friend for the long-haul. This is not a short-term commitment. It is a life-long commitment to help and encourage them on their unfamiliar journey. They will be glad you did and you will too.

Paying for College

One day I was approached by a young woman in front of Home Depot who was holding a small cardboard box in her hand. As I got closer to her I realized she was selling some familiar looking chocolate bars. My initial thought was I don't need any chocolate bars. She asked if I could help her with her college education. She explained she was selling those thin candy bars to raise money to help pay for her college tuition.

You have probably been approached by kids selling the "*World Famous Chocolates*" to raise money for their school band or service club. This was the first time I met an individual selling them to raise money for themselves.

You can probably predict my response. It was short and simple - no thank you. I am embarrassed to say I kept on walking and didn't buy a "*World Famous Chocolate*" bar. I was in a hurry and needed to get some things in Home Depot. I didn't have time for fund raising.

I must admit I felt bad about how I responded to this nice young woman. She looked like she could be a high school graduate. She wasn't pushy or demanding. She just asked a simple question and said thank you as I went into the store.

After I found the items I was looking for I noticed she was still near the entrance asking people for help. As I got into my car I noticed several individuals stopped and talked with her and purchased a Chocolate Bar. I was impressed she was standing alone in front of the store.

I felt I had made a mistake. I should be willing to help too. I got out of my car and walked back to the entrance. I asked her what her college plans were. She said she was enrolling in a nursing program in the fall. I was glad to hear it. Our community needs more nurses. The cost of a small thin *World Famous Chocolate* bar was five dollars. I bought the dark chocolate one. I was glad I went back to help this articulate young student. I should have purchased more.

There are a number of examples in the Bible which record moments when Jesus stopped to help people (Mark 10:46-52). Let me encourage you to stop and help some people too. Don't be indifferent and unwilling like I was. Follow Jesus' example. *Stop and help someone this week.* They will be glad you did and you will too.

Memories of Maui

In August 2023 a firestorm swept through a community in Maui, Hawaii with destructive force. Apparently a hurricane passed north of the islands and battered Maui with 80 mile per hour winds. These powerful winds turned a brush fire into a cyclone of death and destruction.

The greatest devastation was in a tourist town called Lahaina. It had cozy shops and stores which were very popular with tourists. There were also a number of well-known restaurants along *Front Street* like *Cheeseburger in Paradise* and *Kimos* fine dining looking out over the beautiful Pacific Ocean.

Hundreds of homes were destroyed by the fast moving fire which swept down the hillsides and drove the flames all the way to the ocean. Nothing could stop this horrific fire storm. Over 100 people were confirmed dead so far. Final numbers have not been released.

My wife Susan and I were in Lahaina only a few weeks before the fire. One day we had lunch at *Cheeseburger in Paradise* and a few days later we enjoyed a wonderful dinner at *Kimos* watching the sunset over the ocean. We walked along *Front Street* and shopped in a number of stores in Lahaina. When we drove back to our condo in Kihei we actually saw a small brush fire in the area but the winds were normal.

It is hard to believe all of the things we saw in Lahaina are now completely gone. Photos and videos show the total destruction of this small cozy Hawaiian community. Homes, hotels, businesses, and restaurants have been burned to the ground. Shells of rental cars liter the streets. It is unbelievable. We have seen similar devastation in California where Santa Ana winds have driven fires all the way to the ocean. Hundreds of homes were destroyed in cities like Malibu and Laguna Beach. We know it can happen again.

There is a passage in the Bible which says, "As in the days of Noah people will be busy living when destruction will come upon them when they least expect it" (Luke 17:26-29). Let me encourage you to be alert to the potential destruction of all your earthly possessions. Take time to read the words of Jesus which predict similar events in the end times. And let me encourage you to be prepared for the next natural disaster. Pack your emergency clothes and supplies. Be ready to help your neighbors if a disaster strikes. You will be glad you did.

Some Memorable Birthdays

I shared in my previous book how people encouraged me on my first birthday after my wife died. I received a large number of thoughtful cards and text messages and several unexpected gifts. One mother and her daughter made me a fresh batch of chocolate chip cookies. They were amazing. Also a man from our church made me a homemade Apple Pie. It was delicious.

As I approached my next birthday I received another tasty gift. It was another homemade apple pie from my friend Jim. I wasn't expecting it and was surprised to see Him at my door two days before my birthday. This pie tasted just as good if not better than the one he made for me last year. I hope this tradition will continue for many years to come.

I wonder if there are some memorable gifts people have given to you on your birthday. My wife gave me a set of Ping Golf Clubs for my 50th birthday. I still use them today. Another year my son took me and my wife to a Los Angeles Angels baseball game on my birthday. We had dinner at the Diamond Club behind home plate.

One year I surprised my wife with a party on her birthday. I flew two of her best friends from Tucson to California for her birthday. I picked them up at the airport and drove them to Jeanne's school. She was so surprised when these two women interrupted her class.

That evening we went to our favorite restaurant the Whole Enchilada in Diamond Bar for a birthday dinner with our children. After dinner we drove back to our house. She was very surprised to find a house full of friends gathered to celebrate her birthday. It was a memorable day.

There is an example in the Bible of some gifts people gave to Jesus. The Wise Men traveled hundreds of miles to present expensive gifts to baby Jesus in Bethlehem (Matthew Chapter Two). Jesus' mother was surprised to see the visitors from the east. It was an experience she never forgot (Luke Chapter Two).

Let me encourage you to make a plan and do something special to surprise your spouse, children or friends on their birthday *this year.* Make a memory they will cherish for years to come. They will be glad you did and you will too.

Touch and Go

I have flown on many airplanes in my life. Many of them were domestic flights within the United States There have been some flight delays due to bad weather, mechanical problems and waiting for passengers from a connecting flight. You never know what to expect.

I have also flown on many international flights to places like India, China, Russia and Mongolia. I have also flown to England, France, Italy and Israel. Most of these journeys involved changing planes and taking a second flight to my destination.

There have been a few memorable moments in my flying career. One time the ground crew damaged the landing gear on a double decker Air France flight when they tried to push our plane away from the gate. The pilot announced the flight was canceled and several hundred passengers had to go back to the terminal and book another flight.

Another time my wife and I were on a plane which aborted takeoff halfway down the runway at LAX. The plane's computer determined one of our engines was not at full power and stopped our aircraft because we did not have enough speed to get off the ground. We were thankful we didn't end up in Santa Monica Bay.

Recently my wife and I had a new experience on a domestic flight from Ontario, California to Phoenix. When were in our final decent into Sky Harbor Airport and only feet above the runway our pilot aborted our landing. He raced the engines back to life and flew us back into the air. The pilot explained there was a lot of traffic on the runway and he decided to go around and try the landing again. Later he said it was a gust of wind that led him to not land on the first attempt.

You probably have some similar stories from your experience flying across the country and around the world. I remember another time we were stuck on a plane in Beijing, China, because the ground crew could not get the walkway close enough to our plane. It was ten feet short and we sat for over an hour waiting for someone to help us.

There is a familiar verse in the Bible which says, "Trust in the Lord with all your heart. Don't lean on your own understanding. In all your ways trust God and He will guide you" (Proverbs 3:5-6). Let me encourage you to keep on flying. Expect some delays but enjoy your journey.

Birthday Reflections

I was born on August 13, 1950 in Denver, Colorado. My parents were Richard and Donna Hopper. They were born in the 1920's and my father served in the Army Air Corp in World War Two. My parents met at East High School in Denver. I have an older brother Steve Hopper.

I don't remember much about life in Denver. I do remember playing in the snow and visiting my grandmother's cabin in the Colorado Rockies. I remember my parents moving us to Phoenix, Arizona in 1956. One thing were told was always shake out our shoes before putting them on because their might be a scorpion in them.

I remember our first house near 56th Street and Thomas Road. I remember sitting at the job site as a little kid watching our house being built at 5321 E. Pinchot Road. Steve and I attended Ingleside Elementary and we played Little League baseball in the summer.

The 1960's were a fun time in my life. My parents bought a larger tri-level house at 8649 E. San Miguel in Scottsdale. I attended Scottsdale High and graduated from Saguaro High School in 1968. I loved driving my '57 Chevy to school when I turned sixteen. Our family attended the Billy Graham Crusade in 1964 and we began to attend Scottsdale Bible Church. I put my faith in Jesus at a summer camp in Prescott.

I went to college at ASU and I led the youth ministry at the church. I graduated in 1971 and married Jeanne who would be my wife for fifty years. After four years of graduate studies at Dallas Seminary we moved to Tucson, Arizona. Three of our four kids were born there. We have so many wonderful memories leading a small church, raising a young family and making life-long friends at Chapel in the Hills.

We moved to Diamond Bar, California in 1988 and led the Evangelical Free Church for 27 years. Our kids grew up in Diamond Bar and graduated from BIOLA University and Azusa Pacific University. Each of them found a wonderful spouse and have a total of ten kids. We share wonderful memories of our adventures at the church in Diamond Bar. We celebrated our 50th anniversary with our kids and grandkids in Maui. Jeanne died in 2022 from breast cancer. Recently I married Susan who had lost her husband in 2016. We are thankful to share this new season together. I am very thankful for God's love and mercy and for the special people He brought into my life. I hope you are too.

Danny

I met Danny in 1962 when we moved into our new neighborhood on San Miguel Avenue in Scottsdale, Arizona. My birthday is August 13th. His birthday is August 14th. We attended Mohave Elementary School and Scottsdale and Saguaro High together. Since he was a year older than me He was able to borrow his family's car on Friday night so we could cruise down Central Avenue in Phoenix or go to the Rodeo Drive In outdoor theater on Thomas Road.

After high school I enrolled at ASU and Danny joined the US Marines. I remember driving to our pastor's house on the way to the bus station to pray for Danny when he headed for boot camp in San Diego. He served in Viet Nam and was severely wounded in combat. Recently I found some letters in a box which he sent to me during his time in the Marines. I visited Danny a few times at the Navy hospital in San Diego.

After he got out of the military he worked in various jobs and struggled with alcohol. He found help by attending AA and has been sober for over 30 years. I will always remember his phone call on New Year's Day telling me he was celebrating with a group of friends and no one was drinking alcohol.

He eventually got married and became a high school teacher and counselor. He loved his students and made an impact on their lives. Danny continued to experience difficulties from his injury in Viet Nam. Doctors finally amputated his leg to relieve the pain and discomfort but the pain never completely went away. He remains active and still goes hunting with his sons. Danny and his wife Pam continue to serve with AA helping younger men and women.

There are several passages in the Bible which refer to men who were Roman soldiers (Acts 21:37-40 / 22:24-30). These men were considered to the best trained military in the world. Some were actually kind to the Apostle Paul during his travels, trials and imprisonments (Acts 27:1-4 / 42-44 / 28:16).

Let me encourage you to express your appreciation to the men and woman who have served or are now serving in our military. Thank them for their service to our country. And let me encourage you to reach out to some of your old high school or college friends. Make an effort to reconnect. They will be glad you did and you will too.

Helping Those in Need

The impact of the fires which swept through Lahaina on the west coast of Maui was overwhelming. Homeowners, businesses, schools and the tourist industry are just beginning to feel the effect of the devastation.

In August, 2023 a wind driven wild fire raced down from the hillside and burned an entire community in a matter of minutes. Many visitors and residents said they received no warning about the fast moving flames. Over 100 people died in the firestorm.

I have often said it is moments like this that bring out the best and the worst in people. When parts of New Orleans were submerged under water during Hurricane Katrina some people looted stores and vacant houses. On the other hand many more people stepped up to help their neighbors during and after the crisis.

There was a note in my email box from our time share trading company in Maui. They expressed thanks to some time share owners who had already donated their condo to house people displaced by the wild fire in Lahaina. Our time share unit in Kihei is 20 miles south of the burn area. We are thankful there was no destruction in our part of the island and it was nice owners were willing to help Maui residents.

I have not heard any reports of looting in the burn zone. Most stores and their contents were completely devoured by the fire. Maybe there is nothing left to steal. But it was encouraging to hear time share owners were allowing displaced residents to use their condo in Kihei.

There are several passages in the Bible where people welcomed strangers into their home and provided food and shelter. Hospitality was highly valued in Bible times and still is in many cultures today. If a traveler stopped in the village square someone in the community had an obligation to help provide food and shelter for the stranger and his animals (Genesis 19:1-3 / Hebrews 13:1-2 / First Peter 4:9).

Let me encourage you to watch for an opportunity to help someone in *your* community when they need food or shelter. You may not be able to help everyone but you can certainly help someone. And you might consider helping people beyond your community affected by a fire or flood. They will be glad you did and you will too.

233

Shopping

I shared in a previous story about my experience purchasing clothing at stores like Costco and Sam's Club where there are no dressing rooms. I might see a shirt or pair of shorts that looked nice but I have to buy them and take them home to see if they fit. Most of the time they are too large or too small and I have to return them. This seems crazy.

So this time I took a new strategy. I went with my wife to a large department store to look for a casual shirt and a pair of cargo shorts. This store had dressing rooms so I could try things on and know immediately if it fit or not.

Susan and I browsed through the Men's department and found some nice shorts and a couple of shirts. But we soon discovered they did not fit me. I tried on over ten pairs of shorts but didn't find anything I liked.

It was frustrating finding my size on the rack but discovered it was mislabeled or in the wrong place. My wife brought me one pair which the hanger said was my size but the actual shorts were two sizes smaller. I began to break out in a sweat as I continued to try on shorts that didn't fit. It was very frustrating.

We gave up on shorts and started looking for a new belt. This can be frustrating too. One size was too big and the next size was too small. I emptied my pockets in the dressing room. I put my wallet, cell phone, keys and belt on a small shelf. I asked Susan to make sure I didn't leave anything behind.

At one point in this futile search I emerged from the dressing room with several pairs of cargo shorts and several belts in my hands. I told her none of the shorts fit. And none of the belts felt right either. In fact I showed her one of the belts had clearly been worn. Did someone wear the belt and then return it to the store? Were they selling used belts? I was really getting frustrated. Shopping was exhausting!

But then she noticed I wasn't wearing my belt. The used belt was actually my belt! No wonder it looked different from the other ones! We laughed at my mistake and decided we had done enough shopping for the day. Maybe it isn't any easier buying clothes at a store with a dressing room. We may try shopping online instead.

Another Solar Eclipse

In 2017 there was a total solar eclipse which raced across America from the Pacific to the Atlantic. It was the first one to cover the entire country in fifty years. It was a memorable adventure to witness this rare event in person.

I shared some details of our experience in my previous book. We flew from California to Iowa to visit my Aunt Marjorie. We stayed with some friends and enjoyed a few days in Iowa. Then we drove our rental car from Des Moines to St. Joseph, Missouri to be in the path of the eclipse. Our drive went smoothly and we arrived at a site near a regional airport where 20,000 people gathered to witness the event.

However a summer thunder storm rolled through our area blocking our view during the moment when the eclipse reached totality. We did not get to see the ring of fire around the sun when the moon came between the sun and the earth. But we did experience the three minutes of darkness when we were in the moon's shadow. It was amazing.

The next total eclipse is scheduled for April 8, 2024. It will come up out of Mexico and travel northeast toward New England. Many people are already making plans to find a spot to witness the eclipse. I talked with one family who were making reservations to be on a cruise ship which will be in the path of the eclipse in the Gulf of Mexico. We are making plans to view the eclipse in Austin, Texas. The country will be on the move to be in the path of the total eclipse on April 8, 2024.

There is a passage in the Bible which says, "God made the stars, the sun and the moon and set them in the sky to give light to the earth (Genesis 1:14-19). I believe one of the strongest evidences for the existence of God is the order of the stars and planets. The earth literally hangs in space. Its path is predictable. Its days and years are measurable. It seems far too precise to be an accident or a "big bang". One philosopher wrote, "A watch implies a watch maker". A watch is too complicated to have just appeared out of nothing. I believe the same is true of our planet and the universe. The Bible often speaks of the God of heaven and earth (Psalm 121:2). Let me encourage you to open your Bible and learn more about Him. And don't miss the next eclipse. You will be glad you did.

Greeting Cards

I often encourage people to send a card or note to a friend or family member to say hello and tell them you are thinking about them. I know fewer and fewer people are buying and using greeting cards today. It is much easier and faster to send a text, email or other form of internet communication to encourage someone.

However there are a number of benefits to cards verses the internet. A greeting card is more personal. It is hand written. It usually includes a poem or message which expresses your sentiment or sympathy. It can be displayed in your home or office. It is both visual and tangible.

Recently I received a number of thoughtful greeting cards for my birthday. Some arrived in the mail. Others were handed to me in person. It was fun to open them one at a time. It was kind of like a box of chocolates. You never know what you will get.

Some of the cards were humorous. One had a giant cheese burger on the front with birthday candles on top of the burger. Another card was handmade by my six year old granddaughter Janie. She had drawn a birthday cake with candles on the front with the words, "*Happy Birthday Pop Pop*". A third card had the faces of the actors from the *Star Wars* movie. It said, "A Long Time Ago" on the cover. Inside it said, "You Were Born" and "May Birthday Happiness Be With You".

Another reason for the decline in greeting cards is the rising cost. One card may cost six to eight dollars. Plus there is the cost of postage. But smart shoppers can find some nice Hallmark greeting cards for one dollar at the Dollar Store. Sometimes they even sell some two for a dollar. My wife likes to purchase greeting cards at *Trader Joe's*. They only cost one dollar but look like they are from the Hallmark store.

In Bible times people sent letters across the Roman Empire. Many of these were preserved in trash dumps in Egypt and other warmer climates. They included personal messages from one friend or family member to another. The Apostle Paul wrote some personal messages to friends and fellow believers which are preserved in the Bible in *First & Second Timothy, Philemon and Titus*. Let me encourage you to take the time to buy and send a card to someone *this week*. Tell them you are thinking about them as they celebrate a birthday or anniversary or sympathy over the death of a loved one. They will be glad you did.

August 19
What a Mess

We have a large pantry in our kitchen filled with canned goods, baking supplies and other food items. There are boxes of breakfast cereal and brownie mixes. There are bags of tortilla chips and chocolate chips. It is surprising how much stuff can be stored in the pantry.

One day the unexpected happened. As we were searching for something in the pantry a large bottle of olive oil fell off a shelf and shattered on the tile floor. Thankfully no one was hurt but there was shattered glass everywhere and olive oil too. We quickly grabbed a roll of paper towels and began to mop up the mess.

We tried to carefully pick up the broken glass off the tile floor. There were both large and small pieces. We worked slowly to avoid getting cut by the glass. But the olive oil presented a different challenge. How do you soak up and wipe up a slippery liquid on a tile floor?

The paper towels helped but it was difficult to soak up all of the slippery liquid. My wife suggested we get a bucket of soap and water to clean up the oil. It seemed like a good idea but we were not sure it would really get all of the olive oil off the floor.

What would you recommend to clean up the oil spill on the kitchen floor? She decided to ask our internet friend *Alexa* what would be the best way to clean up this mess. She quickly replied – *Baking Soda*! We never thought of that but it did make sense to use a dry powder to clean up a greasy liquid on the tile floor.

We decided to give it a try. After using paper towels to soak up most of the liquid we sprinkled a generous amount of Baking Soda on the slippery mess and it worked! The powder absorbed most of the oil. Then we used a dust pan and small broom to collect the residue. We went back over the area a second time and it was easy to sweep up the dry *Baking Soda*. A simple solution to our slippery mess.

In a similar way you can find simple and practical solutions to your problems in the Bible. It is filled with words of hope, practical instructions and reminders of God's love and forgiveness. Let me encourage you to read one chapter of the Bible each day. Don't start on page one – start in the Book of Mark. Allow God to open your heart and provide peace of mind. You will be glad you did and He will too.

Nehemiah

My wife and I met Lothar (pronounced – Lota) and his wife Nancy many years ago in Tucson Arizona. Nancy joined the staff at our new preschool. She brought lots of fun ideas and memorable children's songs to teach the young students. They had two young children.

Lothar was an electrician and eventually started his own company. He was recognized for the quality and efficiency of his work by one of the largest home builders in Southern Arizona.

He also helped with a number of building and remodeling projects at our church in Tucson. One winter when business was slow he sent some of his crew to re-wire the oldest building on our property at his own expense.

He also helped me with a number of projects at my home in Diamond Bar. He installed ceiling fans in every bedroom in our house. I climbed around in the attic while he guided me from below to the location of each fan. Lothar also ran a new 220 outlet from the electric panel to power the electric dryer in our condo in Scottsdale.

Lothar was from Germany but loved Arizona. He frequently took his dog for a walk early in the morning following trails and dry river beds in the Sonoran desert. He was a good student of the Bible as was not afraid to ask questions when he didn't understand something.

Nancy and Lothar also experienced the death of their daughter when she was in Middle School. It was a heartbreaking journey for them and for our church too. Lothar and Nancy sometimes joined the other couples on some of our "Golf and Shop" adventures even though Lothar did not golf. He was an avid reader and preferred to spend his time with a good book rather than golf.

There was a man in the Bible named Nehemiah. He led the effort to rebuild the walls of Jerusalem around 400 BC. He saw the opportunity to help people rebuild their city. Lothar was like Nehemiah. He was a man of faith who was willing to use his skills and experience to build homes and help people. Let me encourage you to express your appreciation to the couples and individuals who have helped you and encouraged you when you needed help. They will be glad you did and you will too.

The Trash

There are some familiar routines in our daily lives which we do almost without thinking. We do them day after day and week after week. And our neighbors do them too.

One of these routines is putting our trash cans out by the street every week. Tuesday is trash day. Some of our neighbors actually put their garbage cans out on Monday night so they aren't rushing before they leave for work on Tuesday. I put our trash cans out on Tuesday morning because the garbage trucks don't usually come until mid-afternoon.

However, there are some exceptions. Holidays can force us to change our routine. Normally we get an alert from Waste Management informing us trash day will be one day later because of the 4th of July or Memorial Day. Most neighbors adjust their schedule by one day but a few miss the message and are a day early or a day late.

Another thing which can disrupt this weekly routine is when the trucks come earlier than normal. One time the drivers came early Tuesday morning and a number of neighbors like me did not have their buckets on the street yet. The result was confusion and frustration. We missed the trash pickup and are stuck with our garbage for another week.

California is serious about trash. We have three buckets. The Green one is for grass and tree trimmings. The Grey bucket is for recycle. The black one if for trash and garbage. They have introduced a fourth bucket for food waste but I don't think many people are using it yet.

Trash day is only one of many routines which affect our daily lives. The local schools impact our driving habits. We try to avoid going to the store or scheduling a meeting during the hours when parents are dropping off or picking up their children at school. Mail delivery is another part of our daily routine. I often check the mail box before noon to see if the mail person has delivered a letter or package.

There is a passage in the Bible which reveals part of Jesus' daily routine. One verse says, "Jesus got up early in the morning while it was still dark and went out to a lonely place to pray (Mark 1:35). Let me encourage you to add a new routine in your daily life to read a chapter in the Bible and pray every day. You will be glad you did.

Digging through the Trash

I mentioned in a previous story about some of the routines which are part of our daily and weekly schedules. One of them is putting out the trash cans. Tuesday is trash day in our neighborhood. Every Tuesday rain or shine the grey, green and black buckets need to be on the curb.

We learn a lot about our neighbors by the size of their trash cans and the volume of their trash. For example, I could tell when someone was remodeling a bathroom or kitchen when I saw a sink sticking out of their black garbage bucket. I knew when a neighbor got a large screen TV when I saw the big cardboard box in their grey recycle bucket.

Did you know archeologists learned about life in ancient civilizations by digging through their trash dumps? They found ancient Greek vases and broken pieces of pottery buried in the soil from Russia to Africa. They found Cuneiform clay tablets with letters and business documents in the sands of the Middle East.

Linguists learned a lot about the ancient Greek language by exploring garbage dumps in Egypt. Greek words were written on paper-like material made from the Papyrus plant. We still see greeting cards and other things made with Papyrus today. The dry desert climate preserved letters and legal documents which were written on Papyrus. They provided helpful insights into the life of ancient civilizations. And they improved our understanding of the Greek language which was written and spoken around the Mediterranean world in ancient times.

I wonder what archeologists will learn about our modern civilization when they dig through our garbage dumps in the future. I'm sure they will be amazed by the volume of trash we left behind. In California the state legislature mandated we reduce our trash by 50% by 2025. We are encouraged to recycle and reuse items instead of throwing them away. Landfills are reaching capacity.

There is a passage in the Bible which reminds us to not keep accumulating more and more stuff. Life is not measured by how much we own. It is measured by how much we share with others (Luke 12:13-21). Let me encourage you to find a thrift store near you and donate items you don't need. Reduce your spending and increase your sharing. You will be glad you did and others will too!

Cleaning Carpets

One of the biggest challenges we faced when we combined our two households was what to do with all the extra stuff. We had two refrigerators, two washers and two dryers. We had two sets of dishes and two sets of pots and pans. We had extra beds and extra sheets.

Instead of having a garage sale we decided to give many extra things away to a local ministry with a thrift shop. The *Sheep Fold* ministry helps women with children who are dealing with domestic abuse. Our donations could be sold by the store or given directly to women in need. We were glad we had extra things to donate to this program.

Another thing we had were some extra silk rugs. Two of them were very large and very heavy. These throw rugs could fill a dining room or living room. We decided to ask some friends to take these to our condo in Arizona. They were very expensive and had come from India. They were colorful and attractive. But they had been in storage for several years and needed to be cleaned.

Rather than hire a carpet cleaner we decided to do it ourselves. I went to Lowe's and rented a heavy duty Bissell carpet cleaner machine and a bottle of the recommended carpet cleaning solution. We rolled the large Persian Rugs out on the garage floor and went to work. They were heavy and difficult to move around. First we vacuumed each carpet. Then we used the cleaning machine. The residue from the water and cleaning solution revealed the carpets were very dirty from their years in storage. It was hard work but the results were very encouraging.

We were excited and exhausted as we reflected on our effort. The carpets looked very nice but our bodies were very tired. Maybe we should have hired a cleaning company to do the work. But there was a sense satisfaction seeing the results of our labor. There are several passages in the Bible which affirm the value of hard work (Ephesians 4:28 / Colossians 3:23 / First Thessalonians 4:11-12 / Second Thessalonians 3:7-10).

Let me encourage you to get off the couch and get to work on some projects around your house *this week*. Use the strength God has given you to help yourself and help others too. You will be glad you did and they will too.

A Serious Situation

Recently I heard some alarming news from a life-long friend. His note revealed he was facing a serious medical situation which the doctors could not explain. He said he was unable to use his right hand. His brain and his hand were not working together. He was having trouble buttoning his shirt, brushing his teeth and writing with a pen. Something was seriously wrong.

Tom and I had worked together on many building projects at our church in Tucson. We constructed classrooms and laid concrete blocks. We hung drywall and painted classrooms together. He helped me install a new sink in our condo in Scottsdale. He was both handy and helpful.

He had been an athlete in high school and he enjoyed skiing with his wife and children in northern Arizona. He liked to ride his trail bike along the dirt roads through the desert near his home. We played many rounds of golf together. He enjoyed playing and swimming with his children and grandchildren in their backyard pool.

My friend had consulted with some of the best medical professionals in Tucson. Neurologists and rheumatologists were baffled by his condition. Clearly he and his wife were very concerned too. You could probably share a similar story about your friends and family members. People all around us face life-threatening illnesses. Often their doctors and medical professionals do not have a solution to their situation.

What can you do and where can you turn to find help in time of need? One obvious step is to pray. Pray and tell God the concerns on your heart for yourself or your loved ones. Ask God to intervene and guide the doctors as they attempt to diagnosis and treat the situation.

Read the Bible. The book of Psalms is filled with the prayers and cries of people who were facing difficult situations. One author said the theme of the book of Psalms is, "*Life is tough but God is good*". He is like a rock in times of trouble. He hears our cry for help. One author wrote, "God is our refuge and strength, an ever-present help in times of trouble" (Psalm 46:1). Let me encourage you to pray for a friend or a family member who are facing unexpected hardships and trouble. Reach out to them with a thoughtful card or call *this week*. Don't preach to them. Listen to them. They will be glad you did and you will too.

Don't Be in a Hurry

I shared part of this story in another article but I think the lesson is worth repeating. One day we were in a hurry to catch a flight at Ontario airport. We loaded our carry-on suitcases into the car, locked the house, turned off the water and rushed to the airport. We parked our car in the long-term lot and walked to the nearby terminal.

We were not sure how the time got away but it seemed like it took us forever to get out of the house. We should have packed the night before but we were busy with other things. So we quickly packed our bags and hurried out the door. Actually we did get to the airport in plenty of time. The new TSA pre-check helped us get through security without standing in a long line.

When we got to our gate at the airport I walked off to find a snack while Susan stayed with our luggage. I noticed a smile on her face when I returned. She pointed to her feet and laughed as she explained she was wearing two different color shoes. In our hurry to get out of the house she put on one red shoe and one blue shoe. The bedroom was dark when she put on her shoes. She didn't realize what she had done until we got to the airport. All we could do was laugh.

After that experience we adopted a new slogan - *Don't be in a hurry*. We still say this to each other several times a day. Remember to slow down and take your time. *Don't be in a hurry*.

This lesson can apply to many areas of your life. Don't be in a hurry to make a major purchase or financial decision. Don't be in a hurry when you are looking for a spouse to spend the rest of your life with. Don't be in a hurry getting your children to school. Don't be in a hurry when you spend time with family and old friends. The list is endless.

In the book of Joshua the Israelites made a hasty decision with serious consequences (Read Joshua Chapter 9). They were deceived by their enemies and did not pray before making their decision. There is a verse in the Bible which says, "Blessed are all who wait for Him" (Isaiah 30:18). Sometimes the best decision is to wait and not make a foolish choice or dangerous decision. How many times have you made a decision you later regretted? Let me encourage you - *Don't be in a hurry*. Take time to pray. Ask God for guidance. Talk with a trusted friend before moving forward. And make sure you check your shoes!

Mary Jo

My wife and I met Mary Jo and her husband at our church in Diamond Bar many years ago. They bought their home in Walnut at about the same time we purchased our home in Diamond Bar. They took us to dinners at a fancy restaurants. We enjoyed getting to know them.

Mary Jo loved missionaries. She joined the mission's leadership team at our church and faithfully followed the work our missionaries were doing around the world. She also participated in our short-term teams in Russia and worked alongside our missionaries in different countries.

She became active with the widow's group at our church after her husband died. This energetic group enjoyed spending time together and loved to help and encourage one another.

But the thing Mary Jo loved to do the most was pray. She prayed for our missionaries and for individuals she knew who were going through difficulties in their lives. She attended the small prayer group which met early Sunday morning to pray for our church and other people.

She was a faithful member of the Pastor's Prayer Corp too. This group did not have any meetings but prayed for me and our church. These older adults committed to pray for our church every day. I sent them a list of specific needs and requests each month and shared answers and new requests the following month. Mary Jo and others prayed day after day, year after year.

I wonder if prayer is part of your daily routine. We get so busy we rarely make time to pray. I'm talking about sitting down at your kitchen table or finding a cozy chair in your living room and talking with God from your heart. I'm not talking about religious rituals but simple prayers for yourself, your family, your friends and missionaries around the world.

Pastor Bill Hybels of the Willow Creek Community Church in Illinois wrote the book, "*Too Busy To Pray*". He believed we have allowed ourselves to get so busy that we don't spend a few minutes alone with God in prayer. Jesus set the example by spending time alone with His Heavenly Father early in the morning while it was still dark (Mark 1:35). Let me encourage you to follow his example. Set aside some to pray *every day*. You will be glad you did and He will too.

Settling Your Account

I have shared on several occasions about an annual event we shared with some of our close friends from Tucson. We called it *Golf & Shop*. Four or five couples got together once-a-year to continue and deepen our friendships with one another. The men golfed and the women shopped. The women assumed they could spend as much money shopping as the men did golfing.

We met in a variety of locations and enjoyed making many memories together. We typically rented a VRBO with enough bedrooms and bathrooms for each couple. We liked having a kitchen for coffee, breakfast and a closing BBQ. We also went to some very nice restaurants.

At the end of our four day getaway one of the guys totaled up how much each couple owed for the housing, groceries and golf. Each couple paid for their own lunch and dinner but sometimes one of the men had to prepay for golf reservations ahead of time.

Usually Tom did the final calculations and handed each of the men the total amount for their expenses. It was more complicated than it appears. But Tom kept good track of who paid for what and the final amount each couple owed for the short week. Each of us had to settle our account with him. He was always fair and right.

There are some accounting terms used in the Bible to illustrate our standing before God. Each of us have a deficit balance because we are sinners in God's sight. The Bible says Jesus died on the cross and rose again to pay for our debt (sin) and provide us with a home in heaven.

The Apostle Paul wrote, "If you are a hard worker and do a good job, you deserve your pay and we don't call your wages a gift. But if you see that a job is too big for you, something only God can do and you trust Him to do it – that is what gets you set right with God. It is a gift" (Romans 4:4-5 the Message Bible). We are set right with God by faith in Christ alone. His forgiveness is a gift. Our account is settled when we believe in Jesus death and resurrection as the payment for our sins. Let me encourage you to read Paul's letter to the people in Rome and see how God settles your account with Him through faith in Christ. You will be glad you did.

Decisions

There have probably been times in your life where you made a poor decision which had a negative impact on your career and your future. After I completed my four-year program at Dallas Seminary I was invited to enroll in another program to earn a Doctor of Ministry degree. It was a brand new program with a limited enrollment. But after talking it over with my wife I decided to not pursue the degree.

Several factors influenced my decision. It would involve flying to Dallas from Arizona twice a year for classroom instruction. In addition there would be more books to read and more papers to write during the months between the on-campus classes.

I already had a full-time job as the new pastor of the church in Tucson. How would I have time to do academic studies and pastor a church too? My family would also be impacted if I decided to pursue the degree. My first priority was my wife and children.

I was a young pastor with a young children and a limited budget. The cost of tuition, books and travel was beyond my income at the church. How would I find the resources to pay the bills at home and pursue an academic degree too?

I also thought it would be better to pursue a more academic degree than a professional degree. I had completed a Master's degree in Family Counseling at the University of Arizona and planned to apply for their doctoral program. I thought a degree from the U of A would carry more weight than another degree from the seminary.

All of these things led me to not enroll in the new D. Min program at Dallas Seminary in the 1970's. As I look back on my decision I think it was a mistake. The additional training might have helped me be better prepared to lead the church in Tucson and later in Diamond Bar, California. It could have been a time for my wife and me to grow in our faith and trust God to provide the money needed to pay for travel, books and tuition. I might have also benefitted from studying under some of the top professors at the seminary in a smaller classroom environment. Ironically I was accepted in the program in Dallas but didn't go and I was not accepted into the program at the U of A either. Let me encourage you to live by faith and follow the doors God opens for you. You will be glad you did.

Chicken Feathers

I grew up in a suburb of Phoenix, Arizona. It was a beautiful desert setting with orange groves and cotton fields watered by irrigation. My father worked for a bank and my mother was a stay at home mom. The closest thing to farming I had ever experienced was a hayride when I was a teenager. A few friends in high school did ride horses but I didn't I know anyone who lived on a farm.

During my seminary studies in Dallas, Texas, I was invited to speak at a church near Kansas City, Missouri. A small church was looking for a new pastor and the seminary placement director asked if I would like to speak at this church. Our brother-in-law Pat was an officer in the Army and was stationed at a military base in Kansas at that time. So we drove from Dallas to Kansas to visit some family members and to speak at this rural church outside of Kansas City. We stayed in the home of a church member who had a small farm. We enjoyed a nice dinner with our hosts after speaking at the church.

However our Sunday dinner was interrupted when a family member rushed in with news that a predator had gotten into the chicken coup and killed a number of chickens. I don't remember the details but everyone sprang into action. Our hosts explained they needed to deal with the dead chickens immediately. We followed them out to the barn where the chickens had been placed in a large tub of hot water. I remember the husband and wife grabbing a dead chicken out of the bucket and began pulling the feathers off of the chickens.

We joined the effort even though we had never done anything like this before. Jeanne had stuffed and roasted a turkey before but they had already been processed. We had never pulled feathers off a dead chicken. It was an unexpected experience of life on a farm to help this family as they worked against the clock to salvage some chickens.

They didn't teach us how to pull feathers off chickens in seminary. But the Bible does instruct us to be ready to help people in need. There is a verse in the Bible which says we need to be willing to help those around us (First Peter 4:10). Let me encourage you to watch for an unexpected opportunity to help someone *this week*. It could be a good friend or a total stranger. Be ready and willing to help. You will be glad you did and they will too.

Hurricane Hillary

My wife and I live in Southern California. The weather is idyllic with mild temperatures and minimal humidity. Summer days can get pretty warm but the evenings cool off with an ocean sea breeze. We live inland about 30 miles from the beach. Our temperatures can be 15-20 degrees warmer than temperatures at the water. But we really do have some of the nicest weather in the country year round.

However weather forecasters were predicting a rare occurrence over the next few days. *Hurricane Hillary* was barreling toward Southern California. Yes a real hurricane was coming. This had been front page news for the past few days. The last hurricane to hit the Los Angeles area was almost 100 years ago in 1939.

Hillary was off the coast of Baja California. It was a category four storm with winds up to 150 miles an hour. If it continued on this path it would slam into our area in the next 24 hours. Meteorologists predicted it could bring 3-6 inches of rain in one day. That is almost one-half of the usual amount we get in a whole year.

Forecasters predicted the hurricane would lose strength as it moved north into cooler waters. By the time it arrived in Southern California the winds should be down to 40 miles per hour. It will only be considered a tropical storm by the time it hits the mainland. But strong winds and heavy rain were expected from San Diego to Santa Barbara. Areas to the east like Palm Springs would also be impacted.

It is strange to hear these predictions and wonder what we should do to prepare for this once-in-a-lifetime event. People in Florida and the Gulf coast deal with hurricanes year after year. Most are acquainted with hurricanes and act accordingly. But residents near the west coast were unfamiliar with what was coming.

There are several passages in the Bible when Jesus warned his followers to be prepared for future events. He said it will be like the time of Noah when people raised families and went to work every day. Then disaster will come unexpectedly (Luke 17:26-27). He urged his audience to be prepared and not be caught by surprise when unforeseen things happen. Let me encourage you to be prepared for tornadoes in the middle of the country or hurricanes along the coast. You will be glad you did.

Problems with Your Passport

In the years following the end of the Covid19 pandemic people have been traveling by car, trains and planes. Airports are reporting record numbers of passengers. People who were restricted from traveling during the Covid19 crisis are now on the move again.

Those who are making plans to travel overseas need to carry a passport. Thousands of people are applying for a passport for the first time and many others are renewing their existing ones. The result has been a backlog of applications. News reports revealed it could take up to three months to get a new passport. This caused a lot of stress and concern for many travelers.

One of my wife's granddaughters was scheduled to fly to Italy. She and her aunt had planned a two week trip to visit Italy and Sicily. Morgan applied for a new passport but week after week it did not arrive. Finally in desperation she called her local Congressman to ask for help. One of the aides contacted the passport office to intervene for her. Morgan was able to go to the Federal building in Los Angeles the day before her departure to finally get her new passport.

We heard a similar story from a church friend. Nick was scheduled to go on a business trip to South Africa. His old passport had expired so he applied for a new one. He had a similar experience watching the calendar waiting for his new passport to arrive. He also contacted his Congressman and he was able to obtain his new passport the day before his departure.

However I am glad to report my wife had a much less stressful experience renewing her passport. We were scheduled to lead a group from our church to Israel in early October. Susan applied to renew her passport in July hoping it would arrive in time. The wait time for the new travel document was expected to be 12-15 weeks. However we were pleasantly surprised to find her new passport in our mail box in less than five weeks! What a relief.

The Apostle Paul wrote to early Christians to remind them their citizenship is in heaven (Philippians 3:20). When someone puts their faith in Christ they are guaranteed a home in heaven. No paper work required. It is a gift from God not a result of works. Let me encourage you to place your faith in Jesus today and find peace trusting in Him.

September 1
A Tale of Two Showers

I have shared in the past I enjoyed working with my hands to build and repair things in our home and at our church. I learned a lot about construction by working alongside men who had experience pouring concrete, framing walls and installing plumbing. They patiently taught me how to read blue prints and anticipate how a room or building came together from the ground up.

Those experiences gave me the confidence to do build several room additions to our homes in Arizona and California. As our young family grew in Arizona I was able to add a large family room and later a fourth bedroom and third bath. I also added a fourth bedroom and third bathroom to our home in California.

When I added the bedroom and bathroom to our house in California I installed a fiberglass bathtub shell. This was a mistake. I should have installed a walk-in shower instead of a bathtub. I constructed the bed room and bathroom with my children in mind. But in the back of my mind I also knew one of our older parents might need to live with us.

The addition was completed with County permits and inspections. We really liked how well it worked out for our teenage daughters. But when our older parents came to visit the bath tub was a problem. It was especially difficult for my mother-in-law to navigate. The same was true for my father a few years later. I should have installed a step-in shower.

Later my wife and I decided to remodel the other two bathrooms in our house in California. This time I decided to hire professionals to do the work instead of trying to do it myself. These skilled craftsmen did an excellent job. This time we decided to replace the old bath tub with a walk-in shower.

This was the right decision. It was so much easier to use than a bathtub. There is a passage in the Bible where King Hezekiah planned ahead and built a secret water tunnel in Jerusalem (Second Chronicles 32:1-4 & 30). A huge enemy army was marching toward the city. Hezekiah's goal was to conceal water from the Babylonians and provide water for Jerusalem when it came under siege. He planned ahead. Let me encourage you to learn from my mistake. Think ahead. When in doubt don't go with the bathtub. Go for the walk-in shower. You will be glad you did and your family and guests will too!

Invest for the Long Term

I was privileged to be part of two new churches. The first was when I was a teenager and my parents began attending Scottsdale Bible Church in the 1960's. The church began with a handful of people in 1962 in a storefront on Scottsdale Road just south of Thomas Road. My parents began to attend church services in 1964.

It was an exciting time at Scottsdale Bible. The young pastor named Dr. Jim Borror provided energetic leadership and solid Bible teaching. He invested time in the teenagers and added new staff as the church grew. They built their first campus on McDonald Drive just west of Scottsdale Road. Later when other pastors led the church they relocated to a new site on Shea Boulevard just east of Scottsdale Road. Today over 2500 people attend the church 50 years after its inception. The small beginning of a handful of people with a lot of faith continues to touch people in their community fifty years later.

The other new church I was privileged to be a part of was Vantage Point Church in Eastvale, California. Greg and Carol Crawford invited me and a handful of people to start a Bible study in their new home in 2003. A few years later more people joined the effort to launch a new church in this growing community. Two faithful men led these pioneers and launched Vantage Point in 2008. It was not an overnight success. About 200 people attended the first weekly service at a local Middle School. The church moved to the larger high school auditorium and steadily grew through the next decade. Eventually they were able to purchase land and construct their first building. The church has grown from 200 to over 2,000 people in the past 15 years.

The faith and sacrifice of this energetic group continues to impact families and individuals. The investment of their time and finances continues to bring new people to Christ. The long term results have been amazing.

The Apostle Paul wrote, "One plants and another waters but God causes it to grow" (First Corinthians 3:6). He was talking about starting new churches across the Roman Empire. Let me challenge you to invest your time and money to help start more new churches. Your investment will impact many generations to come. They will be glad you did and you will too.

Senior Softball

I know several people my age who are actively involved in a softball league for senior adults. They wear uniforms and play at various locations around the community. This is serious business. They practice one day a week and usually play one game a week.

Softball is not the only sport seniors are involved in. Pickle ball has become the newest interest for active retired adults. Players use one half of a tennis court to play this popular sport. The smaller court makes it easier to play and still provides plenty of exercise too. Someone described it as a blend of tennis and ping pong. There are pickle ball leagues everywhere and I heard they now have national tournaments and playoffs.

In addition to good exercise, activities like softball and pickle ball provide a social component too. People need a partner to play pickle ball and a whole team to play softball. Participants look forward to connecting with their fellow players. You can hear laughter and cheers coming from the softball field and the pickle ball court.

It seems many adults are determined to remain active even as they get older. There are some risks involved for seniors playing competitive sports. We know people who have pulled a hamstring or broken a finger. But most players are careful to avoid contact with other players. I always reminded people at our church's annual Turkey Bowl flag football game the goal was not to win the game. The goal was to not get hurt!

There was a man named Caleb in the Bible who remained active and strong in his senior years. He helped Moses lead the Israelites out of slavery in Egypt and into the promise land in Canaan. When he was 80 years old he said he felt like 40 and was ready to lead the army in battle even at his age (Numbers Chapters 13 & 14 / Joshua 14:6-15).

Let me encourage you to stay active in your senior years. Find a softball or pickle ball league or some other athletic program in your neighborhood. Get off the couch and out the door. Enjoy some fresh air and fellowship with other adults your age. You will be glad you did and they will too.

. **Insanity**

Someone said insanity is doing the same thing over and over again expecting different results. I wonder why I keep doing the same thing even though it has been unsuccessful again and again. I'm not talking about scientific research. I'm referring to buying clothes. I saw a pair of jeans at a reduced price at our local Costco store. It was a name brand – *Levi's*. The fabric was soft and looked sturdy. They were labeled "*505 Regular*" with a straight leg and extra room in the thigh. It looked like the type I like to wear.

I must admit I am not a fan of the newer skinny jeans. I like the ones that have a straight leg fit. Some jeans can fit low on the hip but this pair looked more like the typical blue jeans I grew up with. Against my better judgement I purchased a pair at Costco. The price was listed as $36.95 but they were on sale for $12.00 off. After all who doesn't want to save twelve dollars on a pair of *Levi's* jeans?

One problem with buying clothes at Costco is the absence of dressing rooms. You just have to buy the pants or shirt on faith hoping it will be the right size for you. You have to buy it, take it home and try them on to see if they will fit your unique size and shape. I have done this many times with very little success. My wife Susan often looks for a new pair of walking shorts or a golf shirt for me when she goes to Costco or Sam's Club. She has no problem returning them if they don't fit. I find it frustrating to have to take the items back to the store.

The result of my latest effort to buy a pair of pants at the store and try them on at home was another failure. The label on the Levi's jeans said waist-32 and length-32. When I tried on the jeans the waist was a little snug but I thought it would work. But the length was not even close. The pant legs had to be at least 3-4 inches too long.

Why do I do the same thing over and over again and expect different results. Maybe some people do have success buying clothes at a store or online without trying them on. Maybe they buy six to eight different sizes of the same pants or shirts hoping one of them will actually fit. There is a verse in the Bible which says, "Don't worry about what you will eat or what you will wear. Your heavenly father knows what you need" (Matthew 6:31-34). Let me encourage you to shop where you can try on the clothes before you purchase them. You will enjoy it more and save time and have less stress. You will be glad you did.

Routines

All of us enjoy a summer vacation and an extra day off from work. Life can get busy and we all need some rest and relaxation. But there is something to be said for regular routines. These weekly rhythms provide stability and continuity to our lives.

One of the routines in our family is trash day on Tuesdays. We know the trash truck usually comes around the same time on the same day every week. There are exceptions for holidays but most of the time if it is Tuesday it is trash day. We collect the trash from the kitchen and each of the bathrooms and deposit it in the big black bucket on the side of our house. Then we put the container out on the curb on Monday night or early Tuesday morning.

Another weekly routine at our house is street sweeping on Wednesday. The city tries to keep our community clean by contracting with a private company to clean the streets and gutters. However this is a little more complicated. During the fall and winter months they sweep the streets every week. But in the spring and summer months they only sweep every other week. So we constantly ask each other if the city is sweeping this week because you can get a ticket if your car is parked on the street blocking the sweeper truck.

Maybe the most important routine in our family was going to church on Sunday. Since I was the pastor I had to go. But my wife faithfully got the kids dressed and fed and off to church every Sunday. Actually we liked going to church every week. It was an opportunity to reconnect with friends and a time to recharge our spiritual batteries for the coming week. We loved singing worship songs with other people and studying the Bible together. I loved preaching sermons each week.

Going to church every week was a vital part of our family as our children grew up and still is today even though our kids now have families of their own. There is a verse in the Bible which says, "Let us not give up meeting together each week" (Hebrews 10:25). Let me encourage you to enjoy the routines in your life. Develop some good habits which will benefit you and your family. Find a Bible teaching church in your community and attend services every Sunday. You will be glad you did and your friends and family will too.

Eric & Susan

I met Eric when I was leading the youth ministry at Northwest Bible Church in Dallas, Texas in the 1970's. He and his sister Becky were students at Highland Park High School. Their father was a doctor at Baylor Hospital and their mother was a Bible study leader at church. Eric and some other high school guys played basketball and participated in a Bible with me on Saturday mornings at the church.

Eric went to Wheaton College in Illinois. He also invested one summer leading the fledgling youth ministry at our church in Tucson, Arizona in 1978. After college he enrolled at Dallas Seminary. He came back to Chapel in the Hills in Tucson a few years later for another summer with his new wife Susan. The students loved Eric and Susan.

After he graduated from seminary Eric and Susan joined TEAM mission and set their sights on serving in South Africa. Eric had done a summer internship in the country and felt it was a good opportunity to teach and train future church leaders. They also raised their four children in South Africa.

Eric and Susan lived in South Africa during the time when blacks were given the right to vote and the black majority began to rule the nation. Many people feared there would be a civil war during this transfer of political power. Eric shared with me how Christians across the country prayed for a peaceful transition and there was.

In a recent conversation Eric and Susan shared their thoughts about retirement. Should they remain in South Africa or relocate closer to their family back in the United States. They have had a crucial role in the Bible College where they taught for decades. They have trained and equipped hundreds of church leaders.

The Apostle Paul wrote, "Take the things you have received from me and teach them to faithful people who will teach others also" (Second Timothy 2:2). Let me encourage you to use your training and experience to equip others who want to work in your profession. Whether you are an engineer or an educator, a musician or a minister let me encourage you to help prepare the next generation. They will be glad you did and you will too.

Reconnecting

In the early 1990's our church was invited to help with a church planting effort in Central Russia. The Cold War was over. The Berlin Wall had been torn down. Germany was reunited and Russia opened their borders to travelers from the west. The missionary arm of the Evangelical Free Church of America had an opportunity to partner with a Russian evangelist to start some new churches in one of the southern regions called Tartarstan.

We gathered a group of 8-10 adults from our church and packed our bags for Russia in the summer of 1994. It was a long trip from California to Moscow where we joined several other teams from EFCA churches. It was a long train ride from Moscow to Kazan the capital of Tartarstan and even further to different cities in the region. It was a memorable trip as our team worked with a church in a large manufacturing city called Naberezhnye Chelny. The Russian people we met were very kind and helpful to their American guests.

One of the other American pastors was a man named Noah from a church in Nebraska. He brought a team from his church and worked in another city in the region. I enjoyed his warm heart and confident spirit. He had been to Tartarstan a year earlier and was excited to renew his contacts with the Russian people he had met.

I was pleased to see Noah and his wife again at the national meetings of the EFCA in Fullerton, California. It had been almost 30 years since we led our teams to Russia. He had continued to pastor churches in Nebraska and I had continued to lead the church in Diamond Bar until I handed the baton to a younger pastor on our staff a few years ago. It was good to see Noah and hear about his family and ministry. We talked about the years we worked with churches in Russia and the people we met there.

There is a passage in the Bible where the Apostle Paul wrote about his ministry in different churches he started throughout the Roman Empire. He was thankful for the people he had met and commended them for their continued faith in Christ. He wrote, "You have become a model to all the believers – your faith in God has become known everywhere" (First Thessalonians 1:7-8). Let me encourage you to stand firm in your faith and stay connected to believers you have met around the world. They will be glad you did and you will too.

We are very thankful you and your children became part of the Hopper family. We remember the day you and Tim got married at a cozy beach on Coronado Island in San Diego. It was a bright and sunny day with all of our family gathered together for this special occasion.

The setting for the wedding was perfect with ideal California weather on December 29, 2019. The photos taken at the Del Coronado Hotel were great. You looked beautiful. The wedding reception at Tim's school was very nice too. The grandkids had a great time riding around Coronado Island in a golf cart driven by their favorite uncles.

Both Jeanne and I were so thankful you came into Tim's life. We were happy for him to have a wonderful wife and get two great kids to love too. Thanks for adding the Hopper clan to your life.

We were thankful for your love for the Jesus. We were thankful you and Tim found a church where a number of your friends attended and you found places to serve too. We also enjoyed getting to know your parents and your extended family.

You are energetic and motivated. We marveled you were able to complete a 26 mile marathon. And you keep Tim in shape walking through the neighborhood in Glendora. You have been very brave putting up with the teasing of your three brothers-in-law too. We know you are dedicated to teaching high school kids. You have not only been a classroom teacher for many years but you are also a mentor to younger teachers too. You are impacting students and their families.

It was exciting to attend Emily's college graduation from Cal State San Marcos University and to hear about her new career working with preschool and young children. We were excited Landon finished basic training with the Coast Guard and he was awarded a scholarship for his college education at UC Santa Cruz. Both Landon and Emily have a bright future ahead of them. We continue to pray for you, Tim and your children. Thank you for being part of the Hopper family.

To my readers – Let me encourage you to embrace the men and women who marry into your family. Why not make a call or send a note *this week* and express how thankful you are to have them in your lives.

September 9
The Calm Before the Storm

I wrote in an earlier story about Hurricane Hilary which was bearing down on Southern California in August, 2023. We had been watching news on TV and on the internet predicting the arrival of this storm. It was the first tropical storm to hit California since 1938.

By the time the full storm reached California it was downgraded from a category four hurricane with winds up to 140 miles per hour to a tropical storm with winds around 40 miles an hour. The cooler water of the Pacific Ocean caused the storm to lose strength.

The biggest concern was not the wind but the rain. Even though the wind was expected to weaken as the storm approached forecasters predicted areas could receive 4-6 inches of rain in 24 hours. It was interesting to see how accurate these predictions were.

We experienced steady rain through the night but nothing on the scale of what meteorologists were expecting. The winds were calm and the rain diminished. The worst was yet to come. It felt like the calm before the storm.

There is a passage in the Bible where Jesus painted a similar picture. He said things will look normal before His return. People will be busy working, shopping and living their daily lives. But He will return unexpectedly. He urged his followers to pay attention to events around them and keep watching for His return (Read Matthew Chapter 24-25).

Let me encourage you to stay alert and to not become complacent. The Bible predicts world events will unfold in some dramatic and un-expected ways when we least expect them.

And when you are facing a natural disaster like a hurricane, tornado or an earthquake be ready. Make sure you have some drinking water in storage and canned food ready in case grocery stores are closed and help does not reach you for a few days.

We have an earthquake kit in our garage. It is actually a large clean garbage can on wheels. It contains clothes, blankets and sleeping bags. There is a first aid kit and a portable radio which does not require batteries. It is time to clean it out and see what else is in it. Let me encourage you to do the same. You will be glad you did.

The Plagues in Egypt

One of the highlights of leading the church in Tucson, Arizona was meeting many guests who came to our church during the winter months. We called them *snow birds*. They enjoyed spending the winter in warm Arizona instead of enduring the freezing weather in Michigan or Minnesota.

In the summer of 1982 we drove to Michigan, Minnesota and Pennsylvania to see the homes, gardens, farms and barns of these snow birds. They were amazed we would drive with our four young children across the country to visit them. They welcomed us with open arms and treated our children royally.

We typically stayed two nights with each family. We usually arrived in the afternoon. They had dinner ready for us that evening and gave us a tour of their town the next day. We saw so many interesting things. They also showed us their farms and the crops they were growing. We saw their gardens and picked fresh vegetables for dinner. After spending a second night in their home we drove on the next day.

However one time we did stop just for lunch with a family who had a hog farm. The raised the largest pigs we had ever seen. They were huge. It was a hot and humid summer day so we left the windows on our van open while we enjoyed lunch with our hosts.

When we loaded our kids back in the van we discovered it was filled with flies. There were thousands of flies on the interior roof and on the front and back windows too. It was unbelievable. I think the flies took refuge from the summer heat by seeking shade in our van. We didn't know what to do. We finally decided to start driving with the windows down hoping the flies would escape or be sucked out the windows. We drove a number of miles before we finally got all of the flies out.

This experience reminded us of the ten plagues in Egypt. God used Moses to confront Pharaoh and persuade him to let the Israelites go. One of the *ten plagues* was flies swarming over the land and filling all of their homes including the palace (Read Exodus Chapter 18). Let me encourage you to take your children or grandchildren on a road trip across America *this year*. Let them see this wonderful country we live in. They will be glad you did and you will too. And make sure you don't leave your windows open on a hot summer day!

September 11
A Date to Remember

My parents and their peers always remembered where they were the day Pearl Harbor was attacked by the Japanese on December 7, 1941. Most people heard the news of the surprise attack on the radio. It was a date they never forgot.

November 22, 1963 was a date my generation has never forgotten. It was the day when President John Kennedy was shot and killed while riding in an open limousine in downtown Dallas, Texas. Most people heard about this tragedy on the television from the famous news anchor Walter Cronkite. We cried when we heard his report.

Another date which is remembered by this generation is the attack on the World Trade Center in New York City on September 11, 2001. Two airplanes were hijacked by terrorists and flown into the two tall buildings at the Trade Center in Manhattan. A third plane was flown into the Pentagon in Washington, DC and the fourth plane crashed in Pennsylvania when passengers attempted to stop the terrorists. We learned about this terrible event and watched on TV as the two towers collapsed.

All of these dates hold a special place in the hearts of our countrymen. They remind us there is evil in this world and there are people who are willing to go to any extreme to harm innocent people. My wife Susan was a flight attendant with American Airlines at that time. She was not at work on September 11th but two of the four hijacked planes were from American Airlines.

All of the pilots and flight crews were killed on board the four planes along with all of the passengers. Thousands of people were killed when the twin towers collapsed, the Pentagon was hit and the fourth plane crashed in Pennsylvania. I will never forget watching TV when the second tower went down. A few years ago I was able to visit the site of the 9-11 memorials in New York City and at the Pentagon too.

Let me encourage you to talk with your children and grandchildren about some of the important dates in the history of our nation. Talk with them about Pearl Harbor and 9/11. Share with them where you were when President Kennedy was killed. Remind them why we celebrate the 4th of July. They will be glad you did and you will too.

The Floppy Hat

I have shared in the past how I found almost 20 baseball caps in my closet. This was a surprise to me. I didn't realize I had so many hats. Some were souvenirs from places we had been to like Maui and New York City. A number of them were from our local baseball team the Los Angeles Angels. And a few other hats were gifts from friends and family members. My goal is to give most of these hats away and reduce the number in my collection.

I also have a few nicer hats which I wear when I am doing a graveside funeral. Years ago I noticed all of the staff members of a local funeral park wore attractive white hats like the ones you might see in a Hollywood movie. It made sense to require them to wear something on their heads because of the amount of time the employees spent outdoors.

There is another hat in my collection. I describe it as a *Floppy Hat*. This hat has a broad rim and is light weight. You see them being worn by people who are working outdoors like gardeners and workers doing street maintenance. They provide better protection from exposure to the sun and are more comfortable to wear while you are working.

I wear my Floppy hat when I work in our yard. I wear it when I am pulling weeds or planting new seeds in the garden. If I am painting the house or washing my car I usually wear this light colored hat. I also wear it when my wife and I go for a walk because she is the one who gave it to me. It really does help keep the sun off of my face and ears.

My dermatologist encouraged me to do a better job protecting my face from the bright California sun. I have had cancer removed from the rim of one ear and he warned me there could be more if I did not take steps to shield my face and head from the sun. Our Asian neighbors are very careful to protect their skin from too much sun exposure. There is a verse in the Bible which says, "The sun will not smite me by day nor the moon by night" (Psalm 121:3). People in ancient times were superstitious about the full moon. They believed a person could be "*moon struck*" if they were exposed to a bright full moon. Doctors tell us too much direct sun light can damage your skin and cause cancer. Let me encourage you to wear a hat and sun block when you are going for a walk, sitting at an outdoor sporting event or working in your back yard. You will be glad you did and your doctor will too!

September 13
Moving the Kitchen Table

When my wife and I combined our two households we were able to give away a lot of furniture and appliances. We had two washing machines and two clothes dryers. We had two refrigerators and several flat screen TV's. We had extra beds and extra furniture. It was clear we needed to give some of these things away to other people who could use them.

We also had two kitchen tables. Susan had a very large glass top table which could seat 10 people. I had a small wooden table which could seat four. It could expand by adding an extra leaf to seat six. We decided to keep the glass table and give the smaller wooden table to my brother and his wife.

The challenge was how to get the kitchen table from our house to their house. They lived 4-5 hours away. It would be very expensive to ship the table and four chairs. We wondered if we could get them into our Toyota Highlander or into their Nissan Sentra. It was an engineering challenge to figure out how to get the kitchen table to their house.

We started by measuring the diameter of the table and the opening in our Highlander. The table was 52 inches wide but the opening to the Highlander was only 48 inches. Their car was even smaller. Then Steve and Sharon considered borrowing a passenger van from their son and daughter-in-law. But the back door of the van was too small.

What could we do to get the kitchen table and chairs to their house? There had to be a solution to the problem. One day when we were talking with them on the phone we decided to measure the table and the vehicles again. We were surprised to discover the table was actually only 42 inches in diameter *not* the 52 inches we first thought. Maybe the table and chairs would fit in the Highlander after all. And they did! Success!

I wonder if you are facing a problem or dilemma. Maybe there are logistical problems with furniture or storage space. Maybe your challenge involves a strained relationship with a friend or family member. God loves to come to our side and provide solutions to the problems we face each day. One verse says, "I called out to the Lord and He answered me" (Psalm 34:6). Let me encourage you to pray and ask God for help solving your problems. You will be glad you did.

Chicken Soup

We love the rotisserie chickens from Costco. The number of things you can do with a Costco chicken are endless. I love to have fresh chicken with mashed potatoes and gravy. I prefer to make a sandwich or slider with moist Costco chicken instead of the packaged meat in the refrigerator section.

My wife makes wonderful chicken tacos and enchiladas using chicken from Costco. And Susan loves to make chicken soup from the carcass and the drippings from the bottom of the chicken container. She stores the chicken bones in our freezer. When she has collected several carcasses she pulls out a large stainless steel pot and cooks them in boiling water. Then she strains out the remaining bones, cartilage and skin and keeps the chicken broth.

Recently she decided to clean out the freezer in our garage and she found eight frozen chicken carcasses from Costco. I guess it had been a while since she made chicken soup and it looks like we have been eating a lot of chicken lately.

The discovery inspired her to action. She pulled out two large stainless steel pots and put four carcasses in each pot. She added a large amount of water and boiled them slowly for over an hour. The house smelled so good just like Thanksgiving Day with a turkey in the oven!

Then she followed her usual procedure to separate the bones and skin from the broth. The result was one large pot filled with fresh chicken broth. She had enough to make chicken soup for a professional football team. She plans to share some soup with friends to encourage people who are going through tough times.

Chicken soup is often thought of as remedy for illness and ailments. Adults remember their mother or grandmother making chicken soup for them when they were sick. Do you remember a series of books which were titled, "*Chicken Soup for the Soul*"? These books provided heart-warming stories to encourage the reader. The best remedy for sadness and discouragement is the Bible. God's Word can lift your heart and soul. One passage says, "I have put my hope in your Word" (Psalm 119:114). Let me encourage you to read a chapter every day. And when you make some chicken soup please share some with a friend or neighbor. They will be glad you did and you will too.

The Sun Will Come Out Tomorrow

I love the musical about the life of *Little Orphan Annie*. It was based on the radio program about Annie's life and adventures with Daddy Warbucks. In the movie, Annie sings a song for President Roosevelt who was asking for her help during the Great Depression. Her song was intended to lift the spirits of the president and the nation during the difficult time. The words were, "*The Sun Will Come Out Tomorrow*".

That is how I felt during the buildup and arrival of Hurricane Hillary. Weather forecasters had predicted doom and gloom. They predicted strong winds and heavy rains. They forecasted flooding and the loss of electricity. Politicians and public officials were predicting loss of life and damage to private property and public buildings.

The storm finally arrived on Saturday evening, August 19, 2023. We had light rain during the afternoon which became heavier as the day wore on. However, Sunday morning the rain stopped and the sky cleared. But the real event began on Sunday afternoon and continued into Monday morning. We did have some wind and steady rain in our area but nothing destructive. More rain fell and roads were flooded in the desert near Palm Springs.

By Monday afternoon the clouds were gone and the sun was shining. You would not have known a tropical storm roared through the Los Angeles area 24 hours ago unless you saw it for yourself. Most people were relieved it wasn't worse. Public officials celebrated the fact no lives were lost because of Hillary. Many people stayed home during the storm. Trees and power poles were knocked down and some homes were damaged by the powerful flood waters in some locations. There was a sense of relief from the news broadcasters and government leaders. Southern California had survived its first hurricane and tropical storm in 100 years.

There are a number of verses in the Bible which provide hope and reassurance in times of trouble and uncertainty. There is a Psalm in the Bible which says, "The Lord heard my cry and lifted me out of the mud and set my feet upon a rock" (Psalm 40:1-2). There will be times in our lives when our faith is tested and the future is unclear. But God is our refuge and strength. He will not abandon us in times of trouble. Let me encourage you to listen to the weather forecasts and warnings. And rely on God to help you when you face uncertain times.

Flexibility

I like to plan ahead and put some dates on the calendar. I like to have some things to look forward to like vacations and special occasions. I frequently schedule some flights on Southwest Airlines for future travel because I know we can change our plans and cancel our flights without any penalty.

Recently my wife and I had plans to fly to Arizona for a week of rest and relaxation. We enjoy using our cozy condo and doing some cleaning and maintenance. I usually wait until Southwest has a special sale on tickets and then reserve a flight to Phoenix months ahead.

However a few days before our latest trip we got an idea to visit my brother and his wife in Central California. We enjoy spending time with them and it had been a while since we were together. My wife Susan and Steve's wife Sharon have fun shopping and Steve and I had a project we needed to get done.

Another reason we decided to change plans was comparing the two options. Did we want to go to the hot Arizona desert or the cool California coast in the middle of August? Which one would you choose? We thought cool California looked better than hot Arizona.

So in an uncharacteristic moment we canceled our flight to Phoenix and loaded the car for San Luis Obispo. We set aside the plans we had made months ago and set our sights on Central California.

There are a number of examples in the life of Jesus when he changed his plans in order to help someone. Jesus enjoyed an unscheduled dinner with a tax collector named Zacchaeus (Luke 19:1-9) And Jesus stopped to restore the eyesight of a blind beggar named Bartimaeus (Luke 18:35-43). Clearly Jesus had his sights on going to Jerusalem but he was flexible. He was willing to stop and help people who were lost and hurting.

Let me encourage you to be more flexible in your own life. Be willing to change your plans, cancel your reservations and chart a different course. Be ready to help a friend or neighbor who calls unexpectedly. It is a good idea to dream and plan ahead but it can be helpful to change your plans once in a while. You will be glad you did and your family and friends will too.

September 17
Another Walk in the Park

During our trip to Central California my wife and I stayed in our nephew and niece's house in Atascadero. Matt and Sada and their two young children have a lovely home in this cozy community. Matt is a history professor at Cal Poly University. He has a convenient twenty minute commute down highway 101 from their home to the campus.

They live across the street from Atascadero Lake. It is a peaceful setting in the middle of town with a walking path around the lake. We were surprised by how many people were out walking or jogging on the dirt path. A number of people were walking their dogs along the shady trail. Owners and pets were glad to see each other in the cool morning air. We smiled as we watched the social interaction and conversations as people greeted one another.

We also noticed some beautiful homes on the hillsides overlooking the lake. Some homes looked like the original structures built many years ago while others looked like they had been remodeled and enlarged. We could see reflections of houses and trees on the placid lake.

I think we noticed all of these things because it was so different than where we live in Southern California. Don't misunderstand. We love our neighborhood in Diamond Bar but Atascadero felt different. We didn't hear the noise of the freeway and we didn't see a lot of cars going up and down our street.

Instead it was quiet and peaceful. It was a relaxing atmosphere with a moderate morning temperature. We didn't feel a hectic pace when a few cars drove by on a nearby street. I guess it felt like we were back in time in a small town instead of the busy suburb we live in now. You could feel the contrast.

I'm sure there are busy people and active children in Atascadero. We probably didn't see weary mothers rushing to get their children to school on time. And we didn't hear the noise of cars and trucks which might be found in a different part of town. But it sure was refreshing to go for a walk in this quiet neighborhood. Jesus instructed his followers to slow down and rest (Mark 6:30-31). He promised to give them rest (Matthew 11:28-30). Let me encourage you to slow down and smell the roses. Find a peaceful place in your community to relax and enjoy. You will be glad you did.

The Vine and the Branches

I'm sitting in the kitchen of my nephew and niece's home in Central California. They have a lovely home in a quiet part of town. They invited us to stay in their house for a few days while they were out of town.

The sliding door opens onto the back patio. The patio roof is made of several vertical posts and horizontal pieces of wood spaced apart for the cover. In other words the patio is not completely covered. The wood slats were spaced apart providing some shade but also allowing the sun to shine through too.

I was surprised to see clusters of green grapes hanging down from the patio roof. There were bundles of healthy grapes growing above the patio. I'm not sure if they are ready to eat but they sure look good.

There are vineyards all over this part of California. We saw a number of them as we drove down the highway. Many vineyards had large signs inviting visitors to stop and taste their vintage wine. It looks like Matt and Sada could open a winery of their own.

Vineyards were common in Israel in Bible times. Jesus used the image of grape vines in John chapter fifteen to teach some important spiritual principles. He told his followers, "I am the vine and you are the branches" (John 15:1-10). To grow grapes it is essential the branches stay connected to the vine. Spiritually we cannot grow in our faith unless we stay connected to Jesus. The Vine and the branches are inseparable.

In addition, Jesus said the vine keeper must take care of the vineyard by watering and feeding the grape vines. The keeper of the vineyard also pruned the branches to stimulate new growth and to produce better wine. In the spiritual sense Jesus explained to his disciples they needed to be trimmed and pruned in spiritual their lives. This often comes about when we endure difficulties and persecution. The result will be spiritual growth and more spiritual fruit in our lives.

Let me encourage you to read more about the grape vines and the branches in John Chapter Fifteen. Mediate on the words of Jesus and the analogy of our relationship with him. You will be glad you did and He will too.

Floods in Forest Falls

Recent rains from Hurricane Hillary produced flooding in various parts of Southern California. Most of the city streets and flood channels were not affected. But highways and dry riverbeds were flooded and damaged as a result of the heavy rain. Palm Springs and surrounding areas of the desert did experience extensive flooding. Parts of Interstate 10 in the desert were closed because the road was damaged by raging flood waters.

Another area which was affected were the foothills below Mt. San Gorgonio near Yucaipa, California. The road into the Forest Falls area crosses through a dry riverbed. Normally you can see the large boulders and debris which were carried down the riverbed in past floods. But the torrential rains from Hurricane Hillary produced another devastating flood. The normally dry riverbed was a rushing wave of ragging water and debris.

Most people don't understand how powerful and strong flood waters can be. Many years ago there was a huge flood near Estes Park, Colorado. A large group of people were meeting at a conference center in the area. When a large rain storm struck the area attendees were instructed to leave quickly before the flood waters reached them.

People hurried to their cars and drove on to the main highway. Those who turned right were caught by the flood waters and drowned but those who turned left escaped and survived. In the confusion and chaos some people went the wrong way. It was a terrible tragedy.

Jesus told a story about the damage flood waters can do. One man built his house on a rock while another man built his house on sand. When the flood waters came the house on the rock stood firm but the house on the sand was carried away (Matthew 7:24-27).

Jesus used this image to urge his followers to not only listen to His words but to also apply them to their daily lives. People who heard or read His words and obeyed them were like a wise man who built a house on a rock. But those who heard or read His words and did not apply them was like a fool who built his house on sand. Let me encourage you to not be a fool. Be wise and apply the lessons Jesus taught in your daily life. You will be glad you did and He will too.

Planes and Trains

I mentioned in an earlier story that my wife and I stayed at our nephew and niece's house in Atascadero, California while they were on an extended trip to England with their young children. I had been to their house before but Susan had not. A contractor had built a large addition onto the house with a number of special features to accommodate one of their children with some physical challenges. We enjoyed using their house for a few days.

One of the things I learned about their two sons was their love for planes and trains. I knew Silas enjoyed watching an online internet feed of the airplane traffic at LAX. I did not know this was available to the public but I watched it on the computer with him on a previous visit.

Both boys love airplanes. They have some model planes in their rooms and they have a number of posters on the walls too. Several of the posters are from the "*Planes of Fame*" Air Show in Chino, California. Matt and one of the boys stayed at our house in Diamond Bar several years ago so they could attend the annual Air Show in Chino which is close to where we live.

I also knew the two boys loved trains. They have several posters with trains on their bedroom walls. One large poster features the "*Skunk Train*" and reads "*A Wilderness Adventure in Mendocino, California*". One of the boys actually has a train track which is suspended from the ceiling of his bedroom and a model train runs on it. It is pretty cool.

There is an active train station in Atascadero on the route from southern to northern California. There is also a train museum in the town where the boys like to go. My brother Steve loves to take his grandsons down to the station to watch the trains go by and visit the train museum too.

I don't know why young boys love planes and trains. But they do. Let me encourage you to find some things your children and grandchildren enjoy. Take some time to make some memories with them. They will be glad you did and you will too.

A Veterans Memorial

Several years ago my brother purchased a brick to be placed at the Veteran's Memorial Park in Atascadero, California to honor our father's military service in World War Two. I had seen a picture of the brick but I had never been to the park in Atascadero.

Recently my wife and I drove up to Central California to visit Steve and Sharon. One morning we stopped by the park and found the brick with my father's name on it. It says – *Richard I Hopper / Army Air Corp / 1944 – 1946.*

Our dad tried to enlist in the military near the beginning of World War Two but he was rejected for medical reasons. We don't know what the reason was for his deferment. But as the war dragged on and they needed more men to fill the ranks he was accepted to serve in the Army Air Corp in 1944.

After basic training he was sent to school at Scotts Field near St. Louis for training as a telegraph operator. I couldn't believe they still used the telegraph in World War Two. It was something used in the Civil War in the 1860's. But in the original Hollywood movie about the *Battle of Midway* there is a scene where a scout plane discovered the Japanese fleet and sent a message using a telegraph machine to alert our ships in the area. When the Japanese surrendered in 1945 the war came to an end. Our father was sent to occupy Korea for a year before returning to home in 1946.

When we visited the Veterans memorial at the park in Atascadero we were impressed how well it was maintained. It preserved the names of the men and women from Atascadero who served in the armed forces in a number of wars including recent conflicts like Iraq and Afghanistan.

The brick walkway threads through the memorial grounds. Many bricks have the names of friends and family members from around the country who served in the military. It is a fitting way to honor their service and sacrifice.

Let me encourage you to visit a memorial honoring the military service of people from your community. Take time to show your children and grandchildren the plaques and bricks which honor those who served. They will be glad you did and you will too.

September 22
Words and Sounds

I have heard English is one of the most difficult languages to learn. Our church has sent teams to various countries in Europe and Asia to teach English to non-English speakers. Most students really enjoy learning to read and speak English. But it can be confusing. There are a lot of words that sound very similar but have very different meanings. We call these homophones.

English can be confusing for young students to read and write. When I was in elementary school we were taught there are two kinds of letters in the English language – consonants and **vowels**. Most letters are consonants but five letters are **vowels**. The vowels are A, E, I, O, U. Every English word is a combination of consonants and vowels.

For example there are several words in English that sounds very similar. The word **valves** sounds just like the word **vowels**. A **valve** can refer to something that controls the flow of water in a pipe or the volume of fuel that powers a rocket. Another homophone that sounds very similar is the English word **vow**. As a pastor I have lead many couples through their wedding **vows**. I invite the bride and groom to repeat some words after me to express their love and loyalty to one another.

Susan and I drove along the Central Coast of California from my home in the Los Angeles area to my brother's home in Atascadero, California. He has been a pastor for over fifty years. We had asked Steve to lead us through our simple private wedding ceremony at the church where he served. His wife Sharon and another adult were the two witnesses required by California state law.

Steve read a passage in the Bible in First Corinthians chapter 13 and shared some thoughtful insights related to love and marriage. Then he asked Susan and me if we were ready to share our personal vows to one another. After a brief and uncomfortable pause we both repeated the following – **A, E, I, O, U**! Steve was caught by surprise. He wasn't expecting our reply. Then we all laughed together. Eventually we did express our personal vows to one another. But we still smile when we reflect on our wedding ceremony. Let me encourage you to choose your words carefully and add a little humor to your wedding ceremony. You will be glad you did and we will too!

Two Kinds of Pie

I have shared in the past my two favorite desserts are chocolate chip cookies and apple pie. Over the years many people have blessed me with these two favorite delicacies. The problem is too much of either one is not good for my health or my weight.

Each of us have a few favorite foods or desserts we enjoy. For some people it is ice cream and for others it is candy. Some people like chocolate cake while others prefer carrot cake. Maybe you prefer a cup of pumpkin spice coffee from Starbucks.

It is important to communicate clearly and frequently what your favorite things are. When people want to honor you or express their love for you they want give you something they know you will like. I often shared in my Sunday sermons about how much I enjoyed apple pie and chocolate chip cookies. I wanted to make sure people knew what to give me on my birthday or as a Christmas present. My brother said *he only liked two kinds of pie – hot and cold.*

In the Bible there is an account when David was fleeing from King Saul. David was a fugitive constantly on the run trying to avoid being caught or killed by his arch enemy. One time when he was weary and discouraged David said all he needed to lift his spirits was a drink of water from his home town of Bethlehem.

When several of his men heard his words they went into action. They quietly made their way through Saul's lines and into the center of town. They filled a small jug with water from the well in Bethlehem and carefully brought it to David.

But David surprised them by not drinking the water they had risked their lives to obtain. Instead he poured it out on the ground as a thank offering to God. He refused to enjoy this remarkable gift his men had risked their lives to give to him (Second Samuel Chapter 23:14-17).

Let me encourage you to enjoy your favorite dessert from time to time. Make sure you let your loved ones know what your favorite desserts are. And make sure you accept them and enjoy them as expressions of their love for you. They will be glad you did and you will too.

Morning Moms

Recently my wife and I were walking around a park and noticed how many other people were too. There were a number of people walking their dogs and a few walking alone.

But the sight which captured our attention was a group of women pushing baby strollers. There were four women pushing four young children in strollers. They were lined up side by side extending into a small residential street. It looked like a race but they actually continued walking side by side.

Susan noticed all of these moms were wearing exercise clothes with tight leggings and sweat shirts. It looked like they were getting a workout while walking their young children. These mothers may have dropped off their older kids at school and agreed to meet at the park to keep the little ones busy.

We also commented on the conversation these women were having. They were talking up a storm while they kept pace with one another. It was clearly a social event as well as a physical workout. They were having a good time.

I realize some mothers may not have the luxury of a walk in the park pushing baby strollers. Some may not have access to a local park or recreation center. Some women may not have a friend nearby who could be a walking partner. But these four women looked like they had the friends, the clothes, the time and the location to enjoy spending some time and getting some exercise with other young mothers.

There is a verse in the Bible which says, "Physical exercise is of some value but spiritual exercise is even more valuable" (First Timothy 4:8). One of the best ways to consistently get some physical exercise is to work out regularly with a few people. And one of the best ways to stay spiritually fit is to study the Bible with a few other people too.

Let me encourage you to invite a few friends to get some exercise with you a few days a week. Join a gym or start a walking group. And, let me encourage you to get some spiritual exercise too by meeting once-a-week with a few friends or neighbors to study the Bible and pray together. They will be glad you did and you will too.

Morning Moms (Part Two)

Each generation has some distinct qualities and characteristics. They are rarely the same. For example many mothers stayed home and managed the family in the 1940's and 1950's. The title of a "*Stay-At-Home Mom*" was highly valued and respected. In the following decades more and more mothers joined the workforce and developed careers outside the home.

I remember my mother-in-law sharing her story of being a stay-at-home mom. She lived in one of the original suburbs on Long Island, New York called Levittown. It was built after the end of World War Two. One article I found said, "Levittown was the first mass-produced housing development and set a standard for planned subdivisions for years to come". It was designed with schools and stores close enough for people to walk to.

Like many of the post-war families my in-laws only had one car. If the husband drove to work the mother was left without a car. And if the wife needed the car the husband carpooled with other men who lived nearby.

One of the advantages of being a stay-at-home mother was making friends with other wives on your street. My mother-in-law said she and a few other housewives got together every morning after the kids went off to school. They wore their house coat and walked across the street with a cup of coffee to visit with other mothers before they started their house work for the day. It was part of their morning routine.

There were some disadvantages to this lifestyle. My father-in-law shared a story about driving his car to work. One day after he took the carpool home from work, his wife asked him where the car was. Then he realized he had left the car at work! He forgot he drove the car in the morning and out of habit he took the carpool home that night!

There is a remarkable passage in the Bible which speaks highly of wives and mothers. It reminds us to honor and value all they do to keep a family fed and functioning (Proverbs 31:10-31). Let me encourage you to express your thanks and appreciation to your wife and the mother of your children. They work so hard to make your home and your life as comfortable and restful as possible. She will be glad you did and you will too.

Neighborhood Watch

In recent years there has been growing movement to defund the police. It has become a very divisive issue. Proponents argue the police have abused their authority and have treated some people improperly. On the other side there are people who support the police and want to increase the number of people serving in law enforcement.

Statistics appear to confirm crime is on the increase. Lawlessness is running rampant in some large cities across the nation. Criminal activity has become more frequent from minor shoplifting to mobs of people looting large retail stores. It is a sad commentary on our culture.

However there was a time when things were different. Police officers patrolled the streets and neighborhoods. Residents became familiar with their local police officer. They saw them daily and the officers knew many of the citizens and local shop keepers by name. Criminals were reluctant to expand their activities in neighborhoods where law enforcement officers were known and trusted.

I believe neighborhoods were also safer and crime was lower because a network of adults kept an eye on what was going on. This army of adults were the "*Stay at home mothers*" who lived on every street in most communities. They watched over all the neighborhood kids and knew many of them by name. Parents knew each other and would not hesitate to intervene if a neighbor's child was misbehaving.

I remember a time when people put a sign in their front window which alerted children there was a house on their block where any child could find safety and shelter. I can't remember the name of the program but it was made possible by mothers who were at home during the day.

There are several passages in the Bible which warn of growing lawlessness in our culture (Second Timothy 3:1-6). People will disregard rules and regulations. They will refuse to respect and obey the rule of law. They will ignore common decency and morality and live recklessly irrespective of what they were taught as children.

Let me encourage you to teach your children right and wrong. Be an example of what it means to obey the law and respect the rights and property of others. You will be glad you did and they will too.

Don't Muzzle the Ox

One of my responsibilities as a pastor was to lead a memorial service for someone who had died. I was honored to do this. The loved ones who suffered the loss were grateful to have my help and support. Our church had a team of people who put together a reception after the funeral. They set up the room and served a light meal to the people who attended the service. The buffet usually included sandwiches from a local store plus chips, salads, drinks and dessert.

I usually stopped by the Fellowship Hall before the service to say thanks to the team of adults who organized and prepared for the reception. Sometimes I would eat a small sandwich or cookie just to make sure the food was okay. When people asked if I should be sneaking a snack before the service I always quoted the verse in the Bible which says, "**Do not muzzle the Ox while it is threshing**" (First Timothy 5:18).

Even the animals who helped with the harvest needed to eat. They were allowed to eat some of the grain which was being harvested and processed. They needed nourishment to do the work of pulling a plow in the field and pulling a heavy sledge over the grain on the threshing floor to separate the kernels of the wheat from the shells.

One of the greatest challenges facing an ancient army was feeding the troops and the animals who hauled heavy wagons filled with food and ammunition. This was true of the mounted cavalry too. The animals had to be fed if they were expected to sustain the military operations.

This principle is still true today. Workers still need to eat. Most bring their own food in a lunch box or cooler bag. Some may slip away to get something at a nearby hamburger or taco fast food restaurant.

There is a company which specializes in building churches. Their name is "*Building God's Way*". They challenge people in the church to help with the construction. And they encourage the church to provide lunch for all of the workers on the site one day a week. It is a simple way the church can express their thanks to the contractors and volunteers who helped with the construction. Let me encourage you to do the same for the people who do work for you in your home or at your church. They will be glad you did and you will too.

276

Why Did the Turtle Cross the Road?

Every few years we get a ton of rain in Southern California. Most years are pretty dry but once in a while we get a lot of rain in a short amount of time. Flood channels fill up and some local flooding can occur.

Many years ago I remember driving down Brea Canyon Road on my way into Orange County. It is two-lane country road which connects Diamond Bar to Brea. I like it because you feel you go back in time as you drive down the winding road. Old oil derricks are scattered on the hillsides and old trees line the road. It is a short but pleasant drive.

One time I was heading down Brea Canyon Road after a heavy rain shower when I saw a small rock on the road. This was not uncommon because small boulders and rocks often washed off the hillside and rolled on to the roadway. I carefully navigated over this small rock to avoid hitting it with my tire.

However, when I looked back in my rearview mirror I saw the rock move! I realized it wasn't a rock. It was a turtle! What was a turtle doing slowly crossing the wet road?

I quickly turned my car around and drove back up the road. I parked my car on the side of the road and ran out into the street to rescue the reptile. Thankfully no cars had hit the slow moving turtle and I was able to move him off the street and into the safety of some nearby bushes.

When I shared this story in my sermon on Sunday morning people laughed and applauded my heroic effort. It felt good to rescue this helpless four-legged friend from his dangerous predicament. I must admit I was a little proud of risking my life in order to save his.

However, after church one man pulled me aside and asked me an interesting question. How did I know which side of the road to put him on? He suggested the turtle may have been trying to cross the road all day long and I was probably one of several people who stopped and put him back on the wrong side of the road!

There is a passage in the Bible which says, "Encourage the discouraged, help the week, be patient with all men" (First Thessalonians 5:14). Let me encourage you to stop and help someone *this week*. They will be glad you did and you will too.

September 29
Looking for a Church

When I was a young pastor in Tucson, Arizona, I received a few phone calls from parents who were looking for a church for their adult children to attend. Some of these young couples and young families were connected to Davis-Monthan Air Force Base in Tucson. Some lived on the air base while others found housing in other parts of the city.

Well-intending parents hoped their children and grandchildren would find a new church home while they were stationed in Tucson. The older parents found my name and the name of our church in a directory of Dallas Seminary graduates. They called and asked if I would visit their younger family members and invite them to our church.

The older parents implied their kids were looking for a new church. But in fact, that was not usually the case. The parents hoped their children would go to a church but usually their children and grandchildren were too busy and not really searching for a church.

I usually agreed to visit these new families but soon discovered this was not a very good use of my time. I felt like a carpet cleaning salesman trying to provide a service to a home owner who had tile floor. There was very little connection or incentive for this family to drive across the city and come to our church.

Parents are concerned about the faith and spiritual life of their children and grandchildren. They want them to embrace their faith and raise the grandchildren in a church environment. But the desire has to come from the hearts and minds of the younger generation. Older parents cannot make this choice for their children and grandchildren.

One thing parents can do is pray. Pray for your kids and grandkids every day. Ask God to open their hearts and minds. Pray God will place some followers of Jesus around them in their school and neighborhood. One verse says, "The prayer of a righteous man can accomplish much" (James 5:16). There is a wonderful movement called the "*Legacy Coalition*" which offers resources to grandparents to help them impact the lives of their grandchildren. You can find them online. Let me encourage you to pray for your grandchildren every day. Pray for their faith and their future. Ask God to bring good friends into their lives. They will be glad you did and you will too.

278

September 30
Epaphras

My wife and I met Bruce and his wife Kay when our kids were teenagers. Their daughter and our daughter met at the high school program at our church. They knew their parents had a lot in common. We are thankful these two teenagers connected us with their parents.

Bruce's father was a church pastor. So he had a special understanding of the joys and challenges of the life of a church leader. He always provided support and encouragement to me when he served on our leadership team. Bruce was an effective leader and teacher at our church. He also authored two books related to the Bible.

He also led the Men's ministry at our church and encouraged men to participate in some adventures like Kayaking along the Channel Islands off of the coast of California and going white water rafting on the roaring Kern River. He also challenged men in our church to attend the Promise Keeper gathering on the Mall in Washington, DC.

He started his own software company and was successful in this competitive environment. He and his partner led this company for over 30 years. They found innovative ways to administer benefit funds for a number of large organizations.

My wife and I enjoyed traveling with Bruce and his wife Kay. We went to Park City, Utah and to Hawaii together. We always had dinner together and watched the election returns in November.

Bruce was one of the guys who walked with me during my wife's journey and death from breast cancer. We met weekly with several other men to talk and pray for each of our families. During the Covid19 crisis when many restaurants were closed we got fast food "to go" and sat on lawn chairs under a shady tree the parking lot.

There is a man named Epaphras in the Bible who brought the Good News about Jesus to the city of Colosse in western Turkey in the first century. He was a good Bible teacher and a man of prayer (Colossians 1:3-7 / 4:12-13). Bruce reminds me of Epaphras. I'm thankful for Bruce's love for God, heart for prayer and encouragement to me. Let me encourage you to be a loyal friend to other men God brings into your life. Express you appreciation to those who have been a faithful friend to you as well. They will be glad you did and you will too.

279

October 1
Saying Thanks

Recently I found two *"Thank You"* notes in my house. They were from two of my grandchildren – Caleb and Elizabeth. They live in Europe where their parents are involved in a ministry which reaches out to young people in former communist countries.

I had received the *"Thank You"* notes earlier this year. They were saying thanks for the money I had sent to them and their parents for Christmas. It is much easier for me to send money instead of sending an expensive package with gifts which may not fit or they may not want. They like money so they can pick out something they really want.

Caleb told me he had purchased some *"Air Soft Gear"*. He and his buddies like to have battles in the woods near their house. Several buddies form a squad and do battle with other friends. *Air Soft* bullets are made with a safe foam material so no one gets hurt.

Elizabeth hadn't decided what she planned to purchase but I'm sure she will find something she likes. Both of my grandchildren said they were looking forward to seeing me. One of our favorite activities is to walk from their house into town to enjoy some delicious ice cream together. I can't wait to see them again soon.

One of the letters in the New Testament is basically a long *"Thank You"* note from the Apostle Paul to the believers in Philippi in Northern Greece. They had sent several generous gifts to help Paul while he started churches across the Roman Empire (Philippians 4:15-19). I think they were Paul's favorite church. They were the first group in Europe to respond to Paul's message (Acts Chapter 16).

In several of Paul's letters he expressed how he hoped to visit some new believers again soon. They were looking forward to seeing Paul and he was hoping to see them too (First Thessalonians 2:17-18).

Grandparents love to spend time with their grandchildren. Sometimes distance is a challenge. A number of my grandkids live overseas so I don't get to be with them very often. But it warms my heart when they say they miss me and look forward to being together again soon. Let me encourage you to make a plan and set a date to spend time with your grandchildren soon. Life is busy and time is limited. They will be glad you did and you will too.

An Old Coat

Many years ago our church was invited to send a short-term team to work alongside some missionaries in Romania. Although it was in the middle of summer we were encouraged to bring a warm jacket for the cool evenings in the Transylvanian Mountains.

When we arrived we discovered our Romanian hosts had set up a camp site in a cow pasture. With the permission of the owner they had cleared an area to pitch tents and set up a rustic outdoor kitchen. They dug two out houses in a cluster of trees nearby. The church people had worked hard to create a camp for active children and teens.

Our group was assigned to sleep in a few two-man tents. We were provided with sleeping bags and an extra blanket. The weather was cool in the day time and chilly at night. It rained on several occasions and our tents and sleeping bags were damp with moisture.

I was very thankful to have my warm blue coat. It was a last minute purchase. My wife insisted I buy a new coat for my trip to Romania. I didn't think I needed a jacket in the middle of summer. But I finally gave in and found coat at Costco. I was very glad I had purchased my blue coat.

I tried to sit near the camp fire to keep warm during the evening chapel service. I didn't need the coat during the day but I wore it every night. I was so glad I listened to my wife and brought my warm jacket.

There is a passage in the Bible where the Apostle Paul asked Timothy, "When you come, bring the cloak I left with Carpus in Troas and my scrolls and parchments" (Second Timothy 4:13). Paul knew the value and importance of staying warm when he was being held in prison.

Let me encourage you to be prepared when you travel. You don't need to bring ten pairs of shoes and ten pairs of pants. But you should make sure you are dressed for the climate and alert to the weather where you are going. And let me encourage you to listen to your wife if she says you need to take a warm jacket on your next trip. You will be glad you did and she will too. And did I tell you I still have and still use the old blue coat today!

Kindness

We live in a world where there is a lot of polarization and division. People are frustrated with the status quo and frequently vent their anger with harmful words and actions. Recently I heard someone say they can't remember a time in their life when people were so vocal expressing their frustration and dissatisfaction toward one another. We see demonstrations and proclamations about social, political and economic issues. I wonder where it will lead and when it will stop.

One word I feel is missing in our social and political interaction is *kindness*. Instead of being kind, people voice their criticism and complaints with angry tones and harsh words. Instead of being kind, opponents hurl insults and ridicule at one another. Instead of being kind, people respond and react with anger and bitterness.

There are a number of passages in the Bible which stress the importance of *kindness*. The Apostle Paul explained people were drawn to believe in God because of the kindness He has shown to them (Titus 3:4-7). Several other passages remind us God's divine nature includes kindness (Jonah 4:2 / Psalm 103:8).

Paul listed *kindness* as one of the essential qualities followers of Jesus should show to one another (Ephesians 4:31-32). Kindness can heal wounds and restore relationships. And kindness can be reciprocal. When we are kind to others they are more likely to be kind to us too.

The dictionary defined *kindness* as, "Selfless, compassionate and merciful. Its greatest power is revealed when we practice kindness to our enemies." One author said, "Love your neighbor and show kindness to everyone".

There are many ways you can be kind to other people including those who hold different political or philosophical views than you. Start with your ears. Be willing to listen to people who hold different views than you. Don't launch into an argument. Learn to listen respectfully. "Be quick to hear, slow to speak and slow to anger" (James 1:19).

Change your vocabulary. Stop using words full of criticism and anger. Use words which are carefully selected to not ignite a firestorm of verbal fury. Be careful what you say and how you say it. You will be glad you did and your listeners will too. (Continued)

Kindness (Part Two)

In my previous story I stressed the need for kindness in our culture. It seems people are more and more divided over social, political and economic issues. I believe we need to be willing to listen to those who hold views and opinions which are different than our own. And we need to choose our words carefully when we respond to different views. "Be quick to hear, slow to speak and slow to anger" (James 1:19).

In addition, we need to demonstrate kindness by how we act and react. Actions speak louder than words. A popular theme in the last decade encouraged people to do "*random acts of kindness*". The concept involved doing something kind or compassionate for a stranger or for an opponent. It could be as simple as paying the bill for the car behind you in the drive thru at Starbucks. It might involve putting out and bringing in your grumpy neighbor's garbage cans.

In the political realm it might mean refraining from false accusations against your opponent and not using unflattering photos of him or her in your printed political material. Conduct yourself properly in a public debate and allow your opponent time to respond to your comments and views.

There may be someone in your office or place of work who makes your life miserable. Why not launch a "*Kill them with kindness campaign*"? You could offer to help them with a major project or simply share a plate of cookies with your coworkers. You can take the initiative to help heal the wounds and restore relationships.

Jesus said we should take the initiative to resolve disputes and disagreements. He said, "Before you bring your offering to the temple, go and resolve a matter which may have offended your opponent" (Mathew 5:23-24).

The list is endless. There are many ways to demonstrate kindness to your spouse, family, neighbors, co-workers, classmates and opponents. Let me encourage you to do something kind for someone *this week*. Be willing to forgive them if they have offended you. And ask them for forgiveness if you have offended them. (Ephesians 4:31-32). Take the first step and show kindness to others just as God has shown kindness to you. You will be glad you did and they will too.

October 5
Covered Bridges

We always dreamed of visiting New England to see the fall leaves. I looked at some websites to find out what was the best week to see the leaves at full color. It was Columbus Day weekend in October.

We flew to Boston and rented a car at Logan Airport. After spending the night near the airport we drove west to see New Hampshire and later to Vermont. The autumn leaves were stunning. We ran out of adjectives trying to describe their beauty. It was a dream fulfilled to see the fall leaves in New England.

One day during our travels we stopped at a small general store on a two-lane back road. While we were buying some snacks we noticed a map for sale showing the locations of covered bridges throughout the New England states. We decided to watch for some as we enjoyed the breath taking autumn leaves.

The map included some information about why people built covered bridges in the 1800's. Builders learned these wooden structures lasted longer with a roof over the bridge and wood planks along the sides. By enclosing the bridge it was able to endure the harsh New England winters. Engineers also learned the bridges were stronger with the roof above and wood along the sides. In addition animals were not as fearful of crossing a river if they did not see the water rushing beneath them. A covered bridge remained usable during winter storms and other adverse weather conditions.

Several hundred covered bridges still stand in New England. We found a number of them in Vermont and New Hampshire. Sometimes we went out of our way to find another covered bridge. Some were still used daily by cars and bicycles. However most bridges were on the historical registry and were not accessible to modern transportation.

The autumn leaves were spectacular. It was a long-time dream come true. I highly recommend you make a plan to see them for yourself. And the covered bridges were an added bonus to our fall journey. Let me encourage you to set a date and make your hotel reservations early. You will be glad you did and I will too.

October 6
Complicated

One of the things I stressed to husbands and fathers in our church was servant leadership. Good leaders put the needs of other people ahead of their own. Real leaders help with the kids, help with house work and help with the laundry. One test of leadership was washing dishes and changing diapers. Husbands who love their wives wash dishes and change diapers. Fathers who don't wash dishes and don't change diapers are not effective leaders.

However I think there may be one exception to my recommendation. I'm not sure men should be expected to do the laundry. Washing machines and dryers have become very complicated and confusing. When I was a young husband and father our first washing machine only had one or two settings. Hot water or cold water. Large load, medium load or small load. And we didn't even own a dryer. We used a clothes line in the back yard. It was simple enough for any guy to understand.

It is very different today. Our new washer has a variety of settings. It is complex and confusing. There are so many buttons, settings and dials. It looks like the cockpit of a 747 Jumbo Jet. The operator is required to select different settings for different types of laundry. Is it Denim Jeans or Delicates? Do you want permanent press or heavy duty?

That is only the beginning. Now you need to decide on the water. Do you want hot, warm, cold or "*ecowarm*" - whatever that is? You have to designate the "Soil level" - Heavy, normal or light? What about the spin cycle – High, medium, low or no spin? Plus you get choices like Extra Rinse, Delay End, Self-Clean or Pre-Soak.

The dryer is just as complicated. Do you want the temperature high, medium, low or air dry? Do you want the normal dry, less dry or more dry setting? Do you want the annoying buzzer at the end to be loud or soft? It looks like you need a degree in astrophysics to do the laundry.

There is a passage In the Bible which records Jesus washing the feet of his disciples. He used his hands and a towel to do the job a servant would normally be expected to do (John 13:12-15). Let me encourage you to be a servant to the people in your family. Put their needs ahead of your own. And if possible let your wife do the laundry. She must be a genius to operate such complicated machinery!

285

Complicated (Part Two)

I shared in a previous story the need for husbands to be servant leaders in their home. They need to put the needs of others ahead of themselves. They need to be willing to help with the house work, wash dishes and clean floors. They need to look for ways to use their hands to help their wife and lighten her load.

But there is one area where I believe the wife is far more capable doing – laundry. Not only are the washers and dryers extremely complicated but so are the fabrics the laundry is made of.

There is no end to dirty laundry. When our children were growing up the clothes hamper was always full. No matter how many loads of laundry my wife and I washed each week the hamper magically filled up again and again.

Laundry includes a variety of fabrics. Nylon undergarments, cotton sheets and socks, polyester shirts and blouses, and rayon pants, dresses and other clothes. Each of these items has a tag sewn on it with instructions on how to wash them correctly.

I understand you should wash white clothes with other white clothes. I think you are supposed to wash dark clothes in a separate batch. But I'm not quite clear what you do with bright colors and stripes.

I get confused about washing different fabrics in the same load of laundry. Can you wash cottons with nylon? Can you safely mix polyester with rayon? I wonder if there are any federal or local laundry inspectors who can give you a citation if you wash the wrong colors or the wrong fabrics together.

Jesus taught his followers about old and new wine skins. The lesson is not about laundry or food storage but about trying to put something new on to something old. Jesus said he did not come to patch up an old religion but to introduce something radically new – a personal relationship with a loving God through faith in Jesus (Mark 2:21-22).

If you want to be a servant leader in your family I suggest you watch a few You Tube videos and learn how to operate the complicated washer and dryer in your house. You may want to also ask your wife for some helpful tips. She will be glad you did and you will too.

Assassination

Do you know many people have attempted to assassinate some of the Presidents of the United States? Four sitting presidents have been killed while in office. Abraham Lincoln, James Garfield, William McKinley and John Kennedy. Two other famous Americans were also assassinated in the 1960's – Martin Luther King and Robert Kennedy.

In addition attempts have been made on several other presidents while they were in office including Andrew Jackson, Theodore Roosevelt, Ronald Reagan and Gerald Ford. The Secret Service goes to great lengths to protect each president and prevent anyone from harming them. They are willing to throw themselves in the line of fire and give their life to save the life of the president.

A young man named John Hinckley shot President Reagan when he walked out the back door of a hotel in Washington, DC. Hinckley called Reagan's name when he was getting into his limousine. When the President turned to wave and acknowledge the greeting Hinckley fired several shots before being tackled by police and secret service agents.

The President didn't know he had been shot until they sped away from the scene. Reagan had been wounded in the chest and was seriously injured. He was rushed to a nearby hospital immediately taken into surgery. Before they administered the anesthesia the President asked the doctor if he was a Republican. The surgeon replied, "*Mr. President, today we are all Republicans.*" Reagan survived the gunshot wound and went on to serve two terms as the President of the United States.

We are living in an era where our nation is polarized between different political parties. Common courtesies and respectful debate has declined into shouting matches and angry marches. Both sides lobby for their positions and philosophies. Emotions run high and people are divided over so many issues. I wonder what it will take for us to say "*we are all Americans*" and want the best for our great country.

There is a verse in the Bible where Jesus said "He is the good shepherd and was willing to lay down his life for us" (John 10:14-15). Jesus died on the cross and rose again to pay for your sins and provide a place in heaven for all who would believe in Him. He died to save us. Let me encourage you to read the Book of John and learn more about the life, death and resurrection of Jesus. You will be glad you did.

Israel Tour 2023

My phone rang just after midnight on October 7, 2023. It was a call from the owner of our tour company in Israel. A group of 26 adults from our church were scheduled to fly out of LAX in the morning to begin a twelve day tour of Israel. The news was not good.

She asked me if I had heard what was going on in Israel. No – we had not heard anything. She told me the terrorist group Hamas had launched a surprise attack from Gaza into southern Israel. She said this was a bigger event than the nation had experienced in the past. She was concerned this might not be a good time to bring our group.

After our brief conversation we agreed to compare notes again in a few hours. Our shuttle vans were scheduled to pick us up at our church at 9:00 AM to take us to the airport. Our flight was a few hours later. We prayed for wisdom as we tried to go back to sleep.

She called again at 6:00 AM to tell us the news reports were very serious. Hamas had launched several thousand rockets into Israel and there were reports of terrorists attacking towns inside southern Israel. The situation was not clear but things sounded very serious. She said this might not be a good time to bring our group. At the end of our conversation we agreed to cancel our trip.

This was a very difficult decision and very disappointing. We had been planning this tour for almost a year. People had invested a lot of money to go on this memorable adventure. Months of planning and preparation had suddenly come to an end. I shook my head in disbelief. How could this happen?

She would contact the airlines and the hotels to inform them of our cancelation. I immediately called the airport shuttle to cancel our ride. It was not clear if deposits and payments would be refundable.

Then my wife and I sent out an email and made phone calls to alert everyone on the tour we were canceling the trip and to not come to the church at 9:00 AM. I could hear the disbelief and disappointment in the voices of everyone we talked to. We had planned and prepared for this trip for almost a year and suddenly it was not going to happen. It was like planning for a wedding for a year and then calling it off only hours before the ceremony.   (continued)

288

Israel Tour 2023 (Part Two)

Canceling the trip to Israel was so disappointing. It is hard to explain the variety of emotions we felt at that moment and in the following hours. Did I act too quickly? Should we have at least gone to the airport to see if our flight was still leaving? Should we have canceled the hotels, guide and tour bus so soon?

It felt like the dialog in the movie, "*Apollo 13*" when the space craft with three American astronauts was suddenly damaged in space. There were a lot of unanswered questions and a lot of confusion on the space craft and at flight control. Decisions were being made quickly. Some of those decisions determined whether the crew would be able to land on the moon or even make it back to earth alive.

We had such a short window of time to make the decision to go or not go to the airport and to go to Israel. When we began to see news reports of the events in Israel it became more and more apparent the situation was very serious and we made the right decision.

I was concerned we might get stranded at a location far from home. Our flight went through Istanbul. I worried the airport in Tel Aviv might not allow flights to land and our group would be stuck at the airport in Turkey for days. If we were able to get to Israel we might be confined to a hotel and not allowed to start our tour for safety reasons.

Events over the following days confirmed our worst fears. Hundreds of unarmed civilians had been killed inside Israel by marauding bands of terrorists. One news report said 250 people attending an outdoor music festival were killed by Hamas terrorists. In addition Israelis soldiers and innocent civilians have been taken as hostages inside the Gaza Strip.

Early assessments indicated the surprise attack came from the sea, air and land. Hamas broke through the fenced barrier between the Gaza Strip and Israel at over a dozen locations. Bands of armed militants used pickup trucks with high powered guns to kill people at bus stops, along highways and in homes. It was a very sophisticated and coordinated attack on Israel. Over a thousand people have died and many more were wounded. We were very sad to watch the killing and chaos on TV. We were very glad we canceled our trip to Israel just hours before our departure. We continue to pray for peace in Israel.

Special Children

It is encouraging to see children with special needs getting more attention and recognition. One of the ways this has happened is through the creation of the Special Olympics which are usually held the week after the Olympic Games in various parts of the world.

Schools are offering more help and resources to students and parents with children with special needs. Several have touched our own lives.

Al and Glady Platt were missionaries in Guatemala for many years from the 1950's to the 1980's. They had a wonderful daughter named Brendy who had Cerebral Palsy. She had a good mind and a wonderful sense of humor but had limited mobility. She was loved by the students who attended the Central American Bible Institute in Guatemala City. Brendy and my wife became good friends. She stayed in our home several times when we lived in Dallas and Tucson.

My wife taught special education in the 1970's in Dallas, Texas. She got to know a student named Craig Wood and his mother Janet. Jeanne loved working with students who were facing a variety of physical and educational challenges. She was pleased to see them grow in their ability to communicate and learn.

Some of our immediate family members also have children and grandchildren with special needs including autism, spinal bifida and other physical and visual challenges. The parents do a remarkable job of caring for them and helping these wonderful children.

There are a number of accounts in the Bible where Jesus met and helped children and adults with various physical, emotional and spiritual needs. He reached out and touched and healed a man with leprosy. He stopped to help a blind man and healed several people who were crippled. Jesus felt compassion for people with special needs (Read Mark 1:40-45 / 2:1-12 / 3:1-6 / 5:21-34).

I'm sure you know a friend, neighbor or co-worker who have a child or grandchild with special needs. Let me encourage you to take an interest in their lives. Watch for an opportunity *this week* to lend a hand, provide transportation or welcome them into your home. They will be glad you did and you will too.

October 12
Reminders

We have several items and pieces of furniture that belonged to my parents. One is called a **Dry Sink** which was used in the days before indoor plumbing to wash and dry dishes. My father actually made this small wooden replica himself from a pattern he found. One side of this small cabinet has a flat surface for stacking clean dishes. The other side is recessed a little lower to hold a bucket or pan of water.

Another item we have is a **Rocking Chair**. It is also made from wood. I was told by my parents that my mother rocked me to sleep in this chair when I was a little guy. We still have it today. We also have an old **Telephone**. It is the kind you see in movies mounted on a wall with a hand crank on the side and the mouth piece extending from the front. The ear piece hung in a cradle on the other side of the phone.

My brother and his wife have a **Harvest Table** which belonged to our parents. It was custom made in the 1960's at my mother's request. It is a long narrow wooded table with leaves on each side which can be raised or lowered. The Harvest Table could easily seat 10-12 guests.

There is also an old wooden **Butter Churn** which my parents bought on a family trip to Colorado in the 1960's. It is made of wood slats and stands two feet high. It has a long pole which enabled to the user to stir up the cream and make it into butter. I remember riding from Denver to Phoenix with the butter churn laying between my brother and me in the back seat of our Ford Mustang. It was a long drive.

Another item we still have is a **Wicker Rocking Chair**. It is also made of wood. The seat was fashioned from thin strips of wood woven to make a comfortable seat. We also have an old **Singer Sewing Machine** powered by a foot peddle. It sits on a cast iron frame and is built into a wooden cabinet. It belonged to my Aunt Violet. The furniture made for the Tabernacle in the Old Testament was made of wood too. Each piece had a specific purpose (Exodus 25).

All of these items are reminders of the past. They remind me of my parents and grandparents. At least one of them was made by my father. Let me encourage you to value some of the things your parents or grandparents have handed down to you. The may be old and they may not be in the best condition but they are filled with memories. You will be glad you did.

291

October 13
A Tale of Two Cities

I have shared about our restful week near the ocean in Central California in the town of Atascadero. The weather was very nice and we enjoyed spending time with my brother Steve and his wife Sharon.

We were glad to get back to our home in Diamond Bar in Southern California. But one day when we were on our early morning walk we noticed how different things were between the two communities. One is a large suburb of Los Angeles the other is a small town half way between Los Angeles and San Francisco.

Atascadero is a quiet hamlet with Highway 101 running through it. Diamond Bar is a noisy suburb where two major freeways filled with cars and loud trucks merge together. Even the residential traffic seemed louder in Diamond Bar than it did in Atascadero.

The volume of cars is noticeably different. The main arteries running through Diamond Bar were busy and full of cars. The main streets in Atascadero had very little traffic.

When we went for our morning walk around the lake in Atascadero we could see ducks and geese enjoying the peaceful setting. When we went for a walk in Diamond Bar we were distracted by the cars, trucks and school buses going up and down the streets.

The list could go on and on. It was surprising how we both noticed the difference of one community to the other. Maybe you have experienced something similar comparing where you spent your vacation and where you live.

There is a passage in the Bible which describes the way Jesus got away from the crowds to have some quiet time alone with his Heavenly Father. He experienced the demands of the multitude and realized he needed physical and spiritual rest (Mark 1:35 / Luke 4:42). And when Jesus visited Jerusalem he withdrew at the end of each day to spend the night in the Garden of Gethsemane near the Mount of Olives outside the bustling city (John 18:1-3).

Let me encourage you to make time to get away from the hectic pace of everyday life. Renew your heart and rest your body. You will be glad you did and your family will too.

October 14
The Chosen

There is a new TV series which has been released about the life of Jesus. It is called *The Chosen*. It has been written and directed by Dallas Willard. It has provided a refreshing perspective on the life of Jesus and his twelve disciples.

There has been some controversy about this new depiction of the life of Jesus and his followers. Some critics feel uncomfortable with some of the content which is not specifically mentioned in the Bible. But others feel it provides a helpful and easy way to understand the life and ministry of Jesus.

The title reveals the focus of the series. It gives a very human perspective of the character and personality of each of the disciples Jesus chose. I like to watch how the disciples interact with Jesus and with each other. I enjoy the dialog which includes humor and laughter. They aren't super heroes but normal people just like you and me.

I remember one of my seminary professors said, "If you want to really understand the ministry and teachings of Jesus put yourself in the shoes of the disciples". They make mistakes just like you and me. They ask questions and seek answers just like we do. They are human just like us.

One of the keys to the success of many TV series over the years is the bond which develops between the cast and the viewers. The same is true with *The Chosen*. The viewing audience identifies with different disciples. We smile at some of Matthew's misunderstandings and mistakes. We relate to Simon the Zealot who was a trained assassin but became a loyal follower of Jesus. They are just like us.

Each of the twelve disciples were *chosen* to be Jesus' students and they become his messengers. They start out timid and reluctant. They feel unqualified to serve and represent Jesus. But gradually their confidence and understanding grows.

Let me encourage you to open your Bible and read what it reveals about the life and character of each of the twelve disciples. Start in the Book of Mark. Then find **The Chosen** on your Internet provider or cable channel and see how the director depicts each of the twelve. I think you will be glad you did.

Mother and Daughter

I have shared in the past about the morning routine at our house. My wife and I like to get up early and go for a walk in our neighborhood. During the hot summer days we try to get our walk in before the sun comes up. It can get warm quickly when the sun peaks over the hills.

It is fun to see many of the same people day after day. They have the same routine we do. Two people we see almost every day is an older woman and her daughter. They look a lot alike and they move at a steady pace.

We have spoken to them briefly and enjoyed learning about the mother and her daughter. I believe the mother was recovering from some health issues and was living at a *Board and Care* home in our neighborhood with several other older adults.

The daughter explained she came to visit her mother every day and encouraged her mom to get out and walk together. They seem to enjoy each other and they always greet us when we walk by.

There is a verse in the Bible which instructs younger people to help take care of their older parents and widows. "If a widow has children or grandchildren let them take care of her and let them learn that religion begins at their own doorstep and that they should pay back with gratitude some of what they have received. This pleases God immensely" (First Timothy 5:4 – The Message Bible).

My grandfather died when I was a senior in high school. I enjoyed going to visit my grandmother with my girlfriend and future wife. We spent many evenings talking with Grandma Holliday and enjoying some delicious pound cake and ice cream. We learned a lot about my family's history and about my grandmother's life. I'm grateful we made an effort to spend time with her.

Let me encourage you to spend more time with your older parents or grandparents. Ask about their lives. Learn about things they did when they were young. I regret I did not spend more time with my grandparents when I was a teenager. Don't make the same mistake. I hope you will set aside some time in your busy schedule *this week* to stop by for a visit or speak with them on the phone. They will be glad you did and you will too.

Earthquake Kit

It seems like we hear more and more about natural disasters impacting different parts of our country. Hurricanes devastate the Gulf Coast and East Coast. Tornadoes rip across the mid-west and plain states. And wild fires and earthquakes rattle the West Coast.

There is a big emphasis on *Disaster Preparedness*. Families and individuals are urged to gather together important documents and photos in case you need to evacuate your home or apartment quickly. And we are encouraged to gather food, water and other supplies in a safe place just in case a disaster strikes our city or community.

When my wife and I combined our households a few months ago we realized we had two refrigerators, two sets of kitchen dishes and two flat screen TV's. We also had two earthquake kits. These were in two large clean sturdy plastic garbage cans. Mine was better because it had wheels.

We agreed it was time to go through both of the containers and consolidate them into one and decide what to save and what we could give away. It was interesting what we found inside these two black buckets. There were two hand cranked radios which did not need batteries. There was also a solar powered radio in Susan's bucket.

There were blankets in both but my bucket had two sleeping bags. We also found some cash in my earthquake kit. I had read it is important to have a small amount of cash on hand in case the bank ATM machines don't work due to a power outage. There were a number of envelopes with two five dollar bills and ten one dollar bills. Just in case.

We also found a First Aid kit in each container. There was a limited amount of medicine and some plastic gloves for emergency medical care. We realized there was a limited amount of clothing too.

There are several passages in the Bible which stress the importance of saving for future unexpected needs. "Even the ant knows it is important to save for the coming winter" (Proverbs 6:6-11). Let me encourage you to clean out your earthquake kit *this week*. Who knows what you may find. And if you don't have a *Disaster Preparedness Kit* let me encourage you to start one *this week*. You will be glad you did.

October 17
The Water Filter

One of the problems with our water is the high mineral content. A lot of the water we drink and use in Southern California is imported from the Rocky Mountains and the Sierra Nevada Mountains. Aqueducts transport this water hundreds of miles in a network of open canals and stored in large reservoirs before arriving in our local communities. Even though the water goes through a treatment process at regional facilities it is still considered "hard" water when it comes out of the kitchen faucet or shower head.

Hard water can cause a film to build up on your shower glass door and bath tub. It can clog water pipes over time. It doesn't taste as good or feel as good as filtered and bottled water. There are many companies offering different products to filter the water in your house. Even our refrigerator has an expensive water filter which needs to be replaced every six months. Filtered water is better water for cooking, cleaning, bathing and drinking.

The woman who does my wife's hair recommended a water filter that attached to the bathroom shower. The hair dresser said the water filter would be better for my wife's hair. I was a little skeptical but we did buy one from Lowe's. It was easy to install and I must admit the water feels much better than it did without the filter. It is called a "*Sprite*". It works.

Another thing that needs a filter is our conversation and vocabulary. I am amazed at the volume and amount of foul language included in our public and private conversations. Adults, teens and children are using words and phrases which were unacceptable only a few years ago. The media has contributed to this in movies, TV sitcoms and online websites. It is amazing to hear the profanity used in conversations between actors and actresses. In addition new words, phrases and acronyms continue to be introduced into our vocabulary which are unhealthy and misleading.

These is a verse in the Bible which says, "Watch the way you talk. Let nothing foul or dirty come out of your mouth. Say only what helps" (Ephesians 4:29). "No more lies, no more pretense. Tell your neighbor the truth. When you lie to others you end up lying to yourself" (4:24) (The Message Bible). Let me encourage you to watch your words. Clean up your vocabulary. Speak the truth. You will be glad you did and your friends will too.

Buying Your First Car

After our daughter graduated from college she was offered a teaching position at a local school district. This was unusual. Normally in California college graduates needed to complete a fifth year of education classes and do a semester of student teaching. However when Traci graduated there was a shortage of teachers. School districts were allowed to hire new teachers and let them finish their fifth year and do their student teaching under the supervision of an experienced teacher. And they got paid a full-time teacher's salary.

A few weeks before starting school, Traci and I went shopping for a new car. She told each car salesman her three specific requirements. She wanted a new car with automatic door locks. She didn't want to be fumbling around for her car keys trying to unlock the door. She just wanted to push a button to unlock the car.

Second, she wanted to buy a new car without making a down payment. She didn't have any money after finishing college and she didn't want to ask her parents for help. No down payment was her condition. Third, she didn't want to have to make a car payment until October 1st because that was when she would receive her first paycheck. It all made sense. She was being very practical and reasonable.

I encouraged Traci to consider a Toyota or Honda. These were known to be reliable vehicles that lasted a long time. But salesmen at both dealerships said they could not agree to her three conditions. Then she went to a Saturn dealer and they were glad to sell her a brand new car meeting the specifications she stated. What a contrast. Two dealers refused to sell her a car but the third one was ready and willing.

There is a passage in the Bible where twelve spies were sent to size up the opposition they were facing when they entered the promise land. (Read Numbers Chapter 13 & 14). Ten of the spies focused on the obstacles. The cities were large and fortified. They had vast armies and big soldiers. It couldn't be done. They recommended retreat. But the other two spies who saw the same obstacles believed they could succeed with God's help. They recommended the army attack.

The next time you face some obstacles or challenges let me encourage you to focus on how it can be done with God's help. You will be glad you did and He will too.

New Technology

I am intimidated by technology. I'm afraid I will hit the wrong button and erase the memory of my hard drive or delete some work I have spent hours working on. In contrast my grandchildren are very comfortable with new phones and computers and seem to know how to recover or restart their electronic devices without any problems.

Once in a while I discover something new about my computer or smart phone which becomes very useful. One time my son took a look at my laptop computer screen and asked if he could clean it up for me. I had dozens of icons on my screen and could never find things I needed. So he created a few files and grouped things together.

For example he put all of the items related to our condo rental in one file. He also collected stories and articles from books I have written into a different file. Suddenly my computer screen didn't look so cluttered. Now I am able to find things quickly and easily.

In a similar way my wife Susan continues to introduce me to new features on my smart phone that I didn't know existed. She taught me how to talk to Siri and how to dictate notes and text messages. Wow — why didn't I know about these tools a long time ago?

Part of the problem is I still think of my smart phone as a phone when it really is a computer which includes a telephone function. I know people who run their entire business on their smart phone. They can access files, contact clients and pay bills. They deposit checks and transfer funds using their smart phone. They can interview prospective employees and schedule service appointments with their smart phone.

I believe many people feel the same way when it comes to the Bible. It seems intimidating. How could anyone understand it by themselves? Actually the Bible was written for ordinary people to read and enjoy. It is a library of 66 books with a common theme of God's love, mercy, compassion and forgiveness. The Bible is historically accurate and reliable. It includes real people, real places and real events. It records kings and emperors and pharaohs. Archeology has confirmed many places and people mentioned in the Bible. Let me encourage you to *start reading the Bible this week*. Don't start on page one. Start in the Book of Mark. *Read one chapter a day*. You will be glad you did and I will too.

Progress

We have made many improvements to our home in Diamond Bar since we purchased it 35 years ago. We remodeled the kitchen twice. We remodeled two of the bathrooms. We were one of the first on our block to replace our old sagging wood garage door with a new roll up style.

We added a room addition shortly after we purchased the house. We replaced the old wood shake shingle roof with plywood and asphalt shingles. We have repainted the house twice. I rebuilt the patio roof and replaced the 2X2 slats with a solid roof. I am exhausted just typing this list. We have done a lot to make our house a home to enjoy and share with guests and friends.

I often use the phrase, "Don't be grumpy we need to repair things on the house. We should be grateful we have a house to repair"! Many people would be thrilled to have our one-story, four bedroom house with three bathrooms and a two car garage.

But at the same time there are always more things to repair and improve. Recently I extended the outdoor sprinkler system to include the plants and flower beds. I used to water these by hand with a garden hose. But now all of the planters and flower beds are on a timer so they will be watered even when we are away from home.

In addition, we asked our gardener to remove some old overgrown plants to make way for new flowers and shrubs. We brought in fresh dirt from a local nursery and planted a variety of new things. As a result flowers are blooming and new plants are thriving. Our front courtyard looks attractive to guests and visitors who come to our house. And the back patio looks much nicer with new flowers and colors enhancing its appearance. We also added a new shade screen to reduce the amount of sunlight pouring into the house on a hot summer afternoon.

This did not happen overnight. It was the result of hard work spending time and money to improve the exterior of our house. There will always be more improvements to make and new flowers to plant. But it is satisfying to see the results so far. There is a passage in the Bible that tells about a vineyard which was neglected and how that reflected on the character of the owner (Proverbs 24:30-34). Let me encourage you to take good care of your home, cars, clothes and all that God has given you. You will be glad you did and He will too.

Tim

Your mother and I always remembered the day you were born. You were the first baby in our family. You were not due until November and we wondered if you might be born on your mother's birthday but you came early and were born at Baylor Hospital on October 21, 1974. I remember it was a Monday because I taught an evening class at Dallas Seminary and Dr. Charles Ryrie came to evaluate me that night.

Mom had a lot of experience with young children when she was a babysitter in her teens. But this was new territory for me. You were a happy baby. I remembering reviewing my Greek vocabulary words while I held you on my lap to feed you a bottle of baby formula.

You went off to preschool when you were four years old and learned a poem about "*Mr. Pumpkin*". Mom and I were so impressed how well you memorized the poem and recited it so confidently. When you started at White Elementary School in Tucson you made friends with the Gonzales and Tatum boys.

I enjoyed coaching your soccer and baseball teams when you were young. You and I toured the Titan Missile Site in Green Valley and climbed to the top of Mt. Wrightson together. As you got older we shared some remarkable trips to England, France and Italy together.

You and your mother had a special relationship. She was so proud of you and all you have accomplished. She was frustrated when you didn't get your homework done in high school. But she was proud you became an English teacher and a school principal. You have always had a special place in your heart for students who struggle in school and students with special needs.

We are thankful you married Christine and how you embraced Landon and Emily. Your mother was so pleased you found a wonderful wife to share your life with. I am glad you have encouraged me to visit some of your schools and I was proud to meet your teachers and staff. They always had positive things to say about you.

Let me encourage you to continue to grow in your faith and to love Christine and your kids. Keep on serving the students and teachers at your school. Keep on learning how to be an effective husband, father and leader. I'm very proud of you. You will always be my favorite son.

October 22
Pumpkin Pie

I have shared in the past how much I enjoy Pumpkin Pie. And one of the best places to buy a good pie is at Costco. I know there are other places who make and sell them but none are better than Costco.

Costco only sells Pumpkin Pies for a limited time. Starbucks does the same thing with their Pumpkin Spice coffee. Last year I was surprised to see Pumpkin Pie at Costco the first week of September. So this year I have been counting down the days in August anxiously waiting for them to appear. Sure enough new pies were for sale on August 31st!

I was tempted to buy several and freeze them for the future but I finally decided to only purchase one so there would be plenty for other shoppers to enjoy. I knew there would be a lot more Pumpkin Pies available over the next few months.

I wonder if you have similar interests in other foods or deserts. I know many people enjoy Tamales at Christmas time and Hot Dogs on the Fourth of July. Watermelons are popular at a summer picnic or BBQ. Turkeys are always the number one item at Thanksgiving along with all of the trimmings. Our Chinese friends enjoy Moon Cakes in the fall and celebrate the Chinese New Year with good food in the winter.

There is an account in the Bible regarding the special bread which was made for use in the daily worship. It was called the *Bread of the Presence* (Exodus 25:21-30). New bread was prepared every day and placed on a table in the Tabernacle and later in the Temple. It was considered sacred and only the Priests could eat it.

However one day David came to the Tabernacle and asked for food. The Priest only had the sacred bread and was reluctant to give any to David. The Priest did not know David was a fugitive fleeing from King Saul. But David was starving so the Priest gave him some of the special bread. Jesus referred to this event and explained it was okay to be flexible in order to help someone in need even with the sacred bread (Mark 2:23-27). Let me encourage you to be flexible and make an exception to the rules to help people in need. Share some of your resources with those who do not have enough during this holiday season. Buy an extra Pumpkin Pie at Costco this year and share it with a neighbor or family in need. They will be glad you did and you will too.

It Looks Like Winter

I came across a photo on my computer which I taken several years ago. I didn't check the exact date but I'm sure it was during the winter season. The photo was taken from my neighbor's house. It was a clear picture of my lawn covered with snow.

Southern California rarely has snow. It does snow on the nearby mountains. Sometimes the foothills north of us can get a dusting of snow but snow is unheard of at our elevation. We are only 30 miles from the ocean so it is very unlikely to snow in our community.

But there was my yard covered with white. The driveway and sidewalks were clear but the lawn was white. Although it looked like snow it was actually hail. We had a downpour of hail and it covered the whole yard.

It was pretty amazing to see this unique event. We expect rain in the winter months. Sometimes it can really pour. Sometimes the rain sounds like a tropical storm pounding on our roof. But is unusual to see hail especially enough to cover our lawn.

There are some examples of extreme weather in the Bible. One of the ten plagues in Egypt was a fierce hail storm which killed people and livestock. The hail was so destructive the Egyptian Pharaoh pleaded with Moses to stop the torrential downpour (Read Exodus 9:13-37).

You probably remember a weather event which damaged your home or car. My mother-in-law experienced a summer thunderstorm in Scottsdale, Arizona, where hail damaged the roof of her house and shattered a skylight. One of the national insurance companies set up a temporary claim center in the parking lot of the local Home Depot to inspect hundreds of cars which were damaged by the same storm that damaged my mother-in-law's home.

The Bible predicts there will be extreme weather events in the end times. People will flee for shelter to try and avoid the storms and devastation which will occur all over the world (Revelation 6:12-17).

Let me encourage you to not be caught by surprise when bad weather hits your neighborhood. I recommend you keep your cars in the garage and protect your home and family. And if you see any white stuff on your front lawn take a photo to share with your kids and grandkids.

The Car Wash

Recently we stayed in the condo of a friend where our car was covered with dirt and grime. Our SUV was parked next to the swimming pool when an employee used a power sprayer to clean off the pool deck. I saw him working but didn't realize our car would be affected. Later when I went to the parking lot to get something out of our car I discovered the car was covered with dirt and grime splattered all over it. Just a day earlier we had been to the local car wash. Now it was filthy. We wondered if the employee had used any chemicals in the sprayer which might harm the finish on our car. What a mess.

We decided to find a car wash as quickly as we could to clean off the debris and gunk on the car. We asked our helpful assistant Seri to direct us to a local car wash because we were unfamiliar with the area. She suggested 3-4 places but we couldn't find any of them. Finally we jumped on the freeway hoping to find a car wash near our destination.

Seri was confused about where we were. We kept asking her for a car wash in the direction we were going but she kept giving us directions to places we had already passed. Finally in desperation we got off the freeway and stopped at a gas station. I asked the attendant if he knew where we could find a carwash. He said there was one on the other side of the freeway at a Shell gas station. It was difficult to find but we finally did. The $10 drive thru car wash worked. The gunk and grime were gone and the car looked like new.

As I looked back on our adventure I realized my wife and I had been irritated and frustrated with each other over the dirty car. I was frustrated because she couldn't get Seri to give us clear directions. She was frustrated because I wasn't following her suggestions. You could hear it in our voices and in our responses to each other. A filthy car in an unfamiliar town resulted in irritation and agitation.

There is a verse in the Bible which says, "Don't use harsh words but treat one another with patience and kindness" (Ephesians 4:2/ 4:29). Let me encourage you to be thoughtful how you talk to those you love. Choose your words carefully. Don't respond too quickly. Be kind not critical in stressful situations. You will be glad you did and they will too. And let me suggest you not park your clean car near the swimming pool or you may be searching for a car wash too. By the way - It rained on our clean car the next day. Siri - where was that car wash again?

Ana

San Diego is a beautiful city. Tall skyscrapers tower above the water front and clusters of beautiful boats rest lazily in the harbor below. It was the favorite vacation destination for my family when I grew up in Arizona. My wife Susan lived in San Diego for 20 years. She loved the area and had many fond memories of San Diego.

Recently we spent a few days in San Diego and enjoyed seeing many of the popular places in the city. We visited the Air and Space Museum in Balboa Park and enjoyed Mexican food in Old Town. We also walked along the waterfront and looked at some shops at Sea Port Village. We watched the sun set over the hills surrounding the city.

We also had lunch at the famous *Hotel Del Coronado* resort on Coronado Island. We found an outdoor restaurant with an ocean view at the hotel. The menu was pricy but the food was very good.

We also enjoyed getting to know one of the employees during our meal. Her name was Ana. I noticed her accent and asked where she was from. She told us she was from Romania. She was pleased to hear I had been there and enjoyed my visit to her beautiful country.

Ana explained she was in America on a temporary work program which allowed employers to hire employees from foreign countries. I have met other young people doing the same at a resort in Palm Springs.

She was from Timisoara. It was an important city during the revolution in the 1989 when people removed the dictator from power. She was surprised to hear I had been to her home town. She was pleased to know I had visited Freedom Square and knew about the popular uprising where people were killed when the revolution began.

She told us she had just graduated from college and would be starting her career as an engineer when she returned to Romania in the fall. We asked about her faith and church background too. It was a delightful conversation. There is a verse in the Bible which says, "Always be ready to give an account to anyone who asks you about the hope that is in you" (First Peter 3:15). Let me encourage you to greet the people you meet as you travel. Get to know them and learn about their heritage and faith. You will be glad you did and they will too.

Christmas at Costco

Recently we were walking through our neighborhood Costco store when we noticed an unusual sight. It was a Christmas tree. Actually it is not uncommon to see Christmas trees for sale at Costco but this happened in the month of August!

How can retailers be selling Christmas items in the middle of summer? We still have "Back to School" shopping plus Halloween and Thanksgiving to celebrate before we get to Christmas.

It seems like large and small stores are promoting holidays and introducing new items earlier and earlier every year. Pretty soon we will be purchasing Easter Eggs in November and Thanksgiving turkeys in April. Where will it ever end?

I think I liked it better when we celebrated one season and one holiday at a time. Radio stations did not start playing Christmas music until after Thanksgiving. Now one radio station in LA starts playing Christmas Carols in the middle of November. Easter decorations didn't fill the shelves until February or March.

It is hard to stay ahead of the merchants who are constantly pushing the envelope and promoting new products for new seasons faster than we can keep up. It seems like we are losing the race.

There are a number of holidays mentioned in the Bible which were celebrated by the Israelites every year. They had Passover and the Feast of Unleavened Bread in the spring, Pentecost and the Feast of Weeks in the summer and the Feast of the Ingathering (harvest) in the fall (Exodus 34:18-23). Their purpose was to remind people to give thanks to God and celebrate his love and goodness.

The Apostle Paul wrote, "God has shown kindness by giving you rain from heaven and crops in their season. He provides you with plenty of food and fills your hearts with joy" (Acts 14: 17).

Let me encourage you to not get caught up in the marketing and commercializing of our culture. Make time to pause and remember God's love and mercy as you celebrate each holiday like Thanksgiving, Christmas and Easter. Give thanks to God for his faithfulness and kindness. You will be glad you did and He will too.

Pine Needles

My wife and I have noticed a variety of things as we walk through our neighborhood in the early morning. We enjoy seeing flowering roses and neatly trimmed lawns and shrubs. We are sad to see yards full of weeds and untrimmed plants and trees. Most homes look nice. I hope people think our yard looks nice.

However one thing we have seen more and more are pine needles spread across sidewalks and under tall pine trees. You may remember we had a tropical storm which was the remnant of hurricane Hillary in August. It never rains in Southern California in August. We may get some rain in the nearby mountains which spill over from summer monsoon storms. But normally it doesn't rain here in August.

However hurricane Hillary changed all of that pouring several inches of rain across the region in 24 hours. Along with the rain there were very strong winds which blew down trees. The strong winds also scattered millions of pine needles on the streets and sidewalks. It looked like a year's worth of pine needles were turned loose in our neighborhood in one day.

By themselves the needles don't pose any immediate danger. But during our fall fire season these piles of pine needles increase the risk of wild fires. The street sweeper cleaned up a lot of the needles and some of the gardeners also cleared them from under shrubs and trees. However there are many piles of pine needles collected under the towering pine trees. They look like small match sticks just waiting for a spark to set them on fire. The results could be devastating.

There is a passage in the Bible which used the example of a match stick which could ignite a large fire. The author relates this analogy to our tongue. He says our words can cause emotional damage just like a match stick can cause physical destruction (James 3:5). Another passage says, "Even a fool is thought to be wise if he keeps silent" (Proverbs 17:28).

Let me encourage you to *watch your words*. Use words that encourage not discourage. Build people up don't tear people down. Put aside slander and bad language. Speak with truth. Don't speak lies. Honor God and encourage others. They will be glad you did and you will too. And make sure you clean up your pine needles before fire season!

College Football

I like college football. I love to watch the games on TV and I really enjoy being at a game in person. I love the tradition and pageantry of the college setting. Students fill the stadium and the cheer leaders rally the fans to support their team.

The marching bands contribute to the energetic atmosphere playing songs during the game and preforming on the field during half time. One of the most impressive college bands I have ever seen was from Texas A&M. They have an award winning military band which plays and marches in perfect precision from one end of the field to the other.

My wife and I went to Arizona State University in the 1960's. The school and the football stadium were a lot smaller back then. The Sun Devils won most of their games and began to receive national recognition during the time we were at ASU.

Because of the hot weather in Phoenix most football games were played at night. The football fans endured some very uncomfortable weather during the season and so did the players.

Recently one of the ASU football games was disrupted by a huge dust storm. Just before half-time a wall of dust descended on the stadium followed by thunder and lightning. Officials stopped the game, pulled the teams off the field and told football fans to seek shelter. The game was resumed after the storm passed but was not completed until one o'clock in the morning.

In other parts of the country college football games are sometimes played in freezing snow storms. It looks miserable to be playing football and even more miserable sitting in the stadium watching the game.

Greeks and Romans loved to watch events in the athletic stadiums and open air theaters. People rushed into the theater in Ephesus to protest against the Apostle Paul's teaching (Acts Chapter 19). My mother came to faith in Christ at the Billy Graham Crusade at the ASU stadium in the 1960's. It was a life-changing event my family. Let me encourage you to attend a college football game or other special events at your local college or university. You will be glad you did.

High School Football

When the grandkids are very young most grandparents get to enjoy a lot of time with the little ones. They can do child care when parents are working and they can have sleep overs when the kids get a little older. But once grandkids enter school their availability rapidly declines. They are on a daily routine attending classes during the day and fulfilling homework assignments in the evening. In addition grandkids often enroll in organized baseball, soccer or volleyball programs. A typical schedule involves two practices a week after school and a game or two on Saturday or Sunday.

School, sports and other activities reduce the amount of time grandparents get to spend with their grandchildren. The kids are so busy they have limited opportunities to spend time with their grandparents. One of the ways to address this issue is to attend the grandchildren's sports and school activities.

Recently my wife and I attended her grandson's high school football game. We got to the game in the middle of the first quarter. We had difficulty finding her family so we planted our lawn chairs in some shade near the end zone. It was difficult to identify which team her grandson was on. One team wore white jerseys and the other team wore red and gold uniforms.

The score board was across the field and the glare from the late afternoon sun made it difficult to see who was winning and which team scored a touchdown or field goal. We asked a couple of strangers which one was the home team and then we started searching for *number fifty-one*. We looked and looked throughout the game but never saw him on the field. Maybe he was injured and unable to play. We were disappointed we didn't get to see him in action.

However near the end of the game someone pointed out number 51 playing defense on the other team. He made a solid tackle on the opponent's runner. Suddenly we realized we had been looking for her grandson on the wrong team! He had been playing most of the game and we didn't even realize it. We talked to him after the game and told him what a great job he did. But we didn't have the heart to tell him we had been cheering for the wrong team. Let me encourage you to go to your grandchildren's school and sports events. And make sure you get to the game on time! You will be glad you did and they will too!

A Holiday Weekend

One of the most frequent topics of conversation in California is traffic. No matter where you live traffic is terrible. Freeways do help connect communities but the volume of cars and trucks is staggering. This is especially true on holiday weekends.

Recently we spent several days in San Diego. It is about 100 miles south of where we live in LA County. We drove down on a Wednesday evening. Traffic moved well and we arrived at our destination right on schedule. The freeways really are nice when the number of cars and trucks are minimal. Early in the morning and later in the evening are the best times to be on the freeways in Southern California.

However, we were overwhelmed by what we saw on our drive back from San Diego to our home in Diamond Bar. The GPS on our phone predicted it would take about an hour and forty minutes using Interstate Five to reach our destination. I thought that was a little optimistic but we were willing to give it a try.

We made good time and traffic moved well as we drove north out of San Diego. Even some of the usual slower spots moved at a good pace. But when we reached Carlsbad and Oceanside we glanced over to the southbound lane and were amazed to see traffic going south at a crawl. I was very thankful we were going north and not south!

But we were even more surprised to see how far the traffic was backed up. Mile after mile was bumper to bumper going to San Diego. I felt guilty we were speeding along at 70 MPH in the north bound lanes.

Eventually I called the KNX Radio Traffic Hot Line and left a message asking the traffic reporter what was causing the delay on south bound Interstate Five. A few minutes later the radio announcer reported he had received a number of similar calls by drivers stuck in the traffic. I was sure there was a serious accident but the radio reporter said this was typical on Saturdays and holiday weekends from LA to San Diego. He explained there was a *20 mile backup* of cars going to San Diego. There is a verse in the Bible which says, "Be kind, gentle and patient with one another" (Ephesians 4:2). Let me encourage you to select a different route if you are making plans to visit sunny San Diego. Pack your suitcase with a lot of patience and kindness. You will be glad you did and your passengers will too!

Solar Powered Pumpkins

Halloween has become more and more popular in recent years. One story I heard on the news indicated people are spending more money on this holiday than ever before. Store shelves are filled with candy, costumes and decorations months before the actual event. Grocery stores are selling large and small pumpkins ready for carving and decorating.

I am surprised by how many homes in our neighborhood are decorated for Halloween. There may be more houses decorated for Halloween than there are for Christmas.

Some of the props and decorations have become very elaborate and expensive. I have seen huge skeletons for sale at Costco. They include moving parts and scary voices. One house near us has huge spider webs and scary characters in their front yard.

One of the most unique houses in our neighborhood is decorated with plastic pumpkins. There must be at least 20 happy pumpkins filling the small slope in front of their house. But what makes them even more interesting is the fact they are solar powered. On the top of each plastic pumpkin is a small solar collector which recharges the battery during the day and illuminates the pumpkins at night.

We have come a long way from the days when people carved a pumpkin with a small knife and scrapped out the seeds from the inside. Then they placed a small candle on the inside to illuminate the eyes, nose and mouth. Some people carved friendly faces while others made them look frightening. A lot of creativity went into each pumpkin.

Now you can leave all of the work to the manufactures. No more carving, no more mess and no more candles. You can buy pumpkins ready for use powered by the sun.

Let me encourage you to make some memories with your children and grandchildren on Halloween this year. Find or make a custom costume for each of your family members. Take time to carve a pumpkin with them. Or if you are pressed for time why not buy a few solar powered pumpkins to decorate your house for Halloween. You will be glad you did and your neighbors will too.

Life is Not Better Buzzed

We have seen some amazing and rapid shifts in our culture and in our country. Things which were unthinkable a generation ago have become not only socially acceptable but actually legal. One example is the legalization and accessibility of marijuana in our community and across our country.

When my wife and I were driving on a main road in a local community we saw a sign which vividly illustrated this shift. The sign on a store read, *"Life Is Better Buzzed"*. I believe they were promoting Marijuana and other products laced with the drug.

It wasn't too long ago when Marijuana was an illegal substance. Local, state and federal law enforcement officers worked tirelessly to confiscate and prevent the sale and production of it. Now laws have been passed by local and state legislatures which legalize the production and distribution of the drug.

What is even more ironic is the fact you can purchase it from your car when you use the convenient drive thru window. I have also seen bill boards promoting Marijuana and offering home delivery. Now suppliers will ship it to you or personally deliver it to your house.

Today there are all kinds of restrictions on cigarettes. We used to have cigarette vending machines where any one could purchase a pack for fifty cents. There were billboards featuring the strong looking *Marlboro Man* encouraging consumers to purchase cigarettes. There were TV commercials promoting smoking too. Now smoking, vaping and promoting cigarettes is strictly prohibited. Billboards are outlawed and smoking is not allowed in most public buildings and restaurants. Now there are warning labels to discourage people from smoking cigarettes. But smoking Marijuana is legal and promoted. Now the slogan is, *"Life is better buzzed"*.

We live in a *country of contradictions* where what was once was wrong is now right. And what was once right is now wrong. There is a verse in the Bible which predicts a time will come when people who know what is right will choose to do what is wrong (Second Timothy 3:1-5). Let me encourage you to warn your children about the culture we live in today. Remind them to not conform to the world's values (Romans 12:1-2). They will be glad you did and you will too.

T-Shirts

I was startled the other day when a man came up behind me at a local restaurant. I didn't understand what he was saying so I turned around so I could hear him more clearly. I wondered if I had done something wrong.

But he didn't have a complaint. Actually he offered me a compliment. He said he liked my T-Shirt. At first I was confused but finally remembered I was wearing a shirt from *Cheeseburger in Paradise* in Lahaina.

My children had purchased it for me many years ago. They knew it was one of my favorite restaurants on Maui and they wanted to surprise me with the shirt at Christmas. I didn't wear it very often but always packed the shirt in my suitcase whenever I traveled to Hawaii.

Cheeseburger in Paradise was a popular place for tourist and locals. The burgers were great and the atmosphere was ideal. I loved the view of the ocean and I loved to hear the small waves lapping up on the beach beneath us.

As you know, *Cheeseburger in Paradise* burned to the ground when the terrible wild fire raced through the town in August, 2023. The entire town was incinerated. Over 100 people were killed and many bodies were turned into ash by the horrific inferno.

It has been encouraging to hear about various organizations which are rallying to help families who lost their homes and businesses which were destroyed. One way you can show your support is by contributing to reputable relief organization who is helping people on Maui.

There is a passage in the Bible which reminds us to help those who hurting. "Gently encourage the discouraged and reach out to those who are exhausted, pulling them to their feet. Be patient with each person, attentive to individual needs (First Thessalonians 5:14 – the Message Bible). Let me to encourage you to not forget those who have suffered so much through the fire which destroyed Lahaina or similar disasters in your part of the world. Lend a hand and send a gift *this week*. If you have a T-Shirt from Lahaina or Hawaii wear to express your support for them. They will be glad you did and you will too.

Hondo

We are thankful you married Trisha and became part of the Hopper family. We remember your wedding on December 18, 1999 when Trisha came down a long staircase in her beautiful dress. I will always remember her words when I met her at the bottom of the stairs, "Daddy everyone is staring at me". It was the first wedding in our family.

It was hard to say goodbye when you and Trisha drove off to Portland where you were studying at Multnomah Bible College. But we were thankful for your faith in Christ and your desire to finish college and invest your lives serving him.

It was exciting to be with you in Estes Park, Colorado, when Caleb was born. A few years later we celebrated Elizabeth's birth in Slovenia. You and Trisha are great parents and it is fun to see how much the kids love their mom and dad. We enjoyed staying with Caleb and Elizabeth when you and Trisha were away leading summer camps and training young adults with Josiah Venture. We enjoyed riding bikes around your town with them and going to the ice cream store for a treat.

Both of you are gifted missionaries. You have made Slovenia your home and have adapted so well to a new language and a new culture. You have used your love for the outdoors like Snow Boarding and Skate Boarding to connect with young people in Slovenia. You also created a Bible Training program to disciple college students.

You are a great father and husband. We were amazed when you took Caleb on a memorable camping experience when he turned thirteen. You have encouraged Elizabeth to expand her interests in art and dance. You make time to have a date night with Trisha regularly.

We have enjoyed the times we have been able to spend with you and Trisha and the kids. We remember rock climbing in Big Bear and the help you have given us painting our house. We appreciate you are willing to fix things around your house and how you encourage Trisha in so many ways. We are thankful you are part of the Hopper family.

To my readers – Let me encourage you to express your love and appreciation to the men and women who have married one of your children. Take a moment *this week* to call or send a note and tell them how thankful you are to have them in your family.

Hospitality

One of the lost arts in our culture is hospitality. In previous generations people were inclined to open their homes and invite friends and neighbors over for a BBQ, dinner or dessert. If you watch some old movies you will see a crowd of people filling a small apartment enjoying a meal together on a holiday or special occasion.

It feels like our culture has shifted and people are less willing to host a group of people in their home. You are more likely to see a large gathering at a local restaurant than you are to see them in someone's house.

There may be several reasons for this change. Hospitality is a lot of work. It involves cleaning your house and picking up the clutter on the kitchen counter or dining room table. It requires shopping for food and spending hours preparing a meal. And there is washing all the pots, pans and dishes after the meal. I feel exhausted just thinking about it.

On the other hand it is a lot easier to meet some friends or family members at a restaurant. The chef cooks the food. The waitress serves the food, the bus boy clears the plates and the dish washer does the dirty work.

But a restaurant can be noisy. It can be difficult to talk and hear what others are saying. People at one end of the table can't be part of the conversation at the other end of the table. Plus the cost of a meal at home is usually much less than what you spend at a restaurant.

Recently we were invited to lunch after church with some friends. But my wife and I got the idea it would be nicer to have the group come to our home. We could prepare lunch and we could talk and share in a quieter setting. It did involve some effort on our part. I got to clean the floors and Susan straightened up the house. We prepared the food together. The lunch was a big success with eleven people gathered around our kitchen table.

Many verses in the Bible emphasize the importance of hospitality (First Peter 4:9 / Hebrews 13:1-2). Let me encourage you to open your home to friends, neighbors or strangers *this month*. Share a meal and enjoy some good conversation. You will be glad you did and they will too.

Fixing the Chairs

I have shared in the past about blending two households into one. When my wife Susan and I got married a few months ago we had furniture and appliances from two houses. We had two refrigerators, two washers and dryers and two sets of pots and pans. We actually had four or five flat screen TV's between us.

The question was how would we be able to fit all of this stuff into one small four bedroom house? The answer was we both needed to down size. We needed to decide what we wanted to keep and decide where to donate the extra furniture and appliances we did not need.

One of the things Susan really wanted to keep was her large glass top kitchen table. It was 80 inches in diameter and could seat up to 12 people. I wondered if it would fit in my smaller house but she was confident it would. She was right. It did fit nicely and has become a favorite place to entertain guests.

However, the attractive wooded chairs don't like my tile floor. We have replaced the soft sticky felt pads on the feet of the chairs several times but they keep coming off. The recessed grout between the floor tiles seems to loosen the felt pads when the chairs are moved.

We have looked all over the internet but have not found a suitable solution to our problem. I'm sure there is an answer somewhere in cyber space or on Amazon market place but we haven't found one yet. Recently a friend who owns an upholstery business gave us a few small plastic pieces with a small nail in them which he has used on various pieces of furniture. We are hoping this may solve our problem.

I'm sure you have faced similar challenges as a homeowner. There is plumbing to fix and electrical outlets that don't work. You may have a squeaky door or a dripping faucet. The list is endless. The question is – are you grumpy you have to fix the chairs or grateful you have chairs to fix? It is easy to become discouraged by even little things. But it is more important to be grateful for all the things God has given to you.

One verse says, "Give thanks for everything" (First Thessalonians 5:14). Let me encourage you to watch for moments to be grateful and not grumpy *today*. Give thanks to God for every situation you face. And let me know if you have a solution for my chairs. Thanks!

November 6
Driving Home

One evening we were driving home from a holiday BBQ when we encountered a variety of unexpected obstacles. We had enjoyed our time with family and friends and relaxed on the short drive home. Traffic was light and the freeway was moving at full speed.

Suddenly we came upon an unexpected object on the road. I was driving the 65 MPH speed limit when a large white or yellow bucket was directly in front of us. There were cars in other lanes so I was hesitant to try to swerve around it. I managed to move a few feet to our right and then ran over the unforeseen obstacle.

Thankfully I was able to maintain control of my SUV and it appeared there was not any damage to our vehicle. I think the container may have been an empty five gallon paint bucket or trash container. The bucket had probably fallen off someone's work truck.

We breathed a sigh of relief and kept on going. However moments later we saw a large black object in our lane. It looked like a black or dark blue plastic tarp. It was fairly large. Again I was forced to make a split second decision. Should I stay in my lane and drive over it or try to change lanes and go around it? I decided to stay in my lane and hope for the best. Thankfully it did not seem to do any damage but it was another scary moment on a dark night on a busy freeway.

Finally we got off the freeway and onto Diamond Bar Boulevard. It was good to be on a city street and off the fast moving highway. But then we noticed a car a short distance ahead of us hit his brakes and swerve into the other lane. I slowed quickly but not fast enough to avoid water from a heavy duty lawn sprinkler spraying across the road. Water showered our car from above and dirty water splashed from the road.

Ironically I had just been to a car wash on the way to the BBQ a few hours earlier. Now my clean car was dirty again from the splash of the dirty water on the road from the broken water sprinkler. I was frustrated by this additional obstacle but thankful our car was not damaged and we were not hurt. It was an eventful adventure driving home from the family gathering. When we arrived at our house we gave thanks to God for his unseen protection on our perilous journey. Let me encourage you to thank God for His protection. And you may want skip the drive and invite friends to your house for the next holiday BBQ.

November 7
A Spider in My Face

We have a garden shed at our house which I built many years ago. It has been very useful for storing yard tools and my lawn mower and other things. More recently it has been filled with cardboard moving boxes and plastic storage containers. It is packed right to the door.

One day I was looking for a blue tarp to cover the lawn mower which is now sitting outside the shed. The mower had been displaced by the boxes and containers and I wanted to protect the mower because the weather forecaster predicted a good chance of rain showers.

My wife and I searched for the blue tarp in the garage but we couldn't find it. I knew I had purchased several large plastic tarps to cover moving boxes which we had temporarily stored on the covered patio. After we had emptied all of those boxes on the patio I knew I had saved the tarps for future use.

When we didn't find the tarps in the garage, my wife suggested I look in the garden shed. I was skeptical because every inch of the shed was already full but sure enough I found two blue tarps right by the door. When I reached in to pull out one of the folded tarps I felt a spider web on my arm. As I pulled the tarp out of the shed I looked up I saw a big ugly spider only inches from my face.

Instinctively I yelled and jumped away from the door. I couldn't see the spider but I was worried it was on my head or clothes. I asked my wife to look and see if she could find it. It was creepy thinking the spider might be crawling on me.

I don't like spiders. I have never liked spiders. The term Arachnophobia means fear of spiders. You may have some fears of your own like fear of heights (Acrophobia) or fear of the dark (Nyctophobia). The list is endless.

There are many verses in the Bible which remind us to not be afraid. One verse says, "Fear not for I am with you, don't be discouraged. I am your God and I will help you and strengthen you and uphold you with my mighty right hand" (Isaiah 41:10). Let me encourage you to not allow fear to prevent you from living a fulfilling life. Put your fears aside and live by faith in God. You will be glad you did.

November 8
A Major Plumbing Problem

I was stunned when I opened our monthly water bill. Our normal water bill was usually under $100 a month but the charges were $263.48 for August, 2023. When I thought back over the previous month I did remember having trouble reprograming the timer on my lawn sprinkler system. There were some days when the lawn was watered twice on the same day. And there were a couple of days when it did not get watered at all. I think I finally got the timer figured out.

A few days after the record high water bill arrived I received another piece of mail from the water company. It was a letter informing me they had detected a leak in my system. The newer water meters report water usage to the district office via the internet. People don't manually monitor and read your water meter. It is done electronically. The water district had installed new water meters to implement this new system.

I went out to the sidewalk and removed the cement lid to access the water meter. I was surprised to find the small concrete vault was full of water. I spent an hour emptying the water so I could see the meter. We turned off all of the water in the house. Sure enough the meter kept moving. This confirmed we did indeed have a water leak in the system.

I called the water district office the next day and they dispatched an employee to investigate. He ran a couple of tests and confirmed we had a leak. Then he removed more water and soil from the small concrete vault to expose more of the pipe coming in from the street and going onto my property. If the leak was before the meter it was the district's responsibility to fix it. If the leak was after the meter I would have to hire a plumber to find and repair the leak.

After he had removed more water and debris he turned the main valve on again and he immediately saw the problem. A small washer on the new meter had failed. We could see the leak. He said the washer may not have been installed correctly with the new meter. He replaced the washer in ten minutes. Problem solved. And he said I would get a credit on my huge water bill because it was their fault not mine. There is a verse in the Bible which says, "Don't worry about anything, pray about everything and always give thanks" (Philippians 4:6). Let me encourage you to pray and give thanks to God when you face small and big problems. And make sure your check the small rubber washers when you do your next plumbing project. You will be glad you did!

November 9
The Plumbing Project (Part Two)

If you read the previous story you know how remarkable it was for us to resolve a major plumbing problem. Our water bill was over $250 for one month and the Water District had notified me by mail they detected a leak in the water system at our house.

My heart sank when I began to imagine how expensive this could be. I shared my situation with a couple of men and they both estimated it would cost at least $500 to repair. I thought in these days of runaway inflation it might cost twice that much.

In addition to the financial expenses I worried about how much time it would take to locate the leak and repair the problem. Several years ago I spent a week re-routing some of the copper water pipes through our attic after we had a slab leak. I wrote a story about the adventure in an earlier book. We went for a whole week without running water in our house. It was very stressful and exhausting.

I was trying to remember how we survived for a week without water. We stored water in buckets to flush the toilets and drinking water in several large pots and jugs. It was a vivid reminder how we take running water for granted. Life without running water is a challenge.

When the technician from the Water District looked at our water meter and confirmed we had a water leak he explained the options. If the leak was before the water meter it was their responsibility but if the leak was after the water meter and on my property we would need to hire a plumber. And he stressed the Water District would need to inspect and approve the repairs before turning the water back on.

I envisioned a time consuming project digging up the lawn looking for the leak. And I expected it would be days before the repairs were completed and approved. The outlook was bleak and unknown. It was such a relief when the repairman found the leak and confirmed it was their responsibility and not mine. I was even more amazed when he explained the solution was to simply replace a *small rubber washer*. There is a familiar account in the Bible when a teenager named David used a small stone and a sling to kill the giant Goliath. The problem looked insurmountable but the solution was courage and faith and a *small stone* (First Samuel Chapter 17). Let me encourage you to trust God to provide a solution to your unsolved problems too.

November 10
Reflecting on a Good Day

It seems rare to come to the end of the day with a sense of peace and satisfaction. More often I find myself feeling stressed and exhausted. There were unfinished goals and unfulfilled expectations. Where did the time go? What did I have to show from my busy day?

But recently I found myself feeling relaxed and content at the end of a day. I smiled as I looked back on how I had spent my time and what I had accomplished. The day began early when I had time to sit down and write a couple of stories for this new book. I enjoy putting my thoughts on my computer and hope the stories will encourage people.

Then my wife and I went for our regular morning walk. We talked while we walked and shared what was on our hearts and mind. We looked at the day ahead and reviewed things we wanted to get done. We prayed for our children and grandchildren and other people with needs.

After breakfast we went to the gym for the first time in a while. We had talked about getting back to the gym for weeks but today we did it. I also spent time on the phone talking with a young man who had some questions about the Bible. One of my favorite things is helping people who are interested in growing in their faith and wanting to learn more.

During the afternoon I spent some time making some phone calls related to our upcoming tour to Israel. Some questions had come up and it felt good to gather the information I was looking for. I also scheduled time to meet with a couple who had asked me to do their wedding and schedule breakfast with a friend I had not seen in a while.

I enjoyed a late lunch at home with my wife. We shared a healthy chicken salad and discussed some things which had come up during the day. She was glad to be getting somethings done too. We went for a shorter second walk in the early evening. The exercise felt good.

Did I mention the weather was perfect? It was unusually cool for late summer. Thin clouds kept the hot sunshine away. It felt like spring not summer. At the end of the day we watched part of a movie and had a snack before we went to bed. There is a verse in the Bible which says, "The steadfast love of the Lord never ceases. His mercies never come to an end. They are new every morning" (Lamentations 3:22-23). Let me encourage you to enjoy the time God gives you every day.

World War One

November 11th is the date when World War One ended. Several nations in Europe had been at war since 1914. The United States entered the war in 1917 and the fighting stopped on the 11th hour of the 11th day of the 11th month in 1918. It was a horrible conflict. Armies used poison gas to kill and injure the enemy and fought trench warfare in the fields of France. Millions of men in uniform and many civilians died in the struggle which the United States and its allies finally won.

My grandfather served in the Army during the war. He was shipped overseas to Europe and served in France until the war ended in 1918. We have his "*Dog Tag*" which every soldier wore in case they were killed so their body could be identified. We also have his hand written diary recording his military training and his experience in France. He started writing when he entered the military and kept writing until the day he returned home to Arkansas.

November 11th was originally called *Armistice Day* because it celebrated the day the war ended. But in 1926 Congress changed it to Veterans Day to honor all of the men and women who have served in the military and those who died in war. We also celebrate Memorial Day on the last Monday in May to honor and remember all military members who have died.

One of the ways we honor military veterans who have died is to provide a burial place for the service member and their spouse. There are several National Cemeteries in Southern California in Riverside, Los Angeles and a new one in Orange County. There are additional ones in the San Diego area too.

It is impressive to see these cemeteries decorated with small flags on Veterans Day and Memorial Day. Many service organizations and local Boy and Girl Scout groups place flags at every grave to honor those who served our country. It is amazing to see thousands of flags filling the peaceful green grass at these locations.

Let me encourage you to take time and explain to your children and grandchildren why we celebrate Veterans Day and Memorial Day. Help them understand the importance and significance of these holidays. Tell them about family members who served in the military. And encourage them to thank men and women who wear the uniform.

November 12
A Field of Flags

I had the honor of helping one of the widows in our church bury the ashes of her husband at the Veterans National Cemetery in Riverside, California on the day after Veterans Day. We were amazed to see thousands of small flags had been placed on the graves to honor the lives of men and women who had served in the military.

Volunteers were beginning to remove the flags but thousands of them remained when we arrived early in the morning. It was impressive to see rows and rows of small flags decorating the green grass. We could see snow covered mountain peaks in the distance and a clear blue sky above. It was an unforgettable sight.

The American flag is a powerful visual symbol that represents our country. It is easily recognized by friends and foes alike. During the Viet Nam war people burned the flag protesting the war. People in Iran and other Middle Eastern countries have burned our flag too.

But for others the American flag is a reminder of America's sacrifice to free nations from tyranny and oppression. It is a symbol of America's presence in every part of the world. There is a famous scene in World War Two when the American flag was raised on the highest peak during the bloody battle on the island of Iwo Jima. It was a reminder of the victory and the price paid in human lives to conquer the island and bring the war closer to an end.

The first American flag was designed to represent the new union of the thirteen original colonies. It had thirteen stripes alternating with red and white colors. Each strip represented one of the original thirteen colonies. It also had thirteen stars arranged in a circle based on the idea that all of the states were equal. Later when more states joined the union the number of stripes remained the same but a new star was added for each new state. Today there are 50 states in the union and each one is represented by a star.

I hope you have an American flag at your house. Let me encourage you to fly the American flag on holidays and explain to your children what the stars and stripes represent. Show your pride in your country and express your thanks to those who have served in our armed forces. You will be glad you did and they will too.

The Mustang

One of the most popular and iconic cars of all time was the Ford Mustang. The first ones were produced in 1964. My parents bought one of the earliest models mid-year in 1964 and a second one in 1965. You may still see some of these Mustangs on the road today.

The design was different than most cars at that time. Typically the hood of a car and the trunk of a car were about the same size. But the Mustang was different with a longer hood and a shorter trunk. The interior was different too. Instead of a full bench seat in the front, the Mustang had two bucket seats. It also had the gear shift lever between the front seats instead of the more traditional gear shift lever on the steering column.

My brother got his driver's license in 1964. I was able to ride with him to run an errand or drive to a friend's house. I remember it was like we were in a race car because the front seats had individual belts with a buckle similar to what you were required to wear on an airplane. I think we got a lot of attention when we drove around in the new Mustang.

Eventually my parents sold the first one and later gave the second one to my older brother. But it wasn't very practical for his young family with only two doors and not a lot of room for kids in the back seat.

There was a grandmother at our church in Tucson who owned a Mustang in the 1970's. One way she enticed her grandchildren to go to church was to let them drive her to church in her Mustang.

Years later after my mother died my father gave Grandma Hopper's 1980's Mustang to my son Tim. He drove it from Arizona to California in the early 1990's. It wasn't like the classic cars of the 1960's but he loved it. I remember watching one day when Tim took his three younger sisters for a ride in Grandma's Mustang. My wife and I stood in front of our house and watched our teenage son load his three sisters into his car. We worried about all of our children being in one car driven by our teenage son. But they did fine.

I wonder if there was a Classic Car in your life. Let me encourage you to show some pictures to your kids or grandkids. Share some stories of places you went and memories you made driving that car. They will be glad you did and you will too.

November 14
Spider Webs

I shared in an earlier story about how much I don't like spiders. They give me the creeps especially when I walk into a spider web and wonder if the builder is crawling down my back or caught in my hair. You may feel the same way.

Recently my wife and I were walking through our neighborhood and noticed some large, sophisticated spider webs. One of them in particular was stretched from the roof of a house down to a garbage can. It was one of the largest I have seen. But what was even more interesting is I had not noticed it before. We were walking a little later in the morning and the sun had just come over the horizon. At a particular angle the sun light made the web more visible.

Previously we had not noticed this huge web extending from the roof. But suddenly from our vantage point in the bright sun light made it possible to see the web which we had not noticed before. I suppose this is why spiders have an advantage over their prey. Small bugs and flies don't see the web until it is too late and they are caught in it.

This reminded me of a number of warnings in the Bible which caution people to not be deceived or caught up in false teaching. One verse says, "Do not be deceived by philosophies of this world" (Colossians 2:8). Another passage says, "Don't be caught up in the messages of false teachers" (Ephesians 4:14). Another verse says, "The god of this world has blinded the eyes of unbelievers so they cannot see the truth" (Second Corinthians 4:4).

In Bible times many false teachers misled sincere people who were seeking the truth. Today the internet is filled with people and groups making false claims and spreading half-truths which can confuse and mislead people. Some religious groups look authentic and sound sincere but their message may not be accurate or truthful.

The *two tests* of any religious organization are, "What do they say about the *written word* (the Bible) and the *living word*" (Jesus)? Do they believe the Bible is God's only written revelation or do they have additional books too? Do they believe Jesus is God in human form or do they teach Jesus is just one of many religious leaders? Examine carefully what groups and individuals are promoting. Don't be deceived or misled. Don't get caught up in their web of deceit.

324

Buying Clothes Online

I have expressed my frustration in the past about buying clothes at stores like Costco which do not have dressing rooms. It is difficult to purchase the right size without trying the clothes on first. Inevitably I end up returning them because the clothes don't fit.

In a weak moment of desperation I decided to buy a pair of Wrangler Traditional Cargo Shorts online. It took a while to find them but Amazon did have a full page of cargo shorts. I liked the pair I already owned but they were worn and frayed and I knew my wife would not let me out of the house wearing those old shorts.

I moved through the web page and found the Wrangler brand. They listed over a dozen different colors which came in many sizes. I decided to go for the smaller size hoping they would fit my perfect athletic frame.

It was a little more difficult deciding on a color. My old Wrangler shorts are Khaki color but I didn't see that option on the page. So I selected "Oak". It wasn't white and it wasn't dark so I hope it will be close to my current Khaki color.

I entered my address and credit card information and pressed the *purchase now* button. Success! I was now an official online shopper for cargo shorts. However as I reviewed my purchase I noticed the free delivery date was over a month away. Why would it take five weeks to deliver my new cargo shorts? Where were they manufactured? Were they stored in an underground bunker in some far away country?

Then I tried to go back and see if there were other options better than the "free delivery" five week date? I pressed button after button trying to revise or cancel my order but nothing I tried seemed to work. I was stuck with my online purchase and would need to sit on the front porch for a month watching for my "free delivery".

Why can't shopping be simple? What happened to the old fashion department store where I could walk in, try on and purchase a new pair of cargo shorts? It feels like the internet has taken all of the fun out of shopping. Let me encourage you to shop in person and make sure the item fits before you buy it. You will be glad you did!

Barnabas

I first met Randy when he was the lead pastor of another church in Tucson. His wife taught at our preschool and we enjoyed getting to know them better. When we had a staff opening at our church in 1985 we invited Randy to fill that vacancy.

Randy and his wife Wanda had grown up in Tucson. They were college graduates and had three young children. I enjoyed serving at the church with Randy and appreciated his love for people.

It was a difficult decision for my wife and me to leave Chapel in the Hills Church and become the pastor at the Evangelical Free Church in Diamond Bar, California. But I was thankful the Tucson church invited Randy to become the new lead pastor. He had plenty of ministry experience and was a faithful shepherd.

Randy and Wanda were some of our "Golf and Shop" friends. After we moved to California we began to get together once-a-year with several couples from the Tucson church. The men golfed and the women shopped. Randy was the best golfer in the group. We made many special memories with this special group of friends.

My wife and I were able to visit Tucson from time to time and we were always impressed at how well Chapel in the Hills was doing under Randy's leadership. Eventually they merged with another church in the community and joined the Evangelical Free Church denomination. Our church in California and the Tucson church were part of the EFCA.

Eventually they were able to build a new facility at a strategic location in southwest Tucson. Randy and several other church leaders guided both churches through the merger and the results have been amazing. Randy led the church for over 30 years.

There was a man named Barnabas who was always helping other people. God used him to welcome Paul into the church in Jerusalem and to encourage new believers in the church in Antioch (Acts 9:26-28 / 11:27-30). Randy reminds me of Barnabas. He was a faithful shepherd and encouraged people to grow in their faith. Let me encourage you to send a note or make a call to someone who has been a faithful friend or pastor in your life. Tell them how much you appreciate them. They will be glad you did and you will too.

Building Without Borrowing

I have shared in the past how much I enjoyed construction projects. I have a great respect for men and women who work hard with their own hands to build homes, repair cars, and fix plumbing. I admire the people I see at Home Depot early in the morning gathering materials and supplies for a new day's work.

But one of the biggest obstacles is the cost of these projects. Constructing a new classroom building at a church could cost a quarter to a half-million dollars. It is probably double that amount today. It seemed impossible to think you could complete a building project of that size without borrowing money. But with God's help we did.

We constructed a two story classroom building without borrowing in Diamond Bar and a larger worship center in Tucson on a pay-as-you-go basis. I was able to do the same thing with several room addition projects on my homes too. All of these projects were faith adventures.

There are two parts to an effort like this. The first is raising the money to construct a classroom building at a church or a room addition at home. Churches hold building campaigns. We challenged people to donate money over and above their regular financial support for the church. We asked people to give generously and sacrificially.

We gave each project a name like "Heart to Build", "Heart to Reach" and "The Next Campaign". We invited all of the church family to attend informational meetings in homes to learn more about the building effort. We produced videos and printed material to explain the purpose and need for the project. We wanted to address every question and potential objection people might have. People needed to see the need.

Then we challenged people to make a financial commitment. What would they be willing to give over and above their current financial support for the church as God enabled them? We called these, "Faith Commitments" or a "Faith Promise". It was remarkable how God provided in unexpected ways through many generous donations.

When the Israelites rebuilt the walls of Jerusalem the author said, "They had a heart to build" (Nehemiah 4:6). Let me encourage you to build without borrowing. You will be glad you did!

Building Without Borrowing (Part Two)

I shared in my previous story how we raised funds to construct some buildings at the churches where I served without borrowing money. We bought materials and moved ahead as funds became available. Raising the money was one part of the project. But the construction was the other part.

The same was true with the two room additions I built on to our home in Tucson. We bought materials and built step by step as more money became available. In Diamond Bar church families gave us a generous gift the first Christmas we there. This was a huge boost to completing the room addition without debt. It was thrilling to see how God supplied the money and materials we needed for both the church and the home projects. You can read some of those stories in my previous books.

One of the key ingredients to building without borrowing was doing a lot of the work ourselves and contracting areas where we lacked expertise. In Tucson we hired a contractor to dig the footings, pour the concrete floors and build the block walls. We constructed the interior walls and the wood roof. Contractors from the church ran the electrical wiring and installed the plumbing. We hung the drywall and hired people to tape and texture it. We painted the interior. It was very similar at the church in Diamond Bar. We did a lot of the work ourselves and hired sub-contractors to do work we could not do. I did the same on my room additions too.

Another key strategy of building without borrowing was breaking up some the big steps into smaller pieces. We used contractors who were willing to do their work in phases. We only needed the rough plumbing before we poured the floor. We only needed the electrical wire and conduit roughed in too. Later the contractors could come back to run wires through the walls and even later do the finish work. The HVAC system worked that way too. Step by step we pressed ahead as more money became available. The project took longer than we expected but it was amazing to complete a building without borrowing. There are many examples in the books of Ezra and Nehemiah when God provided in some unexpected ways to rebuild the Temple and repair the walls of Jerusalem. They often said, "*The Hand of God was on us*" (Ezra 7:8-10 & Nehemiah 6:15-16) Let me encourage you to consider building without borrowing and watch how God provides your needs.

November 19
Digging in the Dirt

I'm sure I will be criticized by some people for what I am about to say but I think little boys love to dig in the dirt. I know some little girls do too but I think it is a kind of genetic thing with guys.

I enjoyed watching my young grandsons playing with toy cars and trucks. They liked to build bridges and tunnels for cars and trains to go over and under. They enjoyed digging holes at the beach to fill up with water. They didn't worry about getting their hands or clothes dirty.

Digging in sand and dirt was fun. They could play with plastic army men and create a battlefield in the dirt. They could also make a pretend city with roads, airfields and other features. There was something about dirt which made it better than just playing indoors.

However, when little boys grow up into young men I sense their enthusiasm for dirt declines. Dirt used to be a place for games and fun. But when you are a homeowner dirt becomes associated with work. You dig trenches for sprinkler pipes and dig holes to plant trees and shrubs. You move dirt from the front yard to the back yard. You dig in the dirt to repair broken water pipes and replace lawn sprinklers.

Building a room addition also involved moving dirt too. Digging the footings and making trenches for the water and sewer pipes resulted in a sore back and achy muscles. More dirt was needed to level the site before pouring the concrete slab. It takes a lot of sweat and hard work moving and removing the dirt in any major building project.

There is a passage at the beginning of the Bible which says man will be moving dirt all of his life. This was the result of Adam's and Eve's sin and disobedience to God (Read Genesis Chapters 2&3). One verse says, "The ground will sprout weeds and thrones and you will get your food the hard way, planting and tilling and harvesting, sweating in the fields from dawn to dark" (Genesis 3:17-19).

Digging in the dirt can be enjoyable and rewarding. You can plant flowers and vegetables and enjoy the work of your labor. You can share the results with your family and friends. Let me encourage you to allow your sons and daughters to enjoy digging and playing in the dirt. They will be glad you did and you will too.

November 20
A Leaf in Our Garage

My wife has been very busy sorting through boxes and plastic storage containers in our garage. You have probably already read several stories about combing two households into one home. Both of us have given away furniture, appliances, beds and mattresses which could not fit in our four bedroom house. Eventually we were able to get two cars back in garage and empty the boxes we had stored on the patio.

Actually we are encouraged with the progress we have made. It has taken months to empty boxes and organize things in our house. We have even had time to plant some new shrubs and flowers in the back yard and front courtyard. However there are still many containers to go through in the garage. Susan has spent a number of hours sorting through more storage bins and plastic tubs. She has found a lot of things she hadn't seen in several years while her things were in a storage unit.

Now that the weather has cooled off she has been more comfortable working in the garage. But there is one problem. Every time she opens the roll up garage door leaves blow into the garage. Our neighbor has a nice tree in the front of his house. It has some broad leaves which are falling off the tree now that autumn has arrived.

She is constantly sweeping up more leaves as the wind blows them in our direction. As soon as she gets them all swept up new ones arrive. It is almost like a comedy. As soon as she sweeps them up and puts them in the garbage can more leaves drift into the garage. The leaves are actually faster than she is. It is an unwinnable battle between the homeowner and Mother Nature.

At first it was frustrating but now it has become funny. We laugh as she sweeps up leaves knowing more are on the way. The tree in the neighbor's yard is pretty large and there are a countless number of leaves still on the tree. The wind usually blows in our direction this time of year so it will be a constant struggle for several more weeks. In the book Ecclesiastes there is a passage which says, "There is a time for everything and a season for every activity. There is a time to plant and a time to reap, a time to construct and a time to destroy" (3:1-8). Maybe we could paraphrase, "A time for leaves to grow and a time for them to fall". Let me encourage you to enjoy every season and to not get discouraged when the leaves continue to flutter into your garage.

Rooted

We have a lot of beautiful weather in Southern California. Our climate attracts people from across our nation and around the world. We have lots of sunshine, beautiful beaches and mild temperatures too. However, we also have earthquakes, droughts and wild fires. And we have high taxes, unhealthy air pollution and crowded freeways. One of the unique things we have in Southern California are the Santa Ana winds. These powerful events can tip over eighteen wheel semi-trucks on freeway overpasses and blow down old trees in residential areas.

This usually happens during the fall and winter months when atmospheric systems of high and low pressure cells generate these strong wind patterns. Normally the prevailing winds in California blow in from the ocean and move eastward. But the Santa Ana winds come from the desert and blow west toward the ocean.

They can be very destructive. Winds up to 80 miles an hour can blow down trees which may knock down powerlines sparking wild fires. These wind driven fires can spread rapidly causing extensive damage in urban communities and in remote forest regions.

One of the major causes of these wild fires are old trees which topple over in the wind storms. These trees look strong and healthy but they actually have shallow root systems that cannot stand against the strong winds. I visited a family in the city of San Dimas about 10 miles north of where I live. They had a 100 year old tree tip over in their front yard. The huge tree was lying on its side in the street with its shallow roots were sticking up in the air. Amazing!

How could a huge tree be blown over by these strong winds? The answer is *it did not have deep roots*. The shallow root system did not provide enough strength for the tree to withstand the force of the Santa Ana winds. The Apostle Paul prayed for young Christians to be rooted in their faith and not easily moved by the winds and waves of the philosophies of men (Ephesians 4:14). One of the best ways to have strong spiritual roots in your own life is by reading the Bible daily and attending church regularly. Let me encourage you to dust off your Bible and begin to read a chapter-a-day. Don't start on page one – start in the Book of Mark. And let me encourage you to reconnect with a local church too. These can help give your faith deeper roots to help you remain strong during difficult times. You will be glad you did.

The Fifty Dollar Lunch

In a previous story I shared my dismay over the rising cost of eating out. When my wife and I were in Arizona earlier this year we ate breakfast at a chain restaurant in Scottsdale. We ordered two meals and one cup of coffee. We were surprised to see the meal cost almost $50 plus a tip.

A few days ago we stopped for lunch at a restaurant in Ontario, California. After we shopped for some clothes in a large store we decided to eat lunch in their restaurant. My wife ordered a salad and I chose a crispy chicken sandwich which came with French Fries.
We both ordered water to drink. It seemed pretty simple.

But we were disappointed to see the bill. Each entree cost about $20 and with sales tax the total was almost $50 plus a tip. This felt very similar to what we experienced when we ate breakfast in Arizona. What has happened to an affordable breakfast or lunch? These were not fast food restaurants. These were casual dining where a waiter or waitress took your order at your table and delivered your food.

Prices on most menus have doubled in the past few years. Inflation has driven up the cost of food, gasoline and everything else. The result is the $50 breakfast and the $50 lunch.

The government continues to downplay inflation. They assure us it is not as bad as we think. They hope we won't take time to compare the menu for a breakfast or lunch today with what it was 2-3 years ago.

Everywhere you look prices are far above what they have been. And the quality of the food seems to be lower than it was a few years ago. I believe restaurants are using lower grade ingredients and cheaper slices of meat to try to hold the menu prices down. The food is not as good and the service is not as good as it was in the past.

We continue to feel the pain at the gas pump too. Gas prices in September 2023 were $5.00 a gallon for regular at my local Costco. We paid $6.50 a gallon on a trip through Central California. Let me encourage you to reduce your spending eating out and increase the time you spend eating at home. You will be glad you did and your family will too!

The Junk Drawer

We hired a contractor about ten years ago to remodel our kitchen. It seems this trend started in the last few decades and more and more people were remodeling the interior of their homes. Kitchens are usually the number one priority on a wife's wish list.

We met with a designer who showed us different ways we could increase our storage and counter space to enhance our thirty year old kitchen. My wife was thrilled with all of the ideas and options our designer suggested. I was not as enthusiastic when I saw the price.

Finally we agreed to hire the cabinet company and to purchase new appliances from a recommended dealer. I must admit the result was remarkable. We had a lot more cabinets and drawers to store things and the Quartz countertops were very attractive. The new appliances were a big improvement over the previous ones.

Over the following years we managed to add more plates, cups, and silverware. There was space for Tupperware and other food storage containers. We added some more pots and pans too. The larger food pantry was also a nice feature. My wife was very happy.

However, there was one drawer which became the "*catch all*" for things that didn't have a home. The drawer was near the phone and contained a number of different things like pens and note paper. It had a church phone directory and several rolls of scotch tape. I also found some paper clips and rubber bands. There were some old pieces of mail that we had put off dealing with. There were receipts from the grocery store and the pharmacy. There were two old flash lights with dead batteries. The list could go on. We called it the *Junk Drawer*. It became the last resort. When we couldn't find an item anywhere else we always asked each other, "Did you look in the *Junk Drawer?*"

I don't know if they had a junk drawer in homes in Bible times but there is a passage which described a woman who lost a valuable coin. She looked and looked through her house until she found it (Luke 15 8-13). Maybe she should have looked in the *Junk Drawer* first! Let me encourage you to clean out your *Junk Drawer* from time to time. Who knows what valuable things you might find?

November 24
The Shelf

I wrote a story about building a shelf in the garage in a previous book. My wife wanted some place over the washing machine and dryer to put the laundry detergent and fabric softener. I put it off for years. But finally something motivated me to build her a simple shelf. Success! However, a few years later I had to remove the small shelf in the garage when I was doing a major project re-routing the water pipes up into the attic. The shelf was in the way so I removed it from the wall.

Now several years later my wife Susan asked if there was a way we could mount a small toaster oven in the garage. She felt it could be helpful to have an extra appliance to warm food and other items when we hosted a large group. Could I build a small shelf outside the kitchen door in the garage?

One day while she was away I got out my tools and launched into fulfilling this request. I found an old white shelf made from particle board with a finished edge. I found two metal brackets in the garage and gathered up some wood screws to attach the brackets to the wall. I measured the available space and used my handy skill saw to cut the particle board to the right length. I located the studs in the wall and mounted the two brackets to the wall. Then I used some smaller screws to secure the shelf to the brackets. Success!

However when I set the small toaster oven on the shelf it didn't fit very well. I discovered the appliance extended outward two inches in the back to keep it away from the wall. I'm sure this was a safety feature so the hot oven did not touch the dry wall. I disassembled the shelf and extended it two inches away from the wall and re-secured the shelf to the metal brackets. I put the appliance on the shelf ready to surprise my wife. I don't think she saw the new shelf when she drove her car into the garage. But as she started to walk into the house she noticed it for the first time. Her enthusiasm was muted. I don't think it was quite what she had in mind. Maybe I should have used new materials or painted the old shelf before I mounted it on the garage wall.

I thought she would do summersaults around the garage but she just said a mild thanks and walked inside. Later she looked at it again and seemed to like it a little more. Let me encourage you to do something special for your spouse *this week*. Keep your expectations low. You don't know how they will respond but you will be glad you did.

November 25
Grief

Recently I was watching the *Sunday Morning* show on CBS while I was getting ready to go to church. They had a short five minute feature about a maintenance man who worked for the city. I didn't catch his job title but it looked like he might have been a garbage collector or a road maintenance worker.

As part of his daily routine he looked for opportunities to demonstrate kindness to strangers. The feature showed him paying for groceries for the person behind him at the Super Market. It also showed him paying for coffee for a stranger behind him at Starbucks.

One day he paid for a women's coffee in the drive thru at Starbucks. The surprised woman followed his work truck and personally thanked him for his kindness. It turned out this woman had recently lost her husband of over 40 years. She was grieving his death and very discouraged. The city employee had lifted her spirits and she wanted to thank him.

However, the story didn't end there. The woman decided to follow his example. She began to pay for coffee for strangers behind her at Starbucks. She began to give away gift cards to strangers at a local clothing store. She explained this helped her deal with the grief after the death of her husband.

This brief story on TV reinforced my thoughts on dealing with grief. A woman in our church in Tucson was overwhelmed with grief after the sudden death of her husband Larry due to a heart attack. Mary told me she didn't want to get out of bed in the morning. She didn't feel like doing anything. I suggested she do something for someone else who might be going through a difficult time in their own life. And if she couldn't think of anyone else I suggested she make some cookies her pastor. To my surprise she did! And she told me it did help her when she did something to help someone else.

There are a number of passages in the Bible which instruct us to help other people. The key word is "*one another*". Encourage one another, love one another, serve one another and carry one another's burdens (Galatians 6:2). If you are going through a time of sadness or grief, let me encourage you to do something to encourage those around you. You will be glad you did and they will too.

A Birthday Party

My wife Susan and I were invited to a special Birthday Party in Redlands, California. It wasn't to celebrate a child's birthday. It was to celebrate the birth of a new church called *Portrait Church*. The pastor of the new church had invited me and two other pastors to attend the first weekly Sunday service on September 10, 2023.

The reason the pastors were invited was because we all played a role in starting this church. In 2003 a couple from our church in Diamond Bar moved to a new growing community called Eastvale. They asked me if I would help start a Bible study in their home. Their names were Greg and Carol Crawford. They invited neighbors and we started a Bible study in 2003. Soon we sensed we should start a new church.

In 2007, the Evangelical Free Church in Diamond Bar sent Mark Lee and Tom Lanning from our staff to blend the Bible study group and other interested people from Diamond Bar into a team to launch a new church. Weekly Sunday services started in February, 2008. They called it Vantage Point Church which grew from a few hundred into over 2,000 people over the next 15 years.

As Vantage Point grew they sent a member of their staff and a group of people to launch a new church in Long Beach, California. Then in 2023 Vantage Point sent another staff member along with interested people to launch the Portrait Church in Redlands. Pastor Jay introduced Mark, Tom and me at their opening service to help people understand how Portrait Church is connected to Diamond Bar Evangelical Free Church and to Vantage Point Church in Eastvale.

It was amazing to see over 200 people attend the first weekly Sunday Service and celebrate the birth of Portrait Church together. It was an honor to be with Pastors Jay, Mark and Tom and this enthusiastic group of adults and children. It really was a day to remember.

The Apostles planted many churches across the Roman Empire. Those churches gave birth to more churches in the decades to come. Paul wrote, "One plants and another waters but God causes it to grow" (First Corinthians 3:5-7). Let me encourage you to help plant more new churches in your community. It requires a lot of faith and faithful people to birth a new church. It is not easy. It involves hard work and a lot of prayer. Lives will be changes and God will be honored.

Happy Thanksgiving

Thanksgiving is one of my favorite holidays on the calendar. I have written a number of stories in my first two books about some memorable moments on Thanksgiving. When I was a young pastor in Tucson, I broke two fingers playing Flag Football on Thanksgiving Day. I spent most of the day in the hospital emergency room waiting for the orthopedic specialist to finish his Thanksgiving dinner. My wife was not very happy I missed dinner with our family and guests.

I remember the year when we served a rubber ball instead of a Butter Ball turkey on Thanksgiving Day. I had purchased a store brand turkey at a significant discount because I had spent over $25 on other items for Thanksgiving dinner. The discounted store brand turkey turned out to be a disaster. It tasted like a rubber ball. No one ate it. I learned an important lesson. Always buy a Butterball turkey for Thanksgiving. Don't buy the store brand. You may get a rubber ball.

Another Thanksgiving I remember was when we didn't have any Pumpkin Pies. My wife baked two pies using some cans of evaporated milk with expired dates. We didn't want our guests to get sick with food poisoning so we tossed those out, got some fresh cans of evaporated milk and baked two new pumpkin pies. However when we tasted the new pies they were terrible. My wife forgot to put sugar in the pie filling. So I rushed over to Marie Calendar's restaurant and bought two of the last few pies in the store just before closing so we could have pumpkin pie and Thanksgiving Day.

I also remember a sad Thanksgiving dinner with my grandparents when I was a senior in high school. I remember my grandfather leaving the table in the middle of dinner and laying down on the sofa with discomfort. I knew he had cancer but I didn't realize he would die less than month later. I always remember the tears in my mother's eyes as my grandfather left the table. It was our last Thanksgiving with him.

There is a passage in the Bible which reminds us to give thanks to God in every circumstance (First Thessalonians 5:16-18). I'm sure you have some stories you could tell about Thanksgiving Day dinners and disasters. Let me encourage you to share those memories with your children and grandchildren. Ask other family members to share what they are thankful for. And remember to give thanks to God as you enjoy Thanksgiving with your loved ones. They will be glad you did.

November 28
Looking for a Loaf of Bread

One of the best things about Thanksgiving is having leftovers. Of course all of the food at Thanksgiving dinner is great with turkey, mashed potatoes and gravy, stuffing, yams and all the other trimmings. But there is something special about enjoying leftovers.

When I was a new member of my wife's family many years ago I was assigned the task of finding some bread so people could have some turkey sandwiches on Thanksgiving evening. I was told to go to the store and buy several loaves of bread. Don't come home without it. The problem was most grocery stores were closed on Thanksgiving in those days and only small minimarts like *Circle K* and *7/11* were open. As the new son-in-law I was told to go buy bread so people could enjoy a turkey sandwich made with leftover turkey.

This was like the **Mission Impossible** movies. The main character Tom Cruise was given a difficult task to complete. He is told to rescue a hostage or stop the evil villain from blowing up the planet. He experiences all kinds of obstacles as he tries to complete his impossible mission. I felt the same way. The grocery stores were closed. I went to the minimarts looking for loaves of bread but they were sold out. I guess a lot of other people forgot to buy bread before Thanksgiving and by the time I arrived the shelves were bare.

Finally after searching for over an hour I found a Circle K with some bread. It wasn't the brand my father-in-law requested but at least it was bread. I rushed home with my precious cargo and everyone was able to enjoy a turkey sandwich on Thanksgiving night. My reputation as the favorite son-in-law was saved.

There is a passage in the Bible when Jesus' disciples were hungry. They were tired after non-stop ministry serving the multitude of people following Jesus. When they informed Jesus there were only five loaves and two fish left to feed the huge crowd He multiplied the loaves and fish. The Bible says 5,000 people were fed that day (John 6:5-13). It was one of the greatest miracles Jesus performed.

Let me encourage you to ask God to provide your daily bread and thank Him for his bountiful provision. And make sure you buy a few loaves before Thanksgiving so you and your guests can enjoy the leftover turkey sandwiches. They will be glad you did and you will too.

Connecting with Old Friends

When my wife and I attended the first weekly service at the new Portrait Church in Redlands, California, we were able to reconnect with a number of people who had been part of the mother church in Diamond Bar many years ago.

We saw some young children and their parents. The parents had been teens in the youth ministry in Diamond Bar many years ago. Now they were married and had children of their own.

I was glad to see a couple of men who had served on our church staff in Diamond Bar. Now they were part of the leadership team at the new church. I was thankful they were using their skills and experience to launch a new church in Redlands.

One of the lead singers in the worship team had attended our church in Diamond Bar with her siblings and parents. Her father was one of the leaders who planted the Vantage Point Church. Now she was a mother of three leading the music in the worship service in Redlands.

We enjoyed seeing some children we had not seen in a long time. They had grown up and were teenagers and high school students. One was a cross country runner just like his father who still runs in marathons.

We also saw a young woman we had known in Diamond Bar. Her parents invited me to write a weekly column for their local newspaper many years ago. I would probably not be writing books today if they had not encouraged me to start writing weekly stories for them.

It was nice to see a lovely widow who lost her husband before Covid19. She shared with us she now has 10 grandchildren and a number of great grandchildren. There was another friend who gave us an update on his wife's recent heart transplant surgery.

In Romans chapter 16, Paul wrote to the believers in Rome where he greeted over 30 different people he knew who were attending the church there. He was so pleased to know their faith was strong and they were serving the Lord. That is how we felt as we saw people we knew from the past at the opening of the new church in Redlands. Let me encourage you to reconnect with people from your past. Pray for them and greet them warmly when you can. They will be glad you did.

Jacob

We are thankful you married Teri and became part of the Hopper family. We remember the day you met with us to ask for our permission to marry our daughter. You bought us dinner and an Apple Pie to seal the deal. We remember your plans to propose to Teri on a Hot Air Balloon ride in Temecula and a fancy dinner in Laguna Beach. But Teri got sick the night before and you had to change your plans.

We remember your wedding day on November 15, 2008 at our church in Diamond Bar. Santa Ana winds provided clear blue skies. It looked like a perfect day for a wedding until the winds sparked wild fires and the sky was filled with smoke. The photographer took photos indoors at the reception at the Summit House in Brea because of all the smoke.

We are thankful you and Teri have two beautiful girls. We enjoyed watching Emily and Janie grow up and had fun when they came to our house for a sleep-over. Thank you for starting a new tradition to put up Christmas decorations at our house the day after Thanksgiving.

We are thankful you have been a supportive husband and encouraged Teri to complete her Doctorate Degree in Speech Pathology and teach at BIOLA University. We also love to watch you and Teri work together as a team when you invite guests to your home and cook some delicious meat in your Trager BBQ Smoker.

You are a fun loving father. The girls really love their dad. We are glad you take your family to church and you attend their sports and school events. It was fun to hear you took them to the father-daughter dance. You and Teri have made some wonderful memories with your family.

We are proud of your success in your business. You did not give up when you experienced several setbacks early in your career. Most of all we are thankful for your love for Jesus. It shows in your family life, marriage and business career. We are thankful you and Teri host a Bible study in your home and you serve together on the board at Mariners Christian School. We are thankful you are part of our family.

To my readers – Let me encourage you to write a note *this week* to express your thanks to the men or women who have married into your family. They will be glad you did and you will too.

Help on the Freeway

When I listen to the traffic reports on the radio I often hear about a car or truck stalled on the freeway. When a vehicle has a flat tire or mechanical problem it can bottle up traffic for miles. Our local radio station KNX calls these a "*Sig Alert*" because one of their DJ's was the first to report problems on the freeways in the 1960's in Los Angeles. Hi name was Lloyd Sigmon.

One source explained, "The term "*Sig Alert*" has been adopted by the California Highway Patrol to identify any unplanned event that blocks more than one lane of traffic for 30 minutes or more". Now we have App's on our smart phones which also give us traffic conditions but for decades drivers depended on Lloyd Sigmon.

These traffic alerts were helpful when mapping out your route to work or to an appointment. They rarely reported problems on local streets but they were very useful when you were driving on the freeways. Today KNX also relies on tips from listeners when they call the "*Traffic Tip Line*". Drivers can report a stalled car or truck. I have done this several times and I appreciate the help other drivers provide too.

Many years ago I was driving our Dodge Van east on the 91 freeway when traffic slowed to a crawl. Clearly there was a problem ahead. I had not heard anything on the radio but I knew there was something wrong. As I slowly moved along I saw a car stalled in my lane.

Normally I would just try to squeeze into another lane to get by the stalled car. Instead I got the idea to try and help push this stranger over to the side of the freeway. I pulled up behind him and stepped out to ask him if I could help. I knew my van had a sturdy bumper and I was willing to push him out of traffic. Some truckers saw what I was doing and they blocked the traffic and cleared a path on my right so I could move the car safely off the freeway. It worked!

Jesus told a parable in the Bible about the Good Samaritan. Several people walked past an injured traveler but one man stopped to help the stranger. He was from Samaria (Luke 10:25-38). While others kept walking the Samaritan stopped to help. Let me encourage you to be willing to stop and help someone one the freeway or in your community *this week*. They will be glad you did and you will too.

341

A Cord of Wood

Many years ago I was the speaker at a couple's retreat at a church in Show Low, Arizona. It was a fun weekend meeting with a small group of married couples in this beautiful mountain setting. My wife and I enjoyed getting to know each of the people and shared some lessons from the Bible on how to strengthen their relationships.

After the final session, I filled up our Dodge Van with gas and prepared to get on the road on Saturday night so we could be back at our church in Tucson on Sunday. I asked the host pastor if there was a place where we could purchase some wood to take back to Tucson. We had a wood burning Franklin Stove in our family room and needed more firewood for the winter months.

He directed me to a retailer who sold fire wood which was already cut, quartered and dried. I wasn't sure how much firewood cost and how much we could get into our van. A full Cord of wood is a volume of 128 cubic feet. It is measured by a stack of wood which is eight feet long, four feet high and four feet wide (8X4X4 feet). One source I read said a full cord of wood can weigh up to 5,000 pounds. I was not interested in that much wood so the dealer gave me a set price for all the wood I could load into the back of my van. I don't remember how much I paid.

I proceeded to stack and squeeze as many pieces of wood as possible into the back of my van. It was more than the seller and I thought and it was heavy. I could feel how heavy it as I carefully navigated down the winding mountain road. I'm thankful we got home safely.

It took a while to unload and stack the wood in the back of our house. I was so glad to have some sweet smelling cedar burning in our Franklin Stove through the cold winter months. It was relaxing to sit in front of the fireplace and watch the flickering flames.

In Bible times they needed wood for the Altar in the Tabernacle and the Temple. The Gibeonites we responsible for cutting the wood and carrying the water for the operation of the Tabernacle (Joshua 9:22-23). We don't use firewood in most of our churches today. But let me encourage you to serve at your church on a regular basis. Teach the children, sing on the worship team or welcome guests on the patio. Everyone needs to help. They will be glad you did and you will too.

Schnitzel and Strudel

I have enjoyed visiting my children and grandchildren who live and work in Europe. One family lives in Portugal and the other family lives in Slovenia. Fish is very popular in Portugal and Schnitzel is very popular in central Europe.

In countries across the European continent people enjoy a variety of food and desserts. Restaurants serve both local and international cuisine. And grocery stores are selling more and more products from America. I am surprised at what I can find on the store shelves.

I enjoy rich chocolate from Holland and Belgium. I love the gelato ice cream in Italy and France. I love the Fish & Chips in England. And I really love the Schnitzel and Strudel in Germany, Austria and Slovenia.

Schnitzel is most commonly made from a thin strip of pork, chicken or veal. It is dipped in a mixture eggs and spices and then coated with bread crumbs and fried in a heavy frying pan. A tender piece of schnitzel with some fries is my favorite meal in central Europe.

My favorite dessert is Apple Strudel. It is made from cooked apples, rolled in thin strips of dough and baked until golden brown. You can add more ingredients like raisins and nuts to the mixture depending on your recipe. I love the soft baked apples, the flaky crust and no raisins.

I'm sure you have your favorite foods at home and abroad. It is nice to enjoy the familiar taste of a home cooked meal and eating at your local restaurant. But it is also fun to taste food served in other parts of the world.

It was interesting to discover what kinds of food people enjoyed in Bible times. Fish from the Sea of Galilee was very popular in Israel. Ancient Israelites also raised beef cattle. Fresh dates were enjoyed. Today Falafel, hummus, fresh meat and kabobs are popular in Israel along with a variety of fresh fruit and vegetables. Ice cream is one of the most popular desserts. One verse in the Bible says, "God has given us food to enjoy when it is received with thanks" (First Timothy 4:3-4). Let me encourage you to enjoy the local and international cuisine in your community. And if you have an opportunity to travel to Europe I hope you will enjoy some Schnitzel and Strudel. You will be glad you did!

Saying Goodbye

The famous Italian Opera singer Andre Bocelli recorded a song titled, "*Time to Say Goodbye*". It is a powerful song which fills your heart and mind with emotion. I have it on my smart phone and have listened to it many times.

Saying goodbye can be difficult and emotional especially when you don't expect to see someone for a long time. It is even harder to let go when you don't know if you will ever see someone again.

These emotions were felt by families and loved ones when troops were sent off to war. They faced the uncertainty their loved one might be killed in combat and not come home. We share these feelings when a friend or loved one goes into surgery with a life threatening medical problem. Will we see them again?

On a more personal level it was always difficult to say goodbye to our children who served as missionaries overseas. My wife didn't like driving to LAX so she always said goodbye to our kids and grandkids at our house. She didn't like the traffic getting to the airport and she didn't like the rushed goodbye as we unloaded passengers and luggage on the curb at LAX. There were times when I pulled off the road after dropping off my family at the airport and cried. It was hard to say goodbye.

My friend Ray Redmer used to say goodbye to his aging father with these words, "*If I don't see you again, I will see you in heaven*". We usually said goodbye to our family members by saying, "*We will see you sooner than we think*" and we usually did.

There is a passage in the Bible when the Apostle Paul said goodbye to the leaders of the church in Ephesus. When he told them he did not expect to see them again they wept (Acts 20:36-38). It was hard for them to let Paul go. He had made significant impact on their lives and their faith.

Let me encourage you to cherish the time you have to spend with your family, friends and loved ones. Every day you get to be with them is a gift. Don't waste your time talking about things that aren't important. Share what is on your heart. Clearly express your love and appreciation to them. They will be glad you did and you will too.

December 5
A Memorable Meal

Some of my favorite memories of my father-in-law were on the golf course. I had never played golf before I got married. But my father-in-law was an avid golfer. I realized I needed to learn to play the game if I wanted to be part of the family. My secret goal was to beat my father-in-law in golf and I finally did but not until he was over 70 years old.

We didn't get to play very often. My in-laws lived in Phoenix and we lived in Tucson. But when they came to visit us or when we drove up to visit them we usually found time for a round of golf. The same was true when we moved to California.

Normally my wife would go to lunch with her mother while the men played golf. Since a round of golf can take four to five hours it gave them plenty of time for lunch and shopping. Typically after playing golf we would stop for lunch on the way home.

One time I remember my father-in-law Walt suggested we stop at the store and get some rolls and lunch meat and eat at home. This seemed like a good idea. But when we went to the deli department to select some meat I became alarmed.

My father-in-law was from New York City. He was familiar with all kinds of lunch meat. So he selected things like liverwurst and bratwurst which I had never heard of. He also ordered some different types of cheese too. He was thrilled at the idea of making me an authentic Deli sandwich. I wasn't so sure this was a good idea. Where was the sliced turkey I usually ordered?

I did my best to be enthusiastic about this memorable meal. It was different than anything I had eaten before. He was delighted to enjoy some of the delicacies from his New York days. And he was delighted to share it with me.

There is a passage in the Bible where the Apostle Paul said, "I have become all things to all men so that by all means I might win some" (First Corinthians 9:22). Let me encourage you to step out of your comfort zone and step into the world of your co-workers, neighbors, friends and relatives. Be willing to join them for lunch or dinner even if it is different than what you are used to. They will be glad you did and you will too.

345

A Carpenter

When my wife and I came to the Evangelical Free Church in Diamond Bar, California in 1988 we met a helpful man named Ed. He was a journeyman carpenter who had a career constructing freeways and large buildings in Southern California.

We got to know Ed and his wife Jackie better when we attended a weekly small group with them and several other married couples. Ed and I also worked together on a number of projects at the church. The first thing Ed did for me was build some new adjustable shelves to organize all of the books in my library.

Later he led the effort to construct a new classroom building on our property. His knowledge and experience were invaluable as we built this new facility with our own hands. Later Ed and Chuck remodeled the church kitchen. Everyone loved the new appliances and cabinets.

Ed became one of our most traveled missionaries. After we completed the classroom building we looked for an opportunity to help build in other parts of the world. We took a team to Guatemala in 1992 to help construct a school. Later Ed led a group of men to Mongolia to build a community center. He went to Mexico on some construction projects too. Ed and his wife Jackie went to Romania to work alongside some of our missionaries there. And he also went to Korea with a group of students and adults. He traveled the world.

I knew Ed when he was a soft spoken, kind carpenter. He always had a smile on his face and approached problems with a confident spirit. But earlier in his life he was a rough spoken angry carpenter. When he came to faith in Christ his life and temper were transformed. Hi liked to say a carpenter (Jesus) changed his life.

There are several verses in the Bible which describe how Jesus changed people's lives. I wonder if anger and frustration fill your life. I wonder if your friends and family members would say you are hard to live with and work with. Let me encourage you to ask God to transform your life. Become a follower of Jesus and put aside your old way of life. One passage says, "Get rid of your old way of life and take on an entirely new way of life - a God fashioned life (Ephesians 4:22-24). You will be glad you did and your friends and family will too.

Serving Your Community

One of the things we hear a lot about this time of year is helping people who are less fortunate and in need. We hear about Christmas Toy Drives sponsored by the Police and Fire Department. We see news reports on local TV stations about canned food drives. We see celebrities serving food at the Union Rescue Mission and other locations throughout Los Angeles and Orange County.

The local Rotary Club of Walnut Valley partners with schools in our area to collect canned food and distribute it to needy families in the community. Teachers and students collect canned goods during the annual food drive and assemble 200 hundred boxes which include the canned foods plus fresh vegetables and a turkey for each family.

Your own church or service club may have similar events during the holiday season. Helping other people by donating money and giving your own time makes the holidays more special. It is nice to buy or make a gift for a friend or family member. But it is even more special when we become personally involved in helping other people.

There is a passage in the Bible in the Book of Acts where followers of Jesus took on the task of caring for widows in the early church. They provided a daily food distribution for widows who needed assistance. The Apostles appointed seven reliable and compassionate men to oversee this important responsibility (Acts 6:1-7). Those leaders enlisted the help of other Christians to make sure the widows were cared for.

There are many opportunities to serve and help people during the holiday season. Churches, service clubs and other volunteer groups make a huge impact in local communities across Southern California.

Let me encourage you to help people in your community who need material and spiritual support. I hope you will volunteer some of your time and use your skills to help someone this holiday season. You may want to adopt a family in your church or someone on your street who needs help. You may want to sign up online to partner with a group like the Salvation Army or a local rescue mission or a local service club. It will make your Christmas brighter for yourself and for those you serve. You will be glad you did and they will too.

Love Your Neighbor

Tuesday is trash collection day in our neighborhood. Every week you see people pulling their garbage cans out to the street so the big giant green truck can collect our trash. We actually have three large plastic containers. One for grass clippings, one is for recycling, one for trash.

Our friendly Waste Management Company sends frequent reminders about the rules and regulations regarding trash collection. All items must be placed in the correct container. Any plastic bags or other items placed outside the containers will not be collected.

Recently on a Tuesday morning when I was putting my trash cans out I noticed my neighbor had 4-5 large plastic bags stacked up next the their containers. The first thought that ran through my mind was the garbage man will not take them. He will empty the containers with the lift on his truck but he will not get out and load those by hand.

Without thinking I decided to take action. I rolled my black garbage can over to his house and put two of the large bags in my container. I had room and his container was full. Then I went across the street and got a neighbor's black bucket and put another plastic bag in that one. I did this two more times so all of the bags on the ground were now in a neighbor's trash can.

However while I was doing this my neighbor's garage door opened and he pulled out of his driveway. Busted! He caught me in the act. I hoped he didn't think I was digging through his trash. I was relieved when he understood what I was doing to help him. He told me his wife was going to watch for the trash truck and ask the driver to take the bags. He was grateful for my help and said, "Thanks".

Jesus was asked, "What is the greatest commandment in the Bible?" The religious leaders of the day taught there were 613 commandments in the scriptures. Jesus said the greatest is, "Love the Lord your God with all your heart, mind, soul and strength. And love your neighbor as yourself "(Mark 12:31). Let me encourage you to love your neighbors. It may be simply helping with their trash or providing child care for their children while the adults are at work. You can love your neighbors by making a meal for them during a time of sickness or loss. The list is endless. Watch for an opportunity to love one of your neighbors *this week*. They will be glad you did and you will too.

Compassion

I have shared some amazing stories about rescuing little critters who live outside our house. I saved two lizards from a sticky mouse trap. They had crawled under a pile of boxes and got stuck on the adhesive. I used a flat tool to slowly lift them from the sticky surface. I also freed another lizard from the wire mesh I had installed on our front gate to keep rabbits out of our backyard. I felt like a bomb disposal expert when I used some wire cutters to cut the wire mesh and carefully extract my reptile friend who was caught.

We have some beautiful rose bushes in our backyard. My wife and I have been working hard to improve the soil and to water more consistently. We have harvested some beautiful roses and put them in vases in our house. They look beautiful and smell wonderful.

When I was cutting the leaves off some stems in my kitchen I noticed a small insect among the rose pedals. He was a tiny little guy. He is legs were very thin. It was surprising to see this little tiny creature. It was a *Praying Mantis*. They are a green insect with a stick like body and very thin legs. They are a gardener's friend because they eat other insects which are harmful and destructive to plants. Their name comes from their shape which looks like the creature is kneeling and praying.

I wasn't quite sure how to help my little friend. I didn't want to harm him. I wanted to help him and return him to my rose garden. I picked up a rose pedal and tried to persuade him to crawl onto it. He was hesitant at first but he finally took a step of faith. Then I carefully carried the *Praying Mantis* on the rose pedal to the backyard and gently laid him on a new rose blossom. My friend seemed glad to be back in his garden. I hope he will eat more of the aphids and other things that are feasting on the plants in our garden.

There is a word which is frequently used to describe Jesus. The word is **compassion**. Jesus often felt compassion for people who were in need of help (Mark 1:41). He felt compassion for the blind (Matthew 20:34). He felt compassion for the hungry (Mark 6:34). He felt compassion for a widow who had lost her only son (Luke 7:11-15). But compassion is more than a feeling. *Compassion requires action*. Do something to feed the hungry and give something to help to the helpless. Let me encourage you to show compassion to someone you meet *this week*. They will be glad you did and you will too.

An Amazing Rescue

One of the largest rescue missions of World War Two is also one of the least known. In 1943 and 1944 America and its allies launched air raids on enemy oil fields and refineries in Romania. American airplanes took off from bases in Italy and North Africa and flew over Yugoslavia on these dangerous bombing raids.

Many aircraft were damaged or destroyed during these risky air raids. Pilots and crews bailed out over enemy controlled Yugoslavia. Some crews were rescued by local farmers and citizens. German troops tried to capture the downed airmen but many were rescued, hidden and fed for months by local residents who were opposed to the Germans.

Eventually the United States Air Force drafted a plan to rescue these stranded airmen. It was called *Operation Halyard*. A few special forces parachuted into the mountains and organized the effort to bring these airmen home. They enlisted help from local farmers and supporters to create a runway long enough to land a C-47 airplane. The first plane landed on the runway on the hilltop in the dark. It was dangerous but it proved planes could fly into rural Yugoslavia and get the troops out.

America unleased a fleet of fighter planes to provide air cover for the troop transports. Then the C-47's landed in day light on the small air strip and flew hundreds of stranded airmen back to Italy. More airmen were rescued in the next several months. Over 500 airmen were rescued without any casualties. It was the biggest rescue mission of its kind in history. Read more details in the book, "***The Forgotten 500***".

There are several rescues recorded in the Bible. Abraham rescued his nephew Lot from his enemies (Genesis Chapter 14). David and his men rescued their wives and children from the Amalekites (First Samuel Chapter 30).

The Bible says David risked his life to save one of his sheep from the mouth of a lion and another sheep from the mouth of a bear (First Samuel 17:34-37). Jesus said he was like the Good Shepherd who was willing to give his life to rescue the helpless sheep (John 10:11-14). The Bible says we are the sheep and Jesus is the shepherd who died on the cross and rose again to rescue us from the consequences of our sins. Let me encourage you to come to Him by faith today. You will be glad you did and I will too.

A New Appliance Can Change Your Life

When we remodeled our kitchen about eight years ago we purchased all new appliances. We bought a new refrigerator, new stove, new oven and new dishwasher. Since that time we have replaced the dish washer and have called the service man many times to fix the refrigerator. It seems like appliances aren't what they used to be.

Recently we stepped into the 21st century by purchasing a new toaster. I like toast with my breakfast. I usually buy the *Thomas' Original English Muffins*. You can buy a four-pack for a good price at Costco. I like to spread real butter and seedless strawberry jam on a freshly toasted English muffin.

We did some extensive research before purchasing our toaster. There were a variety of brands at Kohl's, Target and Walmart. I was surprised there were so many makes and models. I didn't realize shopping for a toaster was so challenging and difficult.

We settled on a Cuisinart four-slice toaster. The picture on the box made it look like this was the top of the line. It had four spaces so you could toast up to four slices of bread or muffins at one time. The controls were impressive too. There was a dial to set how long you wanted your toast to heat up. There were also several buttons to identify what you are using the toaster for. There is a special button for Bagels. Another choice is to defrost or reheat.

Maybe the best feature of the new toaster is the fact you can toast four slices at the same time. No more fighting or arguing who gets to do their toast first. Now both you and your spouse can make your own toast at the same time. My wife uses the two spaces on the right and I warm my toast in the two slots on the left. This helps avoid marital discord so early in the day.

Actually there is a passage in the Bible which stresses the importance of putting the needs of the other people in your house ahead of yourself. The Apostle Paul wrote, "Don't just look out for your own interests but also for the interests of others. Put their needs ahead of your own" (Philippians 2:1-5). Paul said we should follow Jesus' example and put others first. Let me encourage you to watch for an opportunity *this week* to put someone else's needs ahead of your own. And if you like toast I recommend the four slice – no arguing - model.

Christmas Traditions

I have shared in my previous books about some of the Hopper family's Christmas traditions. Some of them were passed down from our own parents and some of them started when we had our own family. Every generation keeps some of the old ones and creates new ones. I'm sure this is true for you as well.

One of the Christmas traditions you have read about was making cinnamon rolls. This started with my Grandmother Marie Halliday. She baked the best cinnamon rolls for us when I was young. My brother and I learned how to bake them when we were growing up and continued doing this with our own children in the Christmas season.

I actually included the recipe in the back of my second book, "*Let Me Encourage You More*". My children have modified them or found new recipes but they still bake cinnamon rolls for Christmas in memory of Grandma Halliday.

Another tradition passed down in my family was reading the Christmas Story from the Bible on Christmas Eve. When I was young I remember going to my grandparent's house on Christmas Eve. We enjoyed hot chocolate and warm ginger bread and read the account of Jesus' birth from the Bible in the book of Luke 2:1-20.

On Christmas morning my brother and I were not allowed to open any gifts at our house until we had eaten some breakfast. Who wants to stop and eat when you know there are Christmas presents under the tree in the living room? It seemed like torture but we did it every year.

After we opened presents at our house we drove back to the Halliday's house for Christmas dinner. Then we got to open one present that was waiting for us under the Christmas tree at my grandparent's house.

My father-in-law's heritage was German. My wife's family had a little different twist to their Christmas routine. When she was growing up her parents put the kids to bed and then set up the tree while the kids were asleep and put out all the presents. Around midnight they woke up the sleeping kids and rushed to the window to wave goodbye to Santa. Her parents wanted to do the same with our children. But after a year or two of waking up sleeping kids my wife and I decided to let the kids sleep and open gifts on Christmas morning after they woke up.

More Christmas Traditions

Another tradition we started when we lived in Tucson was going to see the Christmas decorations in a neighborhood called *Winter Haven* a few weeks before Christmas. Several blocks of homes were brightly decorated with lights and other things. It was magical as we drove slowly up and down the street. Our adopted Grandma Pauline always came with us and then we went back to her house for her famous cheese ball, cookies and hot chocolate. This always got us into the Christmas spirit.

When our kids became teenagers Santa always brought them an air filter for their car. This wasn't their favorite gift but it was practical. We had a fleet of old cars which our children drove to school and to work. I knew I needed to change the air filters in their cars. This useful gift came with free installation.

Another family tradition were some small envelopes in the branches of the Christmas tree. These small white envelopes contained some cash so our kids would have some money to buy something they wanted and didn't find under the Christmas tree. They were glad to have some extra money to buy some bargains at the after Christmas sales.

One of the traditions my wife and kids enjoyed was eating tamales on Christmas Eve. We usually had two Christmas Eve services at our church in Diamond Bar. So the family came to the five o'clock service and then went home to enjoy tamales from the Whole Enchilada restaurant. I stayed at church for the second service and then hurried home to join them for dessert.

After dinner and dessert we gathered together in front of the Christmas tree and read the Christmas story from the Bible in Luke Chapter Two. Then each person got to open one present. We saved the rest of the gifts for the next morning. Usually one of the presents on Christmas Eve was a new movie. Some people fell asleep during the movie but it was fun to be together on Christmas Eve.

I'm sure there are some traditions you remember from your childhood and have some other traditions you have started with your own children. Let me encourage you to keep them going and pass them down to your children and grandchildren. And why not start a new tradition *this year*? You will be glad you did and your family will too.

Don't Throw Your Trash

When I was leading a summer youth camp for Jr. High students in northern Arizona I met a remarkable man named Ron Blue. He and his wife served as missionaries in Central America. They established temporary residency in Arizona so they could adopt a child in the state.

Ron agreed to be the speaker for our Jr High camp in Prescott, Arizona. He was energetic and engaging. The students loved him. His enthusiasm was infective. These restless young people listened to every word. It was a great week under the pine trees in Prescott.

During the week Ron captivated the kids with lessons from the Bible. In addition he taught them a song which I still remember today. I have used it with children, teens and adults. The name of the song was, "***Don't Throw Your Trash in My Backyard***". It has a catchy tune and was easy to learn. You may have sung it in Boy Scouts, Girl Scouts or at the YMCA.

There are three parts to the song. The lyrics are:

Don't throw your trash in my backyard, my backyard, my backyard.
Don't throw your trash in my backyard, my backyard is full

Fish and chips and vinegar, vinegar, vinegar.
Fish and chips and vinegar, pickle, pickle, pop.

One bottle of pop, two bottles of pop, three bottles of pop, four bottles of pop, five bottles of pop, six bottles of pop, seven bottles of pop.

These words were sung without music in a round. One group started with the trash words, then repeated them as the second group added the fish and chips. Then both groups continued to sing their lines as the third group joined in with the bottles of pop.

It is hard to explain the tune with written words. I can hear the light peppy tune in my head. When all three groups sing their parts it resulted in a delightful harmony. Let me encourage you to find the lyrics and music online. Sing this simple song with your children, grandchildren or youth group. They will have fun singing it together and you will too.

Christmas Dessert

Our neighborhood has changed over the past 35 years. When we moved in our kids were young and the house we purchased was only eight years old. Three decades later the kids are gone and our house has gone through many changes and improvements. The people living on our street have changed too, so we decided to invite our neighbors to our home during the Christmas holidays. I typed up a simple invitation and invited people to come for dessert.

We were pleasantly surprised by how many people came. Over 20 people filled our living room and family room. Some were neighbors we have known for a long time and others were very new. One family had only lived in their house for a few months. Three couples were original owners and had lived on our street for over 40 years.

People seemed genuinely pleased to meet their neighbors. Two young families discovered their children were in the same grade and in the same class at the local elementary school. They lived on the same street only a few houses apart and didn't realize their children were classmates. The kids were excited to see each other.

Several neighbors were from China. Some spoke Cantonese while others spoke Mandarin. It was fun listening to them speaking to each other in their native language. The newest neighbor spoke very little English but his young fourth grade daughter did an excellent job translating for us so we could get to know her father.

We were so pleased to welcome our neighbors into our home. We enjoyed catching up with some of the older residents and we were delighted to get to know a number of newer ones. We asked each of them to write down their contact information so we could provide a list of names and phone numbers to our neighbors. This could be useful in case of an emergency.

There is a passage in the Bible where people from many nations were in Jerusalem during the holidays. They were pilgrims from Africa, Asia and Europe. They spoke a variety of different languages (Acts Chapter Two). Let me encourage you to open your home and invite neighbors to your house. It can be a Christmas dessert or a summer BBQ. Make sure you provide some names tags to help them get to know one another. They will be glad you did and you will too.

December 16
Planting for the Future

My wife and I have worked hard over the past few weeks planting new plants and shrubs. We hauled in bags and bags of new soil and put new flowers and greenery in the yard. Things look new and bright.

I shared in an earlier story how I worked hard running new PVC pipes to areas around the house which were not connected to the sprinkler system. I ran small drip lines to the new plants to make sure everything would receive water regularly.

We also added fertilizer to the citrus and avocado trees hoping to make them more productive. We planted a new strawberry plant in the front courtyard and it has already produced some nice fruit.

There was a sense of optimism that came from cleaning up the planters and adding new flowers and shrubs around our yard. We ended the day with sore backs and tired muscles but also with a smile on our faces when we saw the transformation happening around us.

I think it is similar to painting a room inside the house with new paint or washing and waxing the car. It is hard work but the results are very satisfying and encouraging.

There is an interesting passage in the Bible where the Prophet Jeremiah encouraged the Israelites who had been taken into exile in Babylon. He told them to settle down and build homes in their new country. He instructed them to plant trees and cultivate gardens in this unfamiliar land.

Jeremiah also told the exiles to raise children and allow them to marry other Israelites who had been taken into exile. He reminded them they would be in exile for many years. He told them God had not forsaken His people and He had a plan for their future (Read Jeremiah 29:4-7).

Let me encourage you to *plant for the future*. Plant some new fruit trees even though they will take time to bear fruit. Start a family garden and grow fresh vegetables for your family to enjoy and to share with friends and neighbors. Plant some new flowers *this week* to remind you of God's love for you. God has a plan for your life. He wants you to be patient and remain faithful even though you don't know what the future holds. You will be glad you did and He will too.

Home Entertainment

Over the years more and more people have installed impressive home entertainment centers in their house. They include huge flat screen TV's and surround sound audio systems that make you feel like you are in a movie theater.

A group of men from our church get together once-a-month to enjoy a delicious BBQ dinner and watch a movie. We always go to Bob's house because he smokes juicy tender meat in his backyard and because he has an impressive home theater.

We don't have a huge big screen theater with a professional quality sound system at our house. But we do have an entertainment center right outside our kitchen window. My wife Susan put out several hummingbird feeders under our citrus tree and near our back patio. We love to watch these tiny birds feed and play outside our window. They are very entertaining.

We use a pair of opera glasses to get a closer look at these little creatures. It is amazing to see them hover beside the feeder and gently drink the tasty nectar. They appear motionless for several seconds while they flap their wings hundreds of times a minute and then dart away at lightning speed.

Each Hummingbird has different markings and colors which distinguish them from one another. We have started to give them names based on the color of their feathers and their individual behavior. We call the hummer with the red neck Charlie and the one with the darker feathers Harry.

They also seem to follow a pattern of behavior. They stop by for breakfast early in the day and then return for dinner at the end of the day. Sometimes the little birds fight or compete over a feeder. They rest in the shady tree but dart out to protect their territory and discourage other birds from drinking from their feeder.

It is fascinating and entertaining to watch these tiny creatures. There is a passage in the Bible which reminds us God created all of the living creatures on our planet. "Where were you when I created each of these things?" (Job 38-40). Let me encourage you to build an entertainment center outside your window and reflect on the God who created it.

357

You've Got Mail

There was a clever movie with the title *"You've Got Mail"* which was made at the beginning of the internet age. The main characters were a young actor named Tom Hanks and the co-star was Meg Ryan. We still enjoy this movie but the technology seems pretty dated. They used the internet to develop a relationship sending emails back and forth on their computers.

Today there are many other ways to chat with people on the internet. My children and grandchildren use *Marco Polo* and *What's App* to communicate with their siblings and cousins. Sometimes they still use text messaging and email too. I know there are many other formats available today. But I still prefer old fashioned snail mail. The kind where you write a note and put the address on the envelope with your own handwriting. The kind of communication that requires a postage stamp to send and receive.

The most popular time to use regular mail is Christmas. Millions and millions of cards are purchased and sent to family and friends through the US Postal service. I realize postage rates have increased this year. One post office employee apologized when she informed me the government had raised the price of stamps twice in the past twelve months. She said it was the first time in history they increased the cost of stamps twice in the same year. But most people don't seem to notice or care anymore.

Many people still mail Christmas cards. Some of them enclose a photo or letter to share updates on their family over the past year. Other people purchase professionally produced Christmas photos with a message on the card. Either way Christmas cards can be an effective way to extend a greeting to family and friends.

The Apostle Paul wrote personal letters to churches and individuals in the first century. He usually dictated his letters to a secretary who recorded his words. And he actually signed some letters with his own hand (Colossians 4:18). Let me encourage you to send some Christmas cards to people this holiday season. Even cards which arrive after Christmas are appreciated. You might find some cards at reduced prices in the after Christmas sales. It's never too late. You will be glad you did and the recipients will too.

Christmas Shopping

One of the more difficult aspects of the Christmas season is shopping for the right gifts for each person in my family. In the past I have walked through the malls and searched the shops looking for ideas. It is like *Mission Impossible* trying to find the right things for my children and grandchildren.

Finally I realized it would be a lot easier to let the parents pick out the gifts for themselves and for their children. They know what they want and what the kids like too. So I usually send a check or transfer money to their bank account so they can do the shopping for me.

It is very expensive to buy and ship gifts to Europe where two of my four children live with their husband and children. Often the cost of mailing a small box filled with gifts was greater than the value of the contents of the box. In addition, most European nations now charge an import tax or tariff on items which come from outside their country.

I have learned to do the same thing for my adult children who live in Southern California. I also send them a check so they can purchase gifts for themselves and for their children. It has worked well over the past few years.

There are several examples of gift giving in the Bible. Abraham gave gifts to the Priest Melchizedek after Abraham's victory over Lot's enemies (Genesis Chapter 14:17-20). King David sent gifts to the leaders of Judah after he defeated some of their enemies (First Samuel 30:26-31).

The most famous gift givers were the *Wise Men* who traveled a great distance to worship the new born King named Jesus. They traveled to Jerusalem and then Bethlehem to give their gifts to honor Jesus' birth (Matthew Chapter Two).

I hope your Christmas shopping has gone well this year. Establish your spending limit and stick to it. It is easy to spend too much money on too many holiday gifts. But I do suggest your allow yourself a little flexibility especially if you are buying gifts for your grandchildren. Get your check in the mail soon. You will be glad you did and they will too!

Christmas in Hawaii

I have never actually celebrated Christmas in Hawaii but we did go to of the Islands in early December with some friends. It was interesting to see the shops and hotels decorated with Christmas trees and playing Christmas Carols.

The local radio stations featured both traditional Christmas music and local Hawaiian songs too. It was kind of weird seeing and hearing reminders of Christmas while enjoying the sunshine, the surf and the sand.

One of the things that was missing were the shopping malls crowded with holiday shoppers. On Maui there are several popular shopping areas but nothing like the huge malls on the mainland filled with shoppers and drivers jockeying for a parking place. The pace is slower, the stores are smaller and the traffic is lighter on Maui and some of the other islands.

It was fun to see some Christmas items for sale with a Hawaiian flavor. We saw a ceramic figure with Santa riding on a surf board instead of riding in his sleigh. We also saw some T-shirts for sale displaying a Hawaiian Christmas themes. They also had tree ornaments for sale with Merry Christmas written on them.

Although I love Hawaii and think it would be fun to celebrate Christmas on the islands, I still prefer to be home for Christmas. I like to be with friends and family during the holidays. I prefer the familiar over some-thing new and different. I don't think it would be quite the same having Christmas in Hawaii.

Wherever you celebrate Christmas this year I hope you will invite your family and friends to share it with you. Let me encourage you to find a Bible teaching church near you so you can celebrate Christmas Eve and Christmas Day. Include time to lift your voice in praise and worship as you celebrate the birth of Jesus.

And let me also encourage you to watch for someone who does not have family in the area. Invite a widow, widower or single mother to join your family's Christmas celebration. You may want to have time alone with your children but why not invite a guest or two to join you for dinner on Christmas Day. They will be glad you did and you will too.

Sing with All Your Heart

I enjoyed spending Christmas Eve and Christmas Day with my daughter Teri and my son-in-law Jacob and their two girls Emily and Janie. We started our holiday celebration by attending the Christmas Eve service at their church on December 24th. Then we drove to their house for dinner. Later in the evening we were joined by my son Tim and his wife Christine. It was our first Christmas without my wife.

One of our family's traditions was reading the Christmas story in the Bible which tells about the birth of Jesus. Emily read the passage in Luke Chapter two which provides many details about the day Jesus was born. Then each person got to open one present before we enjoyed dessert. There would be more presents to open on Christmas morning but it was a nice time together at church and at their home.

We sang a number of Christmas Carols at the Christmas Eve service. Our two granddaughters knew many of the songs because they had learned them in preschool. It was nice to hear them singing along with the other people at the Christmas Eve service.

In fact, you could really hear one of them singing loudly with confidence and enthusiasm. When they were in preschool their teachers encouraged the children to sing extra loud so their parents could hear them. Janie did just that. She sang every song loudly and a little off key. No one minded. I saw a number of smiles from other grandparents who enjoyed hearing her voice.

There is a verse in the Bible that says, "Whatever you do in word or deed, do it with all your heart" (Colossians 3:17). It was refreshing to hear Janie singing the Christmas Carols with all of her heart. I couldn't help but smile as I watched her sing with joy and enthusiasm.

Let me encourage you to do your work and sing your songs with all of your heart. Don't conceal your love for God and for other people. Lift your voice with praise and enthusiasm. You will be glad you did and those around you will too.

December 22
A Special Christmas Gift

My wife was a public school teacher for many years. She taught sixth grade Language Arts and Social Studies. She really enjoyed working with her Middle School students and appreciated the gifts they gave to her during the year.

There were many unusual gifts and some practical ones too. The most useful things she received were gift cards to local restaurants. Teachers have busy schedules and don't always have time to prepare meals for their own families. As our children grew up and went off to college there were only two of us for dinner. It was nice to go out and not have to cook and clean up.

This year my daughter suggested her children give a copy of my latest book, "*Let Me Encourage You More*" to their school teachers for Christmas. My granddaughters were excited to give one of Pop Pop's books to their teachers. One of them shared with me that her teacher often used the phrase "*Let me encourage you*" in class with her students. That phrase sounded just like my book! It was a perfect fit.

In addition, they were excited to give a copy of my book to their teachers because the book included a story co-authored by them. The story was about their experience opening a Lemonade Stand in their neighborhood. I interviewed them about their business venture and how many customers they had and how much money they made. I wrote down their comments and included their story in my latest book. I included their names as the authors of the story. Janie and Emily made sure their teachers read about their *Lemonade Stand* adventure.

My new book also included a story addressed to each of my grandchildren. I shared things my wife and I remembered about the day they were born. I told them how proud and thankful we were for each one of them. I also shared that we prayed for each of our grandchildren every day. We prayed for good friends, a growing faith and for a bright future. Both girls wanted to show their school teachers what I had written about them. Their school teachers were enthusiastic to receive this encouraging Christmas gift. Let me encourage you to give a gift to the hard working teachers who invest so much of their time and energy into your child's life. I recommend a thoughtful gift card to a local restaurant or a new book by a local author. They will be glad you did and you will too.

Living Nativity

Our church is located on Diamond Bar Boulevard which is the main street running through our city. Thousands and thousands of cars pass by our church every day. It is a prime location but I think our church is overlooked by the fast moving cars going up and down the boulevard.

Many years ago my wife suggested we do a Living Nativity in the evening during the Christmas season to emphasize the meaning of Christmas. Several men built a small stage in the church parking lot which could easily be seen by passing motorists.

In addition, we enlisted families and individuals to staff the Nativity set. Each participant wore a costume or gown that depicted what the scene might have looked like on the night of Jesus' birth. Whole families with parents and children participated. The kids loved being on the small stage and parents enjoyed doing this too.

The responses to the Living Nativity were encouraging. Some cars slowed down as they drove by while others honked their horn to show their support. We did the Living Nativity for several nights leading up to Christmas Eve. It was a big success.

One of the benefits of the Living Nativity was the increased visibility in our community. Several people commented about how much they liked what our church had done. I think many people often drove by and didn't pay much attention. It seemed like the Nativity increased awareness of our church in Diamond Bar.

Another unexpected result was how much fun people had participating in the event. A number of people took pictures of their family in the Nativity set and used them on the cover of their Christmas cards. It became a fun family event.

Let me encourage you to get involved in the Christmas program or other activities at your church during this holiday season. Volunteer your whole family for a role in a program or project. You and your family will be glad you did.

Christmas Eve

When I became the pastor at Chapel in the Hills Church in Tucson they did not have a Christmas Eve service. In fact we didn't start one until five years later. In 1980 the associate pastor Dennis and I got the idea to have a service on Christmas Eve and see if anyone would come. We set up 30-40 chairs in our small auditorium because we did not expect many people to show up. But we were very surprised by how many people did come. We had to set up extra chairs. They still have a Christmas Eve services at the church today.

When my family moved to Diamond Bar, California we held our first Christmas Eve service at our church in 1988. We met in our small auditorium and many people came. At the end of the service we gave a candle to all of the children and adults as they exited the building. Then we gathered in the parking lot to light the candles and to sing "*Silent Night*" under the stars. It was a memorable moment as we sang accompanied by a guitar. I will always remember the faces of the children and adults illuminated by the circle of flickering candles.

Now we have two services on Christmas Eve in our new larger building. Younger families come to the first service at 5:00 PM and older adults with teens come to the later service at 7:00 PM. I liked having two services so families and individuals had an option.

We still sing "*Silent Night*" under the stars at the end of each service. One year it rained so we split the congregation in half with one group nestled under the patio of the new building and the other half under the covered area of the old building. It was a memorable moment.

A tradition in our family was to enjoy Tamales after church on Christmas Eve. My wife and kids came to the early service and then went home and ate the Tamales from the Whole Enchilada. I stayed for the second service and then came home so we could read the Christmas Story from the Bible in Luke Chapter Two. This became a tradition in our family and our adult children still read the same passage to their children in their own homes.

Let me encourage you to attend a Christmas Eve service at a church near you. Come as a family and enjoy the music and the message. Then head home and enjoy some warm food and sweet desserts. And read the Christmas story in Luke chapter 2. You will be glad you did.

December 25
The Christmas Train

I have shared in the past about my most memorable Christmas gift but it is worth repeating for those who have not read my previous books. When I was a little guy I remember opening a Lionel Train set complete with train cars and train track on Christmas Day.

The engine and coal car were black. They were made with metal and were very heavy. Years later I would receive another Lionel Train but is was much lighter and made with plastic. The original train set included some other things like a flatbed train car which could transport some automobiles and a box car with a sliding door on each side just like on a real train.

The transformer was a heavy black square box with two levers on it. One lever controlled the speed of the train and the other lever enabled the conductor to sound the whistle on the locomotive. Two wires and a small metal clip connected the transformer to the train track to power the locomotive.

It was fun to assemble the track into different shapes and lengths. Each piece of track was connected with three small pins. Over the years I bought some additional track and train cars to expand my railroad empire.

I wasn't sure what happened to my train after I got married and moved away from home. But my brother Steve found the train in a closet in our parent's home when we helped them move from their old house in Scottsdale to their new house in Gilbert. Steve didn't tell me about this important discovery. But on Christmas morning in 1988 there was an extra gift for me under the Christmas tree. It was my lost Lionel Train.

My father, my son and I assembled the train track and played with the train just as I had done with my father and grandfather a generation before. After we moved to California the train sat on a shelf in a box in my garage for many years. But one of my daughters persuaded me to set up my train around the Christmas tree for my grandchildren to see. The fifty year old Lionel Train was running again.

Let me encourage you to share some of your childhood memories and toys with your children and grandchildren. Make some new memories with them. They will be glad you did and you will too.

December 26
Grandchildren

My wife and I never forgot the day we heard from our daughter she was going to have a baby. It was amazing to learn one of our children was pregnant. We were going to be grandparents.

Jeanne flew to Portugal to be with Traci and Johnathan when our first grandchild was born. My son Tim and my daughter Teri and I flew to Lisbon a few days before Christmas to meet this new little girl named Katie. We felt like the three wise men in the Bible who traveled a great distance to see the new born baby Jesus. I will never forget kneeling beside the living room sofa and admiring little Katie in Traci's arms.

A few months later we traveled to Estes Park, Colorado to be with Trisha and Hondo for the birth of their first baby named Caleb. It was a special memory to meet our second grandchild.

Traci and Jonathan had three more babies in the following years. Carly was next and then Jonah and Ellie. All of them were born in Portugal. Trisha and Hondo added a baby girl. Elizabeth was born in Slovenia. You can see we did a lot of traveling to meet our grandkids.

Teri and Jacob had both of their girls in Southern California. Emily was born on my birthday in August and Janie just missed Jeanne's birth day in November a few years later. We only had to drive a few miles to meet these new family members.

Our son Tim added two more grandchildren to our family when he married his wonderful wife Christine. We are thankful to have Landon and Emily in our family too.

There is a verse in the Bible which says, "Grandchildren are like a crown and a blessing from God" (Proverbs 17:6). Grandparents have an important responsibility. There is a new ministry called, "*The Legacy Coalition*". Its purpose is to motivate and equip grandparents to make a greater impact on the spiritual lives of their grandchildren. You can find more information about this ministry at *Legacycoalition.com*.

Let me encourage you to enjoy your grandchildren. Make some memories they will keep for the rest of their lives. Invest in their spiritual growth and in their future education. Pray every day for their faith, their friends and their future. They will be glad you did and you will too.

December 27
Going Places

As I looked over my day planner I was surprised to see how many trips my wife and I have taken over the past few months. We went to the Central Coast of California in February. In May we drove to Arizona. In June flew to Maui and spent two relaxing weeks by the ocean.

In July we flew to Phoenix and spent a very hot week in the desert. In August we delivered a kitchen table to my brother Steve and his wife Sharon near the cooler central coast. We enjoyed spending several days with them. In September we drove down to San Diego and spent several days in that beautiful city.

As I looked ahead to the remaining part of the year I realized we plan to fly to Phoenix again. Then we are scheduled to lead a tour group from our church on an eleven day trip to Israel in October. We are also scheduled to fly to back Arizona to attend my 55th high school reunion at the end of October.

We have already made reservations for a trip in April, 2024 to visit some friends and watch the total solar eclipse near Dallas, Texas. We also plan to stop at Dallas Seminary and see how much the school has grown and changed since I was a student there in the 1970's.

I am amazed at all the places we have seen and the plans we have made to travel in the future. We have talked about taking a cruise to see the Panama Canal and also visit some new places Susan and I have not seen before. I'm thankful we have the health and opportunity to travel together.

There is a passage in the Bible where the Apostle Paul outlined his desire to expand his ministry into more areas of the Roman Empire. He wrote, "From Jerusalem all the way around to Illyricum (Yugoslavia) I have fully proclaimed the Gospel of Christ. I have been longing for many years to come see you (in Rome). I plan to spend some time with you on my way to Spain" (Romans 15:23-24).

Paul had traveled to many places in the Roman Empire but there were more places to go and more people he wanted to see. Let me encourage you to keep on dreaming and keep on planning new adventures. As we enter a new year I hope you will put a new trip, cruise or flight on your calendar. You will be glad you did and I will too.

The Barking Dogs

We like sleeping with our windows open when the nights are cool in the spring and fall. We secure the window in a partially open position so we can enjoy some fresh air at night. We usually enjoy a restful sleep and wake up refreshed.

However, there are a number of dogs in our neighborhood and they can interrupt our restful sleep when they start barking in the middle of the night. This happened again last night. Something disturbed them and they started barking loudly. There seems to be a big dog and a little one in a yard across the street. The big dog barks with a deep steady voice. But the little one barks with a loud squeaky voice which is more like a yelp than a bark.

Clearly something woke them up and they proceeded to wake us up too. We have seen and heard coyotes in our neighborhood in the past and some neighbors have lost their pets to these aggressive predators. Coyotes can jump over a tall fence and have been known to devour small pets in their own back yard.

I'm not sure why the dogs were barking last night and not sure what to do about this ongoing problem. One neighbor has contacted the city's animal control service asking them for help but nothing has changed.

We love animals but we also love a good night's sleep. We don't want pets to be injured or killed by coyotes but we don't want to be disturbed in the middle of the night. One obvious solution is for the owner to keep the dogs in their house or garage at night. I'm not sure why they don't.

There is a passage in the Bible which prescribes several steps when addressing a problem. The first step is to talk with the individual one on one. Share your concern with them directly. If that doesn't help then go back with one or two other people who share the same concern. If that doesn't work you may need to ask others to get involved. (Read Matthew 18:17)

The goal in every situation is to address and resolve the problem. We want to be on friendly terms with our neighbors and we don't want to create conflict. Maybe we just need to sleep with our windows closed. Let me encourage you to seek a peaceful solution when you have a problem or disagreement with your neighbors. You will be glad you did.

Taking Down Christmas

One of the holiday traditions in our family was putting up the Christmas decorations the day after Thanksgiving. Our daughter Teri and her husband Jacob and their two daughters spent the night at our house on Thanksgiving evening so they could help my wife and me put up the Christmas tree and the outside lights. It meant so much to have their help decorating our house for Christmas.

However, at the end of the holidays it was a lot of work taking the lights and decorations down. Ornaments had to be carefully packed in their individual boxes and the tree had to be put away in the garage. It took a lot hands and a lot of time to put away Christmas.

Do you ever wonder how the shopping Malls and department stores make the switch from Christmas decorations to business as usual? When I was a high school student I was invited to help a church youth group take down all of the decorations at a large department store several days after Christmas. Dozens of students and leaders flooded into the store after closing and began removing everything related to Christmas.

It took several hours to take all of the decorations off the walls and light fixtures. We removed the window displays and floor decorations. We used step ladders to reach the top shelves and other decorations around the store. I was amazed at how many decorations the store had used during the holiday season.

My wife had a number of storage tubs filled with Christmas decorations including the ornaments that covered our nine-foot tree. We had several nativity scenes and several snow globes that enhanced the coffee table in the living room. We also set up my Lionel train around the base of the Christmas tree. The grandchildren loved to take turns driving the train. It was an essential part of the Christmas decorations. It took many hours to decorate our house.

I think it is more fun to put the decorations up than it is to put everything away. Let me encourage you to enjoy the holiday season and help one another put up and take down your Christmas decorations. You will be glad you did and they will too.

Scottsdale

My parents moved from Colorado to Arizona in 1956 when I was only five years old. Scottsdale was a sleepy town in those days. There were no traffic lights and only a few stop signs at the intersections downtown. Sometimes you would see a horse and rider on the street.

On a recent visit I reflected on how so much of my life was shaped by this community. I grew up in Scottsdale. I attended Loloma, Ingleside and Mohave elementary schools. I attended Scottsdale High for two years and then went with many classmates to Saguaro High when it opened in 1966. I graduated with the first full class at Saguaro in 1968. I loved being part of the sports programs at both schools including Cross Country, Basketball and Baseball. I was also involved in Student Government at both schools too.

I met my wife Jeanne at Scottsdale High and we were in Student Council together at both schools. She won every election. I won two and lost two. We went to Arizona State together. We were engaged at the Camelback Inn on her birthday in Scottsdale in 1970. Although our wedding was at a church in Phoenix our wedding reception was at Mountain Shadows in Scottsdale. After 50 years of marriage I placed her ashes next to her parent's in the Paradise Gardens cemetery in Scottsdale.

I started attending Scottsdale Bible Church with my parents and my brother Steve in 1964. The pastors and the church had a big impact on our family and my future. I worked on the church staff during my college years and then went on to Dallas seminary to become a pastor.

We kept in touch with Scottsdale over the years because our parents lived in Scottsdale. We drove from Tucson to Phoenix many times and later from California to visit family and friends. Eventually we purchased a condo in Scottsdale which we continue to enjoy and share with others. It felt like we had come back home.

King David loved his home town named Bethlehem. One time some of his soldiers risked their lives to bring a refreshing drink of water for him from the well in the center of his hometown (Second Samuel 23:15). Let me encourage you to share some memories and stories about your hometown with your children and grandchildren. They will be glad you did and you will too.

A New Year's Resolution

We all need to develop good habits and establish helpful routines in life. My wife Susan and I like to wake up early and go for a walk before the sun comes up. It is the coolest and most quiet part of the day.

We also try to make time to read together from the Bible every day. The best time is during breakfast. Susan likes soft boiled eggs and I prefer my Frosted Mini Wheats with slices from a fresh banana. She usually has a cup of coffee while I prefer a glass of orange juice.

After we finish breakfast and take our vitamins we clean up the dishes and then read together. This year we have been using the *One Year New Testament*. It is a paperback edition from Tyndale Press. The entire New Testament is arranged in 365 daily readings.

Each day includes a passage from one of the four Gospels, the book of Acts or the book of Revelation. Each day also has some verses from one of the New Testament letters. There are also one or two verses from the Book of Proverbs.

The *One Year New Testament* also includes some notes and comments on the passages you read. These provide some helpful insights into the Bible verses. There are also many Bible reading programs available online. There are many different ways to read the Bible on a daily basis. The purpose of these programs is to help you enjoy reading the Bible and help you develop the habit of reading the Bible every day.

I always remember my youth pastor reading his Bible when he woke up in the morning and when he went to bed at night. He never told me to do it the way he did but I wanted to follow his example. I remember a newspaper writer reporting on the daily routine of President Jimmy Carter when he was running for office. His daily routine included reading one chapter in the Bible each morning and the next chapter in the evening before he went to bed.

We challenged people in our church to read one chapter a day. You could read the whole Bible in three years reading one chapter a day. One verse says, "Your word is a lamp to my feet and a guide to my life" (Psalms 119:105). Let me encourage you to start the New Year reading a chapter in the Bible every day. You will be glad you did.

Topical Index

Bible – 22-23, 26, 60, 66, 69, 72, 96, 104, 123, 128, 263, 298, 371

Christmas – 305, 363, 364, 365, 369

Church – 37, 84, 117, 137, 144, 153, 174, 186, 197, 208, 211, 215, 224, 251, 254, 256, 296, 336, 339, 363, 363

Culture – 110, 311, 326

Education – 21, 57, 67, 87, 216, 255

Faith – 28-29, 33, 39, 48, 130, 133, 143, 149, 151-152, 160, 166, 172, 194, 205, 212, 245, 267, 293, 331, 355

Family – 35-36, 40-41, 55-56, 61, 83, 100, 111, 184, 202, 210, 220, 229, 231, 257, 280, 291, 300, 313, 340, 352-353, 370

Food – 124, 136, 272, 301, 345

Friends – 38, 44-45, 91, 118, 135, 163, 165, 232, 236, 242, 244

Forgiveness – 10-11, 58, 70-71

Garden / Lawn – 64, 68, 77, 189, 209, 221, 356

Generosity – 31, 95, 142, 227, 239, 312, 347, 359

Grief – 32, 90, 113, 217, 335, 344

Health – 30, 84, 108, 220, 261

History – 27, 75-76, 159, 177, 190-192, 260. 270, 287, 321-322, 350

House / Hospitality – 20, 88-89, 93, 99, 114, 145, 150, 158, 171, 201, 204, 223, 237, 239, 241, 250, 262, 292, 314-315, 318-319, 333-334

Kindness – 12, 282-283, 306

Marriage / Weddings – 7, 42-43, 46-47, 49, 51-54, 59, 82, 106, 122, 164, 218, 271, 330, 351

Topical Index (Page 2)

Men / Fathers – 13, 19, 112, 120, 138, 178, 185, 226, 234, 253, 286, 323, 329

Music – 17, 18, 19, 354, 361

Money – 24, 73-74, 121, 142, 181, 187, 213, 225, 325, 327-328, 332

Neighbors – 16, 129, 146, 198, 273, 275, 295, 310, 348, 368

Parents, Grandparents – 10-11, 65, 86, 98, 115, 126, 178, 290, 366

Pets / Animals – 103, 116, 154, 156, 214, 277, 317, 324, 349, 357

Serving – 34, 63, 85, 101, 157, 162, 179, 162, 179, 203, 247, 341-342

Sports – 109, 252, 307-308

Travel – 9, 14-15, 92, 94, 107, 119, 127, 132, 139-141, 161, 167-170, 173-182, 219, 228, 230, 235, 238, 249, 259, 265-266, 269, 281, 284, 288-289, 303-304, 309, 316, 343, 360, 367

Thankful – 125, 176, 320, 337-338

Weather – 29, 183, 188, 193, 248, 258, 264, 268, 302

Women / Mothers – 43, 131, 294

Work – 78-79, 80, 105, 147-148, 195-196, 199, 206-207, 276

Writing - 18, 25, 180, 358, 362

Acknowledgements

I want to thank my children and grandchildren for allowing me to share more stories about their lives and our family. I am thankful for all of them and how they have encouraged me in many ways.

I also want to thank my wife Susan for encouraging me to keep writing and complete this new book.

And I want to express my appreciation to Diane Armijo and her editorial team for allowing me to contribute more stories to their newspaper "**Eastvale News**" published by *anapr.com* in Eastvale, California.

You can also read more of my stories in my two previous books – **Let Me Encourage You** and **Let Me Encourage You More**. Please contact me by email at *markh@efreedb.org* or *dbarhop@gmail.com* if you would like to purchase additional books.

I also post stories on my website – ***Letmarkencourageyou.com***

If you enjoyed this book, let me encourage you to give it to a friend after you finish reading it. Don't let it sit on a shelf. Share it with others. You will be glad you did and I will too!